Entrepreneurship

To the memory of my cousin Janet Earp

Entrepreneurship
Theory, Networks, History

Mark Casson

Professor of Economics, University of Reading, UK

In association with

Peter J. Buckley
Ken Dark
Marina Della Giusta
Andrew Godley
Mohamed Azzim Gulamhussen
Teresa da Silva Lopes
Nigel Wadeson

Edward Elgar
Cheltenham, UK • Northampton, MA, USA

Published by
Edward Elgar Publishing Limited
The Lypiatts
15 Lansdown Road
Cheltenham
Glos GL50 2JA
UK

Edward Elgar Publishing, Inc.
William Pratt House
9 Dewey Court
Northampton
Massachusetts 01060
USA

A catalogue record for this book
is available from the British Library

Library of Congress Control Number: 2009940660

Mixed Sources
Product group from well-managed
forests and other controlled sources
www.fsc.org Cert no. SA-COC-1565
© 1996 Forest Stewardship Council
FSC

ISBN 978 1 84980 039 6

Printed and bound by MPG Books Group, UK

Contents

Preface and acknowledgements

This book reports the results of my recent research into entrepreneurship. It focuses on the relationship between entrepreneurship studies and other disciplines, including economics, sociology, social psychology, international relations, management, economic history and business history. Given the breadth of the subjects covered, I have been very fortunate in receiving help and support from a number of collaborators, who are listed on the title page. These collaborators are either colleagues or former colleagues, or former doctoral students; some are both former students and current colleagues. All are associated with the University of Reading in one way or another.

Whilst most of the chapters incorporate previously published results, all the chapters have been re-written to eliminate wasteful duplication and to provide continuity of argument for those readers who wish to read through the book as a whole. At the same time, each chapter is presented in a reasonably self-sufficient form for the benefit of readers who wish to dip into the book to study specific topics; cross-references to other chapters are supplied for their benefit. Since each of the chapters has been re-written, my co-authors do not necessarily agree with everything that is said in the version that appears in this book.

Entrepreneurship is a lively area of research with enormous potential, and so I hope to produce another volume in a few years time – colleagues and students please take note! As usual, I should like to thank my wife Janet – my staunchest critic – for spotting numerous errors in the first draft of this book, and for offering to correct some of them. I should also like to thank the publisher, Edward Elgar, for his support and friendship throughout my career, and also the members of his editorial team who have pressurized me into completing this book.

Chapter 1 is based on an entry in the *Oxford Encyclopaedia of Economic History* (Oxford: Oxford University Press, 2005), and the Editorial Introduction to the *Oxford Handbook of Entrepreneurship* (Oxford: Oxford University Press, 2006), supplemented by material from 'Entrepreneurship and Historical Explanation' (with Andrew Godley), in Y. Cassis and I.P. Minoglou (eds), *Entrepreneurship in Theory and History* (Basingstoke: Palgrave), pp. 25–60.

Chapter 2 is a synthesis of 'The Discovery of Opportunities: Extending the Economic Theory of the Entrepreneur' (with Nigel Wadeson), *Small Business Economics*, **28** (2007): 285–300, and 'The Search for Entrepreneurial Opportunity' (with Nigel Wadeson), *History of Economic Ideas*, **15** (1) (2007): 137–58.

Chapter 3 is a revised and shortened version of 'Entrepreneurship and Macroeconomic Performance' (with Nigel Wadeson), *Strategic Entrepreneurship Journal*, **1** (3-4), (2007): 239–62.

Chapter 4 is an unpublished paper co-authored with Peter J. Buckley. The ideas in this paper were applied to international business issues in 'Edith Penrose's *Theory of the Growth of the Firm* and the Strategic Management of Multinational Enterprises' (with Peter J. Buckley), *Management International Review*, **47** (2) (2008): 151–73.

Chapter 5 is a revised version of a paper presented at the Tenth Symposium of Economic History at the Universitat Autonoma de Barcelona in January 2005.

Chapter 6 is a revised version of a paper in *International Small Business Journal*, **25** (3) (2007): 220–44. It incorporates material from 'The Costly Business of Trust' (with Marina Della Giusta), *Development Policy Review*, **22** (3) (2004): 321–42 and 'The Economics of Trust' (with Marina Della Giusta), in R. Bachmann and A. Zaheer (eds), *Handbook of Trust Research* (Cheltenham: Edward Elgar, 2006), pp. 332–54.

Chapter 7 is based on an unpublished paper 'The Place of Co-operatives in the Institutional Theory of the Firm' (with Marina Della Giusta) (2005).

Chapter 8 is a revised and shortened version of 'Culture and Economic Performance', in Victor Ginsburgh and David Throsby (eds) *Handbook of the Economics of Art and Culture* (Amsterdam: North Holland, 2006), pp. 359–97.

Chapter 9 is a revised and shortened version of 'Revisiting the Emergence of the Modern Business Enterprise: Entrepreneurship and the Singer Global Distribution System' (with Andrew Godley), *Journal of Management Studies*, **44** (7) (2007): 1064–77.

Chapter 10 is based on 'Entrepreneurship and the Development of Global Brands' (with Teresa da Silva Lopes), *Business History Review*, **81** (Winter

2007): 651–80, incorporating some material from an unpublished paper on trademarks with Nigel Wadeson.

Chapter 11 is a revised version of 'Entrepreneurship in Victorian Britain, 1830–1900' (with Andrew Godley), in David S. Landes, William Baumol and Joel Mokyr (eds), *The Invention of Enterprise* (Princeton, NJ: Princeton University Press for the Kauffman Institute, 2009).

Chapter 12 (with Ken Dark and Mohamed Azzim Gulamhussen) is a synthesis of ideas in 'Multinational Enterprise, Imperialism and the Knowledge-Driven State', in J.H. Dunning and P. Gugler (eds), *Foreign Direct Investment, Location and Competitiveness*, (Amsterdam: Elsevier, 2008), pp. 3–28, and 'Extending Internalisaton Theory: From the Multinational Enterprise to the Knowledge-Based Empire', *International Business Review*, **18** (2009): 236–56.

PART I

Theory

1. The economic theory of entrepreneurship: an overview

The aim of this book is to provide a rigorous and up-to-date account of the economic theory of the entrepreneur, and its practical applications to business behaviour and policy formation. The theory emphasizes the importance of good judgement in economic success. Entrepreneurs are people who specialize in the application of judgement to economic decisions. Good judgement leads to timely innovation and profitable arbitrage; it eliminates waste caused by the misallocation of resources, and reduces the risks associated with major projects. Entrepreneurs establish firms through which they can exploit their superior judgement, although they may take over the control of existing firms instead. Entrepreneurship is not confined to small firms. Reputable entrepreneurs may be employed as salaried strategic managers – they do not always have to own the firms for which they work. The demand for entrepreneurship is driven by volatility in the economic environment, whilst the supply of entrepreneurship is determined by the number of people with suitable personality characteristics. The interaction of demand and supply determines the reward to entrepreneurship and the number of entrepreneurs who are active in the economy.

1.1 INTRODUCTION

The Fundamental Significance of the Entrepreneur

Entrepreneurship is a fundamental concept linking different academic disciplines – notably economics, sociology and history. Entrepreneurship is not just an ordinary interdisciplinary subject; it is a core subject that links the conceptual frameworks of different social sciences. Indeed, it may be regarded as a key building block of an integrated social science.

But if entrepreneurship is so important, why has its significance been overlooked? Two factors account for the problem:

- mainstream economists have perceived entrepreneurship as a complicating factor in explanations of the way that markets work, and have therefore sought to avoid the subject;
- there has been disagreement over the most appropriate definition of the entrepreneur.

These two factors have reinforced each other: confusion over the definition has been used as a pretext for marginalizing the entrepreneur in economic theory.

Marginalization of the Entrepreneur

Economics is the logical discipline in which a theory of entrepreneurship should emerge. Yet – paradoxically – mainstream economic theory of the twentieth century largely ignored entrepreneurship (Baumol, 1968). Mainstream economists have taken the existence of markets as given and regarded competition as an impersonal process. In practice markets are not given – they are created on the initiative of entrepreneurs – and the personal qualities of entrepreneurs are a significant influence on the outcome of the competitive process.

Despite its central role in economic theory, the market has, until recently, remained something of a black box so far as mainstream economists are concerned. Inside the black box is a process, usually referred to as 'competition', but its only observable outcome is a set of equilibrium prices and quantities (Richardson, 1960). Entrepreneurs are firmly locked up inside the black box, and therefore out of view. In practice, of course, entrepreneurs are highly visible to ordinary consumers, and indeed most business history and much economic history is written from the records that entrepreneurs leave behind. This creates a fundamental gap between the low profile of the entrepreneur in economic theory and the prominent role of the entrepreneur in both popular culture and the historical record.

The problem persists to this day. When describing markets, modern economic textbooks rely heavily on Marshallian supply and demand analysis (Marshall, 1890) and Walrasian general equilibrium theory (Walras, 1954) as refined by Arrow and Debreu (1954). Whilst Marshall recognized the practical importance of entrepreneurship, his explanation of market forces relied heavily on the 'scissors' formed by intersecting schedules of supply and demand. Considered as producers, entrepreneurs were placed on the supply side of the economy, but as distributors and marketers they were placed on the demand side, with the wholesale price linking the two. As a result of this division, entrepreneurs disappeared from view (Casson, 2003).

Walras, by contrast, completely abolished the entrepreneur by postulating that markets were adjusted by an auctioneer instead. The auctioneer was an altruistic individual who, despite possessing a monopoly of trading opportunities in the entire economy, set no margin between buying price and selling price and therefore appropriated no profit for himself. His information was so perfect that he incurred no costs in the adjustment process; he therefore did for free what entrepreneurs do for a profit – namely establish markets and intermediate the trade in them.

Both Marshall and Walras therefore presented markets as impersonal institutions regulated by the force of competition. Two anomalies arise from this view. First, when entrepreneurs are eliminated from the market process, buyers and sellers must interact directly with each other. Buyers compete with other buyers, and sellers with other sellers. In practice, however, buyers and sellers in most markets are relatively passive; it is entrepreneurs that publish price quotations, and buyers and sellers simply choose from the menus provided by the entrepreneurs. In reality, it is the entrepreneurs that compete most intensely with each other. One entrepreneur sets up a market, others enter if the venture is successful, the rivals compete, and only the most efficient survives. Second, when entrepreneurs are eliminated from the market process, economists tend to regard firms as mere producers. As a result, the knowledge exploited by firms is assumed to relate to production technology, whereas in fact it relates mainly to demand and supply. This confusion between economic knowledge of market conditions and technological knowledge used in production has bedevilled a good deal of policy debate.

This book expounds a theory of entrepreneurship that has been developed specifically to resolve the paradoxes set out above. The theory explains how entrepreneurs initiate market processes and develops a range of hypotheses suitable for historical study. The theory is not overtly heterodox – it embraces many of the core assumptions of modern economic theory, such as rational action, although it qualifies these assumptions in certain ways. It does, however, open up the black box labelled 'the market' and examine what is inside. As a result, the personal qualities of entrepreneurs are revealed as an important influence on the outcome of competition. Competition rewards entrepreneurs who demonstrate good judgement, and penalizes those who do not. Entrepreneurs who possess good judgement gain market share at the expense of others, and so the distribution of market share and the distribution of profit both reflect the distribution of entrepreneurial ability within the population.

Definition of the Entrepreneur

Outside the realms of mainstream economics, two main ways of defining entrepreneurship can be found in the literature. One defines the entre-preneur as the founder or owner-manager of a small or medium-sized enterprise (SME) with growth potential, whilst the other defines the entre-preneur in terms of the economic function that he or she performs. (For a comprehensive review of the relevant literature see, for example, Shane, 2003; Acs and Audretsch, 2003; Casson et al., 2006).

The first approach grew out of the crisis in Western capitalism during the early1970s caused by the rise of competition from Japan and South-East Asia. Post-war policymakers believed in scale – big government to provide a welfare state and big firms to exploit economies of scale in production. These firms were often bureaucratic and their industrial relations poor; they were meant to create jobs, but once import com-petition intensified their inefficiency destroyed jobs instead. The more entrepreneurial redundant employees started their own firms. Small – not large – was now 'beautiful' in the eyes of policymakers. To encourage the formation of SMEs, an enterprise culture was created, based on a positive role model and a rhetoric of 'wealth creation'. 'Entrepreneur' became the favoured appellation for anyone who was self-employed or a small-scale employer; even economists got in on the act, and described anyone who chose self-employment as an alternative to unemployment or waged employment as an 'entrepreneur' (Blanchflower and Oswald, 1998). In industries where self-employment was the norm – for example, household plumbing – almost everyone was called an entrepreneur, whether their business grew or not. By contrast, the CEOs of high-growth firms were not described as entrepreneurs – even in high-technology high-growth firms – because they received a salary and did not own their firms outright.

1.2   THE CANONICAL LITERATURE OF THE THEORY OF ENTREPRENEURSHIP FROM CANTILLON TO KIRZNER

From an economic perspective this first approach made little sense. It is the function of the entrepreneur that is important – 'an entrepreneur is what an entrepreneur does'. But what does an entrepreneur do? The canonical literature suggests a variety of tasks, including 'high-level' activities like innovation and risk-taking, and also 'low level' activities such as spotting opportunities for arbitrage. The theory presented in this book is based on a synthesis of the principal insights set out by the canonical authors on the subject.

Cantillon and risk   The term 'entrepreneur' appears to have been introduced into economic theory by Richard Cantillon (1755), an Irish economist of French descent. According to Cantillon, the entrepreneur is a specialist in taking on risk. He/she 'insures' workers by buying their output for resale before consumers have indicated how much they are willing to pay for it. The workers receive an assured income (in the short run, at least), while the entrepreneur bears the risk caused by price fluctuations in consumer markets.

Knight and uncertainty   This idea was refined by the US economist Frank Knight (1921), who distinguished between risk, which is insurable, and uncertainty, which is not. Risk refers to recurrent events whose relative frequency is known from past experience, whilst uncertainty relates to unique events whose probability can only be subjectively estimated. Knight thought that most of the risks relating to production and marketing fall into the latter category. Since business owners cannot insure against these risks, they are left to bear them by themselves. Profit is a reward for bearing this uninsurable risk: it is the reward of the pure entrepreneur. With freedom of entry into industries, profits in one industry can exceed profits in another industry in the long run only if the uncertainties are greater in the more profitable industry – in other words, if the demands on entrepreneurship are greater in that industry.

Schumpeter and the entrepreneur-hero   Popular notions of entrepreneurship are based on the heroic vision proposed by Joseph A. Schumpeter (1934). The entrepreneur is visualized as someone who creates new industries and thereby precipitates major structural changes in the economy. The entrepreneur innovates by carrying out new combinations; the role is neither that of a pure inventor, because the entrepreneur adopts the inventions made by others, nor that of a financier, because of a reliance on bankers to fund investments. The entrepreneur takes the crucial decision to commit resources to the exploitation of new ideas. An element of calculation is involved, but it is not pure calculation, because not all of the relevant factors can be accurately measured. Profit is a motivating factor, but not the only one: the other motivators include the 'dream and the will to found a private kingdom'; the 'will to conquer: the impulse to fight, to prove oneself superior to others'; and the 'joy of creating'.

Marshall and low-level entrepreneurship   Schumpeter was concerned with the heroic or 'high-level' kind of entrepreneurship that, historically, has led to the creation of railways, the development of the chemical industry and the growth of integrated oil companies. A weakness of his analysis is that it leaves little room for the much more common, but no less important, 'low-level' entrepreneurship carried on by small firms. Few economic histories nowadays would ignore the important role of small firms in economic development. Alfred Marshall (1919) emphasized their importance and described the role of these firms in some detail, but critically omitted them from his formal analysis of supply and demand. Given the techniques that were available to him, Marshall could only model equilibrium situations, and so could not fit entrepreneurship into his analysis.

The Austrian School and arbitrage   The essence of low-level entrepreneurship can be explained by the Austrian approach of Friedrich A. von Hayek (1937) and Israel M. Kirzner (1973). Entrepreneurs are middlemen who provide price quotations as an invitation to trade. While bureaucrats in a socialist economy have little incentive to discover prices for themselves, entrepreneurs in a market economy are motivated to do so by profit opportunities. They hope to profit by buying cheap and selling dear. In the long run, such differentials, once discovered, generate a profit for the entrepreneur.

The difficulty with the Austrian approach is, however, that it isolates the entrepreneur from the organization of routine activities that is so characteristic of a firm. It fits an individual dealer or speculator far better than it fits a small manufacturer, say, because the latter has to oversee an organization whereas the former does not. For a fuller understanding of entrepreneurship we need to clarify the link between the entrepreneur and the firm.

1.3   JUDGEMENTAL DECISION-MAKING

The insights of these economists can be synthesized by identifying an entrepreneurial function that is common to all approaches. This is the exercise of judgement in decision-making (Casson, 1982). Judgement is the ability to come to a sound, defensible decision in the absence of complete information. A middleman who buys before he/she knows the price at which he/she can resell must make a judgement about what the future price will be, for instance. Or an arbitrager must make a judgement about where price differentials are most likely to be found in order to focus his price discovery effort on a suitable segment of the market. An innovator must assess whether a new product will prove attractive to consumers, or whether a new technology will really cut costs by as much as its inventor claims.

Judgemental decisions normally require the synthesis of different types of information. The high-level entrepreneur of the Schumpeterian type, for example, needs to synthesize information about new inventions with information about trends in product demand and in the prices of raw materials, in order to determine whether an innovation is worthwhile. If entrepreneurs do not possess this information they must know where to acquire it. If some of the information is confidential then it will have to be acquired through personal contact rather than from published sources. Entrepreneurs therefore need to create a network of contacts that can feed them the information that is required.

A synthesis of information has commercial value only if it relates to a profit opportunity. If everyone recognizes the same opportunity at the same time then profits will be competed away. As rival entrepreneurs bid up the price of inputs and the prospect of increased supplies drives output prices down, everyone's profits will disappear. The only beneficiaries will be the customers and the suppliers.

Profit opportunities arise on a regular basis when economic conditions are volatile, because the allocation of resources continually needs to be adjusted in response to change. In addition, long-term trends, such as the accumulation of knowledge, the growth of population and the depletion of non-renewable resources, also create a need for change. When incentives work well, profit is the reward that the entrepreneur obtains for expediting economic adjustments and, in some cases, for making adjustments that might otherwise never occur.

If information were freely available, and could be costlessly processed, then there would be no need for judgement. Every decision would be correctly taken and no mistakes would ever be made. But in practice information is costly. It is time-consuming to make and record observations. Human memory capacity is limited. Interpretative skills are scarce. Above all, communication is an expensive process. It follows that people do not have all the information they need when taking a decision.

When decision-makers cannot afford to collect all the information they need, they have to act under uncertainty. But the uncertainty faced by one person may be different from the uncertainty faced by another person. Sources of primary information are highly localized; for example, only people 'on the spot' can directly observe an event. Different people in different places will therefore have different perceptions of any given situation. They may therefore make different decisions. Consequently, the nature of the decision depends on the identity of the person who makes it. The entrepreneur matters because each individual's judgement of a situation is potentially unique.

Not all information is reliable. The senses may be confused; but the biggest risk relates to information obtained from other people. Other people may be unreliable, or their messages may be misunderstood. Alternatively, they may set out deliberately to mislead, so that they can extract more profit from their information for themselves. One person may check their information sources more carefully than another, and therefore stand less chance of being misled.

The interpretation of information may differ too. Different people may hold different theories about the way the environment works. As any social scientist knows, it is difficult to test conclusively between rival theories because of data limitations. Thus different theories coexist because of data limitations, leading to different interpretations of similar evidence. In a business context, entrepreneurs may act differently on the basis of similar information because they interpret the situation in different ways (Harper, 1996).

If a situation recurs frequently, it is worth investigating it carefully in order to find the theory that fits it best. This theory identifies which information is required to make the correct decision. Arrangements can be made to collect information on a regular basis, so that it is always to hand when required. Whenever a decision needs to be made, this information is processed using an appropriate decision rule in order to arrive at a correct decision. If some information is very costly to collect, then its costs have to be traded off against its benefits in arriving at the correct decision rule. This rule does not guarantee the correct decision; but it is optimal in economic terms, in the sense that it trades off the risk of a mistake against the saving in information cost.

Once this optimal decision rule is known there is no further need for the entrepreneur. Everyone knows how the decision rule has been specified, and so no reward can be earned by those who take the decision properly.

Now consider the opposite case in which no such rule is available. This is likely to involve a novel situation. It either has no precedent, or is so unusual that it would not pay to investigate it fully. Nobody knows the correct decision rule, and nobody systematically collects information on the situation. The more complex the situation, the more inadequate the theory is likely to be. There may be no theory at all, or there may be a range of rival theories which it is difficult to choose between. There may be no information, or a surfeit of information, because no one is quite sure what information is relevant and what is not. Matters are even worse if the decision has to be arrived at quickly – for example, because the situation is unstable and will continue to deteriorate until something is done. This is the kind of situation that calls for the most intensive judgement. To improvise a decision quickly, people have to rely on the theories with which they are already familiar, and the information that they can retrieve from their memory. Differences in theories, combined with differences in memories, lead to differences in decisions.

In the intermediate case, the situations are less complex, more relevant information may be available and situations less volatile. But once again, the people with the most relevant theories and the most comprehensive memories will tend to make the best decisions. These are the entrepreneurs – they possess the quality of judgement required to improvise a decision successfully when no agreed decision rule is available. Entrepreneurs – whether at a high or low level – are therefore those who exercise entrepreneurial judgement.

To fully operationalize this theory, it is necessary to specify the nature of complexity. Complexity is best defined in terms of the size of the model that is required to represent the principal features of the situation. So far as entrepreneurship is concerned, the involvement of other 'major players' in the situation is a major source of complexity. Other firms are important players, whether as competitors or as potential partners in alliances. The government is also obviously an important player, particularly in industries connected with defence, where it is a customer as well as the policymaker. The greater the strategic skills of the other players, the more complex the situation becomes. International business issues are more complex than domestic issues, for instance, because there are a larger number of skilful players involved.

Examples of judgemental decisions include the following:

- An opportunity to exploit a new technology has been identified and a quick decision is required in order to pre-empt a rival. The investment is irreversible – that is, the costs are sunk – so that a mistake cannot be corrected afterwards. The revenue stream is uncertain, and cannot be guaranteed by forward sales of output. Should the investment be undertaken right away?
- A new source of competition has just emerged from a firm in a newly-industrializing country. Should the dominant firm in the industry cut its price, or can it rely upon its existing customers not to switch to the rival firm? Is the rival firm producing more cheaply because of low-cost labour and/or subsidies, about which nothing can be done, or is it using more efficient techniques which ought to be imitated?

1.4 MARKET-MAKING OPPORTUNITIES

One of the most important types of opportunity exploited by an entrepreneur involves the establishment of a new market, or the widening of an existing one. The entrepreneur reconfigures patterns of trade by establishing a new centre for trade in a particular product or in a range of products. A low-level entrepreneur might set up a local shop to stock a range of products that is otherwise only available in a neighbouring town. On the other hand, a high-level entrepreneur might set up a multinational enterprise producing a new branded product using a patented technology. Both of these entrepreneurs require an organization in order to exploit their opportunity effectively. The shop owner requires a simple organization for staffing the till, banking the cash, ordering stock and keeping the shelves filled. The head of a multinational enterprise requires a more sophisticated organization to handle the logistics of international transportation, exchange rate exposure management and so on. Many managers will be employed for this purpose.

Once the low-level entrepreneur has made the initial judgement to set up the shop, much of his/her subsequent work is routine. Only intermittent shocks, such as a major change in tastes or the entry of a local rival, will require further judgemental decisions. By contrast, calls for judgement will be much more frequent in the multinational enterprise, because it is exposed to a variety of shocks in different markets around the world. The head of the organization may become so busy that he delegates entrepreneurial discretion to the managers of local subsidiaries. These managers then become entrepreneurs in their own right. They initiate local responses to local problems, and consult only with colleagues and superiors when they judge that international strategies are affected.

1.5   ENTREPRENEURIAL STRATEGY: PRE-EMPTING OPPORTUNITIES

Information about a profit opportunity has the properties of a 'public good' because it can easily diffuse to other people. An entrepreneur will therefore want to keep his/her information synthesis secret until he/she has pre-empted the profit opportunity. There are three main ways of pre-empting an opportunity, but not all of them are available in every case.

- *Acquisition of special legal privileges*   This is the most direct way to attain a monopoly position. The privilege may consist of a state charter, licence or franchise, or a patent linked to the technology employed. The privilege will normally be valid for a fixed term, after which it may or may not be renewed.
- *Speculation and arbitrage*   In practice, many patents and licences are difficult to enforce. In the absence of effective legal enforcement, the best alternative is to appropriate the profit from a speculative

deal in some resource. This provides a basis for rapid capital gains; the entrepreneur can buy up the resources which appear undervalued in the light of his/her information, and then sell these resources on to others at higher prices once the information has entered the public domain. Commodity and currency traders appropriate profit in this way on a daily basis. The same strategy can be applied to land, mining rights and the like: for example, buying up land that is used for agriculture and selling it off to a builder for housing.

- *Loyalty*   Where manufacturing and commerce are concerned, profit cannot usually be appropriated through a once-for-all transaction. The opportunity involves creating a market for a type of product that did not previously exist, or making an existing product in a different way. It involves a succession of trades over a long period of time. The closest analogy to the speculative strategy is to tie in suppliers and customers using long-term contracts. This would prevent the suppliers and customers from switching to rival firms later on. These long-term contracts would capitalize the flow of future costs and benefits in the same way that the price of the speculative asset did before. The transactions costs associated with this strategy are likely to be high, however. Furthermore, once alerted to the situation, customers and suppliers will be reluctant to sign such contracts, since they will realize that they can get a better deal once competitors arrive on the scene. Under these conditions, the best strategy is to win the loyalty of their customers and suppliers, so that they are reluctant to switch to rivals when they appear. If rivals expect the clients to be loyal to the innovator, then this will discourage them from entering in the first place.

The practical difficulties of pre-empting profit opportunities mean that entrepreneurs usually want to keep their information secret for as long as possible. This explains the culture of commercial confidentiality and business secrecy that is found in many businesses. Small firms are particularly vulnerable to 'theft' of information by bigger firms, since it is easier for a big firm to enter a small firm's market than the other way round. Founders of small firms who lack business experience may also overestimate the commercial value of the privileged information in their possession. For example, they may believe that they are the only people to know the identities of their customers, whereas in fact larger firms know about these customers but find their demands too small to bother with. A combination of over-optimism and perceived vulnerability may explain why the culture of secrecy appears to be particularly strong in small firms.

1.6   THE SUPPLY OF GOOD JUDGEMENT

People differ in their quality of judgement. Some people have a personal comparative advantage in exercising judgement, and others do not. Those who own resources do not necessarily possess the quality of judgement needed to utilize them properly. Wealthy aristocrats, for example, do not necessarily make good businessmen. Economic efficiency requires that people with the best judgement are matched to the most judgemental decisions.

There are various reasons why people differ in their quality of judgement. Some people may be very observant, and notice things that others miss. Others may have strong powers of concentration, that enable them to process information more quickly than other people. Older people may have longer memories, so that they can retrieve more information about similar situations that have arisen in the past. This is particularly useful in areas where theory is weak – for example, in understanding the motivations of others. Some people may be more methodical than others, and better at checking information. For all these reasons, some people have either more information or better interpretative models, and so face lower information costs than others. For a given expenditure of effort, they are more likely to arrive at a correct decision.

Not all entrepreneurs are successful. There is a strong bias in the historical literature towards successful entrepreneurs, for fairly obvious reasons: successful entrepreneurs make an impact on the national economy, they are inclined to self-promotion and the enterprises they create survive long enough to leave good records. The successful entrepreneurs are those whose confidence in their judgement turns out to be well-placed. For every high-profile success, however, there tend to be numerous failures. Small start-up businesses are notoriously prone to failure in the first two or three years (Storey, 1994; Parker, 2004). Failures are normally caused by overconfidence, though bad luck and incompetence may also play their parts. Luck is also a factor in business success, because ill-founded judgements may occasionally be validated by chance events. However, the proportion of luck to judgement in entrepreneurial success remains unknown.

Given the scarcity of entrepreneurship, the question naturally arises as to whether its supply can be increased, and if so how. For a given size of population, there are two main ways of increasing the overall supply of entrepreneurs. The first is to improve the quality of judgement in the population, and the second is to give people more confidence in the judgement that they have. The first approach raises the question of whether entrepreneurs are 'born' or 'made'. There is little historical evidence that entrepreneurship is inherited: the evidence on family firms suggests that sons usually display less initiative than the fathers they succeed. There is some support for the idea that entrepreneurial qualities are incubated in adversity. Fatalistic acceptance of poverty is certainly not an entrepreneurial characteristic, but determination to reverse an economic set-back often seems to be (Brenner, 1983). The idea of 'proving oneself' in order to live down some humiliation may also be a factor, although the evidence is only anecdotal on this point. Many entrepreneurs claim to be 'self-made', but it is impossible to know whether, in making this claim, they are simply unwilling to give credit to parents, teachers and others who have helped them along their way.

The second approach suggests that people should be encouraged to become more self-confident, and to take greater risks. This attitude was characteristic of the 'enterprise culture' of the 1980s and 1990s (see below); the problem is that by encouraging people with poor judgement to make risky decisions, more resources may simply be wasted.

1.7   HUMAN CAPITAL AND THE MARKET FOR ENTREPRENEURS

There is a close connection between the theory of entrepreneurship and the theory of human capital. Some of the propositions derived from the theory of entrepreneurship can be tested in the same way as propositions derived from human capital theory (Schultz, 1971). Entrepreneurship can be regarded as one of the components of human capital. It is a skill relating to the processing of information. It is not the routine managerial skill of taking decisions according to procedures, but rather the skill of judging what these procedures should be. It is also the skill involved in taking decisions in unexpected business situations where ordinary procedures do not apply.

From this point of view, entrepreneurship is one of a number of inputs that contribute to the overall performance of the economy. Together with the other components of human capital – skilled manual labour and routine management – it may be considered as a factor input into the economy. It is an input that improves the allocative efficiency of the economy. Like any factor of production, it is a substitute for other factors of production. Thus if managers are abundant, but entrepreneurs are scarce, decisions that would have been taken by entrepreneurs may be taken by managers instead. This means that a decision that might have been improvised, on the basis that existing procedures are inappropriate, will be taken using routines instead.

According to this approach, the demand for entrepreneurship, like the demand for any other factor of production, is a derived demand. Unlike more conventional factors of production, however, the demand for entrepreneurship derives not from the overall level of product demand, but rather from the volatility of such demand. If the pattern of product demand were completely stable, so that nothing ever changed, then every firm could repeat the same production plan from one period to the next without any difficulty. Furthermore, if product demand simply alternated between the same small number of states, the firm could prepare its plans in advance for each possible state, and simply implement the pre-specified plan appropriate to whichever of these states appeared. The demand for entrepreneurship arises from the fact that product demand is likely to enter new and unprecedented states for which no plan already exists, because it is uneconomic to devise in advance a plan for every conceivable state, since many conceivable states exist that may never actually occur.

It is not only the state of demand that is volatile in this way. In an open international economy, supply shocks are a regular occurrence. Then there are technology shocks arising from new inventions and discoveries, and cultural and institutional shocks that affect the contractual basis on which business is carried on. In general, the more volatile the environment, the greater the demand for entrepreneurs.

This means, in practical terms, that when volatility increases there will be an increase in the demand for entrepreneurs and a corresponding decline in the demand for substitutes, such as managers. This will normally be reflected in the formation of more small firms and the restructuring of large firms. The large firms may disappear through bankruptcy, or be split up through management buy-out and 'asset-stripping'; alternatively, they may be re-organized in a more flexible form, as a coalition of internal entrepreneurs. Greater competition to hire entrepreneurial employees means that pay structures will tend to become more flexible, because it will no longer be possible to offer both entrepreneurial employees and non-entrepreneurial employees the same rates of pay.

1.8   THE ENTREPRENEUR AND THE FIRM

Many people make entrepreneurial judgements from time to time, for example, choosing a career and a place in which to live. It might appear, therefore, that almost everyone is an entrepreneur. But whilst many people act entrepreneurially on occasions, few do so on a regular basis. Entrepreneurs *specialize* in taking judgemental decisions. This means that they take judgemental decisions not only on their own behalf but on behalf of other people too. They do this by exercising control over resources owned by other people.

In a free society, people are allowed to decide for themselves whether their judgement is good. In choosing their occupations, people who are confident that their judgement is good will tend to gravitate to jobs that call for intensive use of judgement, whilst those who believe that their judgement is bad will gravitate to jobs where other people take decisions for them.

The process of specialization is facilitated by the formation of firms. Firms provide a convenient institutional framework through which people can entrust their resources to the entrepreneur. Investors entrust financial capital, for example, whilst employees agree to allow the entrepreneur to direct their work.

In order to exercise judgement, the entrepreneur needs a suitable degree of discretion. This may be acquired through outright ownership of the firm. Most entrepreneurs are not sufficiently wealthy, however, to own large firms outright, and so they borrow from other people, in the form of bank loans, debentures and equity shareholdings. They may also lease rather than own the physical assets they control.

An entrepreneur does not require absolute control in order to exercise judgement; control may be shared with others (for example, business partners) or delegated to subordinates. Indeed, if they give their subordinates freedom to improvise decisions then these subordinates in effect become entrepreneurs themselves. A large firm may therefore be run by a team of entrepreneurs. The team is likely to have a leader, but not necessarily an autocratic one. A chairman or chief executive may act simply as 'first amongst equals', by taking responsibility for resolving differences of opinion between the other entrepreneurs (Casson, 2005).

Where a single person is in control, they do not necessarily act as an entrepreneur all the time. In a small firm, for example, there may be insufficient judgemental decisions to keep them fully occupied. In this case they may carry out routine managerial functions as well, and even perform manual work (for example, in a craft-based business).

It is sometimes suggested that an entrepreneur must own the firm for which he/she works, but this is not necessarily the case. To begin with, control does not require complete ownership, because when shareholdings are diversified, a dominant minority shareholding may be quite sufficient to exercise control. But control may not require any shareholding at all. The judgement of an entrepreneur with a strong reputation for both competence and integrity might be trusted by shareholders with or without the entrepreneur having any pecuniary interest in the firm. In practice, of course, few potential entrepreneurs are so poor that they cannot afford to buy some shares and so risk-averse that they would decline to do so. Furthermore, few people are trusted so much that shareholders will not require some form of performance bond. A performance bond does not have to be based on equity ownership, however. If the entrepreneur enjoys a high salary and attractive perks then the threat of dismissal may become an important sanction for shareholders. Share options are an alternative – they expose the entrepreneur to substantial capital gains and losses without requiring any heavy investment in the firm.

In general, the extent of a person's reputation governs the amount of other people's resources that they can bring under their control. A person who is not trusted must rely entirely on their own resources. This explains why so many people identify the entrepreneur with a capitalist: they implicitly assume that personal capital is a necessary requirement for the entrepreneur. This explains the popularity of some of the following strategies in the early phases of business growth:

- *Inheritance* The entrepreneur's parents or wealthy relatives may die while he/she is still young. Being the first son under primogeniture and having elderly parents are advantages in this respect. Wealth can be augmented by strategic marriage too – for example, acquiring other people's inheritance from wealthy widows (except when their property is entailed).
- *Hard work and saving* This is a slow method, but has the advantage that the entrepreneur may acquire useful skills whilst in employment, especially if the employment also involves responsibility.
- *Starting on a very small scale and steadily re-investing profits* This method is also potentially slow but can be expedited if the initial venture is high-risk. Thus a merchant may begin by smuggling, gunrunning or piracy, and then become legitimate once sufficient capital has been accumulated to support a proper import-export business.
- Other means include gambling and insurance fraud (for example, over-insuring warehouse contents and then committing arson).

Entrepreneurs with local reputations may acquire resources from family and friends –for example, elderly relatives may finance the younger generation in a family firm. Friends and acquaintances may combine their resources to establish a partnership – this is a common arrangement in professions such as accountancy and law. Manufacturers may obtain resources through trade credit extended by customers or suppliers who have dealt with them on a regular basis. Businessmen and women with a reputation in a local community may rely on local sources of finance channelled through social networks.

1.9   THE ENTREPRENEUR AS PROJECT MANAGER

Not all entrepreneurial activity requires a firm. Simple arbitrage opportunities can be carried out by a private individual. The main reason why entrepreneurship benefits from being organized through a firm is that most coordination activity involves projects. In this context, the key characteristics of a project are that:

- it takes time to complete – particularly when new trading hubs have to be created, and the trading linkages are likely to persist for a significant length of time;
- the outcome is uncertain, so risk is involved; furthermore, the risks involved are subjective, since people with different judgements may assess the risks differently;
- resources must be irreversibly committed – costs are sunk and cannot be recovered; for example, although shop premises may be flexible, costs connected with shelving, display and staff training cannot easily be recovered if the project fails; and
- there is a minimum scale on which the project must be implemented; it is impractical to try out an experiment on a small scale and only scale up if it succeeds; thus if a shop is opened with too little stock it is likely to fail even though a larger shop might well succeed.

The need to manage projects explains the key institutional features of the firm.

- As a virtual person, the firm has unlimited life, so that a project can continue to operate after the death of the entrepreneur.
- Unlike an ordinary partnership, a joint-stock firm can issue bonds and shares in small denominations and therefore can raise finance from a variety of sources.
- Limited liability reduces shareholder risks and promotes a secondary market in shares; this makes shares more liquid and encourages external finance.
- The firm can act as an impersonal network of contracts; thus it is easier to create a production team through contracts between the firm and its individual employees than it is through contracts between each team member and the others.
- The requirement to comply with minimum standards of governance and accountability protects the interests of 'stakeholders' and thereby enhances the reputation of the entrepreneur when dealing with shareholders, employees and suppliers.

Table 1.1   Four stages of entrepreneurial decision-making

Stage	Aspects	Relative reliance on disputed knowledge	Diversity of knowledge base	Output
Project identification	Discovery of potential opportunity Validation of opportunity by looking for hidden snags	High	High	Project opportunity
Project specification	Range of inputs and outputs Locations Contractual arrangements (boundaries of firm) Organizational structure and administrative procedures	Medium	Medium	Project plan
Project development	Research into technology Development of product or process	Low	Medium	Project know-how
Project implementation	Sign contracts Manage workers, sell output Measure performance	Low	Low	Going concern

The formulation and implementation of a project involves several stages, and the type of knowledge involved at each stage is different. Although in principle each stage could be controlled by a different entrepreneur, in practice the same entrepreneur usually needs to take control of every stage.

Four main stages of entrepreneurship may be identified, although each stage has several different aspects, as indicated in Table 1.1. The most fundamental stage is the first; it is often referred to as the 'discovery of opportunities'. The entrepreneur reviews the state of the economy and then compares the efficient allocation of resources to the prevailing allocation in order to identify an opportunity for coordination. In practice, of

Table 1.2　Typology of shocks generating coordination opportunities

	Transitory	Persistent
Demand	Fashion	Change in population and social structure
Supply	Weather, strikes, etc.	Scientific advance Discovery or depletion of raw material supplies
Matching	Numerous minor crises requiring immediate assistance	Development of transport and communication systems

course, an individual entrepreneur does not have the capacity to review the state of the entire economy and will focus on some specific, familiar field. In particular, this is likely to be a field in which the entrepreneur believes that he or she possesses the practical skills required to exploit an available opportunity, because it will not be a valuable prospect in an unexploited form. The entrepreneurial approach is essentially modular – an assumption is made that an opportunity in a chosen field can be exploited successfully, independently of whether simultaneous opportunities in other fields are exploited or not.

To identify a coordination project the entrepreneur will require a knowledge of demand conditions, supply conditions, and the most appropriate way to match supply to demand (see Table 1.2). Identifying changes in these conditions is also important, as the economy is unlikely to have adjusted to them already. Speed of response is important, because some changes may be purely transitory, and even where changes are persistent, pre-emption of rivals may be important.

An entrepreneur will therefore need to synthesize information from a diverse range of sources. Prudent entrepreneurs will also recognize that their own interpretation of this information is likely to be controversial. It is therefore necessary for them to discover any 'hidden snags' in the project by collecting additional information – particularly the kind of information considered relevant by a potential critic. Only when it appears that there is no obvious hidden snag will the 'due diligence' investigation be completed and the entrepreneur proceed to the next stage.

The next stage involves deciding how profit is to be extracted from the project. This stage links the theory of entrepreneurship to the theory of the firm, because the entrepreneur will be thinking of these decisions in terms of setting up a new firm or expanding an existing firm. The best location for the project must be chosen. If the project has national or global implications, multiple locations may be selected, with a view to the

Table 1.3   Obstacles to the marketing of projects at intermediate stages

Obstacle	Project opportunity	Project specification	Project know-how	Going concern
Lack of evidence on economic performance	x	x	x	
Lack of evidence on technical viability	x	x		
Lack of intellectual property rights and consequent need for secrecy	x	x	Possible	
Lack of detailed specification	x			

ultimate establishment of a multi-regional or multinational firm (Buckley and Casson, 1976).

Transaction cost considerations also play an important part at this stage. The entrepreneur will seek to optimize the boundaries of the firm, carrying out some activities internally, and licensing, franchising or subcontracting other activities to independent firms. The economic logic of such decisions is well known, and will not be repeated here (see, for example, Williamson, 1985; Casson, 1997). It is worth noting, however, that these decisions will be contingent on the nature of the project involved, and without some knowledge of the project it is impossible to predict the decisions the entrepreneur will make. Similarly, it must be recognized that some of the knowledge employed to make these decisions will be controversial, so that different entrepreneurs exploiting similar projects might adopt different strategies. Simple transaction cost models, therefore, which ignore the nature of the knowledge employed by the entrepreneur are likely to perform badly in explaining firm behaviour compared with a theory like the present which synthesizes relevant aspects of the theory of the firm with relevant aspects of the theory of the entrepreneur (Barney, 1999).

An entrepreneur who excels at the first stage – opportunity recognition – may be relatively weak at the second stage – strategy formulation – and it is therefore potentially beneficial at this point to engage in collaboration with a strategy specialist. An entrepreneur may be unable to sell a project concept because it is too vague and is unprotected as intellectual property – even if he/she could explain it properly this will only result in giving the idea away (see Table 1.3). It may be valuable to take advice, however. Although strategy formulation involves controversial knowledge, it is not so controversial as the knowledge used at the first stage. It may therefore be possible for the entrepreneur to hire a strategy adviser, even though the strategy adviser would be unwilling to buy into the project. Because much of the knowledge used by the strategy adviser is relatively uncontroversial, it is easy for such an individual to demonstrate competence and to have this underwritten by an educational institution or professional association. A strategy adviser may therefore either become part of the entrepreneur's salaried management team or work for a consultancy fee.

The third stage is project development – often known as R&D. There is some confusion in the literature on the relationship between entrepreneurship and R&D. In principle they are quite distinct: the entrepreneur makes economic judgements, including judgements about the value of technologies, whilst R&D involves scientific and engineering judgements about the conduct of experiments and the interpretation of their results. However, because many economic models of R&D have no formal role for the entrepreneur, the role of the entrepreneur is sometimes ascribed by default to those responsible for the management of R&D.

Although R&D involves – by definition – the quest for new knowledge, much of this new knowledge is uncontroversial, or is regarded by practitioners as uncontroversial, because it has been obtained though scientific methods that are above suspicion. From the standpoint of entrepreneurship, therefore, the controversial element in R&D is relatively low. The range of knowledge required may nevertheless be high. Although basic research is often highly specialized, near-market research concerned with product development often involves a range of technological issues, from quality assurance of raw material inputs through to consumer safety. The relatively low level of controversial knowledge makes it straightforward for the entrepreneur to hire consultants and specialist employees, although the diversity of the knowledge base means that a number of different specialists may need to be hired and moulded into a team.

Once the product concept associated with the project has been scientifically proven, it might be possible for the entrepreneur to sell out, particularly where there is patent and trademark protection in force. Otherwise the entrepreneur might have to continue into the final operational stage, hiring workers and managers and testing the market directly. Once a customer base has been built up and a pricing strategy established, the project can be valued using standard accounting techniques, and it can be sold if so desired. A specialist entrepreneur may choose to exit at this stage in order to develop another project. If the entrepreneur believes that the existing project has unexploited potential however, he/she may wish to remain attached to it in order to implement various growth and diversification options (Penrose, 1959).

1.10 ENTREPRENEURSHIP AND NETWORKS

Social networks are important at all stages of entrepreneurship. Opportunity-seeking entrepreneurs may collect second-hand information from family, friends and acquaintances as a substitute for making direct observations themselves. Access to elite social networks is particularly useful at the discovery stage, as this is where confidential information about high-value opportunities is most likely to circulate. An entrepreneur who wishes to be the first to exploit the news will cultivate access to journalists who handle it prior to publication. Location in a major metropolis is a great advantage from this point of view. This is the place where travellers often call first when arriving from overseas, it is where journalists collect information for their stories, and where groups of people assemble to take important decisions – politicians in Parliament, business leaders at their headquarters and so on. This explains why so much high-level entrepreneurial activity in any country is concentrated in the metropolis.

Reputation is closely associated with network membership. A person's reputation is likely to be strongest in a network to which they belong. Networks often thrive on gossip about other members. Elite networks confer external reputations on their members, especially when only suitably qualified people are allowed to join.

Given that access to key networks is often restricted, the entrepreneur needs a strategy to gain access (for example, making friends with influential people who are 'gate-keepers' to the networks). There should also be a strategy for identifying key members after joining – whilst others may be socializing for relaxation or pleasure, the entrepreneur will be socializing strategically in pursuit of an opportunity. While no single contact may prove decisive, the entrepreneur can synthesize information from different people and use different sources to cross-check information. In this respect, membership of multiple networks is advantageous, especially when the sources of information that need to be synthesized are very diverse.

Networks can also be useful in validating opportunities. Other people may be better than the entrepreneur at spotting hidden snags, since the entrepreneur may become over-committed to, and therefore uncritical of, a new project. People need to be trustworthy, however, if they are to act as a 'sounding board' for an entrepreneur's ideas without the risk of their stealing them. Potential financial bankers such as backers and venture capitalists can be useful in this respect. They have an incentive to give impartial advice because they will also suffer if they fail to spot a hidden snag. While they need to be sufficiently critical to identify snags, they should not be so critical that they cannot recognize the positive potential of the project.

Physical networks are also important. Without physical networks, products and services cannot reach a wide market. Without long-distance transport networks, projects remain small; entrepreneurs are confined to replicating small operations in numerous locations rather than establishing a single large operation to serve a global market. Long-distance communication networks are also important; they allow information for diverse locations to be synthesized in the project discovery process, and they facilitate the coordination of long-distance trade (for example, through post and telecommunications).

This analysis suggests that the trading networks created by entrepreneurs are incubated by the social networks through which entrepreneurs gain access to information. These social networks are supplemented by communications networks which allow information of a more impersonal nature to be synthesized from widely dispersed locations. At the same time, transport networks allow entrepreneurs to distribute their products widely and, where appropriate, to concentrate their production operations on a single large-scale plant fed by components and raw materials from distant sources. In addition, transport networks facilitate social networks by encouraging travel and migration which bring entrepreneurs from different towns and cities into face-to-face contact.

1.11   PARTNER SELECTION

The importance of partner selection came to the fore through the fashion for strategic alliances in the 1980s and 1990s. It was observed that many alliances lasted for only short periods of time. In some cases there was a good reason for this: termination was a natural outcome because the alliance was devised for collaboration on a specific R&D project, or as a means for one of the partners to enter or exit an industry.

Strategic alliances are examples of inter-firm partnership. But there is another form of partnership which is of greater historical significance: namely the partnership between the shareholders in an enterprise. The enterprise may involve either a single project, such as a trading voyage, or recurrent activities of the kind undertaken by an ordinary firm. Prior to the emergence of the joint-stock enterprise and modern equity markets, many firms were financed as partnerships between two or more individuals, each of whom held a substantial share of the overall stake.

Partnerships of this kind required a great deal of trust. This is particularly true where all the partners hold equal shares, so that there is ambiguity about ultimate control. In some partnerships the prime responsibility for decisions clearly lies with just one of the partners, and the other partners have a 'sleeping' role. This corresponds to the case in which an entrepreneur seeks out finance from investors who play an essentially passive role (so long as the venture appears successful). But in other partnerships, several of the partners may share the decision-making role. They may establish a division of labour, based on their relative expertise in different areas of the business, or they may take all the decisions collectively.

Choosing the right partners requires a good knowledge of other people. This is not just a question of 'networking', but of psychological insight. It involves the capacity to 'decode' the signals that people give through everyday behaviour in order to infer what their underlying motivations are likely to be. This capacity also requires a certain degree of self-awareness. It is difficult for a person to understand other people's motivations if they do not first understand their own. Successful entrepreneurs are likely to choose their partners well, and therefore to have enduring relations with them.

It is not always appropriate to maintain a partnership, however, even where trust is high. Conditions may change as a result of changes in the industry or in the personal circumstances of those involved. An appropriate choice of partner allows the partnership to be dissolved in amicable fashion, so that all the partners retain their reputation for integrity. A successful entrepreneur may therefore build a career through a succession of partnerships rather than a single enduring one: but if their partner selection is effective, they will enhance their reputation as their partnerships progress, and avoid the damaging recriminations that arise when partnerships turn sour.

1.12   MOBILITY OF THE ENTREPRENEUR

It was noted above that everyone takes judgemental decisions from time to time. These decisions concern choice of occupation, where to live and selection of partner – in business and marriage. Entrepreneurs will reveal their qualities by the kind of choices they make. Some choices will be distinctly entrepreneurial and others non-entrepreneurial; others will simply reveal differences between various types of entrepreneur. It was also noted above that it can be difficult to identify what makes a true entrepreneur. Because they reveal underlying attitudes, the personal choices that people make may prove useful in this respect.

Through their personal decisions, entrepreneurs sort themselves out into different fields: some go to live in one country or region, and others in another; some go into one occupation, and others into another; some marry for love or beauty, and others for connections and money.

Geographical Mobility

Everyone has to decide, at some stage, whether to remain in the place where they grew up, or to move on to somewhere else. People tend to be most mobile between the time that they leave school and the time that they settle down to pursue their main career. It may be suggested that, at this stage, entrepreneurs are more likely to move and non-entrepreneurs to stay. This is particularly true of people brought up in isolated rural areas where there are few opportunities for profit. Such areas tend to lose their more entrepreneurial young people. Conversely, large cities tend to attract entrepreneurial young people. They offer greater profit opportunities, a wider choice of jobs and access to larger amounts of specialized information through the clubs and societies that flourish there. Those who succeed in the city may well retire to the countryside, buying their way into the local gentry, and acquiring positions of status – for example, becoming a magistrate. Some may retire to the area where they grew up, but envy of their success by those who remained behind may sometimes keep them away.

If entrepreneurs are prepared to move long distances they have, in principle, a wide choice of destinations; they also have a choice of political regimes under which to operate. Short-run profit opportunities may be an important consideration for the very young, who may be attracted by mining booms or the like to emigrate to underdeveloped parts of the world. Once these booms are over, they have to decide whether to return home, or to move on somewhere else. At this stage, the long-run attractions of political regimes may be important, particularly if they are concerned to protect their new-found wealth from taxation.

Even some of the most entrepreneurial people may not wish to move long distances to alien societies on economic grounds alone. A 'push' may well be required. A good example of this is the expulsion of ethnic minorities by totalitarian political regimes. This may range from the persecution of religious sects to the dispossession of peasants and the expropriation of a wealthy merchant class. While such measures do not discriminate between entrepreneurs and non-entrepreneurs in terms of which people leave, they may well discriminate in terms of where the migrants terminate their travels. The least entrepreneurial may well stop at the first place of refuge, whilst the more entrepreneurial may continue in search of the most conducive regime.

While immigrants who have been expelled from other countries might be thought to be, on balance, less entrepreneurial than the purely 'economic' migrant, the effect of adversity on their motivation should not be overlooked. If loss of wealth and status stimulates a desire to restore the family's fortunes, then expulsion may turn into a very powerful motivator of success.

Occupational Mobility of the Entrepreneur

It used to be the case that young men who remained behind in a locality would be likely to follow their father into the same line of business. Where the father was an employee, they followed him 'into the works' or 'down the pit'. A father might even have used his influence to get his son a job, even though it might have been in a 'sunset' industry. To those with narrow horizons and a parochial outlook, any long-standing local industry may still appear secure. But those entrepreneurs who remain behind will reveal their qualities by getting jobs, or starting firms, in newer industries instead. The non-entrepreneurial workers may eventually join the ranks of the 'structurally unemployed'.

The same mechanism applies in a family firm (Church, 1993). Tradition has a father telling his son, 'One day all this will be yours', and the son feeling morally obliged to succeed his father, even though his interests might lie elsewhere. More entrepreneurial offspring might turn down the offer and set up in business in a different industry, forcing the father to look outside the family for a successor – possibly with beneficial results for the firm.

Business owners who remain behind in a declining industry or region may join forces to lobby for protective tariffs or industrial subsidies. They harness organizations, such as trade associations, which were originally established to promote the provision of industry-specific 'public goods' like training, for collusive purposes. They attempt to maintain profit levels through (covert) price-fixing; to counter trades union power by bargaining collectively and so on. A secretive and conspiratorial business culture develops, reflecting the entrepreneurial weaknesses of the business group.

Inter-Sectoral Mobility

Entrepreneurs not only move between industries within the private sector: they can also move between the private sector, the non-profit sector and the government sector. The initial choice of sector will reflect the entrepreneur's preferences. Some entrepreneurs may place considerable weight on pecuniary rewards, whilst other may weigh non-pecuniary rewards, such as status, more heavily instead. Some entrepreneurs may thrive on taking financial risks, while others are more risk-averse.

Entrepreneurs who value money rather than status and are happy to bear financial risks are likely to become the owners of private firms. Those who value both money and status, but are more averse to financial risk, are likely to become private sector employees. Those who value status rather than money, and are financially risk-averse, are likely to enter government service. Those who value status rather than money, and are willing to take some financial risks, may enter the non-profit sector.

As an entrepreneur's career progresses, his/her circumstances are likely to change, with concomitant behavioural change as well. Having acquired a substantial amount of wealth from private ventures, the entrepreneur becomes fearful of losing it, and so switches it into a 'liquid' asset such as land. The demand for money being satiated, status becomes the next target. A gentry property and local politics might be the next stage, until the consumption of money and status is restored to balance.

There is a strong tendency in much of the historical literature to see the private sector as the sole arena for entrepreneurial activity. This is particularly true of writers who wish to emphasize the greed and avarice of the entrepreneur. Proponents of free enterprise tend to reinforce this bias by attempting to show that entrepreneurship can only flourish when it is driven by the profit motive working through a competitive market system. Theory lends little support to this ideological view. It merely suggests that, not surprisingly, entrepreneurs who seek pecuniary rewards gravitate to the private sector, whilst those who seek non-pecuniary rewards gravitate to other sectors instead.

1.13   THE INSTITUTIONAL FRAMEWORK

The regimes that are most attractive to mobile entrepreneurs are likely to possess the classic institutions of the liberal market economy. Good judgement is most likely to thrive in societies that recognize the controversial nature of much of the knowledge exploited by entrepreneurs and that tailor their institutions to benefit from the 'creative tension' caused by rival opinions. Such societies are likely to be individualistic rather than collectivist, in the sense that they seek to control autocrats and dictators who believe that they know better than everyone else on every issue.

They will have some or all of the following characteristics:

- private property, which is freely alienable, subject to certain minimal restrictions;
- freedom of movement, and freedom to associate with business partners;
- confidentiality of business information, especially regarding the relations with customers and suppliers;

- protection of creative work through patents, copyright, design protection and so on;
- access to impartial courts which will enforce property rights and which have the competence to settle complex commercial claims;
- a stable currency, based on a prudent control of the money supply;
- democratic government, with sufficient balance of power between opposing interests to reduce the risks of draconian interventions in industry and commerce;
- openness to immigration by entrepreneurs and skilled workers (and possibly other groups as well)

Differences in regime can also be found, to a more limited extent, between regions of the same country. Different regions acquire distinctive cultures, often as a result of historical patterns of interregional migration. Regions with a dominant but declining industry may have strong trades unions (or craft guilds), whose inflexible attitude to working practices is a major deterrent to entrepreneurs in 'sunrise' industries. This suggests that successive waves of innovation will move around a country, avoiding areas where previous waves of innovation have ossified into traditional working practices. Only the metropolis will remain vibrant because of its continuing ability to attract young entrepreneurs. If the metropolis too goes into decline, then the outlook for the entire national economy is bleak.

Adopting an international comparative perspective, Jones (1981, 1988) has argued that entrepreneurship is a natural feature of human behaviour that government can either encourage or suppress. Encouragement is provided by a regime of freedom under law, which allows people to carry out experiments in commercial and industrial organization at their own expense. Suppression is effected by governments that fall into the hands of elites, who think they know best which experiments are socially desirable and which are not. They subsidize prestigious experiments out of taxes, and repress ordinary experiments because they are seen as either useless, immoral or politically subversive.

Thus while the presence of liberal market institutions may account for economic success, their absence may lead to poor performance. This may explain the failure of many less-developed countries to commercialize and industrialize on a significant scale. Assuming that the leaders of these countries are seeking economic progress, their persistence in maintaining inappropriate institutional structures remains to be explained. One possibility is that their time horizons are very short and their motives are venal; their objective is to maximize the perks of holding political office for as long as they can cling to power. This approach appears quite common in countries where military dictators hold ultimate power.

Another possibility is that leaders have misguided beliefs about the way in which economies function. They overestimate the 'gains from raids' and underestimate the 'gains from trade', and therefore focus their attention on waging wars against neighbouring countries. They fail to appreciate that sources of information are highly decentralized, and therefore underestimate the value of competitive profit-seeking whilst overestimating the benefits of state control. A third possibility is that attitudes are so traditional and inward-looking that change of any kind is resisted, including change to a more entrepreneurial economy. Cultural attitudes may be so parochial that a leader may be unaware, or unconcerned, about how far their country is lagging behind the most advanced economies.

1.14   ENTERPRISE CULTURE

When there is a general perception in a society that volatility has increased, social and political attitudes may change as well. Considered as an historical phenomenon, the enterprise culture of the 1980s and 1990s was a natural reaction to some of the anti-entrepreneurial attitudes that had taken root in the West in the early post-war period (Della Giusta and King, 2006). The growth of the welfare state allowed public investment to 'crowd out' private investment, whilst the Cold War focused inventive activity on military projects. Productivity stagnated, while Keynesian full employment policy sustained unrealistic wage aspirations.

It should not be inferred, however, that the enterprise culture of the 1980s and 1990s was based on a correct understanding of the role of the entrepreneur. The highly competitive and materialistic form of individualism promoted by 'enterprise culture' is not necessarily conducive to good judgement. Indeed, competitive and materialistic values can actually impair economic performance. People who are aggressively selfish often find it difficult to trust other people, because they believe that other people are aggressively selfish like themselves. Trust is important to entrepreneurs because it reduces their transaction costs. Entrepreneurs need to be trusted by investors and customers, whilst they in turn need to trust their employees and suppliers.

A reputation for being trustworthy is often based on unselfish objectives – such as compassion and a desire for justice. Commitments to traditional moral values such as honesty and diligence also promote trust. The greater the moral commitment of the entrepreneur, the more likely they are to be trusted; as a result, their reputation increases and they can gain control of more resources with which to put their judgement to work.

It is not so much a spirit of competitive individualism as the principle of *voluntary association* that is important. While competitive individualism tends to undermine trust, voluntary associationism encourages cooperative behaviour and therefore builds up trust and reputation. It allows individuals the freedom to choose which associations they join, but demands that once a member joins they commit to serving that association wherever their short-term material self-interest might lie (see Chapter 8).

1.15   ETHNIC ENTREPRENEURSHIP

Variations in institutional regimes also appear to influence the entrepreneurial patterns of particular groups of migrants. Almost everywhere immigrant arrivals have selected to work in ethnic labour markets in order to reduce the costs of adjustment to the new host society. The reduced assimilation into the host culture also leads to varying degrees of social exclusion. This has often given rise to patterns of so-called ethnic entrepreneurship, where ethnic minorities pursue self-employment in order to avoid economic discrimination. Variations in institutional regimes and in ethnic backgrounds appear to make significant differences in how ethnic entrepreneurs are able to overcome economic discrimination, build prosperous businesses, and acquire social acceptability (Godley, 2001).

   While currently the dominant view among specialists is pessimistic (that the entrepreneurial route to ethnic assimilation and social inclusion typically fails), the theory of entrepreneurship developed here could better explain the determinants of failure. Focusing on entrepreneurial judgement, for instance, would clarify whether self-employed ethnic minorities are actually entrepreneurial, or whether in fact many small-business owners are simply being managerial. Focusing on the entrepreneur's interpretative skills would highlight whether cultural backgrounds either help or hinder the entrepreneurial function. Focusing on the costs of information would highlight whether ethnic entrepreneurs are particularly disadvantaged, and, if so, whether this arises from host society discrimination or some other factor, such as opting to remain in an industry where the long-term prospects are poor.

1.16   IMPLICATIONS FOR ECONOMIC AND
BUSINESS HISTORY

The theory set out above has important implications for economic and business history. To begin with, it shows that entrepreneurship has been an important factor in stimulating economic growth throughout recorded history. However, the roles that entrepreneurs have occupied have changed significantly over time. These changes have occurred because of advances in knowledge, the evolution of sophisticated institutions – notably commercial law – and the accumulation of wealth, which has created a growing demand for luxuries.

In the twentieth century the most prominent entrepreneurs were the CEOs of large Chandlerian corporations, who initiated 'three-pronged' investments in production, marketing and distribution that enabled them to capitalize, first on the growth of national markets, and then on the growth of the global market (Chandler, 1990).

In the nineteenth century some of the most prominent entrepreneurs were engineering consultants advising on major infrastructure projects, such as canals, railways, harbours and town improvements (Smiles, 1862). The local promoters of these schemes often lacked the wider perspective of the consulting engineer, who had undertaken similar projects in different localities. It was not, therefore, just the consultant's technological knowledge that was valued, but also his knowledge of the strategic issues involved in raising capital and defeating rival schemes (Casson, 2009).

Business partnership was an important feature of eighteenth-century entrepreneurship. The opportunities of an expanding economy could not be fully exploited by purely family firms. At the same time, the establishment of joint-stock limited liability companies was an expensive process, and so partnerships between people from different families became increasingly common. The partners pooled their resources – at the time of the Industrial Revolution it was not unusual for one partner to be an impoverished inventor and another a wealthy merchant or financier. The partners divided responsibilities according to their expertise, and took the key decisions together – in effect, sharing the role of the entrepreneur.

Once the historian looks behind the legal construct of the firm to the people who control it, the role of entrepreneurship becomes quite clear. Firms are designed to outlive the people who found them, and given the importance of people, the strategy and performance of the firm are both liable to change once the key personnel change. The death or retirement of an entrepreneur is therefore a crucial stage in the development of a firm. Even very able entrepreneurs find it difficult to manage succession – they groom unsuitable successors, or fail to address the issue altogether, and leave the firm to be fought over by rival factions once they have gone. Family firms are often criticized for their failure to cope with succession; the criteria used for the selection of a successor are often ambiguous, so that an incompetent eldest son may be preferred to a more competent daughter or son-in-law (Jones and Rose, 1993). Failure is particularly likely with dynastic families that are reluctant to bring in non-family entrepreneurs; on the other hand, families that simply want to maximize their income may out-perform the owners of non-family firms because a small number of powerful shareholders are better able to discipline a salaried entrepreneur than is a diverse group of small shareholders (Casson, 1998).

Theory indicates that the personal qualities of the entrepreneur are an important factor in the success and failure of a firm. Historical biography is therefore invaluable in testing theory. Until recently, biographies of both businesses and businessmen were often dismissed as anecdotal and therefore unscientific, whereas in fact they can provide vital evidence with which to test theories of the entrepreneur. Taken as a whole, the biographical literature confirms many of the predictions of entrepreneurship theory, although there is insufficient space to do full justice to all the issues here. It is clear that the early lives of entrepreneurs have a significant impact on their subsequent performance. Access to vocational education (for example, dame schools, technical colleges) has been important, together with a religious education that emphasizes impersonal moral principles rather than personal status as the legitimate source of worldly authority (for example, Methodism). The wide-ranging life experiences of immigrants also seem to have given them advantages – especially those groups that were attracted to major urban centres by the prospect of economic gain (Godley, 2001).

Given that entrepreneurship is such an important historical force, its effects should be discernable at every period of time. It is therefore surprising that many historians suggest that entrepreneurship appears in intermittent bursts – most notably during the Industrial Revolution of 1760–1830. In fact many other 'revolutions' can be discerned using the lens of entrepreneurship theory. Some of the most important are presented in Table 1.4. Whilst the knowledge exploited in these revolutions eventually diffused to every country, diffusion was sometimes slow, and so the revolutions have been dated using a particular country – England – in which several of the nineteenth-century revolutions first occurred. This historical interpretation agrees with Schumpeter's (1939) account of waves of innovation, which he believed also triggered long-period cycles in economic activity (see also Solomou, 1987; Freeman and Louca, 2001).

The application of entrepreneurship theory to history combines elements of both economics and sociology. It is difficult, for example, to consider the role of business partners and family owners without considering not only the economic opportunities they discover but also the webs of social obligations in which they are embedded. This underlines the point made at the outset – that entrepreneurship theory acts as a bridge between social sciences, such as economics and sociology, that were at odds with each

Table 1.4   Economic revolutions in England, 800 – date

Period	Revolution
800–1200	State formation
1100–1300	Urbanization
1200–1500	Market organization
1300–1700	Financial revolution
1400–1600	Overseas discoveries
1600–1700	Chartered trading companies
1700–1800	Agricultural revolution
1760–1830	Industrial Revolution
1830–1900	Railway and infrastructure revolution
1900–date	Telecommunications revolution
1900–date	Commercialization of science
1900–date	Mass production

other throughout much of the twentieth century. While economics has de-personalized entrepreneurship by emphasizing the impersonal forces of the competitive market, sociology has also de-personalized the entrepreneur by treating entrepreneurs as faceless members of an exploitative capitalist class. Once entrepreneurs are recognized as real people, the need for a theory to address economic and social aspects of individual behaviour in an integrated fashion becomes clear. The theory of entrepreneurship set out in this chapter attempts to do just this. It treats entrepreneurs as rational agents capable of good judgement in their economic affairs, but also as people whose objectives are not purely venal, but also reflect moral values and social responsibility.

1.17   IMPLICATIONS FOR ECONOMIC THEORY AND POLICY

The theory set out in this chapter has implications, not only for history, but also for economics. Entrepreneurs are the human face of the market economy. Markets are sets of linkages between buyers and sellers. They need to be understood not just in terms of general forces of supply and demand, but also as products of individual initiative. Entrepreneurs set up and intermediate market linkages, often using hubs. Rival hubs are often co-located to facilitate price comparison and innovation. As hubs proliferate, competition intensifies between entrepreneurs as substitute linkages emerge, and so rents increasingly accrue to consumers and factor suppliers

Information collected from the marketing and distribution activities of these 'market making firms' often initiates manufacturing innovations by the suppliers. Market-making should not be confused with production, and economic knowledge of profit opportunities should not be confused with technological knowledge about how to organize production. Entrepreneurs specialize in collecting information about profit opportunities. They can delegate the supply of technological know-how to the scientists and engineers that they employ.

Entrepreneurship is a theory of success. Success is not purely a matter of luck. It stems from good judgement, which is individual-specific. The procedures on which good judgement is based are tacit and unpatentable, and are therefore impossible to sell. Good judgement has many manifestations: scientific judgement, for example, may determine what laboratory experiments are carried out. The characteristic of entrepreneurs is that they make practical economic judgements, and specifically judgements about the way that resources are allocated. Furthermore, they specialize in making such judgements. They make these judgements, not only on their own behalf, but on behalf of other people as well.

The process of specialization is facilitated by the formation of firms that provide an institutional framework through which people entrust their resources to the entrepreneur. Investors entrust financial capital, for example, whilst employees agree to allow the entrepreneur to direct their work. The success of a firm therefore derives from the personal qualities of the entrepreneur. These qualities are more specific than those referred to in economic theory of 'human capital' (Schultz, 1971) or 'resource-based' theories of the firm (Barney, 1999).

Good judgement is not the same thing as low risk-aversion, or a preference for innovation; indeed, taking unnecessary risks and innovating prematurely indicate bad judgement. Whilst good judgement is not the only factor in success – persistence, hard work and a desire for achievement are also important – it is the crucial factor in successful innovation and risk-taking. Other qualities by themselves are not enough.

Entrepreneurship does not necessarily lead to self-employment or the founding of a firm or the sole ownership of a firm. The more reputable an entrepreneur, the more willing are investors to contribute capital, and the less concerned they are that the entrepreneur should carry risk himself. A highly reputable entrepreneur may therefore function as the salaried CEO of a large firm, and not as the owner of a small one.

Unlike other views of entrepreneurship, which focus only on small firms, or only on high-tech innovation, the theory presented here encompasses all forms of entrepreneurial activity. It is truly a general theory of entrepreneurship, and not a theory that offers spurious generalizations based upon a special case.

The consequences for policymakers are obvious. Entrepreneurship should not be equated with self-employment or the ownership or management of SMEs. Self-employment is a natural role in many occupations – for example, plumbing – simply because it is difficult for an employer to monitor the activity of the employee; SMEs may remain small for a good reason – the limited competencies of the entrepreneur.

Government support for entrepreneurship should not automatically focus on SMEs. Large firms too may need government support – in particular large high-growth firms. Government should focus on doing what government does best, investing in infrastructure – in particular transport and communications – and in social networks. Because social networks often operate on a non-profit basis, there is a risk that networking opportunities may be under-supplied through private initiatives. Because government needs to maintain contact with a wide range of citizens and interest groups, it is well positioned to develop social networks, and where it also has a reputation for integrity, confidentiality and impartiality, it is in a good position to preside over them. Government can therefore support non-profit networks that intermediate between entrepreneurs and financiers, business partners, major customers and so on. Finally, government can support entrepreneurs by setting tax rates that lead to socially efficient decisions about whether or not to become an entrepreneur and about which particular projects to promote (Baumol, 1990).

1.18   CONCLUSION

The entrepreneur is a leading character in many accounts of economic growth, appearing in business biographies as a charismatic founder of a company; in industry studies as a prominent innovator, or a leading figure in a trade association or cartel; and in national histories as one of the hordes of self-employed small-business owners who confer flexibility and dynamism on a market economy. Entrepreneurship is not confined to the private sector; it can also be discerned in the personalities of people who establish progressive charitable trusts and reform government administration.

Yet this very ubiquity of the entrepreneur is a cause for concern. Entrepreneurship means different things to different people. It is rarely defined explicitly, and controversies over entrepreneurship often involve questions of semantics as well as fact. Few definite hypotheses have been deduced from theory, and few law-like generalizations have been advanced from case-study evidence.

An adequate account of entrepreneurship must address the following issues:

- What does the introduction of the entrepreneur add to our understanding of economic development? Do accounts of entrepreneurial behaviour supplement statistical evidence, or merely re-tell the same story through biographical anecdote?
- Is entrepreneurship just a label for an area of ignorance? Does it – like 'culture' and 'institutions' – sometimes just denote residual causes of growth that cannot be properly measured?
- Can anyone really know what goes on inside the mind of an entrepreneur? If not, what is the point of speculating about the subject?

These questions can be addressed only by a systematic theory of the entrepreneur. This theory must generate hypotheses, either about entrepreneurs themselves, or about the economies to which they belong. These hypotheses must explain both contemporary and historical evidence of the kind that ordinary theories that leave out the entrepreneur cannot address.

This chapter has outlined a theory of entrepreneurship that has been developed specifically to address these issues. The theory explains how entrepreneurs initiate market processes, and develops a range of hypotheses suitable for historical study. The theory facilitates a more sophisticated assessment of the factors influencing the rise and decline of firms, regions and nations. It also allows historical evidence to be harnessed to the testing of economic theory, outside of the narrow confines of conventional 'cliometrics'.

The theory emphasizes that both cultures and institutions matter. Like the canonical theories, it recognizes that the economic environment faced by the entrepreneur is not the textbook ideal-type of perfectly competitive market. Firms and governments do not instantly adjust their behaviour in response to price changes. Volatility, and the consequent emergence of disequilibria, occurs continually in the world economy. Entrepreneurs both create and respond to these disequilibria by exercising their commercial judgement.

The theory presented in this chapter has an important advantage over the earlier theories in the canonical literature. It goes beyond canonical thinking by focusing very sharply on the nature of judgement. By examining the factors influencing the demand and supply of judgement, and the role of profit in rewarding judgement, a number of powerful propositions can be deduced. Amongst the range of propositions generated by the theory, several are of particular interest to the historian.

Because judgement improves with age and experience, successful entrepreneurs are likely to be mature people in early middle age rather than those who are very young. Previous experience of working for another firm often provides insights and contacts that are useful to the self-employed entrepreneur.

Because independent judgement is required to identify profitable opportunities, successful entrepreneurs may well be outsiders (ethnically, socially or religiously). Furthermore, because reputation typically increases with successful outcomes to business interactions, so successful entrepreneurs are likely to be well-connected.

Because the volatility of the business environment changes over time, the interpretative abilities of the population of entrepreneurs at one point may fail to meet demands at a later stage. When the supply of entrepreneurs is demonstrably inadequate, political dissatisfaction may encourage institutional changes designed to improve the supply of entrepreneurs.

The theory of entrepreneurship demonstrates clearly the strong links between economic concepts such as markets, firms and competition, sociological concepts such as networks and trust, and historical concepts such as institutional innovation and structural change. Controversies over definition, and a reluctance by economists to confront the complexity of market dynamics led, until recently, to the marginalization of the economic theory of the entrepreneur. Despite the high professional standing of the canonical writers in the field, mainstream economists have preferred to ignore their intellectual contribution. Now that this resistance is beginning to crumble, the opportunity exists to integrate the disciplines of economics, sociology and history by restoring the entrepreneur to his/her rightful place at the centre of the market process. By bringing greater realism to economics, this will act as a bridge between economics and other disciplines and facilitate the development of a rational action social science. This integrated social science can be based on the principle of rational action, provided that rationality is construed as purely instrumental, and as something framed by culturally contingent values and beliefs. Institutions, networks and history will all have a prominent role in this integrated theory, as will the concept of the entrepreneur.

REFERENCES

Acs, Zoltan J. and David B. Audretsch (2003), *Handbook of Entrepreneurship Research: An Interdisciplinary Survey and Introduction*, Dordrecht: Kluwer.

Arrow, Kenneth and Gerard Debreu (1954), 'Existence of an equilibrium for a competitive economy', *Econometrica*, **22**, 265–90.

Barney, Jay (1999), 'How a firm's capabilities affect boundary decisions', *Sloan Management Studies*, **40** (3), 137–45.

Baumol, William J. (1968), 'Entrepreneurship in economic theory', *American Economic Review (Papers and Proceedings)*, **58**, 64–71.

Baumol, William J. (1990), 'Entrepreneurship: productive, unproductive and destructive', *Journal of Political Economy*, **98**, 893–921.

Blanchflower, D. and Andrew Oswald (1998), 'What makes an entrepreneur?', *Journal of Labour Economics*, **16** (1), 26–60.

Brenner, Reuven (1983), *History: The Human Gamble*, Chicago: University of Chicago Press.

Buckley, Peter J. and Mark Casson (1976), *The Future of the Multinational Enterprise*, London: Macmillan.

Cantillon, Richard (1755), *Essai sur la Nature du Commerce en Generale*, ed. and trans. H. Higgs (1931), London: Macmillan.

Casson, Mark (1982), *The Entrepreneur: An Economic Theory*, 2nd edn (2003), Cheltenham, UK and Northampton, MA, USA: Edward Elgar.

Casson, Mark (1997), *Information and Organization: A New Perspective on the Theory of the Firm*, Oxford: Oxford University Press.

Casson, Mark (1998), 'The economics of the family firm', *Scandinavian Economic History Review*, **47** (1), 10–23.

Casson, Mark (2003), 'Marshall and marketing', in J. Creedy (ed.) *From Classical Economics to the Theory of the Firm: Essays in Honour of D.P. O'Brien*, Cheltenham, UK and Northampton, MA, USA: Edward Elgar, pp. 194–219.

Casson, Mark (2005), 'Entrepreneurship and the theory of the firm', *Journal of Economic Behaviour and Organization*, **58**, 327–48.

Casson, Mark (2006), 'Culture and economic performance', in V.A. Ginzberg and D.Throsby (eds), *Handbook of the Economics of Art and Culture,* Amsterdam: North-Holland, pp. 359–97.

Casson, Mark (2009), *The World's First Railway System*, Oxford: Oxford University Press.

Casson, Mark, Bernard Yeung, Anuradha Basu and Nigel Wadeson (eds) (2006), *Oxford Handbook of Entrepreneurship*, Oxford: Oxford University Press.

Chandler, Alfred J. Jr (1990), *Scale and Scope: The Dynamics of Industrial Capitalism*, Cambridge, MA: Harvard University Press.

Church, Roy (1993), 'The family firm in industrial capitalism: international perspectives on hypotheses and history', *Business History*, **35** (4), 17–43.

Della Giusta, Marina and Zella M.E. King (2006), 'Enterprise culture', in M. Casson, B. Yeung, A. Basu and N. Wadeson (eds) *Oxford Handbook of Entrepreneurship*, Oxford: Oxford University Press, pp. 629–47.

Freeman, Christopher and Francisco Louca (2001), *As Time Goes By: From the Industrial Revolutions to the Information Revolution*, Oxford: Oxford University Press.

Godley, Andrew (2001), *Jewish Immigrant Entrepreneurship in New York and London, 1880–1914,* Basingstoke: Palgrave.

Harper, David A. (1996), *Entrepreneurship and the Market Process: An Inquiry into the Growth of Knowledge*, London: Routledge.

Hayek, Friedrich A. von (1937), 'Economics and knowledge', *Economica*, n.s., **4**, 33–54.

Jones, Eric (1981), *The European Miracle*, Cambridge: Cambridge University Press.

Jones, Eric (1988), *Growth Recurring*, Oxford: Clarendon Press.

Jones, Geoffrey G. and Mary B. Rose (eds) (1993), *Family Capitalism*, London: Frank Cass.

Kirzner, Israel M. (1973), *Competition and Entrepreneurship*, Chicago: University of Chicago Press.

Knight, Frank (1921), *Risk, Uncertainty and Profit*, Boston, MA: Houghton Mifflin.

Marshall, Alfred (1890), *Principles of Economics*, 9th edn, ed. C.W. Guillebaud (1961), London: Macmillan.

Marshall, Alfred (1919), *Industry and Trade*, London: Macmillan.

Parker, Simon C. (2004), *The Economics of Self-employment and Entrepreneurship*, Cambridge: Cambridge University Press.

Penrose, Edith T. (1959), *The Theory of the Growth of the Firm*, Oxford: Blackwell.

Richardson, George A. (1960), *Information and Investment: A Study in the Working of the Competitive Economy*, (revised edn, ed. D. Teece) Oxford: Oxford University Press, 1990.

Schultz, Theodore W. (1971), *Economics of Human Capital: The Role of Education and of Research*, New York: Free Press.

Schumpeter, Joseph A. (1934), *The Theory of Economic Development*, ed. R. Opie, Cambridge, MA: Harvard University Press.

Schumpeter, Joseph A. (1939), *Business Cycles*, New York: John Wiley.

Shane, Scott (2003), *A General Theory of Entrepreneurship: The Individual – Opportunity Nexus*, Cheltenham, UK and Northampton, MA, USA: Edward Elgar.

Smiles, Samuel (1862), *Lives of the Engineers*, London: John Murray.

Smith, Adam (1776), *An Inquiry into the Nature and Causes of the Wealth of Nations*, Glasgow edn, Oxford: Oxford University Press.

Solomou, Solomos (1987), *Phases of Economic Growth, 1850–1973*, Cambridge: Cambridge University Press.

Storey, David (1994), *Understanding the Small Business Sector*, London: Routledge.

Walras, Leon (1954), *Elements of Pure Economics, or the Theory of Social Wealth*, ed. W. Jaffe, London: Allen and Unwin.

Williamson, Oliver E. (1985), *The Economic Institutions of Capitalism*, New York: Free Press.

2. The discovery of opportunities

With Nigel Wadeson

This chapter presents a conceptual framework that can be used to analyse the process of entrepreneurial opportunity discovery. An opportunity can be considered as a project whose exploitation would be advantageous to the entrepreneur. The entrepreneur has to use judgement in deciding which projects are most worth implementing. One important aspect of this is the question of how the entrepreneur is to apply judgement in deciding what information to gather, given the need to economize on the costs of doing so.

2.1 INTRODUCTION

The concept of opportunity plays a central part in entrepreneurship theory (for example, Kirzner, 1979; Shane, 2003; Sarasvathy et al., 2003), though the term 'opportunity' has been employed in different ways by different writers, and this has created some confusion. Kirzner (1973), for example, suggests that opportunities are like dollar bills blowing around on the sidewalk, waiting for an alert individual to pick them up. Schumpeter (1934), by contrast, suggests that opportunities require large amounts of capital to exploit, and that the commitment to exploit them can be found only in minds of the highest order.

When used in some contexts, 'opportunity' seems to signify merely an idea about how to earn a profit. In the economic literature, it often relates to an unexploited 'activity', but it remains unclear what sort of 'activity' this would be. The purely metaphorical nature of Kirzner's example, and the very exceptional activity described by Schumpeter, reinforce this notion that the concept of opportunity is difficult to apply in practice. This chapter argues that an opportunity is best conceived as a potentially profitable but hitherto unexploited *project*. There are specific qualities that distinguish projects from activities, and these qualities demonstrate how the concept of opportunity can be brought 'down to earth' in a relevant manner. The shift from activity to project does not require a radical rethinking of the subject; rather, it is an exercise in clarification.

There are relatively few opportunities that simply lie around waiting for people to stumble across them by chance. The discovery of an opportunity generally involves a commitment of scarce resources; in some cases this may be simply the time of the person involved, but in other cases physical resources, such as offices and IT systems, can be tied up as well. In a world of scarcity, these resources could have generated value if they had been deployed to an alternative use. The costs are sunk, for example, the time an entrepreneur has spent in seeking out a project cannot be recovered if it is abandoned (although any unspent time can, of course, be saved).

Although the concept of opportunity is well known, many economists continue to have difficulty understanding why it plays such a central role in entrepreneurship. They tend to question why there are unexploited opportunities. If these opportunities exist, and could be exploited right away, why have they not already been exploited? This seems to point to an inefficiency in the economic system which is difficult to explain.

The short answer to this question is that the existence of unexploited opportunities does not imply any inefficiency at all. The misunderstanding arises because the costs of discovery have been ignored. More opportunities could be discovered if more resources were devoted to their discovery. But diminishing returns are liable to set in. The easiest opportunities to identify are likely to be discovered first, and so the costs of each additional discovery increase as more people join in the search and the stock of easily discovered opportunities is depleted. Secondly, duplication of effort becomes more likely as more people join in and make the same discoveries. Duplicated discoveries are not only socially wasteful: competition by rivals exploiting similar projects dissipates rents and thereby, in the long-run, discourages entrepreneurial effort (Casson, 1994). Thus there is a margin at which the expected profit afforded by a further opportunity becomes equal to the expected cost of discovering the opportunity. Beyond this margin lie all the undiscovered opportunities that await discovery at a later date.

If there were a fixed stock of opportunities, then as new opportunities were discovered the stock of unexploited opportunities would decline until no new opportunities remained to be discovered. Such 'stagnationist' thinking was once quite common (Keynes, 1936), but it overlooks the implications of learning and volatility. Experience gained as a by-product from exploiting existing opportunities creates new opportunities by making additional projects viable. Changes in the environment can also make new projects worthwhile, whilst making others obsolete. As the economy adapts to changing conditions, new opportunities arise as fast as others are destroyed.

The exploitation of opportunities is a vital part of the economy's response to external shocks. When new scarcities arise, or existing scarcities tighten their grip, opportunities arise to economize on the scarcer resources and substitute other resources for them instead (Baumol, 2002). The prospect of profit arising from exploiting opportunities encourages entrepreneurs to seek out the projects that help the economy to adapt to changing conditions. In Austrian theory, it is the prospect of profit from an opportunity that motivates the search that leads to discovery (Kirzner, 1973).

Opportunities, therefore, are a natural consequence of economic volatility. At any given time some opportunities will be recognized and exploited, and others will be overlooked. The set of potential projects from which opportunities are drawn is always very large, and so it is important for the entrepreneur to choose the right field in which to search. A set of possible search strategies is delineated below. The long-run success of the entrepreneur can then be explained by good judgement in the choice of search strategies. In summary, search strategy impacts significantly on the performance of the entrepreneur.

2.2   THE CONCEPT OF OPPORTUNITY

The key to the framework set out in this chapter is a view of the economy as a system of interdependent projects, linked by flows of information and material resources. Each project generates goods and services; a simple project may generate a single good or service whilst a more complex project may generate a mixture of them.

Both information and material resources are scarce and costly. The economic problem for a society is to select the most appropriate portfolio of projects. In a free enterprise system this selection is generated by the interaction of numerous decisions made by different individuals, and aggregated through market institutions. All the individual decisions are subject to uncertainty. Given the state of the economic environment at any one time, there is a set of projects that would best meet the needs of society. This set cannot be identified, however, because of the scarcity of information. Some of the projects in the set may be already in operation, but others may not. An opportunity is a project which is not in operation but which would be profitable given the state of the economic environment. The starting up of new projects and the closure, growth or shrinkage of existing projects are among the factors that change the economic environment for new projects.

In this framework, individuals are rational, but they incur information costs. They address the scarcity of information by economizing on its use.

This explains why they face uncertainty: collecting all the information required to guarantee a correct decision would not only be difficult, but hopelessly uneconomic. Thus the amount of uncertainty that a person faces is to some extent a consequence of their own decisions on how much information to collect. Gifford (1995) has made a similar point, but she follows Radner (1992) in assuming that individuals have fixed and finite computational capabilities. In the interests of simplicity, the framework below assumes, on the contrary, that individuals can always process additional information if they are willing to incur the cost. The two approaches complement each other; they lead to similar conclusions, but the cost-based approach is simpler then the capacity-based approach for present purposes.

It is assumed that individuals are 'meta-rational' in the sense that they optimize the amount of information they collect. This implies that they face a trade-off between the costs of collecting additional information and the benefit of reducing the risk of a mistake. There are two types of mistake: missing a profitable opportunity, and exploiting an unprofitable opportunity by confusing it with a profitable one. To effect the trade-off, an individual needs to know their information costs. They also need to have a theory that identifies the risks they face, and the instruments available to manage these risks. Meta-rational individuals are 'instrumental' and 'purposeful' in the sense that they pursue given ends (Mises, 1949), but they are only 'boundedly rational' rather than 'substantively rational', in the sense that they do not normally act upon full information (Simon, 1983).

The ends pursued by entrepreneurs may be non-materialistic: some choices may offer them emotional rewards, based on personal recognition and social status, as well as purely financial rewards. Whilst Austrian theory tends to emphasize material rewards, Schumpeter was very clear that emotional rewards based on status (the will to win) and the creation of a legacy (the desire to found a dynasty) are important to outstanding entrepreneurs.

It is not only information that is costly to acquire: theories are costly to acquire as well. Theories are required to interpret information; raw data does not 'speak for itself'. A rational individual may well select a theory that they know is highly simplified because a more complex theory would be too expensive to learn, and would be of little use if the information required to apply it was difficult to collect. Although a meta-rational individual might be aware of more sophisticated theories, therefore, they might choose not to use them because of the cost involved.

Entrepreneurs are people who believe that they have lower information costs than other people. They might also believe that they have better theories, because they find theories easier to learn, and can therefore invest in more sophisticated ones. Entrepreneurs believe that they have a comparative advantage in collecting and processing information. The type of information in which they believe that they are most advantaged determines the type of information which they specialize in collecting, and this in turn determines the kinds of opportunities that they are likely to discover.

To undertake large projects, entrepreneurs need reputation, because they require access to resources they do not own – in particular, to other people's funds (Knight, 1921). Reputation means that other people accept their claims. An entrepreneur becomes a specialist decision-maker when other people place their resources under the entrepreneur's control by lending funds, for example, by investing in a firm.

If an entrepreneur's claims are valid then his/her decisions will, on balance, be better than the decisions that other people would have made in the same circumstances, and therefore the value of the resources placed under the entrepreneur's control will increase, for example, the firm will be profitable and grow. Conversely, if the entrepreneur's claims are false then, in the long run, poor decision-making will lead to the failure of his firm and the loss of reputation.

Overall, a good entrepreneur, with good judgement, will tend to select good projects, whilst a bad entrepreneur, with bad judgement, will select bad projects. Of course, given the prohibitive cost of collecting full information, there will always be residual uncertainty; good judgement shortens the odds, but does not guarantee success. The new projects promoted by a good entrepreneur will tend to be true opportunities, whilst the projects promoted by a bad entrepreneur will be false opportunities – that is, projects that appear promising to people who use over-simplified theories and poor information. Investing in false opportunities represents a waste of resources. The key to entrepreneurial success is to possess sufficient judgement to recognize true opportunities and to screen out false ones.

2.3   PROJECTS

In conventional economics, resources are allocated between activities. An activity involves a continuous flow of inputs and outputs. When an activity is in a steady state, the rates of input and the rates of output are constant over time. The level of the activity is variable; if conditions change then the scale of the activity can be either increased or decreased instantaneously with no cost of adjustment, so the system can easily move from one steady state to another. Hence operations are never 'locked in' to any particular scale of activity.

By contrast, a project involves a stock of resources which are committed to a particular use over a specific period of time. These resources include land, labour and physical capital such as office and factory buildings, plant and equipment. Setting up a project may incur substantial sunk costs: it involves a commitment of resources which cannot be recovered if the project is abandoned later. The scale of a project cannot be easily changed, although various real options may exist for reducing its scale (for example, by not replacing worn out equipment) or expanding its scale (for example, developing new projects as spin-offs of the existing one) (Dixit and Pindyck, 1994). The values of the various types of real options inherent in the project form part of its overall value (McGrath, 1999).

The benefits generated by a project are usually realized only after many of the costs have been incurred. Projects therefore need financing: someone needs to pay the costs before the revenues come on stream. These costs and revenues are not necessarily monetary: the cost may be represented by unwaged voluntary effort, whilst the revenues may be payments in kind, such as the satisfaction that volunteers obtain from a job well done. In some cases financing may be provided by the project team as a whole, but in other cases it is supplied by a specialized group of shareholders.

There are many different types of project, and even projects of the same type are different, although some of the differences may be small. Thus all retail projects have important characteristics in common, but there is still heterogeneity: shops differ in their location, the date they were established, and the range of products that they stock.

In principle, all projects compete for resources. Land, labour and finance are all scarce. However, because of interdependencies, many projects also complement each other. The outputs generated by one type of project are the inputs required by some other types of project. It is therefore more accurate to say that clusters of complementary projects compete for resources.

Projects need to be managed. The implementation of a project normally requires that some processes are carried out before others: it is difficult, for example, to put up a building by painting it first and digging the foundations later. Someone has to plan the activities in the correct sequence and supervise the implementation of the plan. Internal coordination therefore requires project management. Volatility can disrupt schedules, and so it is inconvenient to adhere to a completely rigid sequence. Risks associated with absenteeism, bad weather and shortages of materials all favour flexibility, as does learning that takes place as part of the project (Wadeson,

2005). A manager therefore needs to be in constant attendance, and in a large and complex project, management becomes a specialized role.

Choices between projects can be made either within firms – for example, where different divisions compete for internal funds (Chandler, 1962; Williamson, 1975) – or between firms, as when different firms compete for venture capital to undertake the projects they have decided to promote. Whilst the distinction between internal and external project selection is of considerable significance for the theory of entrepreneurship as a whole, it is of only secondary relevance to the theory of opportunity, and so the distinction will not be pursued further here.

2.4   PROJECT POSSIBILITY SETS

In an activity-based view of the economy (for example, Koopmans, 1951), there is a set of *possible* activities and, within this, a subset of *feasible* activities. The set of possible activities which are not necessarily feasible comprises all the available inputs combined in every conceivable proportion. The set of feasible activities is determined by the state of technology at the time. The set of production activities, for example, is specified by the activities that enter into the production functions in various industries.

In a project-based view of the economy, the corresponding notion is that of project sets. When analysing entrepreneurship it is tempting to reject the notion of a given set of possible projects and to argue that the entrepreneur creates new possibilities through the exercise of his/her imagination. The difficulty with this approach is that, without a well-defined set of possibilities, it is impossible to apply the theory of meta-rational choice, as set out above.

The approach in this chapter therefore retains the notion of a given set of possibilities – that is, a set of possibilities which is exogenous to any decision made by the entrepreneur. The project set is fixed for all time, and is the same for every entrepreneur. Differences between entrepreneurs arise because they have different perceptions of the project set, and not because their project sets are different. Highly imaginative entrepreneurs are able to visualize more of the possible projects than less imaginative entrepreneurs, but they cannot visualize projects that do not already exist as part of the project set.

Not all projects are feasible. A possible project is specified by the steps that must be taken to implement it, and by the outputs that it is expected to generate. If the steps are wrongly specified then the project will not be feasible because the expected output will not materialize.

There are four stages involved in implementing a project: discovery, design, development and operation. Entrepreneurial judgement is involved in all four stages, though the level of judgement typically diminishes with successive stages (see Chapter 1). The same entrepreneur does not have to undertake all the stages, but under normal conditions this will be the case. If there were markets in discoveries ready for design, designs ready for development, and developments ready for operation then an entrepreneur could sell a partially completed project to another entrepreneur. This would allow different entrepreneurs with different skills to specialize in different stages of project innovation. In practice, however, selling projects is usually difficult, as rights to unexploited projects are difficult to appropriate and defend.

It is assumed that each project competing for resources is championed by a single entrepreneur. Entrepreneurship is defined as a role rather than a person, which means that the entrepreneur, as a person, may fulfil other roles a well. Conversely, individuals with similar views, and mutual trust, may partner each other in the entrepreneurial role. An entrepreneur (or partnership of entrepreneurs) may promote several projects rather than just a single one.

An entrepreneur does not know in advance whether a possible project is feasible. Moreover, even if a project is believed to be feasible in a technological sense, it may not be viable in an economic sense, because the benefits conferred by the project do not outweigh its costs. Although activity-based models typically assume that the feasibility of activities is common knowledge throughout the economy, the assumption in a model of entrepreneurship must be that neither the feasibility nor the viability of a project is common knowledge. Indeed, there is often no agreement between people on either of these questions. Optimists may believe that a project should be undertaken, whilst pessimists believe that it should not. In a free market economy, the optimists can go ahead despite the reservations of the pessimists provided that they can mobilize sufficient resources to carry out the project at their own risk.

The basic notion of a trade-off, encapsulated in conventional activity-based models of the economy, remains valid because all projects compete for the same collection of resources. However, project sets are much more heterogeneous and diverse than activity sets, and hence the trade-offs are far more subtle.

When modelling entrepreneurship it is easier to focus on a set of projects rather than a set of opportunities, which is more subjective. Beliefs about the set of opportunities are subjective because they reflect individual entrepreneurs' perceptions of prospective profits. Furthermore, the set of opportunities is endogenous because some of the unexploited projects only exist because entrepreneurs decided not to exploit them previously.

Much of the confusion over opportunity has arisen because of the failure to distinguish properly between the project set and the opportunity set.

2.5   COORDINATION IN A PROJECT-BASED ECONOMY

Coordination of the economy hinges crucially on selecting the most appropriate portfolio of projects. In a volatile economy, the project portfolio needs to be continually updated. Because projects are long-lived, this is not a matter of instantaneously changing the entire portfolio, as would occur in a conventional activity-based economy. Neither is it simply a matter of adjusting the scale of existing projects. With the scale of existing projects largely fixed, adjustment often involves starting up entirely new projects. As already noted, at any one time there are a large number of projects that are not in operation, and hence there is a wide range of new options to choose from.

To undertake new projects it is necessary to find supplies of land, labour and finance. There may be spare supplies because of 'frictions' in the market process: for example, 'brown-field' land which became idle in a previous period and has not yet found an alternative use; unemployed labour, and workers returning to employment after maternity leave; idle cash balances waiting for an investment opportunity, and so on. Some resources may be liberated by reducing the scale of existing projects. When start-up projects are small, contractions in larger long-established projects are a natural way of releasing resources. In some cases, however, large projects may have reached the end of their life, through depreciation or obsolescence, or both, and may therefore be ready to be shut down altogether.

A simple way of viewing this process is to say that in each period all the possible projects in the economy are placed in competition with each other for scarce resources (Witt, 1998). The focus is on competition in the factor markets for land, labour and finance. Although rival projects will ultimately compete with each other in product markets too, this competition will only occur once the projects have been successfully set up (Sarasvathy, 2001). Their claims on resources will, of course, be assessed on the basis of how well they are expected to compete with rival projects in the future, but this is competition based on expectations regarding the future outcome of product market competition rather than the reality of the competition itself (Shackle, 1979).

From this perspective, existing projects are competing with new projects to retain the resources already under their control. Thus entrepreneurs in charge of established projects are fighting to retain the allegiance of key employees who might be tempted away to join new projects or existing projects which plan to expand. Established projects have an advantage over new projects because their costs are already sunk, whereas those of the new projects are not. On the other hand, some existing projects may have failed to fulfil their expectations regarding product market performance, and so may be ripe for killing off.

2.6   COMPLEMENTS AND SUBSTITUTES

If all the projects considered at any given time are substitutes for each other, then it is relatively straightforward for the factor markets to allocate resources to the most promising ones. As rival entrepreneurs bid up the wages of labour, the price of land and the interest rates on loans, so the values of projects (as reflected in their share prices, for example) fall. Once its value becomes negative, a project is eliminated from the bidding. Eventually there are just sufficient projects remaining to use up the available resources.

If entrepreneurs' expectations are correct then, provided certain other conditions also hold, this process will generate an optimal portfolio of projects. But if some of the entrepreneurs have mistaken expectations, then the outcome may be less favourable. However, if each entrepreneur is meta-rational then the portfolio will be subjectively optimal, conditional upon the information available at the time, and on the distribution of that information amongst the entrepreneurs (as suggested by Hayek, 1959).

In certain cases, however, the value of a project may depend upon whether certain other projects are undertaken at the same time (Young, 1993). These projects may either complement or conflict with the project concerned – for example, they may generate outputs which improve or damage the environment in which the original product is produced (Richardson, 1960). Such 'externalities' should, in theory, be 'internalized' by negotiations between the entrepreneurs concerned. In an entrepreneurial economy these agreements need to be made before any of the projects has been implemented, because afterwards its will be too late to reverse the investment decisions taken. The negotiation and enforcement of such agreements is extremely costly, and the total cost of internalizing all the externalities between every conceivable set of possible projects is clearly prohibitive.

A practical way of addressing complementarities is to group the projects together and evaluate them as a whole. For example, the projects may be internalized within a single multi-plant firm, and promoted as an integrated entity by a single entrepreneur.

The most direct way to address conflicting projects is to place the projects into separate groups with the provision that only one group can be undertaken. For example, a single licence to operate may be created for which rival firms, promoting conflicting projects, compete. The firm that makes the highest bid obtains the contract. Only then does it go to the factor markets to obtain the resources it requires.

An alternative is to plan the economy by centralizing the selection of projects with a planning authority. The resulting portfolio selection problem is extremely complex, however. It is unlikely to be solved effectively because the planner will not have all the required information and has little incentive to apply the practical judgement that is characteristic of the successful entrepreneur.

In a free market economy these problems are addressed pragmatically. Local planning is often used to avoid wasteful pollution, duplication of facilities and the like. This reflects a view that distant projects are more likely to be independent of each other than projects in the same locality. When entrepreneurs need to get planning permission before they can enter factor markets, their discussions with the planners help to coordinate project selection at the local level.

2.7   INFRASTRUCTURE AND KNOWLEDGE

There is a special form of complementarity that has particular significance for entrepreneurship, because it affects the sequencing of investment decisions. It arises when one type of project needs to be completed before another type of project can commence.

Infrastructure is an obvious example. It has long been recognized that transport infrastructure – in particular roads, bridges, railways, ports and airports – needs to be in place before mass production and heavy manufacturing can get under way; without it there is no affordable means of importing materials or exporting products. It follows that knowledge of where appropriate infrastructure exists is essential to the manufacturing entrepreneur.

This leads to the second point, which is that certain specialized forms of knowledge are also a prerequisite for certain types of project. Knowledge of the problems encountered with the existing technology in an industry is a useful guide to projects that can improve upon it. Knowledge spillovers occur not only within industries but between industries: spillovers between textiles and engineering, for example, have exerted a strong influence on the development path pursued by newly industrializing countries (Audretsch and Keilbach, 2006). Understanding the implications of the knowledge gained in one project for the performance of another can be crucial in optimizing the sequencing of project investments.

Spillovers are also important in the commercialization of the economy. The establishment of markets can boost production by making it easier to realize profit from output. Quite small investments in market-making can often have quite remarkable effects. The establishment of a general store near a crossroads may attract artisans to use the store as a retail outlet. As the local population increases, additional services are provided. Entrepreneurs with new ideas are attracted to the area once it has become an established market place. Innovative practices stimulate competition and give the emerging market town a good reputation, which expands its geographical catchment area.

In principle, spillovers could be taken into account in a central plan. The planner would devise an intertemporal development plan for the entire economy. This would specify a sequence of project investments that adjusted the project portfolio at each period so that it followed an optimal path. In practice, of course, the information requirements of such an exercise are prohibitive, being even greater than the requirements of the other planning exercises described above. As a result, the responsibility for exploiting spillovers devolves to individual entrepreneurs.

2.8   EVALUATING NEW PROJECTS

The project-centred approach to the economy highlights the importance of the process by which projects are evaluated by individual entrepreneurs. There are an enormous number of projects for entrepreneurs to investigate. The projects already in operation represent a tiny proportion of the projects that need to be considered. Although some projects not in operation may have been previously tried and subsequently shut down, they too are small in proportion to the number of wholly untried projects.

If every project in the set of all possible projects were promoted every period by some entrepreneur, then the number of entrepreneurs required would be enormous. Indeed, expenditure on the evaluation of projects and the selection of successful bids would probably exhaust the entire resources of the economy. It is therefore vitally important to find a strategy for economizing on the costs of entrepreneurial discovery.

A strategy for discovery must address three main issues:

- selection of the field of search;
- method of investigation of the selected field; and
- fine-tuning project proposals to avoid hidden snags.

Selection of the Field

Selection of the field is primarily governed not by the entrepreneur's views of the economy, but by his/her perception of their own capabilities. There is no point in entrepreneurs discovering opportunities that they lack the skills to exploit. Entrepreneurs therefore take the earliest possible opportunity to weed out those types of projects that they cannot undertake themselves.

- If the entrepreneur plans to operate the projects he/she has discovered then it will pay to screen out projects for which the relevant management skills are known to be lacking.
- If the entrepreneur needs to manage on the spot, he/she might be confined to those projects located near his/her place of residence.
- If the entrepreneur needs to borrow funds to undertake large projects, it will pay to screen out large projects for which funding will be difficult to procure.
- A lifestyle entrepreneur may only consider fields which are of personal interest or amusement, or which provide the status to which such an individual aspires.
- An entrepreneur may reject areas which are considered morally objectionable, and even decide to concentrate only on areas which are considered particularly worthy from a social perspective.

The weakness of this approach is the obverse of its strength. It makes no use of information about the state of the economy. Instead of looking inward, to their own capabilities, it could be argued that entrepreneurs should be looking outwards to the current state of the economy.

Investigation of the Field

Once a field has been selected, the entrepreneur will identify a range of factors that influence demand and supply in the chosen field. It is at this stage that information about the state of the economy becomes especially relevant. If the focus is on long-term projects then the entrepreneur will be seeking to identify long-term trends, such as rising population, changing lifestyles, depletion of natural resources and so on. For some factors, such as population growth, historical statistics are available, whereas lifestyle trends can only be measured by more subjective indicators.

If the entrepreneur thinks like a conventional economist then the natural approach will be to work with a model of the economy. The focus will be on changes in economic conditions that have not yet been recognized by other entrepreneurs, with the assumption that change is driven by exogenous shocks to the business environment. If the focus is long term, transitory shocks will be ignored, though persistent ones will be taken into account (despite the fact that it is often difficult to distinguish between the two). In the absence of a formal forecasting model it may be simply enough to extrapolate recent trends and use historical analogies to forecast their likely consequences. The entrepreneur may also draw upon personal experience of analogous situations.

As well as analysing long-term trends, the entrepreneur may look for symptoms of short-term disequilibria. A symptom of unsatisfied short-term demand is that a high proportion of existing output is being returned to suppliers as defective; this suggests that consumers would value substitute product of higher quality. Likewise, complaints from producers of falling orders and late payment may be taken as an indication that they would be willing to diversify into the supply of an alternative product if the opportunity arose. A chorus of complaints from both buyers and sellers would be convincing evidence of a short-term opportunity awaiting discovery.

Another short-term strategy is to analyse the current profitability of existing projects. Improving the quality of a profitable product makes more economic sense than improving the quality of an unprofitable one, since an unprofitable product may have no future anyway. Profitability alone is a poor indicator of opportunity, however. Profit measures are based on accounting costs rather than opportunity costs, and like other statistics are essentially historical: thus extrapolation can be misleading. Taken in conjunction with other symptoms, however, profitability measures can refine an entrepreneur's assessment of an opportunity.

Fine-Tuning Project Proposals

Once the field has been investigated, the search for opportunities will have been narrowed down to a particular product niche. The project set is so large, however, that even in this niche there will be many different projects. The projects are all variants of the same general type, however.

It is at this third stage that the detailed examination of project possibilities is carried out. To ensure that the project is feasible, the entrepreneur must search for any 'hidden snags'. Given that 'the devil is in the detail', this will involve examining factors that are specific to the particular type of project involved. A rational entrepreneur will adopt a sequential approach, collecting first the information that is easiest to obtain and that is likely to eliminate the largest number of possibilities and therefore narrow down the search for the best practical solution in the most effective way (Lippman and McCall, 1976; Weitzman, 1979; Casson and Wadeson, 1998; Wadeson, 2004). Once the entrepreneur has identified a suitable project, and is satisfied that a better project could only be found at considerable cost, the process will stop. The chosen project becomes the basis for a finely-tuned proposal presented to the factor markets.

2.9 DISTINCTIVE QUALITIES OF THE ENTREPRENEUR

The discovery process requires a special combination of imagination and practical judgement which, it can be argued, is the hallmark of the successful entrepreneur. While it requires imagination to visualize the logical structure of the project set in order to make an intelligent choice of field, this kind of abstract thinking is common to artists and intellectuals as well as entrepreneurs; they too are able to take a broad view of the general field of possibilities. But 'armchair theorists' cannot identify the practical possibilities available in a promising field and develop one of these possibilities to the point where it can be successfully implemented.

The early stages of the discovery process do not require the entrepreneur to have a detailed knowledge of all the projects which populate the various segments of the project set. It is sufficient for the entrepreneur to whittle down the categories under consideration using information gained from general factors that govern the average performance of projects in particular segments of the project possibility set. But once a specific field has been selected for detailed investigation, it is necessary to populate the field so that a specific project can be selected.

This requires practical judgement. If the entrepreneur is familiar with similar projects that have been carried out at other times or in other places then it is possible to adapt these precedents to populate the set. Elements of related projects might be incorporated to form a new hybrid, based on the assessment of the strength and weaknesses of previous projects in the field. These project possibilities are constructed by a form of 'intellectual arbitrage', in which projects already implemented in one field are transferred to another field. Successful intellectual arbitrage requires the fields to be sufficiently similar that only minor adaptations are required when the concept is transferred.

Most artists and intellectuals are incapable of taking the crucial final step involved in specifying a viable project proposal in a selected field. They may lack the detailed knowledge that is required to arbitrage project specifications from other fields. Whatever the cause, when it comes to collecting detailed information that affects the practicalities of a particular project, they are often reluctant to take responsibility; they dismiss the issues as trivial, and claim that someone else should do them instead. The hallmark of the entrepreneur is that his/her imagination goes beyond the purely abstract and extends to the practical and mundane.

2.10   COMPETITION BETWEEN ENTREPRENEURS

The analysis of entrepreneurial decision-making has so far focused upon a single entrepreneur. In practice, of course, there are many entrepreneurs in the economy, and no analysis of entrepreneurship would be complete without an examination of the relationships between them.

In principle, entrepreneurs could be allocated to sub-fields by a central planner who delegates the discovery of opportunities in each particular field to a particular entrepreneur. To avoid wasteful duplication of effort, the fields may be sub-divided to the point where there is only one entrepreneur in each field. This principle is quite commonly applied within conglomerate firms, where senior managers are each allocated to a product division in which they operate as an internal entrepreneur (Penrose, 1959).

Market economies operate on a different principle, however, in which there is no control over the number of entrepreneurs in a given field. As a result, in choosing their fields of specialization, entrepreneurs must take account of the choices of field made by other entrepreneurs.

There is little point in choosing a crowded field unless it is highly profitable. Sunk costs are incurred in entering a field, and so entrepreneurs will tend to stay in a field once they have entered it. This makes it easier for other entrepreneurs to assess how many people there are in the field, and how 'crowded' it is relative to other fields. Overcrowding is most likely in fields that involve low sunk costs: not only are these easier to enter, but people can enter and leave so quickly that the number of people in the field at any given time is difficult to assess. Overcrowding is a particular risk when there is highly publicized discovery, and people act on extrapolative expectations – the 'gold rushes' of the nineteenth century are a case in point. With 'free for all' discovery, entrepreneurs may gain an advantage over others simply by being better at estimating the number of people already in a field.

Sophisticated entrepreneurs may be able to gain further advantage by influencing the expectations of their competitors. An entrepreneur may start a rumour that a new discovery is false in order to discourage competitors from entering the field. Alternatively, an entrepreneur may fabricate a new discovery so that he can lure people into buying up resources that he already owns. A classic case of social manipulation concerns the profit

made by the Rothschild family from the spreading of misinformation in
the financial markets regarding the outcome of the Battle of Waterloo.

2.11   SUMMARY AND CONCLUSIONS

This chapter has presented a simple framework of entrepreneurship which
explores how the entrepreneur might go about the discovery of opportunities. An opportunity is defined as an unexploited project that would yield
a profit to the entrepreneur if undertaken. Entrepreneurs specialize in
exercising judgement regarding project selection decisions.

Writers on entrepreneurship who stress imagination and creativity sometimes suggest that the field of entrepreneurial endeavour cannot be mapped
out – that there are no coordinates by which one entrepreneur can position
themselves relative to another (Shackle, 1979). They suggest that opportunities have no independent existence but are essentially products of the
imagination of the entrepreneur. This is not the view taken here. It is argued,
instead, that there is an objective set of projects which remains the same over
time. Projects may be classified according to various characteristics, such as
type of product, location of facilities, the sorts of tasks involved and so on.

Not all projects are feasible, however; although the set of possibilities
remains constant, feasibility changes due to technological progress over
time. In this context, imagination remains important, but it takes on a
specific form: it is the ability to visualize the overall structure of the project
set, and to populate a chosen segment of it with possible projects whose
viability can be investigated in detail.

Some types of information are more costly to collect and communicate
than others. Simple models are cheaper to specify and learn than more
complex models. Entrepreneurs have a comparative advantage in project
selection because they have lower personal information costs than other
people and have better theories with which to interpret observations.
Entrepreneurs therefore become the owners and managers of firms in
which other people invest. Different firms specialize in different fields
because the entrepreneurs that control them have personal comparative advantages in processing information relating to particular types of
product and particular sectors of the economy.

ACKNOWLEDGEMENTS

Previous drafts of this chapter were presented at the Conference on
Entrepreneurship at Ohio State University, October 2005, the Schumpeter

Society Conference at Trest, June 2006, and the Austrian Economics colloquium at New York University, October 2006. Nigel Wadeson and I are grateful to the organizers, discussants and audiences, and in particular to Sharon Alvarez, Jay Barney, Peter Hammond, David Harper, Israel Kirzner, Peter Klein, Mario Rizzo and Christian Seidl for their comments. None of these people necessarily agree with the views expressed in this chapter, however.

REFERENCES

Audretsch, David B. and Max Keilbach (2006), 'Entrepreneurship, growth and restructuring', in M. Casson, B. Yeung, A. Basu and N.S. Wadeson (eds), *Oxford Handbook of Entrepreneurship*, Oxford: Oxford University Press, pp. 281–310.

Baumol, William J. (2002), *The Free-Market Innovation Machine: Analyzing the Growth Miracle of Capitalism*, Princeton, NJ: Princeton University Press.

Casson, Mark (1994), 'Cultural factors in innovation', in Y. Shionoya and M. Perlman (eds), *Innovation, Technology, Industries and Institutions: Studies in Schumpeterian Perspectives*, Ann Arbor: University of Michigan Press, pp. 271–96.

Casson, Mark and Nigel S. Wadeson (1998), 'Communication costs and the boundaries of the firm', *International Journal of the Economics of Business*, **3** (3), 307–30.

Chandler, Alfred D., Jr (1962), *Strategy and Structure*, Cambridge, MA: MIT Press.

Dixit, Avrinash and Robert S. Pindyck (1994), *Investments under Uncertainty*, Princeton, NJ: Princeton University Press.

Gifford, Sharon (1995), 'A model of project evaluation with limited attention', *Economic Theory*, **5** (1), 67–78.

Hayek, Friedrich A. von (1959), *Individualism and Economic Order*, London: Routledge & Kegan Paul.

Keynes, John M. (1936), *The General Theory of Employment Interest and Money*, London: Macmillan.

Kirzner, Israel M. (1973), *Competition and Entrepreneurship*, Chicago: University of Chicago Press.

Kirzner, Israel M. (1979), *Perception, Opportunity and Profit*, Chicago: University of Chicago Press.

Knight, Frank H. (1921), *Risk, Uncertainty and Profit*, Boston: Houghton Mifflin.

Koopmans, Tjalling C. (ed.) (1951), *Activity Analysis of Production and Allocation*, New York: Wiley.

Lippman, S.A. and J.J. McCall (1976), 'The economics of job search: a survey', *Economic Inquiry*, **14**, 155–89.

McGrath, R. (1999), 'Falling forward: real options reasoning and entrepreneurial failure', *Academy of Management Review*, **24** (1), 13–30.

Mises, Ludwig von (1949), *Human Action*, London: William Hodge.

Penrose, Edith T. (1959), *The Theory of the Growth of the Firm*, Oxford: Blackwell.

Radner, Roy (1992), 'Hierarchy: the economics of managing', *Journal of Economic Literature*, **30** (3), 1382–415.

Richardson, George B. (1960), *Information and Investment*, Oxford: Oxford University Press.

Sarasvathy, S,D. (2001), 'Causation and effectuation: towards a theoretical shift from economic instability to entrepreneurial contingency', *Academy of Management Review*, **26** (2), 243–63.

Sarasvathy, S.D., N. Dew, S.R. Velamuri and S. Venkataraman (2003), 'Three views of entrepreneurial opportunity', in Z.J. Acs and D.B. Audretsch (eds), *Handbook of Entrepreneurship Research,* Dordrecht: Kluwer.

Schumpeter, Joseph A. (1934), *The Theory of Economic Development*, trans. R. Opie, Cambridge, MA: Harvard University Press.

Shackle, George L.S. (1979), *Imagination and the Nature of Choice*, Edinburgh: Edinburgh University Press.

Shane, Scott (2003), *A General Theory of Entrepreneurship: The Individual-Opportunity Nexus*, Cheltenham, UK and Northampton, MA, USA: Edward Elgar.

Simon, Herbert A. (1983), *Reason in Human Affairs*, Oxford: Blackwell.

Wadeson, Nigel S. (2004), 'Multi-dimensional search: choosing the right path', *International Journal of the Economics of Business*, **11** (3), 287–301.

Wadeson, Nigel S. (2005), 'Projects as search processes', *International Journal of Project Management*, **23** (6), 421–7.

Weitzman, M. (1979), 'Optimal search for the best alternative', *Econometrica*, **47** (3), 641–54.

Williamson, Oliver E. (1975), *Markets and Hierarchies: Analysis and Anti-Trust Implications*, New York: Free Press.

Witt, Ulrich (1998), 'Imagination and leadership: the neglected dimension of an evolutionary theory of the firm', *Journal of Economic Behaviour and Organization*, **35**, 161–77.

Young, A. (1993), 'Substitution and complementarity in endogenous innovation', *Quarterly Journal of Economics*, **108** (3), 775–807.

3. Entrepreneurship and macroeconomic performance

With Nigel Wadeson

This chapter develops a formal model of the impact of entrepreneurship on macroeconomic performance. It examines the role of entrepreneurs in creating markets for novel products. Entrepreneurs specialize in collecting information that permits them to make judgemental decisions about innovation. The quality of their judgement determines the success of innovations, and thereby impacts on the long-run performance of the economy. The model demonstrates rigorously that constraints on the supply of entrepreneurship reduce economic performance, and serves to identify the policy instruments that can improve performance by alleviating these constraints.

3.1 INTRODUCTION

In response to the industrial depression of the 1970s and the rise of 'supply-side economics' many Western governments began to promote entrepreneurship and enterprise culture as a means of improving macroeconomic performance (see Chapter 1). By 2000 the budgets for supporting small-business start-ups, strengthening university–business linkages and promoting high-technology industrial districts had become very substantial. Recently, policymakers have begun to question whether the benefits of these policy interventions outweigh their costs. For example, while small firms have undoubtedly created new jobs for workers made redundant by large firms in 'sunset' industries, many of these new start-up firms have failed to grow as quickly as expected (Storey, 2006).

Economic theories of entrepreneurship suggest that entrepreneurship brings wide-ranging benefits, including greater innovation, more risk-taking and a general improvement in the coordination of the economy (Harper, 1996). In principle, these theories should provide a simple framework for evaluating the contribution of entrepreneurship to the macro-economy. But in practice these theories are generally micro-oriented, focusing on individual products or firms rather than on the economy as a whole (Ricketts, 2006). As a result, there is growing concern that theories of entrepreneurship are of little practical use in policy formation. This chapter addresses the challenge of transforming the economic theory of entrepreneurship into a form which can be used to assess its benefit to the macroeconomy.

Macroeconomic performance is typically measured either in terms of the standard of living, or the rate of growth (for example, GNP per head and its proportional rate of change). Whilst growth has been a major political objective throughout the post-war period, entrepreneurship is most often used to explain differences between countries (and regions) in *levels* of economic activity. Using this approach, the persistence of different levels of performance is typically explained by long-run differences in cultures and institutions. This chapter therefore concentrates on explaining the impact of entrepreneurship on levels of productivity and welfare, rather than on the rate of growth. This approach is consistent with the view that policy in the twenty-first century will be gradually redirected to maximizing sustainable levels of economic activity rather than maximizing growth per se.

3.2   ISSUES ADDRESSED BY THE MODEL

The economic theory of entrepreneurship is usually expounded in a discursive manner. It is quite usual to begin with a brief historical introduction showing how key insights into entrepreneurship have developed over time. Considerable attention is paid to philosophical issues, such as the nature of entrepreneurial knowledge and why there is so often a difference of opinion between entrepreneurs and others over the value of projects that entrepreneurs intend to carry out (see Chapter 2). The thrust of the discussion is microeconomic, with a focus on individual firms producing specific products innovated by an entrepreneur. The approach to economic modelling is informal. Although the theory aspires to rigour – as exemplified by the careful use of definitions and recourse to standard economic logic – it is not usually expressed in mathematical terms.

Where macroeconomic modelling is concerned, however, it is difficult to guarantee logical consistency without recourse to mathematical methods. This is because of the complexity of the macroeconomy. In line with this view, this chapter adopts a mathematical modelling approach. Although the method of analysis differs from that of the preceding chapters, the basic theoretical approach is nevertheless the same.

A commitment to formal modelling is, in fact, useful in its own right, whether or not the model is macroeconomic. A modeller is forced to confront key issues that can be easily fudged in a purely verbal discussion. It is necessary to be absolutely explicit about all the assumptions employed, and to defend these assumptions, however implausible they may at first seem. The model presented in this chapter clarifies a number of key issues in the theory of entrepreneurship:

- the nature of the link between innovation and risk-bearing;
- the nature of the demand for entrepreneurship, and the role of volatility in the economic environment as a driver of that demand;
- the distribution of entrepreneurial ability within the population, and the influence that this has on the supply of entrepreneurship;
- whether entrepreneurship can be regarded simply as a fourth factor of production – in addition to land, labour and capital – and, if so, whether it is just a variant of human capital;
- the nature of entrepreneurial reward – whether it is a wage or a rent, or a combination of the two, and whether it is monopolistically or competitively determined;
- the role of competition in markets for innovative products; and
- the question of whether competition operates differently in the 'market for entrepreneurs' than it does in other markets.

It must be emphasized, however, that the treatment of these issues in this chapter reflects the underlying assumptions of the theory on which the model is based. If these issues were examined in the context of a different theory, involving different assumptions, then different conclusions might be reached. Having said this, the conclusions derived in this chapter are entirely consistent with those reached in the other chapters of this book. This reflects a common emphasis on the role of judgement, and a common commitment to analysing judgement in the context of a rational action approach.

3.3 OUTLINE OF THE MACROECONOMIC MODEL

The model is an algebraic model of the kind commonly employed by economic theorists; in common with these models, all the variables are assumed to be continuous and non-negative, unless otherwise stated. The key variables are listed for ready reference in Table 3.1.

A macroeconomic model describes a closed system. The model presented below concerns a system in general equilibrium. Each decision-maker faces a budget constraint that requires income and expenditure to be equal. The division of labour creates different types of decision-maker;

Table 3.1   Key variables and parameters of the formal model

Algebraic symbol	Definition	Significance
Variables		
c_0	Consumption of the standard product	If no novel products were produced then this would measure the standard of living in the economy
c_j	Consumption of the novel product in niche j	Consumption occurs only as a result of successful entrepreneurial activity
CS	Consumer surplus	Expected aggregate consumer surplus in the economy
l_0	Employment in the mature sector	Employment in production of standard good, not controlled by entrepreneurs
l_1	Employment in the innovative sector	Employment controlled by entrepreneurs, involving the production of novel products or the standard product as each entrepreneur deems appropriate
m	Number of entrepreneurs	The number of individuals who forsake waged employment to act as full-time entrepreneurs
n	Number of active niches	Number of niches in which entrepreneurs are active, making judgements about whether to produce novel products
P	Price of a successful novel product	$P - 1$ is the premium earned by the successful production and sale of a unit of a novel product
P^+	Limit price	The maximum price that an entrepreneur can charge in any given niche to deter competitive entry
π	Expected profit margin	The expected value of the profit appropriated by an entrepreneur from a unit of a novel product produced in a niche
s_j	Opportunity indicator for niche j	A binary random variable indicating whether consumers face a problem that can only be satisfactorily solved by consumption of a novel product in a given niche
u	Individual utility	Individuals choose between becoming workers or entrepreneurs, and between consuming standard or novel products, according to which of these strategies maximizes their utility
U	Social welfare	The sum of individual expected utilities
w	Real wage	The payment made to each worker per period, measured in units of the standard product

Table 3.1   (continued)

Algebraic symbol	Definition	Significance
x_j	Innovation indicator	A binary variable that indicates whether a novel product is produced in a given niche
y_0	Output of the mature sector	Output of the standard good that is not controlled by entrepreneurs
y_1	Output of innovative products	Output of novel products controlled by entrepreneurs
y_2	Output of the standard product by entrepreneurs	Output of the standard products controlled by entrepreneurs who believe that there is no opportunity for innovation in their niches

Parameters

a	Entrepreneurial ability	The number of niches in which an entrepreneur of the first rank can operate successfully in any given period
b	Labour productivity	The physical amount of product, either standard or novel, that can be produced by an individual worker in a given period, using given technology and working practices
c^+	Satiation consumption	The maximum quantity of product (whether standard or novel) that is demanded by a consumer in any niche
e_{11}	Type I error generated by a superior symptom	The probability that an entrepreneur will misjudge a situation by missing a profitable opportunity to produce a novel product
e_{21}	Type II error generated by a superior symptom	The probability that an entrepreneur will misjudge a situation by producing a novel product when there is no demand for it
e_{12}	Type I error generated by an inferior symptom	The probability that a competitor would misjudge a situation by missing a profitable opportunity to produce a novel product
e_{22}	Type II error generated by an inferior symptom	The probability that a competitor would misjudge a situation by producing a novel product when there is no demand for it
H	Population	The total number of individuals in the economy
k	Degree of interpersonal inequality in entrepreneurial ability	A measure of the extent to which the number of niches in which an entrepreneur can successfully operate diminishes as the number of active entrepreneurs increases. A high value of k (close to unity) indicates that the supply

Table 3.1   (continued)

Algebraic symbol	Definition	Significance
		of entrepreneurs will respond elastically as the expected profitability of innovation increases relative to the real wage
N	Number of niches	The maximum number of different novel products that could conceivably be produced in the absence of resource constraints. It is an indicator of the degree of heterogeneity, and complexity, in the economy
q	Frequency of opportunity	The probability that in any given period there is a profit opportunity in a given niche
v	Reservation price of a novel product	This parameter measures consumers' valuation of novelty: $v - 1$ is the maximum premium for novelty that a consumer is willing to pay
z	Unconditional probability of an outcome of an innovation decision made by either an entrepreneur or by one of his/her competitors	There are eight distinct z-factors. They are functions of q and the four e-parameters. The z-factors are intervening variables which together capture all of the economically significant content of q and the e-factors. This facilitates the modular structure of the model by allowing a different account of the entrepreneurial decision process to be substituted without altering the principal formulae derived in the model

Note: The key variables relate to fundamental factors that govern the demand and supply of entrepreneurship and transmit its effects to the macroeconomy. A number of intervening variables that are employed mainly to simplify the presentation of equations have been omitted from the table.

the key distinction in the present model is between manual workers and entrepreneurs. The budget constraints of different decision-makers are consistent, so that when they are aggregated total income and total expenditure in the economy are equal.

The model is not a simple variant of a standard macroeconomic model, however, but is radically different in a number of respects. This is because it is entrepreneurs, rather than a self-adjusting set of Walrasian markets, that lie at the core of the model. The environment of the economy is volatile rather than stable. Consumers buy goods because they face specific problems, and consumption is therefore a 'problem-solving' activity. Entrepreneurs contribute specialized problem-solving services by making decisions about the mix of products to be produced. Good decisions are rewarded with profit and bad decisions with losses. This profit incentive encourages entrepreneurs to be careful in the decisions that they make. Good entrepreneurs are attracted into judgemental decision-making, and bad entrepreneurs are deterred by the opportunity cost of alternative earnings forgone.

A major challenge when introducing entrepreneurship into a macroeconomic model is to do justice to the heterogeneity of the economy. Entrepreneurial projects are very different from one another, and allowing explicitly for all the differences would produce a very complicated model (see Chapter 2). The solution is to assume that the economy has many specialized niches but that all the niches have the same parameters. Although each niche is subjected to its own specific shocks, the behaviour of each niche is on average the same.

Consider an economy with a fixed population of *H* individuals. Individuals differ in their abilities, but have identical preferences, as explained below.

The economy has two sectors: an innovative sector and a mature sector. The innovative sector produces a range of novel products, whilst the mature sector produces a single standard product. Entrepreneurship is concentrated on the innovative sector.

The analysis is based on a single representative time period. The key decisions are all taken at the beginning of this period, in a specific sequence that is explained below. Throughout the rest of the period the consequences of these decisions work through the system. The relevant period corresponds to a decade, rather than just a year. This is because innovation decisions typically relate to production projects whose economic life is about five to twenty years. The 'fiction' of the model is that innovation decisions do not occur continuously throughout the period, as they do in practice, but take place only intermittently at the start of each period.

Each individual is both a producer and a consumer. In line with the discussion in the previous chapter, everyone is assumed to be rational. In addition, it is assumed for simplicity that everyone (including entrepreneurs) is risk-neutral. People evaluate options on the basis of expected rewards, and do not prefer some option simply because the probability distribution of rewards has lower variance. This reflects the view that the most important distinguishing feature of entrepreneurs is not their personal preferences but their superior judgement. Entrepreneurs make better judgements not because they are less risk-averse, but because they are more accurate in their estimation of expected values.

Considered as producers, individuals may operate as either workers or entrepreneurs. Entrepreneurs employ workers for a wage and receive profit from the sale of the products that the workers produce. For each individual, overall consumer expenditure is equal to their income from production – whether as a worker or as an entrepreneur.

Consumers derive utility from consumption of both the standard product and the novel products. The standard product is a versatile multi-purpose good which provides consumers with a basic level of quality in many possible uses. Novel products are more specialized, and provide consumers with higher quality – but only in a specific use.

3.4   VOLATILITY

In the context of this model, the behavioural significance of entrepreneur-ship stems from the fact that novel products are only valued by consumers under specific circumstances. There is always a risk that a novel product may not be required; conversely, there is also a risk that the need for novelty may not be recognized unless entrepreneurs are suitably alert. The role of the entrepreneur is to manage these risks by making judgements about whether the circumstances warrant the production of a novel product.

By contrast, anyone can produce the standard product. Because the standard product is always in demand, employers in the mature sector incur no risks (unlike the entrepreneurs) and operate under perfectly com-petitive conditions; as a result, they earn no profit.

All consumers have the same preferences (that is, the same utility func-tion). Consumers are interested in a very large number, N, of possible product niches. Each niche corresponds to a different type of problem that a consumer may encounter – for example, an unsatisfied need for a particular type of food or shelter.

A key assumption is that each consumer problem is independent of other consumer problems. The solution to one problem does not depend on the solution to some other problem, and solving one problem is not a substitute for solving some other problem. The mutual independence of consumer problems means that each consumer's utility is the sum of the utilities that he/she derives from consumption in each niche.

Volatility in the environment is reflected in the nature of the problems that consumers face. Many problems can be routinely addressed by con-sumption of the versatile standard product, but from time to time excep-tional problems occur that create a demand for an innovative product in a particular niche. Although the standard product can address an excep-tional problem, it cannot address it as well as can a novel product.

Demand in each niche is easily satiated. It only takes a certain amount of product to solve a particular problem, whether this is normal or serious. Whatever the problem, once the consumer has consumed c^+ units in any niche, further consumption in that niche affords the consumer no additional utility, whatever type of product is used. It is assumed that c^+ is small, so that even the poorest consumer (a wage-earner) can achieve satiation in a large number of niches (see below). The total number of niches, N, is so large, though, that no consumer, however great their income, is ever satiated in every possible niche.

The marginal utility of the standard product is constant up to the satiation level, and is the same in all niches. Without loss of generality, therefore, the marginal utility of the standard product may be normalized to unity; thus utility is measured in units of standard product equivalence.

Since this is a general equilibrium model, individual behaviour depends only on relative prices rather than absolute prices, and it is therefore convenient to choose one of the products as a *numeraire* (that is, to set its price to unity by convention). The standard product makes a suitable choice for *numeraire*, as this means that real income and expenditure are measured in the same units as utility.

As noted above, a novel product is only demanded in a given niche when consumers face a serious problem. When a serious problem occurs, the problem is common to all consumers – for example, fashion may dictate that each consumer has a specific need to be seen to be consuming a particular type of novel product. The binary variable s_j indicates whether special circumstances prevail in the jth niche ($s_j = 1$ indicates demand for a novel product and $s_j = 0$ indicates no such demand ($j = 1,\ldots, N$)).

The marginal utility of a novel product is also constant up to the satiation level. When consumers face a serious problem, the marginal utility of a novel product is $v > 1$. Thus v is the reservation price for each novel product. When these circumstances do not prevail, however, the novel product is valueless (its marginal utility is zero). It is therefore a mistake for an entrepreneur to innovate when there is no demand for a novel product.

While each niche requires a distinctive type of novel product, all niches have the same parameters of product demand; the model therefore recognizes heterogeneity whilst facilitating aggregation. Let u be the utility of an individual consumer; let c_0 be their consumption of the standard product, and c_j their consumption of the novel product in the jth niche. Because the standard product is versatile, and complete satiation is impossible, demand for the standard product is never satiated. In the light of previous assumptions, it follows that:

$$u = c_0 + v \Sigma_j s_j \min[c_j, c^+] \qquad j = 1,\ldots, N \qquad (3.1)$$

Equation (3.1) indicates that there is an insatiable demand for the standard good and a set of rapidly satiated demands for novel products that arise only under specific circumstances in particular niches. The summation of niches illustrates that the problems in different niches are independent of each other, as mentioned above.

Production of each product requires labour only and takes place under constant returns to scale. Every individual in the economy is equally productive in manual work. Each individual can produce b units of any product in any given period. Labour productivity is the same for all products and reflects technology and working practices, both of which are exogenous.

Entrepreneurs hire workers competitively at a wage w. Wages are bid up to the point where the marginal employer makes no profit. It follows that the unit cost of each type of product is w/b. Because of labour market flexibility, the economy operates at full employment. Because all novel products are produced under similar conditions and face similar patterns of demand, they all sell (when they are produced) for the same price, P.

The economy can operate in three regimes, each of which is associated with a distinctive type of equilibrium. Only one of these regimes is of interest for the study of entrepreneurship; namely the one in which the innovative and mature sectors coexist side by side. The second regime involves production of only the standard product; this is of no interest because it involves no entrepreneurship. The third regime involves every niche being controlled by an entrepreneur. It is more complicated to analyse than the first regime. Since it provides few additional insights, it is not discussed in this chapter. Sufficient conditions for the first regime to prevail are derived below.

Under the first regime the marginal worker is employed in the production of the standard commodity, which is also the *numeraire*. Competition between producers of the standard product bids up the real wage to b:

$$w = b \qquad\qquad (3.2)$$

Thus each worker receives their average product. As a result, the unit cost of producing any product is unity, $w/b = 1$. Thus there is no profit for producers of the standard product, and there is no consumers' surplus for consumers of this product either. All the reward from production of the standard product is appropriated by labour instead. Profit comes only from the innovation of novel products, as explained above.

3.5   THE ROLE OF JUDGEMENT IN INNOVATION

In each niche, the probability that conditions create a demand for a novel product is q. Demand conditions in each niche are random (that is, s_j is a random variable, $j = 1, \ldots, N$). Conditions in any niche in any period are statistically independent of conditions in previous periods, and of past or present conditions in any other niche.

By the time that consumers recognize that they have a demand for novelty in some niche, it is too late for entrepreneurs to produce the relevant product. Demand conditions in each niche therefore need to be predicted. They cannot be predicted with any certainty, however. There are symptoms available, though, which can be used to make predictions with a margin of error that may be acceptable.

Once a commitment to produce a product has been made, the labour costs are sunk. By this stage it is impossible for an entrepreneur to switch to the production of another product. Because the standard product is versatile, there is no risk involved in its production. Because novel products are niche-specific, however, and are worthless if there is no demand for them, considerable risk is involved in their production. Consumers only purchase a novel product once they have evaluated it, and they are not obliged to purchase an unwanted product. The entire wage cost of an unwanted novel product therefore constitutes a loss to the entrepreneur.

To avoid a problem with loss-making entrepreneurs attempting to consume out of negative income, it is assumed that interest-free consumption loans are available which allow entrepreneurs to sustain their consumption at a level equal to their expected profit. When consumers are confronted by unwanted supplies of a novel product, they transfer the income they have saved on the unwanted product to the standard product. Consistency of decisions is ensured because the consumers can purchase supplies of the standard product that have been released by the reduced demand of the creditors who are financing the losses of the entrepreneur.

In the absence of any symptom, it is assumed, it would be uneconomic to innovate in any niche. Otherwise 'hit and miss' innovation would occur throughout the economy without any need for entrepreneurs. A sufficient condition to prevent hit and miss innovation is that the probability of there being a demand for a novel product is less than the reciprocal of its reservation price:

$$q < 1/v \tag{3.3}$$

This implies that the expected revenue generated by innovation in a state of ignorance is less than the corresponding revenue that would be obtained by producing the standard product instead.

The use of symptoms generates two types of error: a Type I error, in which demand conditions favouring innovation appear unfavourable, so that there is no production of a profitable product, and a Type II error in which unfavourable demand conditions appear favourable, so that an unwanted product is produced.

In each niche there are two symptoms that can be used to predict demand. One of the symptoms (symptom 1) is more accurate than the other (symptom 2). In any given niche, the superior symptom (symptom 1) can only be observed by one particular person. The inferior symptom (symptom 2) can be observed by anyone.

The identity of the inferior symptom is only revealed to other people once an entrepreneur has begun to observe the superior symptom. Information about where to find the inferior symptom is a 'spillover' or byproduct of the exploitation of the superior one. It takes time for a person to observe the superior symptom, but not the inferior one. Thus observers of the inferior symptom can 'free ride' to a limited extent on the observer of the superior one.

A person who decides to observe a superior symptom becomes an entrepreneur. Such an individual sacrifices labour income in order to devote time to observing the symptom. Having observed the symptom, it is necessary to exercise judgement about whether to produce a novel product. If the individuals' judgement is good then he/she will make a profit and if it is bad then he/she will make a loss.

It is assumed that an entrepreneur who has observed the superior symptom does not bother to observe the inferior one as well. Under the assumed conditions it does not normally pay the entrepreneur to use both symptoms, unless either the reservation price or the probability of favourable conditions is low, when it may pay to innovate only if both symptoms are favourable.

On the basis of the observation of the superior symptom, the entrepreneur decides whether or not to produce a novel product. If the decision is not to produce the novel product, the standard product will be supplied instead.

The risk that an entrepreneur makes an error of judgement depends upon the quality of the superior symptom. It is assumed that all the superior symptoms incur the same probability of error in each niche. The probability of a Type I error is e_{11} and the probability of a Type II error is e_{21}; that is, given favourable conditions, the probability that a symptom indicates unfavourable conditions is e_{11} and, given unfavourable conditions, the probability that it indicates favourable conditions is e_{21} ($e_{11}, e_{12} < 0.5$). It follows that the unconditional probability of the successful exploitation of an innovation opportunity is $z_{111} = q (1 - e_{11})$, and the unconditional probability of a wasted opportunity is $z_{121} = q e_{11}$. When the opportunity is wasted the entrepreneur, believing wrongly that there is no opportunity, produces the standard product by mistake.

The unconditional probability of a failed attempt at innovation is $z_{211} =$

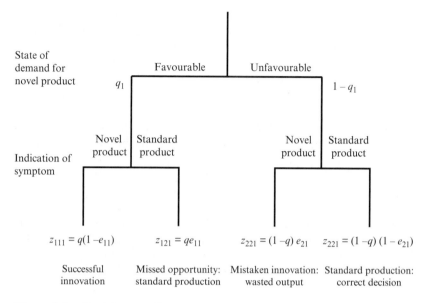

State of
demand for
novel product   Favourable   Unfavourable

q_1 $1 - q_1$

Indication of
symptom

Novel product | Standard product   Novel product | Standard product

$z_{111} = q(1 - e_{11})$ $z_{121} = qe_{11}$ $z_{221} = (1 - q)e_{21}$ $z_{221} = (1 - q)(1 - e_{21})$

Successful innovation | Missed opportunity: standard production | Mistaken innovation: wasted output | Standard production: correct decision

Figure 3.1   Decision tree for an entrepreneur

$(1 - q) e_{21}$; this generates worthless output. Finally, the probability that a correct decision is taken to produce the standard product is $z_{221} = (1 - q)$ $(1 - e_{21})$. The decision process is illustrated schematically in Figure 3.1.

Entrepreneurs are aware that they face competition within their niche from people exploiting the inferior symptom. They do not wish to share the market with these people, because there are so many of them that the entrepreneur's resultant share would be very small. Others can be deterred from entering by the entrepreneur committing in advance to a price so low that if it were to be matched by rivals they would make a loss. This determines a limit price – the highest price that can be charged that will have this effect; this is equal (apart from a infinitesimal amount) to the price, P^+, at which a rival will just break even. The entrepreneur then honours this price commitment in selling to consumers, in order to retain credibility. The limit price is the same in each niche because the parameters on which it depends are the same.

The inferior symptom (symptom 2) has higher errors of misclassifying the state of demand than the superior symptom (symptom 1); in other words, the inferior symptom provides a less powerful test of the true state of demand. The errors are respectively:

$$e_{12} > e_{11}; \qquad e_{22} > e_{21} \qquad (3.4)$$

where e_{12}, $e_{22} < 0.5$. The probability of the favourable conditions, q, is common knowledge, and so too are the errors, e_{ij} ($i, j = 1, 2$). The entrepreneur therefore calculates the corresponding probabilities for his rivals:

$$z_{112} = q\,(1 - e_{12}); \qquad z_{122} = q\,e_{12} \qquad\qquad (3.5)$$
$$z_{212} = (1 - q)\,e_{22}; \qquad z_{222} = (1 - q)(1 - e_{22})$$

The break-even condition for the rival is that the expected profit margin is zero. Recalling that unit production cost is unity, the break-even condition implies that the limit price is:

$$P^+ = 1 + (z_{212} / z_{112}) \qquad\qquad (3.6)$$

If the inferior symptom is very poor then the limit price may exceed the consumers' reservation price v. In this case the rivals are unable to compete with the entrepreneur because the symptom they use is so poor. Thus the actual price set by the entrepreneur in each niche is the minimum of the limit price and the reservation price:

$$P = \min [v, P^+] \qquad\qquad (3.7)$$

The expected profit margin of the entrepreneur is:

$$\pi = (v - 1)\,z_{111} - z_{211} \qquad\qquad P^+ \geq v \qquad (3.8)$$
$$(z_{111}\,z_{212} / z_{112}) - z_{211} \qquad\qquad P^+ < v$$

If the superior symptom is poor, or the novelty premium $v - 1$ is low, then the entrepreneur's expected profit margin may be zero or negative. In this case it pays no one to act as entrepreneur. As explained above, this case is of no interest to a study of entrepreneurship, except as a limiting case, and so it is assumed that the Type 1 and Type 2 errors are sufficiently low that the profit margin is always positive, $\pi > 0$.

Given the expected profit margin π, the profit in each niche depends upon the quantity of product supplied. This will be sufficient to satiate every consumer's demand in the relevant niche. When the limit price P^+ is below the consumers' valuation, v, consumers derive a surplus per unit $v - P^+$. Since they derive no surplus from consumption of the standard product, they will prioritize the consumption of novel products. (It is assumed for simplicity that they follow the same approach even if $P^+ \geq v$, although in this case no consumers' surplus is available on novel products.)

Let $x_j = 1$ when an entrepreneur innovates a novel product in the jth niche, and $x_j = 0$ otherwise. The consumers' budget constraint is:

$$c_0 + P \Sigma_j c_j = Y \qquad (j = 1,\ldots, N) \qquad (3.9)$$

where Y is individual income (from labour or entrepreneurship, whichever is the greater). The consumer also faces supply constraints that are common to all individuals:

$$c_j = 0 \text{ if } x_j = 0 \qquad (j = 1,\ldots, N) \qquad (3.10)$$

Maximizing utility (1) subject to the constraints (3.9) and (3.10) is quite straightforward. The solution is to consume novel niche products whenever circumstances create a demand for them, and to devote the remaining income to the standard product:

$$
\begin{aligned}
c_j \quad &= c^+ \quad \text{if } s_j = 1 \text{ and } x_j = 1 \quad (j = 1, \ldots, N) \quad &(3.11.1)\\
&= 0 \quad \text{otherwise} \\
c_0 \quad &= Y - P \Sigma_j c_j \quad &(j = 1, \ldots, N) \quad &(3.11.2)
\end{aligned}
$$

The total quantity consumed in each innovative niche is therefore:

$$Q = c^+ H \qquad (3.12)$$

and so profit per niche is:

$$\Pi = \pi Q \qquad (3.13)$$

3.6 THE SUPPLY OF ENTREPRENEURSHIP

While the modelling of product demand is unconventional because of the emphasis on volatility and judgement, the modelling of the supply of entrepreneurship is relatively conventional. The supply of entrepreneurship, like the supply of any other human resource, depends upon the individual's expected reward, and the relationship of that reward to the rewards available from alternative occupations. In the present model, the only alternative to entrepreneurship is manual labour.

It is assumed that most individuals know of some niche in which they could observe a superior symptom, and for every niche there is at most one person with this capability. This means that almost anyone can, in principle, become an entrepreneur. Not everyone will want to become an entrepreneur, however, because the opportunity cost may be too high. Individuals differ in their entrepreneurial ability because some of them find it easier to observe superior symptoms than do others.

The most able entrepreneurs can observe symptoms very quickly, and so can operate in several different niches in any given period. When individuals are ranked in order of their entrepreneurial ability, the number of niches, n, that can be covered by the most able m entrepreneurs is:

$$n = a\, m^k \tag{3.14}$$

where a is an entrepreneurial productivity parameter and k $(0 < k < 1)$ measures the elasticity with which the number of niches with entrepreneurial activity responds to the number of entrepreneurs. An entrepreneur who operates in several niches may be identified as the owner or manager of a multi-product firm, whilst an entrepreneur who operates in a fractional niche may be identified as being in partnership with other entrepreneurs.

The marginal productivity of the mth entrepreneur is derived by differentiating (3.14); given that k is less than unity, the marginal productivity of entrepreneurship diminishes continuously as the number of entrepreneurs increases:

$$dn/dm = ak/m^{1-k} \tag{3.15}$$

Let Π be the expected profit that an entrepreneur can obtain from any niche. The marginal value product of entrepreneurship is $\Pi\, dn/dm$, and for the marginal entrepreneur this will equate to the real wage:

$$\Pi\, dn/dm = w = b \tag{3.16}$$

Let an asterisk denote an equilibrium value. Substituting (3.15) into (3.16) gives the equilibrium level of entrepreneurial activity:

$$m^* = (a\, \Pi k\, /\, b)^{\,1/(1-k)} \tag{3.17}$$

Equation (3.17) determines the supply curve for entrepreneurs. Supply is greater, the greater is the entrepreneurial productivity parameter, a, the expected profit from a niche, Π, and the greater the elasticity of response, k, as determined by the distribution of entrepreneurial ability.

3.7 MARKET EQUILIBRIUM

It may seem anomalous to talk about the equilibrium of an entrepreneurial economy, given that disequilibrium creates the opportunities that entrepreneurs exploit. There is, however, no paradox. The model has been

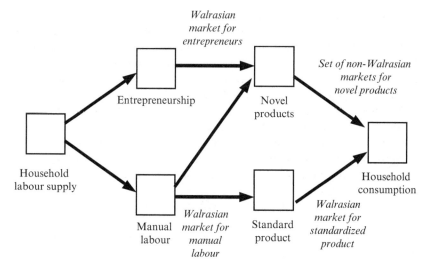

Figure 3.2   The market system in a simple entrepreneurial economy

carefully constructed so that disequilibrium affects only one group of markets – namely the markets for innovative products that are operated by entrepreneurs. For the sake of simplicity, the other markets operate as though they were intermediated by a Walrasian auctioneer. This applies to both the factor markets – the market for manual labour and the market for entrepreneurship itself. It also applies to the final market in which the *numeraire* commodity is traded – namely the standardized product.

Furthermore, the markets for the innovative products are so numerous that their interaction with the rest of the economy can be analysed on the assumption that the short-period fluctuations in the different markets effectively cancel each other out. There are many markets, and the shocks affecting each market are independent of each other, so that 'central limit' theorems apply. This means that the expected number of niches in which innovations occur can be related to the number of entrepreneurs in the economy in a deterministic way.

The situation is illustrated in Figure 3.2, which presents a variant of the familiar 'wheel of wealth diagram'. The role of a representative household as supplier of labour is illustrated by the box on the left-hand side, whilst the role of the household as consumer is shown on the right. Households can work either manually or as entrepreneurs. Novel products require inputs of both entrepreneurship and manual labour, whilst the standard product requires only manual labour. There are four markets in the economy: two factor markets and two product markets. Three of the four markets are Walrasian. The fourth is, in effect, a collection of a large number of small non-Walrasian markets, each intermediated by a monopolistic entrepreneur. Despite the complex strategic issues raised by these non-Walrasian markets, the model is easily soluble. This is largely because the innovative markets all have similar parameters, they are small in size and large in number, the shocks they experience are statistically independent and the impacts of novel products on consumer welfare are additive. It is, therefore, a judicious choice of assumptions that creates a simple model of a complicated situation.

The algebraic solution proceeds as follows. Substituting equation (3.14) into (3.17) gives the equilibrium number of innovative niches:

$$n* = a^{1/(1-k)} (\Pi k / b)^{k/(1-k)} \tag{3.18}$$

The total output of novel products that satisfy consumer demand is:

$$y*_1 = z_{111} Q n* = q (1 - e_{11}) Q n* \tag{3.19.1}$$

and the output of the standard product from the innovative sector (in response to unfavourable symptoms) is:

$$y*_2 = (z_{121} + z_{221}) Q n* = (q e_{11} + (1 - q)(1 - e_{21})) Q n* \tag{3.19.2}$$

The total manual labour requirement in the innovative sector is:

$$l*_1 = Q n* / b \tag{3.20}$$

Let $l*_0$ be equilibrium employment in the mature sector (devoted entirely to competitive production of the standard good). Full employment implies that:

$$l*_0 + l*_1 + m* = H \tag{3.21}$$

and so the output of the standard good from the mature sector is:

$$y*_0 = b l*_0 = b (H - m* - l*_1) = b(H - m*) - Qn* \tag{3.22}$$

To guarantee that the economy is in the appropriate regime, each manual worker must be able to afford to consume all of the successfully innovated products:

$$b > Pc^+ z_{111} n* \tag{3.23}$$

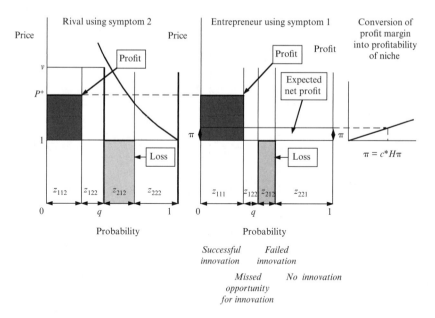

Figure 3.3   Determination of the expected profitability of a niche

Since $P \leq v$ and $vq < 1$, a sufficient condition is that:

$$b \geq c^+ n^* \qquad (3.24)$$

Since n^* increases with respect to c^+ and decreases with respect to b, the gist of the condition is that b must be sufficiently large and c^+ sufficiently small – but not so small as to make entrepreneurship uneconomic altogether. In other words, productivity must be sufficiently high to give workers a reasonable wage, while the size of each niche must be sufficiently small that consumption of each novel product takes up only a small proportion of this wage.

3.8   DIAGRAMMATIC ANALYSIS

The model can be readily summarized in graphical terms. There are two main steps in the determination of the general equilibrium. The first step, illustrated in Figure 3.3, is to calculate the expected profit generated by a representative niche. The second step, illustrated in Figure 3.4, is to use this expected profit to determine the equilibrium level of entrepreneurship.

The first step involves three stages. The first is to determine the limit

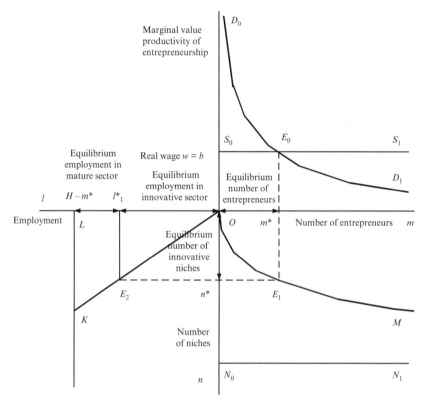

Figure 3.4 Demand and supply of entrepreneurs

price; this is illustrated in the left-hand panel of Figure 3.3. The panel shows how the profit of the entrepreneur's rival is determined, given that the rival must match a price commitment announced by the entrepreneur. Profit is measured in terms of a representative unit of output rather than the output of the niche as a whole. The limit price P^+ is set by the entrepreneur so that the area of the black rectangle, which measures the rival's expected profit on a successful innovation, is just equal to the area of the grey rectangle, which indicates the expected loss incurred by the rival on a failed innovation. The height of the profit rectangle corresponds to the profit margin generated by the limit price, and its width reflects the rival's unconditional probability of success. The unit height of the loss rectangle corresponds to the cost of labour, while the width corresponds to the rival's unconditional probability that the novel product is unwanted and has only been produced by mistake. The figure illustrates a case in which the limit price is below the consumers' reservation price, which means that the rival firm would be profitable if it had the field to itself. If the rival had access to only a very poor symptom then the limit price might lie above the reservation price, indicating that the rival would not be viable whether it was in competition with the entrepreneur or not.

Given this limit price, the expected profit of the entrepreneur can be determined from the entrepreneur's own probabilities of failure and success, which differ from those of the rival. The determination of the entrepreneur's expected profit is shown in the central panel. Once again, the analysis is conducted in terms of a representative unit of output. The entrepreneur's expected profit is indicated by the area of the black rectangle and the expected loss by the area of the grey rectangle. The difference between these two areas is measured by the area of the rectangle of unit width whose height is equal to the profit margin on a unit of output, π.

The profit margin is then converted into the profit generated by the niche as a whole, Π, by scaling up by the number of units demanded, Q. This scaling is effected by the sloping straight-line schedule in the right-hand panel of the figure.

The top right-hand quadrant in Figure 3.4 illustrates the demand and supply of entrepreneurs. This equilibrium between the demand and supply of entrepreneurs is the basis of the entire model. The demand for entrepreneurs is derived from the volatility of preferences in the innovative sector, and the consequent need for good judgement in managing that volatility.

Both the height and shape of the demand schedule $D_0 D_1$ are important in locating the equilibrium. The *height* is directly proportional to the profit per niche, Π, as derived in Figure 3.3. The *shape* is derived from the supply schedule of entrepreneurial ability, OM, shown in the bottom right-hand quadrant of the figure. The schedule OM relates the number of entrepreneurs, m, measured horizontally, to the number of niches in which entrepreneurs can operate, n, measured vertically and in a downward direction along the axis ON_0. The schedule OM is bounded from below by the horizontal line $N_0 N_1$ which represents the total number of niches in the economy. The slope of the schedule OM determines the marginal physical productivity of entrepreneurs, which is then converted into their marginal value productivity by scaling it up using the profit per niche. For any given number of entrepreneurs, m, therefore, the height of the demand schedule $D_0 D_1$ shown in the upper quadrant is proportional to the slope of the ability schedule OM shown in the lower quadrant.

Each entrepreneur has the same opportunity cost of time, w, which is measured in real terms by labour productivity, b. This determines the supply curve of entrepreneurs $S_0 S_1$, which is infinitely elastic at the level b.

The intersection of supply and demand at E_0 determines the equilibrium number of entrepreneurs. Projecting this equilibrium point down into the lower right-hand quadrant determines the number of innovative niches, n^*, as indicated by the height of E_1. The number of niches is converted into the number of employees in the innovative sector by a scaling factor indicated by the slope of the straight line OK in the bottom left-hand quadrant. Employment in the innovative sector, l^*_1, can then be read off from the point E_2 along the horizontal axis (reading to the left from the origin O).

By assumption, the economy is incompletely specialized in innovation, and so there is residual employment in the mature sector, where only the standard product is produced. After deducting the number of entrepreneurs, m^*, from the total population, H, the total supply of manual workers, $H - m^*$, is given by the intercept OL of the vertical schedule LK with the horizontal axis. The distribution of the population between entrepreneurship, employment in the innovative sector and employment in the mature sector is therefore indicated by the partitioning of the horizontal axis.

3.9 WELFARE ANALYSIS FOR THE MACROECONOMY

Social welfare, U, is measured as the sum of individual utilities. Since utility is measured in units of the standard good, total utility is simply a weighted sum of the output of the standard good and the novel goods, with the novel goods that are acceptable to consumers being valued at their reservation price v and the unwanted goods being valueless.

$$U^* = b(H - m^*) + ((v - 1) z_{111} - z_{211}) Q n^* \qquad (3.25)$$

The first term, $b(H - m^*)$, corresponds to total wage income, W, and the other terms relate to profit. The term $(v - 1) z_{111} Q n^*$ indicates the addition to welfare contributed by valuable novel products, whilst the second term, $- z_{211} Q n^*$, reflects the loss of welfare caused by the mistaken production of valueless novel products.

If the limit price is less than the reservation price, $P^+ < v$, then reported national income, Y^*, is less than utility:

$$Y^* = b(H - m^*) + ((P^+ - 1) z_{111} - z_{211}) Q n^* \qquad (3.26)$$
$$= W^* + T\Pi^*$$

where W^* is total wage income and $T\Pi^*$ is expected total profit income.

The discrepancy between utility and income is accounted for by consumers' surplus on the successful novel products:

$$CS^* = U^* - Y^* = (v - P^+) z_{111} Qn^* \qquad (3.27)$$

To appreciate more fully the properties of the model it is useful to consider a simple special case. This case is one in which there is a moderate elasticity in the supply of entrepreneurship, $k = \frac{1}{2}$, and the reservation price rather than the limit price is a binding constraint on the profitability of entrepreneurship, $P^+ \geq v$.

Substituting

$$m^* = (a\Pi / 2b)^2 ; \qquad n^* = a^2\Pi / 2b \qquad (3.28)$$

into (3.25) gives

$$U^* = bH (1 + ((a\ c^+/ 2b)((v - 1)z_{111} - z_{211}))^2\ H) \qquad (3.29)$$

Equation (3.29) shows that social welfare is an increasing function of entrepreneurial ability, a, labour productivity, b, the satiation level of consumption, c^+, and the reservation price of a novel product, v. In the absence of entrepreneurship, welfare would be merely bH. Thus all of the additional terms in (3.29) contribute to social welfare.

3.10   DISCUSSION OF THE RESULTS

Social welfare depends crucially on the z-factors, which indicate the unconditional probability of successful innovation, z_{111}, and the unconditional probability of failed innovation, z_{211}, the former having a positive effect and the latter a negative one. Expanding the z-factors shows that social welfare varies positively with the probability that novelty is demanded, q, and negatively with the two error probabilities – the probability that the entrepreneur will fail to recognize an opportunity to innovate because he/she is not alert, e_{11}, and the probability that the entrepreneur will innovate by mistake because of over-optimism and poor judgement, e_{21}.

It is interesting to note that the contribution of entrepreneurship to macroeconomic performance depends quadratically on population size. This is because the entrepreneur's time devoted to observing symptoms is a fixed cost independent of the number of people who consume novel products. Thus large economies give greater encouragement to entrepreneurship than small economies. The greater the degree of integration between individual regional economies, therefore, the greater is the incentive for entrepreneurship.

It is also worth noting that other factors also enter non-linearly into the social welfare function. Entrepreneurial ability, a, enters quadratically, as do the parameters of demand for novelty, v, c^+. Entrepreneurial ability and the demand for novelty increase the profitability of innovation activity, and thereby attract additional people into entrepreneurship. Given the assumed value of k, the supply of entrepreneurship is reasonably elastic, and it is this elasticity that generates the quadratic effect. This elasticity is in turn a reflection of the relatively high degree of interpersonal equality in the distribution of entrepreneurial ability. The more equal the distribution of ability, the more elastic is the supply of entrepreneurs.

Although high labour productivity enhances social welfare as a whole, its impact is moderated by the fact that, by raising manual earnings, it increases the opportunity cost of entrepreneurship. This helps to explain the emergence of 'petty entrepreneurship' in poor countries in which manual labour productivity is low (Motsuenyane, 1989).

The utility (3.29) represents the maximum obtainable under the assumed conditions. This is because novel products are priced at their reservation price, v. When a limit price lower than v prevails, utility will be lower too because the level of entrepreneurship will be lower. Some of the profit that would otherwise accrue to the marginal entrepreneur accrues to consumers as a surplus instead, and so too few people become entrepreneurs.

The patent system provides a partial response to this problem. By guaranteeing the innovator a monopoly, the need for limit pricing is removed. This shifts the demand for entrepreneurship back up to the schedule illustrated in Figure 3.4. In practice, however, the scope of the patent system is limited, being confined mainly to innovations that exploit new technology. This means that some types of innovation opportunity, involving patentable technologies, become more profitable than others, even though, according to the model, they are all equally beneficial to society. As a result, entrepreneurs who are competent at technological innovation are favoured over those that are not. With a limited number of novel products protected by patents, it is still likely that the marginal entrepreneur is not fully compensated through profit. The main effect of partial patent protection may well be therefore, not to promote entrepreneurship as a whole but rather to divert entrepreneurial activity towards high-technology innovations and away from low-technology innovations. When viewed from this perspective, general business support for entrepreneurs may be more beneficial in social terms than the selective support delivered by the patent system.

3.11 POLICY IMPLICATIONS AND TESTING OF THE MODEL

As explained in the introduction, the model is designed to demonstrate to policymakers that entrepreneurship boosts the standard of living. The model therefore relates macroeconomic performance, as indicated by national income and aggregate consumer surplus, to institutional and environmental factors such as the valuation of novelty, size of the market, and the elasticity of supply of entrepreneurs. The model generates other results as well, for example, the proportion of output accounted for by novel products is related to the level of entrepreneurial activity.

Because the approach is deductive, policymakers will demand empirical evidence to support the model. Such evidence could be provided by cross-section regressions showing how the economic performance of different countries is related to the institutional and environmental factors that are conducive to entrepreneurship. It is worth noting, however, that evidence on small-firm start-ups is only peripherally relevant to tests of the model; for while the model recognizes the importance of small-firm start-ups, it does not identify entrepreneurship exclusively with the small-firm sector. The validation of the model therefore calls for a rather different kind of empirical work than that which has dominated entrepreneurship research up to now.

3.12 EXTENSIONS OF THE MODEL

The model has a simple modular structure and is therefore easily extended. Additional sources of volatility can be introduced. In practice it is not only the demand for novelty that is volatile, but the supply of novelty as well. Lack of scientific knowledge may create a barrier to the supply of novel products. The entrepreneur may therefore need to consult two symptoms rather than one – one for demand and the other for supply. These symptoms can be examined simultaneously or sequentially, and in the sequential case either of them may be considered first (see Chapter 2). The larger the number of volatile factors, the more symptoms the entrepreneur has to consult, and the wider the range of options that are available concerning the order in which they are observed (Casson and Wadeson, 1998).

Spatial and temporal dimensions may be introduced as well. The economy may be subdivided into regions, each of which has its own independent local sources of volatility. These volatilities will be driven by local institutional changes and fluctuations in the availability of local resources. Local entrepreneurs will tend to take responsibility for managing local risks as they can observe local symptoms directly rather than at second-hand.

The period of analysis may also be divided into sub-periods, during which demand is affected by short-term changes in fashion, and supply is affected by accidents, absenteeism and strikes. This creates a demand for continuing entrepreneurial involvement in the production and marketing of novel products. It is only when the entrepreneur has acquired sufficient experience to devise routines for handling the more common types of short-term volatility that responsibility for this can be devolved to ordinary managers.

In general, the management of different types of volatility will tend to be specialized with different types of entrepreneur. Entrepreneurial teams will emerge, in which entrepreneurs with different specialisms collaborate to manage complex innovation processes. This collaboration may take place within a single firm which the entrepreneurs jointly own, or between separate firms which are owned by different entrepreneurs. The analysis of multiple volatility, and the emergence of a division of labour to deal with it, can therefore provide important insights into the organizational structures of entrepreneurial firms and the role of inter-firm alliances in innovative industries.

3.13   SUMMARY AND CONCLUSIONS

This chapter has developed the economic theory of entrepreneurship set out in the preceding chapters into a formal model which demonstrates the contribution of entrepreneurship to macroeconomic performance. The primary function of the entrepreneur, according to this model, is to exercise judgement, and most important economic judgements involve decisions about which products should be produced, and in particular which products not currently produced should commence production.

The model highlights a number of important points.

- The contribution of entrepreneurs to macroeconomic performance depends crucially on their quality of judgement, as indicated, in this model, by their ability to predict the demand for novelty correctly. The size of the market, the premium that consumers place on novelty, and the elasticity of supply of entrepreneurship are all important factors too.
- The volatility of consumer demand for novelty is important in generating a demand for entrepreneurship in the first place. Successful entrepreneurs understand that consumers are problem-solvers, and

that because of lags in the system it is important to predict consumer needs correctly.

- Profit must be used with care as a measure of the contribution of entrepreneurship. When entrepreneurs face competitive constraints some of the contribution of entrepreneurship appears as consumers' surplus. It is only when the best entrepreneurs are far superior to the second-best that all the contribution of entrepreneurship is captured as profit.
- The general equilibrium of a free-market economic system is essentially a speculative equilibrium in which the individual judgements of entrepreneurs are aggregated by the market system. Labour is a key resource for entrepreneurs, for without it, novel products cannot be produced. According to the model, innovative entrepreneurs bid away labour from a mature sector that produces only a standardized commodity and direct the labour into the production of novel products instead. In this sense innovation involves an act of arbitrage in the labour market, rather than in the product market, as is usually assumed.

REFERENCES

Casson, Mark and Nigel S. Wadeson (1998), 'Communication costs and the boundaries of the firm', *International Journal of the Economics of Business*, **5**(1), 5–28.

Harper, David A. (1996), *Entrepreneurship and the Market Process: An Inquiry into the Growth of Knowledge*, London: Routledge.

Motsuenyane, A. (1989), *The Development of Black Entrepreneurship in South Africa*, Lagos: Nigerian Institute of International Affairs.

Ricketts, Martin (2006), 'Theories of entrepreneurship: historical development and critical assessment', in Mark Casson, Bernard Yeung, Anuradha Basu and Nigel Wadeson (eds), *The Oxford Handbook of Entrepreneurship*, Oxford: Oxford University Press, pp. 33–58.

Storey, David (2006), 'Evaluating SME policies and programmes: technical and political dimensions', in Mark Casson, Bernard Yeung, Nigel Wadeson and Anuradha Basu (eds), *Oxford Handbook of Entrepreneurship*, Oxford: Oxford University Press, pp. 248–78.

4. Entrepreneurship and the growth of the firm: an extension of Penrose's theory

With Peter J. Buckley

Edith Penrose is one of the most important figures in the development of the modern theory of the firm. Entrepreneurship played an important role in her thinking. Penrose believed that entrepreneurship provided a continuous dynamic that sustained the growth of successful firms. She argued that many of the factors that the Edwardian economist Alfred Marshall believed influenced the size of firms actually influenced their rate of growth instead. Behind Edith Penrose's *Theory of the Growth of the Firm* lies a formal model that guarantees the internal consistency of her theory. This model – set out below – illuminates many issues in the theory of the firm including not only growth, but also the composition of the management team, the degree of decentralization and the size distribution of firms. The model also facilitates a detailed examination of the different dimensions of corporate diversification. The results of this model call into question some of the recent interpretations of Penrose's thought. Contrary to recent claims, her approach to economics was not overtly heterodox – rather, she applied traditional economic techniques in a novel way. This novelty was inspired by her emphasis on entrepreneurship as the driving force in the growth of the firm.

4.1 INTRODUCTION

Edith T. Penrose (1914–96) published the first ever theory of the growth of the firm in the May 1955 issue of the *AER, Papers and Proceedings* (Penrose, 1955). The theory built upon her previous controversy in the *AER* with Armen A. Alchian, which had been stimulated by her critique of biological analogies in the theory of the firm (Penrose, 1952; Alchian, 1953).

Penrose suggested that 'the predisposition to grow is inherent in the very nature of firms'. This disposition reflects not just the demands of survival, but fundamental human motivations – the 'businessman's search for profits in particular' (Penrose, 1955, p. 531). This idea was developed in *The Theory of the Growth of the Firm* (1959) – a book recently hailed by management scholars as a pioneering exposition of the resource-based view of the firm (Foss, 2002; Penrose and Pitelis, 2002).

Rugman and Verbeke (2002) have challenged the resource-based interpretation, arguing that Penrose's major contribution was not the anticipation of modern management theory but the formulation of an economic theory of the optimal rate of growth of the firm (see also Kor and Mahoney, 2004, p. 185). Penrose believed, in fact, that entrepreneurship was the major factor driving the growth of the firm. It is not so much resources in general, as entrepreneurship in particular, that accounts for the growth of the firm.

This chapter presents a formal model of the growth of the firm derived from Penrose's work. It encapsulates her key insights and affords significant extensions. Penrose discusses two objectives of the firm – shareholder value maximization (which she terms profit maximization) and growth maximization subject to a dividend payout constraint. In fact, there is not a great deal of difference between the two, and the model presented here can be solved for both, although the focus below is on value maximization.

Penrose's fundamental research question is this: given that entrepreneurship lies at the heart of the firm, why does the size of the firm not spontaneously adjust to reflect the vision of the entrepreneur? Her answer is that firms cannot be created out of nothing, but need to be grown from small beginnings. The key to understanding the growth of the firm is to understand better the scope of the entrepreneurial vision, which determines the potential size of the firm, and the constraints that prevent the firm from attaining this size at the outset.

In addition, Penrose argued that entrepreneurial firms could continually expand by capitalizing on their previous experience. Entrepreneurial learning meant that the steady state size of an entrepreneurial firm could be infinite, so that an entrepreneurial firm could continue to grow indefinitely at a constant rate.

The chapter sheds new light on the controversy surrounding her work. Penrose emphasized the firm's resources because she saw them as both the key to the firm's success and as the key constraint on its growth. The tacitness of information, on which resource-based theory places so much emphasis, is not only a stimulus to growth but, most importantly, a factor limiting the growth of the firm. The driving force for growth in Penrose's theory is the entrepreneurial quality of the firm's management team, which enables it to identify opportunities for diversification before other firms. Tacitness is a positive factor only in so far as it protects the information advantages of the entrepreneurial team. The growth rate of the firm there-fore reflects a balance between entrepreneurial dynamism on the one hand and the difficulty of enlarging the firm's management team sufficiently quickly to exploit the resultant opportunities on the other.

Fifty years on, Penrose's paper remains a 'state-of-the art' contribution; subsequent important work by Jovanovic (1982), Evans (1987), Audretsch (1995), Geroski (1998) and others has complemented her insights, but it has not superseded them.

4.2   SIZE VERSUS GROWTH

Penrose believed that the standard theory of the firm derived from Marshall (1890) confused the factors that limit the size of the firm with those that limit its growth. She argued that there is, in theory, no limit to the size to which a firm can grow.

- There are limits to growth within a single market, which are set by overall market size and competition for market share, but a firm can evade these constraints by diversifying into other markets.
- While U-shaped average cost curves determine a unique optimal size at which average cost is a minimum, this logic applies to physical plant rather than to a managerial unit such as a firm. A firm can expand beyond optimum plant size by increasing the number of plants through horizontal and vertical integration, or product diversification.
- Marshall's biological analogy between the firms in an industry and the 'trees in a forest' is misleading because it ignores the fact that firms are institutions that can regenerate themselves continually through managerial succession. Firms can also merge to accelerate their growth, and metamorphose into new forms, as when a small firm with highly-centralized autocratic management merges with other small firms and turns into a large highly-decentralized multi-divisional firm. As a legal and contractual entity, a firm can in prin-ciple endure for ever.
- Managerial diseconomies of scale are often said to limit the size of firms, but such limiting factors are actually diseconomies of growth. Bureaucracy, for example, does not limit size because it can be addressed through decentralization (see below); on the other hand, the additional training costs incurred by faster growth cannot be avoided. Thus the future size of a firm is not limited by the existence of a finite optimum size but by a finite optimal rate of growth.

When analysing growth, the natural analogue of a theory of optimal size is a theory of optimal growth, and this is essentially what Penrose provides. Factors which are commonly said to limit size are irrelevant to size, she said, and limit growth instead. Because size of firm does not matter, there is no reason to believe that the firm's growth rate will vary systematically over its lifetime, and so it is reasonable to postulate the existence of a steady state rate of growth. The existence of such a steady state implies that firms can last for ever and so, with a constant rate of growth, they can (theoretically) eventually approach infinite size. To many observers of the corporate scene in the 1950s, it seemed as if large firms like General Motors would, indeed, continue to grow for ever.

4.3   THE VALUE OF A GROWING FIRM AND THE DETERMINATION OF OPTIMAL GROWTH

Let the size of the firm at time t be measured by $x(t)$, and its instantaneous proportional rate of growth by $g(t)$. In Penrose's theory, size is measured by the number of markets served by the firm; for convenience, it is assumed that a newly-established firm operates in a single market, $x(0) = 1$. All variables are non-negative unless otherwise stated. Discrete variables, such as the number of markets, are treated as though they were continuous.

The entrepreneurial capability of the firm is measured by the profitability of the markets it is able to enter; the operating profit generated by a representative market is a constant, A, independent of the size of the firm. Thus gross operating revenue is Ax. Growth is achieved by entering new markets, with a unit entry cost per market of B. The number of markets entered per period is gx, giving a total cost of entry Bgx. The crucial feature of the Penrose model is that managerial costs increase with the speed of growth; this generates a 'cost of growth' component which is linear in scale, x, but quadratic in growth, g, namely Cg^2x. Linearity ensures that the firm's total costs remain proportional to scale, whilst the quadratic term ensures decreasing returns to growth.

Future profits are discounted at the cost of capital, r. For simplicity, the costs of setting up the firm and entering the first market are ignored, since these are sunk costs at the time that growth begins. The value of the firm is the sum of discounted operating profit, net of investment cost and the cost of growth:

$$v = \int_0^\infty exp(-rt)(A - Bg - Cg^2)x\,dt \qquad (4.1)$$

There are two ways of determining the value-maximizing growth trajectory. The first is to maximize v with respect to $x(t)$, using the Euler-Lagrange equation as the first-order condition. The second is to assume a constant proportional rate of growth, and then to solve for the optimal rate. The two approaches yield the same result and so, in the interests of brevity, the second is used here.

Substituting

$$x = \exp(gt) \tag{4.2}$$

into (4.1) gives the fundamental formula for the value of the firm in the Penrose model:

$$v = (A - Bg - Cg^2)/(r - g) \tag{4.3}$$

This is the net profit per unit size, capitalized at the rate $r - g$. Note that the value of the firm is finite and positive only when $g < r$ – a restriction that is relaxed later.

The first-order condition for value-maximization is

$$v_g = ((A - Bg - Cg^2)/(r - g)^2) - ((B + 2Cg)/((r - g)) = 0 \tag{4.4}$$

where the derivative v_g measures the sensitivity of the firm's value to changes in its rate of growth. The derivative comprises two terms: the first measures the impact of a change in growth on the capitalized value of initial profits, assuming that the profit stream remains unchanged, whilst the second measures the marginal reduction in the profit stream induced by growth, assuming that the capitalization rate remains unchanged.

Placing both terms over a common denominator gives a quadratic equation which has two positive real roots when:

$$Cr^2 > A - Br > 0 \tag{4.5}$$

These inequalities imply that growth is profitable when $g = 0$ $(A - Br > 0)$ and that the firm as a whole is unprofitable when $g = r$ $(A - Br - Cr^2 < 0)$. Only the smaller of the two roots lies in the permitted range, and it is this root that corresponds to the maximum:

$$g^* = r - (r^2 - ((A - Br)/C))^{1/2} \tag{4.6}$$

Differentiation of the growth equation shows that under the assumed conditions the partial derivates can be signed as follows:

$$g^*_A > 0; \qquad g^*_B < 0; \qquad g^*_C < 0; \qquad g^*_r < 0 \qquad (4.7)$$

Growth is higher, the higher is the profitability of the representative market, A, and the lower are the cost parameters, B, C. B is less important than either A or C because its impact is mediated by the cost of capital, r, which is normally substantially less than unity. Thus growth is governed by a fundamental trade-off between the profitability of the representative market, A, and the strength of decreasing returns to growth, as measured by C. Growth is also higher, the lower the cost of capital: an increase in the rate at which future profits are discounted discourages the firm from sacrificing current profit to promote future growth.

The solution implies that all growth can be internally financed. No set-up costs are incurred on the formation of the firm, and the profit earned in each market covers the expense of diversifying into the next market. This accords with the common view of firm finance at the time that Penrose wrote.

The remainder of this chapter explores the determinants of the key parameters A, B, C. A family of models is presented, each of which endogenizes these parameters in a different way. For this purpose, A now represents net revenue per unit size, B a cost component which is proportional to growth, and C a cost component which is quadratic in growth.

4.4 MANAGEMENT TRAINING COSTS

A prominent feature of Penrose's theory is the need to train managers through an induction programme in which recruits are apprenticed to experienced managers. This takes up the time of experienced managers. The need to train a growing number of entrepreneurs is a sufficient reason for diminishing returns to growth.

Suppose that two types of manager are employed by the firm. Let m_1 be the number of managers carrying out routine activities, and m_2 the number carrying out entrepreneurial activities connected with the discovery of new diversification opportunities.

The demand for routine management is directly proportional to the number of markets in which the firm operates, while the demand for entrepreneurial management services depends on the number of new market opportunities that need to be discovered:

$$m_1 = a_1 x; \qquad m_2 = a_2 x g \qquad (4.8)$$

Let m_3 be the number of managers engaged in training recruits. Let a proportion of managers q retire or quit each period. The number of recruits is equal to the number of staff who need to be replaced, qm, plus the number needed to accommodate growth, gm. Each recruit takes u_1 periods to learn the job, and teaching them the job costs u_2 in the time that experienced managers devote to training. Hence the total time cost of training is:

$$u = u_1 + u_2 \qquad (4.9)$$

Total demands on management are now:

$$m = m_1 + m_2 + m_3 = (m_1 + m_2)/(1 - uq - ug) \qquad (4.10)$$

To eliminate the non-linearity in g, a first order approximation is made, which is valid so long as d and g are reasonably small:

$$m = (1 + uq + ug)(m_1 + m_2) \qquad (4.11)$$

It is assumed that managers can perform all activities equally well. There is therefore a single integrated market for management services in which the prevailing salary is s.

Operating profit per market is now z, and the sunk cost of investment on entering each market is i. Net profit is:

$$(z - a_1(1 + uq)s - (i + (a_1u + a_2(1 + uq))s)g - a_2usg^2) x \qquad (4.12)$$

which corresponds to the general model with:

$$A = z - a_1(1 + uq)s; \qquad B = i + (a_1u + a_2(1 + uq))s; \qquad C = a_2us \quad (4.13)$$

The number of markets, and the number of managers of each type, all grow exponentially at the same rate g^*. Investment expenditure on market entry also grows at the same exponential rate.

Value-maximizing growth is higher, the higher is profit per market, z, the lower are the set-up costs of market entry, i, the lower are the demands on management overhead per market, a_1, a_2, and the lower are salary rates, s. As before, growth is higher, the lower the cost of capital, r.

Growth decreases, the higher the turnover of managerial labour (due to retirement and quits), q, and the longer the training process required, u. Minimizing turnover implies recruiting managers young and giving them 'jobs for life' (since this strategy maximizes their working life with the firm) as well as encouraging loyalty through age-related and experience-related pay. The more tacit and less codified is the information used by managers, the greater the investment required for training is likely to be. Tacit information, in this model, therefore increases the costs of growth.

4.5   DECENTRALIZATION

Penrose needs to refute the argument that large firms grow more slowly because they become bureaucratic. She claims that decentralization, and in particular the increasing use of multi-divisional structures by large US firms, can neutralize the diseconomies of bureaucracy.

Bureaucracy may be identified with an escalating cost of routine management. It is therefore postulated that the routine costs of management increase quadratically with the size of firm, rather than linearly as before. To focus on bureaucracy, training costs are eliminated by setting $u = 0$, but decreasing returns to the rate of growth are retained by making the demand for entrepreneurial management a quadratic function of growth.

Decentralization is associated with an increasing use of internal markets, as measured by an index, k, which runs from unity for a purely bureaucratic management system based on internal central planning to infinity for a firm which is coordinated entirely by market forces. Both of these cases represent extremes that are rarely observed in practice. The quadratic component of cost is reduced by an increase in decentralization, such that a 1 per cent increase in decentralization generates a 1 per cent reduction in costs.

Given the advantages of decentralization, it might be asked why only large firms avail themselves of this option. The answer is that there are fixed costs of operating decentralized systems. These include the costs of implementing multi-divisional accounting, performance measurement for individual managers, procurement strategies to promote competition amongst individual subcontractors, and so on. These fixed costs are independent of the size of the firm but vary directly with the degree of decentralization.

The overall demand for routine management services at scale x with degree of decentralization k is:

$$m_1 = (e_0 x^2 / k) + e_1 k \qquad (4.14)$$

where e_0 is a parameter measuring the intensity of demand for routine management and e_1 a parameter measuring the costs of operating decentralized systems. The first term measures the direct demand for routine management under decreasing returns, whilst the second term measures the number of managers occupied in implementing the decentralized systems. It is assumed that the number of managers required to implement decentralization is directly proportional to the degree of decentralization involved.

The demand for entrepreneurial management services is

$$m_2 = a_2 x g^2 \tag{4.15}$$

A value-maximizing firm will set the degree of decentralization, k, to mini-mize the routine management input, m_1. The relevant first order condition is:

$$m_{1k} = - (e_0 x^2 / k^2) + e_1 = 0 \tag{4.16}$$

where m_{1k} is the marginal change in routine management requirements induced by a unit increase in k. The solution of this equation determines the optimal degree of decentralization:

$$k^* = (e_0 / e_1)^{1/2} x \tag{4.17}$$

Decentralization is directly proportional to size – the larger the firm, the more decentralized it becomes. Decentralization is higher, the greater the intensity of demand for routine management services, e_0, and the lower the unit costs of decentralization, e_1.

Back-substitution of k^* into m_1 indicates that when the firm adopts an optimal degree of decentralization at every size, the demand for routine management once again becomes a linear proportional function of size:

$$m_1 = 2(e_0 e_1)^{1/2} x \tag{4.18}$$

The proportionality factor is directly related to the intensity of demand for management, e_0, and to the cost of decentralization, e_1.

Substituting the new expressions for m_1 and m_2 for the original ones, and setting $u = 0$, generates the new parameter values:

$$A = z - 2(e_0 e_1)^{1/2} s; \qquad B = i + a_2 s; \qquad C = a_2 s \tag{4.19}$$

The most important consequence is that both the value-maximising growth rate and the growth-maximizing growth rate increase as the cost of decentralization, e_0, falls. Effective decentralization promotes growth because it reduces its bureaucratic burden on the firm.

4.6 THE PROFITABILITY OF INDIVIDUAL MARKETS

So far the size of firm has been measured simply by the number of markets, x, in which it operates. This section introduces two other measures of size: the total value of sales, and the value added by the firm. The size of the firm is now measured by the size of the market scaled up by the number of markets in which the firm operates, rather than by the number of markets alone.

It is assumed that all markets have the same parameter values for demand. The demand curve in a representative market is linear:

$$y = b_0 - b_1 p \qquad (4.20)$$

where y is physical output, p is price, b_0 is a parameter measuring the size of market and b_1 is a parameter measuring the price sensitivity of demand. Output is generated under constant returns to scale using manual and clerical labour, n, as the sole factor input. It requires a_0 units of labour to produce one unit of output:

$$n = a_0 y \qquad (4.21)$$

Labour is hired at a wage w_0. Unlike managerial employees, manual workers do not need to be trained. The input of manual labour is additional to, and independent of, the input of management required to co-ordinate the firm as a whole.

Penrose distinguishes different stages of production in her discussion, and it is therefore appropriate to assume that production may utilize inputs of raw materials and semi-processed products from an earlier stage of production. The cost of such inputs, per unit output, is w_1.

The unit cost of production is therefore:

$$c = w_0 a_0 + w_1 \qquad (4.22)$$

and profit per market is:

$$z = (p - c)y \qquad (4.23)$$

A value-maximizing firm will maximize profit per market. The firm can choose either p or y, but not both. The first order condition for a maximum of profit determines the optimal level y^*, and so, by implication, the optimal value p^*:

$$y^* = (b_0 - b_1 c) / 2; \qquad p^* = (b_0 + b_1 c) / 2 b_1 \qquad (4.24)$$

whence the unit mark-up and the profit are respectively:

$$p^* - c = (b_0 - b_1 c) / 2 b_1; \qquad z^* = (b_0 - b_1 c)^2 / 4 b_1 \qquad (4.25)$$

This second result gives a formula, $z = z^*$, that can be inserted into the formulae for A above. It is readily established that z^* increases with the size of the market, b_0, and decreases with the price-sensitivity of demand, b_1, the labour intensity of production, a_0, the wage rate, w_0, and the cost of raw material inputs, w_1.

The result for b_1 is particularly interesting. Since profit decreases with the price sensitivity of demand, the ability of the firm's entrepreneurs to discover new markets with insensitive demand is crucial. Entrepreneurs who can discover unique opportunities for essential products with no competitors will earn a high rate of profit per market, and therefore be able to achieve an exceptional rate of growth.

It can also be argued that the tacitness of information tends to reduce the sensitivity of demand, as measured by b_1. Tacitness was identified above as a managerial barrier to growth, but it can also play the role of a barrier to entry which protects the diversifying firm from imitators. The more tacit the information used by the management team, the more difficult it is for rivals to copy the firm's product, and so the less price-sensitive will be the firm's demand in any market. This stimulates profit and therefore growth.

Finally, it should be noted that when the number of markets is treated as a continuous rather than discrete variable, the effect is to reduce the size of the market but leave the distribution of prices that different customers are willing to pay unchanged. The market is subdivided into l equal segments, each with demand curve:

$$y = (b_0/l) - (b_1/l)p \qquad (4.26)$$

each of which sustains an optimal output y^*/l sold at price p^*, resulting in profit z^*/l. When these figures are aggregated across the segments, the results are the same as in the discrete model. Continuity of x is achieved by increasing l towards infinity.

4.7   RISK AND UNCERTAINTY

Penrose regards uncertainty as manageable. It is the existence of uncertainties that generates the demand for managers to run the firm. In

Penrose's theory managers behave as individual members of an entrepreneurial team. But unlike the entrepreneurs described in Chapter 1, they have such good judgement that they can eliminate entirely all risk to the profits of the firm. Managers collect sufficient information to dispel all uncertainty before decisions are taken. It is because the information collected is completely correct that a firm can sustain a steady rate of growth in a volatile environment. This is very much in line with popular thinking at the time Penrose was writing. It was the era of long-term forecasting, indicative economic planning, and management by objectives. The managers employed by large firms were believed to have all the technical qualifications necessary to control business risks successfully.

By taking such an extreme position, Penrose overlooked – or at least underestimated – two types of risk which have important implications for business growth; namely that:

- *The market into which the firm has diversified may subsequently disappear* This might be the result of either changes in demand, driven by changes in tastes or the emergence of substitute products, or changes in supply, driven by rising costs or the entry of competitors.
- *The market into which the firm has diversified may not exist at all* The information used to assess the market opportunity may have been inadequate or misleading. No profit is ever generated from the market because the expected demand never existed in the first place.

These risks can be handled very easily by making minor modifications to Penrose's theory. However, incorporating these risks radically changes some of her conclusions.

Let each market in which the firm operates have a probability h_1 that it disappears in any given period. The impact of a shock is the 'sudden death' of the market rather than the onset of a slow decline. The probability that a market disappears is independent of the length of time that the firm has been operating in it. Firms often exit mature markets at the times of periodic 'shake-outs', and managers frequently report that the loss of such markets has stimulated diversification – for example, the weakening of the domestic market encourages diversification into export markets. This strategy of building on an apparent weakness no longer appears paradoxical once the role of diversification in sustaining steady-state growth is examined in the context of disappearing markets.

Let the probability that any given market turns out to have zero profit potential be h_0. If a market does not have profit potential then the firm must find some other market into which to diversify in order to sustain its growth. Set-up costs are incurred before the market is discovered, as are entrepreneurial management costs. Both types of cost are sunk costs; they can never be recovered when the firm exits a market.

To compensate for the disappearance of existing markets the firm must enter $h_1 x$ new markets each period, just to make good the loss of markets. To this must then be added the gx new markets required to sustain growth. The total number of new markets that must be entered is therefore $(g + h_1)x$.

This higher figure represents the number of *successful* entries that is required. To compensate for a reduced rate of success in correctly identifying profitable markets, the number of markets that the firm must attempt to enter must be increased by a factor $1/h_0$. Thus the total number of attempted entries becomes $(g + h_1)x / h_0$. The new components of cost are therefore:

Investment cost of market entry	$=$	$i(g + h_1)x / h_0$
Routine management cost	$=$	$a_1 sx$
Entrepreneurial management cost	$=$	$a_2 sx((g + h_1)/h_0)^2$

Thus:

$$\text{Profit} = (z - a_1 s - i(h_0/h_1) - a_2 s(h_0/h_1)^2) - ((i/h_0) + 2(a_2 sh_1/h_0^2))g - (a_2 s/h_0^2)g^2$$

which corresponds to the general framework with:

$$A = z - a_1 s - i(h_0/h_1) - a_2 s(h_0/h_1)^2;$$
$$B = (i/h_0) + 2(a_2 sh_1/h_0^2); \qquad\qquad (4.27)$$
$$C = a_2 s/h_0^2$$

Growth diminishes as both h_0 falls and h_1 increases – that is, as the probability of successful market entry falls and as the frequency of markets disappearing increases. Conversely, growth increases as the probability of successful market entry rises and the durability of markets increases. The first factor is related to the quality of entrepreneurial judgement, whilst the second is related, amongst other things, to the ease with which the firm's market entry can be imitated by others. In so far as the firm faces competitors who adopt a 'follow the leader' strategy, the durability of markets is liable to diminish.

It is worth noting that some of the replacement market entry may involve re-entering markets in which the firm was previously represented, but which later disappeared, and have reappeared again. Another possibility is that the firm re-enters a market that has only just disappeared because it has identified a method of revitalizing the market. For example, a firm facing changing tastes in some market may decide not to abandon the market but to reinvest by relaunching its brand with a more up-to-date image (see Chapter 10).

The disappearance of existing markets reinstates the relevance of bio-logical analogy to the growth of the firm. It shows that while Marshall's metaphor of the 'trees in the forest' may not apply to large corporations enjoying steady-state growth, it still applies to the individual markets in which they operate. Penrose's contribution is therefore not to demonstrate the limitations of biological analogy so much as to show that the analogy needs to be applied in the appropriate way – that is, to markets rather than to firms.

4.8   THE SIZE DISTRIBUTION OF FIRMS

Penrose considers the implications of steady-state growth for industrial concentration and the size distribution of firms in the later chapters of her book. It is the least convincing part of her work. Penrose notes that if firms grow faster than the economy as a whole then large firms will become dom-inant and concentration, especially through merger, will increase. Whilst this was a popular political view at the time, it is contrary to the statistical evidence – both then and now. In most developed countries the propor-tion of output accounted for by large firms is either stable or decreasing; an increase in large-firm dominance, when it occurs, is often caused by a small number of very large mergers, rather than by a systematic process of diversification pursued over a long period of time (Hart, 2001).

The simplest way of addressing this issue is to suppose that firms are liable to sudden death at any stage of their growth. Unlike the previous section, in which sudden death was applied to individual markets, this form of sudden death applies to the firm as a whole. It could be due to an external cause, such as radical innovation, wiping out all firms in some mature sector, or to an internal cause specific to the firm, such as a cata-strophic failure in the management team. At some stage in the life of most firms, it could be argued, management succession fails; for example, an ageing entrepreneur refuses to retire or appoints an incompetent relative (the classic 'family firm' problem). Although there may be some conta-gion when firms collapse – with large firms bringing down their suppliers, for example – the assumption of independent collapse driven by internal factors seems to be the most common scenario, and is therefore assumed below.

Let h_2 be the probability that a firm collapses in any given period.

There are no assets to sell off when the firm collapses, and so no money is returned to the shareholders; there are no debts either, since the firm has no borrowing, as explained above. The probability of collapse reduces the rate at which profits are capitalized to $1/(r + h_2 - g)$. There is no reason for the cost of capital itself, r, to change, since there is no additional risk of default. The firm is therefore revalued at:

$$v^+ = (A - Bg - Cg^2)/(r^+ - g) \tag{4.28}$$

where:

$$r^+ = r + h_2 \tag{4.29}$$

A significant implication of the reduction of the capitalization rate is that the value of the firm will remain finite even if g exceeds r; the firm's value only becomes infinite when $g \geq r + h_2$.

With firms being formed at a constant rate, and collapsing at a constant rate h_2, the size distribution of firms is exponential with a decay factor h_2. Let $f(t)$ be the frequency with which firms of age t are represented in the population of firms in the steady state. Then:

$$f(t) = h_2 \exp(-h_2 t) \tag{4.30}$$

where the first term h_2 is a constant of proportionality chosen to ensure that total frequency across all ages sums to unity. If all firms grow at the uniform steady-state growth rate g, starting from unit size, as assumed above, then every firm of age t has size $x(t) = \exp(gt)$, which, when inverted, implies that a firm's age is a logarithmic function of its size:

$$t = (1/g) \ln(x) \tag{4.31}$$

Substituting this expression into the frequency distribution of age, and making an appropriate adjustment to the constant of proportionality, gives the frequency distribution of size:

$$f(x) = \begin{matrix} 0 & x < 1 \\ ((h_2/g) - 1)x^{-h_2/g} & x \geq 1 \end{matrix} \tag{4.32}$$

This distribution is valid only if $g < h_2$ – that is, if firms grow at a slower rate than they collapse. It is a Pareto distribution whose form depends crucially on the ratio h_2/g. The higher this ratio, the more equal the distribution of size. A low growth rate, together with a high probability of collapse, implies a relatively equal size distribution of firms, with relatively few very large firms, whilst a high growth rate, combined with a low probability of collapse, implies a relatively unequal distribution, with a significant number of large firms and relatively few small and medium-sized firms.

If $h_2/g \leq 2$ then both the mean firm size and the variance of firm size are infinite. Thus although the distribution exists, it has a very 'fat tail' of large firms. If $2 < h_2/g \leq 3$ then the mean is finite but the variance remains infinite, whilst if $h_2/g > 3$ then both mean and variance exist:

$$\text{Mean} = (h_2 - g) / (h_2 - 2g) \tag{4.33.1}$$
$$\text{Variance} = (h_2 - g) \, g^2 / (h_2 - 2g)^2 \, (h_2 - 3g) \tag{4.33.2}$$

The existence of the third and higher moments of the distribution depends upon even stricter conditions. It is evident, therefore, that a distribution of firm size with both finite mean and finite variance exists only when the growth rate is low compared with the rate of firm collapse.

The fact that the Penrose model with firm collapse generates a Pareto distribution of size is not a mathematical peculiarity or mere coincidence. The Pareto distribution approximates the outcomes of stochastic processes which comply with Gibrat's Law of Proportionate Effect, which simply restates Penrose's proposition that growth is independent of size. Penrose applies the Gibrat principle without the element of stochastic variation introduced by Gibrat (1931). The independence of growth and size is also reflected in the fact that the Pareto distribution is 'scale-free' – the relative frequencies of firms at different sizes depends only on the ratio of their sizes and not on their absolute sizes.

In terms of statistical analysis, therefore, Penrose was following a well-trodden path when she argued that the growth of firms was independent of their size. She was not the first person to postulate this, but she was the first economist to explain why growth would be independent of size and to identify the economic and managerial factors which determine that rate of growth.

Penrose's model would be strengthened even further if it could be extended to include random, or so-called 'higgledy-piggledy' growth for the individual firm, along the lines postulated by Gibrat. In this extension, only the firm's average growth rate, rather than its actual growth rate, would remain constant from one period to the next. Another extension would allow for cross-section differences in the rates of growth of individual firms. These could be cross-sectoral differences (for example, reflecting differential rates of growth of demand in manufacturing and services) or regional differences (for example, reflecting differences in the supply of managers at different locations). The extension most attuned to Penrose's own approach, however, would be to postulate inter-firm differences in the quality of entrepreneurship which could exist within the same sector and the same region. Unfortunately, however, such extensions present serious analytical challenges, and cannot be addressed within the scope of the present chapter.

4.9 ALTERNATIVE DIMENSIONS OF DIVERSIFICATION

Penrose discusses three main dimensions of diversification:

- horizontal integration;
- vertical integration, and
- pure diversification (sometimes called conglomerate integration).

Wolf (1977) has argued that growing firms will choose strategically between these alternative dimensions. A firm that favours horizontal integration, for example, may opt for multinational expansion, replicating the same activity in different countries, whilst another may opt for pure diversification, undertaking different activities, but confining its activities to a single country. This creates two alternative forms of firm: the single-product multinational and the multi-product domestic firm. Introducing vertical integration raises further possibilities, such as becoming a vertically-integrated single-product domestic firm. More ambitious firms may tackle two of the three dimensions of diversification simultaneously. This creates three additional forms: the single-product vertically-integrated multinational, such as the classic US multinational of the 1960s; the multi-product vertically integrated domestic firm such as the 'national champion' in a strategic industry such as defence; and the vertically-disintegrated multi-product multinational, such as a modern firm exploiting the extension of global brands (see Chapter 10).

To accommodate different dimensions of diversification, it is necessary to extend the basic framework introduced in section 4.3. For simplicity, only two dimensions are considered. These dimensions represent the number of countries or regions in which the firm operates (horizontal integration), the number of stages of production (vertical integration) or the range of products (diversification). Sizes along the two dimensions are measured by x_1, x_2 respectively.

Interplay between the two dimensions means that the total number of activities, x, in which the firm is involved is:

$$x = x_1 x_2 \qquad (4.34)$$

Thus if the firm is both horizontally integrated (dimension 1) and vertically integrated (dimension 2) then it operates in x_1 locations at each of x_2 stages, which implies $x_1 x_2$ separate plants. Each of these activities is assumed to be equally profitable, as before.

If the firm expands along each dimension at a constant proportional rate then both x_1 and x_2 grow exponentially. The rates of growth along the two dimensions, g_1, g_2, can be chosen independently. It follows that the overall rate of growth of the firm is the sum of the growth rates along the separate dimensions:

$$x = \exp((g_1 + g_2)t) \qquad (4.35)$$

To remain close to the one-dimensional model, it is assumed that every activity incurs an entry cost, just as before. However, this cost now varies according to the direction of expansion, with cost parameter B_1 along dimension 1 and cost parameter B_2 along dimension 2, giving a total entry cost per period $(B_1 g_1 + B_2 g_2) x$. Similarly, the costs of expanding the entrepreneurial management team to promote growth are quadratic functions of the rate of growth along the relevant dimension, with parameters C_1, C_2.

Given these assumptions, the fundamental formula for the valuation of the firm takes the form:

$$v = (A - B_1 g_1 - B_2 g_2 - C_1 g_1^2 - C_2 g_2^2) / (r - g_1 - g_2) \qquad (4.36)$$

A value-maximizing firm will maximize v for any given value of overall growth, g. Forming the relevant Lagrangian and solving the first-order conditions determines g_1, g_2 as functions of g:

$$g_1 = (C_2 / (C_1 + C_2))g - ((B_1 - B_2) / (2(C_1 + C_2))) \qquad (4.37.1)$$
$$g_2 = (C_1 / (C_1 + C_2))g + ((B_1 - B_2) / (2(C_1 + C_2))) \qquad (4.37.2)$$

Back-substitution into v gives:

$$v = (A^* - B^* g - C^* g^2) / (r - g) \qquad (4.38)$$

where:

$$A^* = A - ((B_1 - B_2)^2 / 4(C_1 + C_2)) \qquad (4.39.1)$$
$$B^* = (B_1 C_2 + B_2 C_1) / (C_1 + C_2) \qquad (4.39.2)$$
$$C^* = C_1 C_2 / (C_1 + C_2) \qquad (4.39.3)$$

Maximizing v with respect to g then gives, exactly as before, the solution:

$$g^* = r - (r^2 - ((A^* - B^*r)/C^*))^{1/2} \qquad (4.40)$$

The individual growth rates g^*_1, g^*_2 are then determined by back-substitution. Comparison with equation (4.6) shows that the previous results for a single dimension are quite robust.

The direction of growth g^*_1/g^*_2 encapsulates the long-run growth strategy of the firm. It depends crucially on the ratio of the 'cost of growth' coefficients C_2/C_1. The firm will grow faster along the dimension with the lower cost of growth. Thus if one dimension requires the exploitation of very tacit information, which is costly to impart through training, then the firm is mostly likely to grow along the other dimension instead. This reinforces the point noted earlier: in Penrose's analysis, tacitness is more important as a constraint on growth than as a source of growth.

4.10   OVERALL ASSESSMENT

Optimal Size of Firm and the Necessity of Growth

Penrose maintains that there is no optimal size of firm but only an optimal rate of growth. More precisely, the logic of her model implies that the optimal size of firm is either infinite or zero. If the firm is capable of making a profit, after allowing for all opportunity costs, then its optimal size is infinite, because there is no reason why the rate of profit should diminish as the firm expands. If, on the other hand, the firm makes only losses, then its optimal size is zero: it should never have been set up in the first place.

Growth is an issue because profitable firms cannot be created infinitely large. They have to grow from small beginnings. If they could be created large then there would be no need for them to grow. But if there were no limits to growth then a small firm could grow to an infinite size in an infinitely short space of time. To fix a finite optimal rate of growth there need to be decreasing returns to the rate of growth at every size. It is this requirement that is embodied in the fundamental equation (4.3).

Goodwill and the Value of the Firm

In Penrose's model the value of a growing firm increases continually over time because it is always proportional to the firm's current size. This is because the rate of profit is constant. This growing value represents the cumulative impact of sustained entrepreneurship within the firm. Growth is sustained through progressive diversification, coupled with the use of decentralization to neutralize increases in the costs of bureaucracy.

Tacit Information as a Constraint on Growth

Penrose's remarks on tacit information have been taken out of context by advocates of the resource-based theory of the firm. Tacitness plays a very specific role in Penrose's theory: it explains why there are decreasing returns to the rate of growth. Because managerial information is partly tacit, managers need to be trained in the firm's customs and procedures in order to assimilate them into the existing team. As the rate of growth increases, the proportion of managers engaged in training, either as mentors or recruits, increases. The more tacit the information handled by the management team, the greater the demand for training, and the sooner decreasing returns set in.

Penrose's view of tacit information needs to be distinguished from the argument in resource-based theory that the tacit nature of managerial know-how acts as a barrier to imitation in the markets in which the firm operates (Teece, 1981). Section 4.6 captures this aspect of tacit information by making the intensity of the firm's demand in a representative market increase with the tacitness of the information it exploits. This effect does not play a central role in Penrose's own analysis, however. It is therefore a mistake to suggest that the tacitness of information is a source of 'competitive advantage' in Penrose's theory – rather it is a source of weakness.

Entrepreneurship

It is not tacitness, but entrepreneurial ability, that is the source of competitive advantage in Penrose's model. Without entrepreneurial ability the firm would be unable to identify opportunities for diversification, and without these opportunities it will be unable to grow, for in Penrose's view any single market will soon exhaust the growth potential of a firm.

Penrose recognizes that differences in the quality of entrepreneurship explain differences in the growth of firms. It is not resource endowments in general that explain growth, because these endowments are constantly changing as a direct result of the process of growth. It is the endowment of entrepreneurship that is crucial for growth. The initial endowment of entrepreneurship will be determined by the personality and abilities of the founder of the firm (Penrose, 1960). As the founder takes on more managerial staff, the opportunity arises to delegate to them, thereby freeing the founder from the threat of time-consuming routine demands. Instead it becomes possible to devote more time to identifying new market opportunities. But the staff who take decisions on the founder's behalf need guidance on the principles and procedures they should use, and this is where the tacitness of information comes in.

A World of Infinite Opportunities

Penrose's analysis of entrepreneurship is complicated by the fact that she offers two separate accounts of how opportunities for diversification are discovered, as well as two accounts of how the growth of entrepreneurial management resources is sustained.

Penrose implicitly assumes that opportunities are always available to sustain the growth of the firm. The firm's ability to recognize these opportunities derives both from the external vision of the founder-entrepreneur, and from the firm's subsequent internal ability to learn from experience in the markets it has entered. Sometimes Penrose emphasizes one source of information, and sometimes the other. This does not affect our formalization, however, so long as the internal and external sources combine to maintain a steadily increasing flow of opportunities that the firm can exploit. As the firm grows, diminishing returns may set in to external search, but if they do, then internal learning can make good the deficit, so that the profitability of new opportunities is sustained.

Similarly Penrose offers two accounts of the growth of the management team. In the first account, used in the model above, the firm sets out to grow the management team in line with its optimal rate of growth. The founder of the firm recruits ambitious graduates and head-hunts entrepreneurial managers from rival firms. The second – and better known – account emphasizes indivisibilities. Penrose argues that entrepreneurship is supplied by unused managerial resources caused by indivisibilities in the recruitment process. Routine managers with nothing to do turn to entrepreneurship instead. This second account is incompatible with steady-state growth because the supply of indivisible resources does not increase as the firm grows, and cannot therefore provide the requisite expansion of the entrepreneurial management team. For this reason this chapter has focused on the first account alone.

4.11 CONCLUSION

This chapter has argued that behind Penrose's theory, as expounded verbally, lies a simple formal model which guarantees the consistency of her

Table 4.1   Summary of the model

Endogenous variable	Symbol	Exogenous variable / parameter	Symbol
Size (number of markets)	x	Age	t
Growth rate	g	Cost of capital	r
Output per market	y	Wage of manual labour	w_0
Price in representative market	p	Cost of raw materials per unit output	w_1
Degree of decentralization	k	Salary	s
Routine managers (not involved in training)	m_1	Set-up cost of market entry	i
Entrepreneurial managers (not involved in training)	m_2	Marginal cost of increased decentralization	e_1
Managers in training	m_3	Turnover rate amongst managers due to retirements and quits	q
Manual and clerical labour employed in representative market	n	Time cost of training a manager (varies positively with tacitness)	u
		Size of representative market	b_0
		Price-sensitivity of representative market (varies inversely with tacitness)	b_1
		Probability that a market is unprofitable on entry (per unit time)	h_0
		Probability that a market disappears (per unit time)	h_1
		Probability that a firm collapses (per unit time)	h_2
		Labour-intensity of production in representative market	a_0
		Routine management-intensity of market operation	a_1, e_1
		Entrepreneurial management intensity of market discovery	a_2

theory. This model is encapsulated by a general formula for the value of a steadily-growing firm. This formula can be applied to numerous issues in the theory of the firm, which span both economics and management: these include not only growth, but also the composition of the management team, the degree of decentralization, and the size distribution of firms.

Penrose's theory is an intriguing application of the concept of entrepreneurship. Although Penrose endorsed entrepreneurship as a fundamental driver of the growth of the firm, many modern interpretations of Penrose have overlooked this aspect of her work. Even self-styled heterodox economists, who are overtly critical of conventional economics, have perpetrated the same error as those they criticize – namely they have marginalized the role of the entrepreneur.

Table 4.1 lists eleven endogenous variables which are explained by Penrose's theory, together with seven exogenous variables and ten parameters. Almost without exception, the impact of each exogenous variable or parameter on each endogenous variable can be unambiguously signed using the comparative static results above (either singly, or in conjunction with each other). This table, together with the model behind it, provides a convenient summary of Penrose's pioneering contribution to the theory of the firm. It is striking evidence of the power of Penrose's insights that so many different results can be obtained from such a parsimonious set of assumptions.

ACKNOWLEDGEMENTS

Thanks are due to Christos Pitelis, Alan Rugman and Alain Verbeke for very insightful comments on an earlier version of this chapter. Peter Buckley and I would also like to thank Jane Humphries and Michael Best for providing some interesting biographical material. None of these people necessarily agree with the interpretation offered in this chapter, however.

REFERENCES

Alchian, Armen A. (1953), 'Biological analogies in the theory of the firm: comment', *American Economic Review*, **43** (4), 600–603.
Audretsch, David B. (1995), *Innovation and Industry Evolution*, Cambridge, MA: MIT Press.
Evans, David S. (1987), 'Tests of alternative theories of firm growth', *Journal of Political Economy*, **95**, 657–74.
Foss, Nicolai J. (2002), 'Edith Penrose, economics and strategic management', in

C.N. Pitelis (ed.), *The Growth of the Firm: The Legacy of Edith Penrose*, Oxford: Oxford University Press, pp. 147–64.

Geroski, Paul (1998), 'An applied econometrician's view of large company performance', *Review of Industrial Organization,* **13**, 271–93.

Gibrat, Robert (1931), *Les Inegalities Economique*, Paris: Librarie du Recueil Sirey.

Hart, Peter E. (2001), 'Theories of firms' growth and the generation of jobs', *Review of Industrial Organization*, **17**, 229–48.

Jovanovic, Boyan (1982), 'Selection and evolution of industry', *Econometrica*, **50**, 649–70.

Kor, Yasemin Y. and Joseph T. Mahoney (2004), 'Edith Penrose's (1959) contributions to the resource-based view of strategic management', *Journal of Management Studies,* **41**, 183–91.

Marshall, Alfred (1890), *Principles of Economics*, 9th edn, ed. By C.W. Guillebaud, London: Macmillan.

Penrose, Edith T. (1952), 'Biological analogies in the theory of the firm', *American Economic Review*, **42** (5), 804–19.

Penrose, Edith T. (1955), 'Limits to the growth and size of firms', *American Economic Review, Papers and Proceedings*, **45** (2), 531–43.

Penrose, Edith T. (1959), *The Theory of the Growth of the Firm*, Oxford: Blackwell.

Penrose, Edith T. (1960), 'The growth of the firm: a case study: the Hercules Powder Company', *Business History Review*, **3**, 1–20.

Penrose, Peran and Christos N. Pitelis (2002), 'Edith Elura Tilton Penrose: life contribution and influence', in C.N. Pitelis (ed.), *The Growth of the Firm: The Legacy of Edith Penrose,* Oxford: Oxford University Press, pp. 17–36.

Rugman, Alan M. and Alain Verbeke (2002), 'Edith Penrose's contribution to the resource-based view of strategic management', *Strategic Management Journal*, **23,** 769–80.

Rugman, Alan M. and Alain Verbeke (2004), 'A final word on Edith Penrose', *Journal of Management Studies,* **41** (1), 205–17.

Teece, David (1981), 'The multinational enterprise: market failure and market power considerations', *Sloan Management Review*, **22** (3), 3–17.

Wolf, Bernard M. (1977), 'Industrial diversification and internationalisation: some empirical evidence', *Journal of Industrial Economics*, **26**, 177–91.

PART II

Networks and institutions

5. Networks: a theory of connectivity and interdependence

The concept of a network is common to both the social and natural sciences. The use of the network concept in entrepreneurship research therefore places entrepreneurship studies in a wider context. There are many different types of network, however. This chapter sets out the main dimensions of network structure, and explains the factors that determine the structure of any given type of network. It considers social networks, commercial networks involving trade and investment, and local business networks, such as those found in industrial districts. It is argued that the structure of a network can usually be understood as the efficient solution to a coordination problem. As a result, explanations can be developed of why different network structures emerge in different situations. To develop explanations along these lines, however, the conventions on which network research is currently based will need to be changed.

5.1 NETWORKS AS AN INTERDISCIPLINARY SUBJECT

Networks play a crucial role in the theory of entrepreneurship. As explained in Chapter 1, networks are used by entrepreneurs to synthesize information from different sources in order to discover profit opportunities. Once an opportunity has been discovered, networks can help entrepreneurs make contact with prospective financial backers. With financial backing, entrepreneurs can set up trading networks on their own initiative. New shops and factories act as hubs which intermediate new linkages and redirect trade into novel channels. Trade itself utilizes transport and communication networks to deliver products to customers; these networks may themselves have been created through infrastructure investments made by a previous generation of entrepreneurs.

The fact that entrepreneurship has been omitted from – or at least marginalized by – conventional economics means that networks have to some extent been marginalized as well. Networks have played a much smaller role in economic theorizing than they have in other related disciplines.

The concept of a network plays a central role in both natural and social sciences. In physics, there are electrical circuits; in civil engineering, structures like bridge trusses; in information technology there are telephones and the internet; while in geography there are transport systems, such as motorways and railway systems. Agriculture and industry depend upon distribution systems (pipelines, electricity grids) and disposal systems (drainage ditches, sewage systems). In biology, the brain is analysed as a network of neurons, and in anthropology, family networks are created and sustained through reproduction. Economists refer to networks of trade, investment and technology transfer when discussing international and interregional resource flows. Sociologists analyse social groups in terms of interpersonal networks, and use network effects to explain 'chain migration' flows, whilst business strategists analyse networks of strategic alliances between firms.

The concept has recently become very popular in historical research in international business, and in economic and social research more generally (Jones, 2000; Jones and Amatori, 2003). Networks are a powerful way of understanding the historical evolution of economic and social institutions such as national governments and multinational enterprises. Institutions are often classified using a three-fold distinction between firms, markets and the state (North, 1981). Networks are then introduced as a fourth type of institution, with the claim that, until recently, their significance was overlooked.

Indeed, it can be argued that the concept of a network, like the concept of entrepreneurship, is a key component of an emerging paradigm around which an integrated social science can be built. To some writers, however, the concept is just a passing fad. This chapter argues that the concept of a network is indeed an emerging paradigm, but that the new paradigm will be successful only if researchers can agree on appropriate definitions of terms.

Networks are complex and they can be structured in many different ways. Different networks involve different types of element connected up in different ways using different types of relationship. There are crucial differences between different types of network that are often overlooked. Confusion is created when researchers fail to specify which type of network they are writing about.

The mathematical theory of networks is, rather misleadingly, termed the 'theory of graphs'. Although graph theory claims to be general, it involves a number of simplifying assumptions that restrict its application to economics and business. In particular, it ignores differences in types of element, and considers only a limited set of relationships, because its main concern is network configuration. This chapter outlines a different approach to modelling networks that is better adapted to the needs of social science research in general, and to the study of entrepreneurship in particular.

5.2   AMBIGUITIES OF THE SUBJECT

When analysing networks, different disciplines refer to the same concepts by different names. The members of a network are variously referred to as elements, nodes, vertices and points, whilst the connections between them are referred to as linkages, edges, paths and so on. These differences of terminology obscure important commonalities: for example, all these terms are simply different ways of expressing the notion of connectivity. Important differences are obscured as well, because the term 'network' is used in different ways by different disciplines.

Ambiguities exist even within a single discipline. For example, international business historians have used the term 'network' in several ways (see Thompson, 2003). All four of the concepts described below have been applied to export-oriented industrial districts based on flexible specialization, but it is not always clear, in any given instance, which type of network a writer has in mind.

- *A 'network' as a distinctive organizational form, intermediate between firm and market*   In this context, a network comprises a web of long-term cooperative relationships between firms. It is distinctive because the relationship between the firms is not authoritarian like an employment relationship, and differs from a spot market relationship because it involves a long-term commitment. It is intermediate between firm and market because, like the employment relationship, it is long-term, whilst like the spot market relationship, it involves firms of equal status.
- *A 'network firm' as a set of quasi-autonomous subsidiaries*   Japanese *keiretsu* and Italian business groups are often described in these terms. This type of network involves a small central locus of authority – namely an investor or group of investors who use a set of holding companies to control a range of businesses in which independent minority investors may also be involved. However, there is significant devolution of day-to-day decision-making to individual subsidiaries. This concept of a network firm has also become popular in mainstream international business literature on the strategic management of multinational enterprises, where it is seen as combining the global vision of an influential headquarters with the flexibility of autonomous subsidiaries.
- *A 'local business network' which involves key actors, such as bankers, entrepreneurs and government officials, who informally coordinate activities within an economic region or urban centre*   Unlike the previous cases, the network involves a mixture of organizations

of different types. The relationships are used to finance strategic investments in local public goods, such as training colleges or dock improvements, whose benefits accrue to businesses in general rather than to any single business in particular.

- *A 'network industry', such as transport, water, energy and other utilities* Network industries typically sink large amounts of capital into specialised infrastructure that links different locations and facilitates the movement of resources between them (Foreman-Peck and Millward, 1994). The network refers to the spatial linkages and the hubs at which they meet. Connecting an industrial district to a long-distance transport network is often crucial in promoting its export trade.

There is a tension between these specific connotations of a network, and the generality of the underlying concept. It can be argued, for example, that firms and markets are not alternatives to networks, but simply special types of network – the firm being a relatively rigid and hierarchical network, and a market a flat and flexible one. On this view, almost everything is a network, and so it is fruitless to argue about what is a true network and what is not. The research question is not so much 'Is it a network?' as 'What type of network is it?' The key to understanding networks is to have a scheme by which to classify them.

To make this general approach successful, there needs to be greater standardization of terminology, both across disciplines and within them. This requires more social 'networking' between researchers – ironically, networking is something at which researchers on networks have hitherto been rather poor.

5.3   THE ROLE OF NETWORKS IN THE COORDINATION OF ECONOMIC ACTIVITY

In some disciplines, such as geography, networks are of intrinsic interest. Networks of rivers and their tributaries are explained as the outcomes of geological processes and climatic conditions, while the location and development of ports is explained by the geographical requirements of inter-modal freight transfer between sea, road and rail. In other disciplines, such as economics, networks are not so much a phenomenon to be explained, as an explanation of other phenomena. Networks are the answer – not the question. In economics the basic policy question is how to improve the performance of the economy, or to enhance the quality of life, and the answer is to invest in networks of the appropriate type. An important research challenge is to explain how social activity is driven by the demands of economic activity, and conversely, how economic activity is influenced by social activity.

Where networks are a subject of intrinsic interest, it is natural to focus simply on describing them. Geologists, for example, spend a lot of time mapping river systems. But where interest in networks is mainly instrumental, as in economics, emphasis naturally switches to understanding why they matter. What function do they perform that cannot be performed by other mechanisms?

The key economic role of networks, it is claimed in this chapter, lies in their contribution to the coordination of activities. Whatever the activity, networks are crucial in communicating crucial information, controlling conflict and fostering cooperation. Without the benefits of coordination, it would not be worth investing in networks.

A common objection to this approach is that networks are created because people like to belong to them. In other words, the benefits generated by networks are intrinsic, rather than instrumental. Intrinsic benefits are certainly an important benefit of belonging to small and cosy groups like a happy family. But not all networks are a pleasure to belong to: some professional networks can be very competitive, for example, and, far from welcoming new members, act more like a clique or a cartel. People still seek entry, however, because of the economic advantage that can be obtained. If emotional benefits were the only benefits that people derived from networks, it seems likely that networks would be much less common than they are.

Taking an instrumental view of networks helps to explain why there are so many varieties of network in use. Different network structures are best adapted to coordinating different types of economic activity. If emotional benefits were the only reward then it is likely that networks would be much more homogeneous: in particular, they would be much smaller and friendlier than many of them really are. To explain why network structures vary, it is necessary to recognize that different types of network coordinate different types of activity.

5.4 A TYPOLOGY OF NETWORKS

Social Networks versus Physical Networks

If 'everything is a network' then clearly there must be different types of network. There is a basic distinction between *physical* and *social* networks. A river and its tributaries, for example, form a physical network that distributes water, whilst an extended family forms a social network that connects descendants of common ancestors (Haggett and Chorley, 1969). More precisely, a physical network connects material elements such as natural features, buildings and plants, whilst a social network connects people.

Physical networks have *spatial* characteristics. These are usually represented in two dimensions – for example, by a map of a road or river system – although some networks are inherently three-dimensional – for example, crystalline structures and aircraft flight-paths.

The spatial dimension is also relevant to social networks, but not to the same extent. An individual's social network may be summarized by the names in their address book, but it would be a mistake to suppose that those who live further away are contacted less frequently. In social networks, *social distance* is more relevant than *Euclidean distance* – thus two people who live either side of a national border may be 'further apart' than two people who live at opposite ends of the same country. Social distance may be expressed using a metric of communication costs, provided that these costs include not merely the cost of a letter or telephone call, but also the costs of overcoming linguistic and cultural barriers (Wasserman and Faust, 1994).

Networks can be analysed at different levels of aggregation. An element of a physical network may comprise a single unit, such as an individual factory, or a collection of units, such as a town or region; this leads to a difference between the inter-plant network studied in industrial complex analysis (Isard et al., 1959) and the interregional network studied by regional policy analysts (Armstrong and Taylor, 2000). In the social sphere, single individuals constitute an interpersonal network whilst groups of people make up an inter-organizational network. Inter-organizational networks are often best analysed in interpersonal terms, however, since relations between organizations are usually mediated by representatives, and relationships may alter radically when the representation changes.

Stock and Flow Relations

When economists talk of networks, they usually refer to flows: in particular, trade flows and international capital flows. In geography, by contrast, there is more emphasis on stocks: in particular the stock of infrastructure, such as roads and railway lines. In practice, almost all networks comprise both stocks and flows. For example, trade and capital flows require trust between transactors, which means that they draw upon a stock of trust – or social capital – to facilitate the flow. Conversely, road and rail infrastructure is constructed specifically to facilitate a flow of traffic comprising vehicles that carry passengers, freight and mail.

Table 5.1   A simple typology of network relationships

Type of network	Flow relationship	Stock relationship
Physical	Resource flow (traffic)	Physical infrastructure (channels)
Social	Communication	Relationships (social infrastructure)

Thus while a network can, in principle, be defined purely in terms of flow relations, there is, in practice, almost certainly a set of stock relations that facilitates the flows. Conversely, when a network is defined in terms of stocks, these stocks almost always exist in order to facilitate some flows. In the case of a river network, for example, the river channel is the stock and the water – together with the ships and barges that float upon it – represents the flows. Thus while it is logically possible to have a network comprised entirely of stock relations, or entirely of flow relations, the economic fundamentals of network operation make such cases very rare.

Within a social network a stock connection is exemplified by reputation: an individual who has a reputation for integrity is trusted by another. Although reputation and trust are somewhat subjective factors, their durability makes them stocks rather than flows. By contrast, a flow connection is represented by communication, such as the announcement of a meeting, or the negotiation of a trade. Once a meeting has been held, or a trade completed, another is set up, and so information flows continuously.

Once again, a stock connection facilitates a flow. It is difficult, for example, to communicate with someone who does not speak the same language or share the same beliefs, or who simply cannot be trusted. Thus a flow connection benefits from an underlying stock connection based on membership of the same linguistic and cultural group. The connection between stock and flow relationships is summarized in Table 5.1.

Investment in Networks

Another important distinction is between *natural* networks and networks *engineered* by human agency. Rivers and families are both examples of natural networks, determined respectively by geological and biological factors. Both physical and social networks can be engineered: thus a canal is an analogue of a natural river, whilst a club is an analogue of a family (see Table 5.2).

Engineering a network can involve a major investment. Canals were financed using an early form of joint-stock company, whilst the

Table 5.2   Overview of different types of network (with examples)

Physical / social	Natural	Engineered by investment
Physical	River	Canal
Social: bonding	Family	Club, charity, church, trade union, professional association, political party, alumni group. . .
Social: commercial		Firm, government, market

establishment of early professional societies required major commitments of time by their founders and trustees. An engineered network is an intrinsically economic phenomenon, since it requires some person – or a group of people – to incur substantial present costs in anticipation of future benefits. This applies whether the objectives of the network are commercial or social. In general, engineering major networks requires entrepreneurship and leadership of a high order.

Engineered networks are typically embedded in natural networks: thus canals developed from cuts made in navigable rivers, and railways followed river valleys because the gradients were easy. In the social sphere, members of clubs and communities may also be linked by extended family connections.

Any given network is almost invariably part of a wider system. Each element is also connected to members of other networks; this is known as 'bridging' in the sociological literature. The importance of an element within any given network, such as a local business network, often derives from the number of external linkages that the elements possess, for example, the number of contacts that a businessmen has in the nearest metropolis.

The only network that is not part of a wider system is the global network that encompasses the totality of all the networks: it is the network that links every person, every resource and every location, directly or indirectly, to every other, through different types of physical and social connection. Every other network is a sub-set of this encompassing network. It is necessary to base analysis on subsidiary networks because this encompassing network is so complex that, while it can be analysed at a high level of aggregation, it is too large to analyse fully at a disaggregated level. It must be recognized that every subsidiary network selected for study is therefore an 'open system' which connects with the rest of the global network at various points. For analytical purposes it is often useful to ignore these external connections in order to focus on the internal structure of a subsidiary network, but it is important not to forget that the analysis is then based on the assumption that the structure of the wider network remains constant.

5.5   COORDINATION

The Interdependence of Physical and Social Networks

Physical networks are often analysed as though they were independent of social networks, and vice versa, but in reality the two types of network are closely linked. Social networks are used to coordinate flows through physical networks, and to coordinate strategic investments in them. Conversely, social networks require supporting services supplied by physical networks – for example, transport to and from the meetings organized by a club. Geographers often study physical networks in isolation from social networks, whilst sociologists often study social networks in isolation from physical ones. Such partial perspectives provide a distorted picture of networks, and can lead to misleading conclusions.

Physical networks involving flows of goods and services emerge because the *division of labour* leads individuals to specialize in particular tasks. A single complex task is broken down into a set of simpler tasks, each performed by a different person. The different elements of the physical network are created by this differentiation of tasks. A social network is created to coordinate the actions of the people who have been assigned to these different tasks, using special channels of communication.

Different stages of production may need to be carried out at different locations, due to local availability of natural resources or special labour skills. This requires a physical network to transport intermediate products and ensure that scales of activity at different locations are compatible with each other.

Different products may also be produced at different locations. When consumers like variety, a high proportion of the output at each location must be exported. This requires a distribution network to transport the product and a social network to ensure that each consumer obtains the particular mixture of goods that he/she desires.

Alternative Mechanisms of Coordination

The coordination of a division of labour needs everyone to be clear about their own responsibilities: they need to know which decisions they are expected to take and which they should leave to other people. The allocation of responsibilities is established through the ownership of property rights. It is not necessary for everyone to know the owner of every resource, but to avoid confusion it is important for each person to know which resources they own and to be able to demonstrate their ownership to others if required (Putterman, 1990).

Coordination can be achieved either by placing the resources under common ownership and control, or by arranging for independent owners and managers to reach agreement over their use. By placing all the resources under common ownership an organization is created to plan the allocation of resources, whereas when owners are independent, resources are allocated through trade. An organization typically invokes authority to implement its plans, whereas trade relies on voluntary agreement. It is often implicitly assumed that social networks are based on voluntary agreements, but in practice many networks actually involve authority relations.

In a private enterprise economy the ownership of resources may be pooled by vesting ownership in a single individual, such as an entrepreneur, or in a group of shareholders who have set up a joint-stock company. Operatives may then be employed by the owners for a wage or salary. In this case the social network used for coordination resembles a profit-maximizing firm. If the operatives are also owners then the network will resemble a producer cooperative. If the owners have altruistic motives, then the organization may operate on a non-profit basis; in this case the network may resemble a charity or a club.

If resources are vested in the state then politicians will set the objectives and civil servants will administer production; in this case the social network resembles a part of government. If different resources are owned by different people then coordination will be effected through trade, and in this case the social network resembles a market.

If the number of market participants is too small to generate competition then they may agree upon some other principle, such as custom, for determining price. In this case the social network may resemble the kind of cooperative inter-firm network mentioned in the literature on industrial districts, and alluded to above.

5.6   VOLATILITY AND INNOVATION

If a physical network operated in a totally stable environment then there would be little day-to-day need for coordination. Each day the same routine would be followed. A rigid system of command and control working on a regular cycle would be perfectly adequate to coordinate physical flows – much like a railway signalling system driven by the dictates of a daily timetable.

In fact the economic environment is constantly changing, creating a continual need to modify levels of production and patterns of trade throughout the global economy (see Chapter 1). As new trade routes open up, new demands for infrastructure arise. Networks of transport and communication evolve, breaking some connections, but also bringing distant places into closer contact with each other.

In addition, intellectual curiosity and the quest for greater economy stimulates scientific discovery. In a private-enterprise economy individuals can profit from discoveries through innovation. To produce and distribute new products, entrepreneurs create new networks of customers and suppliers, and possibly destroy the networks built up by their established competitors in the process. Thus while established networks influence the type of information discovered, the discovery of new information feeds back to alter the structure of networks too.

Social networks also spread news, including information about new investment opportunities. The diffusion of news speeds up adjustment to change. News can be spread in two main ways: by local contact, through conversation with neighbours in a small group, or through broadcasting to members of a larger group.

A leader may emerge who controls broadcast information. The leader may promote particular beliefs about the environment and censor or discredit competing views. He/she may also favour certain types of institution over others, for example, preferring large firms to markets, or government to private enterprise. He/she may decide to promote certain moral values as conducive to trust, such as honesty, loyalty and hard work.

5.7 INTERMEDIATION

The division of labour applies not only to production activities, but also to the design and operation of a network. In a physical network, specialized hubs may emerge where different traffic flows converge. These hubs provide flexibility by allowing traffic to be switched from one route to another.

In social networks, entrepreneurs and leaders act as information hubs. Individual consumers go to entrepreneurs to buy their goods, relying on the entrepreneurs to procure the goods on their behalf from the producer, who is the ultimate source of supply. Individuals who need to make contact with other individuals might go to a leader and ask them to arrange an introduction. The leader might expect the individual to join their group, and possibly to pay a membership fee, in return for receiving this service.

In a private enterprise economy entrepreneurs compete with each other for custom. Similarly, leaders of rival groups compete for members and to gain influence for their views. As a result, both physical networks and social networks develop a multiplicity of competing hubs. Ordinary members use these hubs as gateways to the rest of the network. In effect, relationships between ordinary members of the network are mediated by the entrepreneurs from whom they buy, the leaders of the groups to which they belong, and the hubs through which they travel and through which the goods they buy are consigned to their homes. While individuals also have direct connections to other individuals, the number of such direct connections is very small compared to the number of people to whom they are indirectly connected through the hubs. This would make the hubs extremely powerful if it were not for the competition between them. This competition reflects the fact that an individual usually has more than one hub through which they can reach another individual who is able to fulfil their needs.

5.8   CONNECTIVITY AND CONFIGURATION

Four Key Dimensions

As explained above, the basic principles of network representation are set out in the mathematical theory of graphs (Biggs et al., 1986; Diestel, 1997). A set of *elements* that are connected to each other form a *network*. Every pair of elements belonging to a network is connected up, either *directly* or *indirectly*. Indirect connections are effected through other elements of the network.

From an economic and social perspective, there are four key dimensions along which networks vary:

- *size*, as measured by the number of elements that belong to the network;
- *diversity*, as measured by the number of different *types* of element that belong to the network;
- the types of *relationship* that connect the members; and
- the *configuration* of the network, which describes the pattern in which the different elements are connected up.

Entrepreneurship researchers have discussed relationships in considerable detail, but have said surprisingly little about size and diversity, that is, about the characteristics of the elements that are connected up. Configuration has been studied even less, and it is therefore useful to begin by addressing this issue.

Considerable research has been carried out into the configurations of physical networks, but remarkably little into the configuration of social networks. Conversely, far more research has been carried out into the nature of relationships in social networks than in physical networks. Only a small number of writers, such as Leibenstein (1978) and Burt (1992), have integrated the analysis of relationships with the analysis of configurations.

There are many different ways of connecting up a given set of elements. The configuration of a network is defined by the set of direct pair-wise linkages between its elements. As the number of elements increases, the number of different ways in which elements can be connected up increases dramatically. Network analysis is bedevilled by the complexity created by this 'combinatorial explosion'.

Complexity can be reduced by focusing on a small number of standard configurations, such as the hubs, webs and branches described below. These standard configurations can be combined in modular form to create large networks from sets of smaller networks, for example, a web of hubs, or a hub of webs.

In this context, it is important to establish that the standard configurations referred to above are reasonably efficient for most economic purposes, for otherwise it is unlikely that they will be used in economic networks. While a formal proof of efficiency lies outside the scope of this chapter, simple heuristics show that each of the standard forms is indeed efficient under appropriate circumstances. It also confirms that efficiency is often enhanced by intermediation effected by specialist intermediators which emerge as local hubs. Thus the logic of intermediation explains the emergence of networks with simple modular forms.

Diagrammatic Representation

Because networks are so complex, it is useful to develop a diagrammatic representation that is more accessible than the abstract algebra employed in graph theory. The diagrams are constructed according to an explicit set of rules. These rules may be illustrated using a linear network.

Figure 5.1.1 shows four elements connected up in a line. Each element is represented by a circle. Each element is directly connected to its neighbours, and all are indirectly connected to each other. *A* and *C* are connected via *B*, and *B* and *D* via *C*, whilst *A* and *D* are connected via two intermediate elements, *B* and *C*.

Linear networks are widely used in transport systems – such as stations along a railway line – but are little used in social networks because they deliver poor service to the elements at the end of the line. The terminal elements are only directly connected to one other element, and are connected to each other only by a path through all the other elements in the network. Repeated intermediation distorts communication in a social network but only slows down communication in a transport system, so a linear network is better suited to transport than to social interaction.

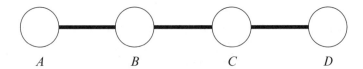

Figure 5.1.1   Linear network

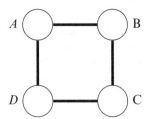

Figure 5.1.2   Ring network

Redundancy

There may be more than one path between two elements. In Figure 5.1.2 the four elements are connected up in a ring. Because only four elements are involved, the network takes the form of a square. It could represent a ring road around a town, connecting up different suburbs, or a group of people seated round a large table. A ring is generated from a line by joining the two ends of the line together: that is, by connecting *A* and *D*. This eliminates the relative isolation of the end points, but at the expense of an additional connection.

When travelling along the ring road, there is always an alternative route: for example, it is possible to get from *A* to *C* via either *B* or *D*. Alternative routes make round-trip itineraries possible: for example, from *A* to *B* to *C* to *D* and back to *A*.

Alternative routes provide an element of redundancy in a network. While 'redundancy' sounds wasteful, it imparts flexibility to a network: if one linkage breaks, another can be used instead. Thus if the link between *A* and *B* fails, a traveller from *A* can reach *C* via *D* instead.

Similarly, in a social network, if *A* wants to get in touch with *C*, they may have a choice of being introduced to *C* by either *B* or *D*. If one of the intermediaries falls ill, they can use the other one instead. Again, if *A* falls out with *B* as a result of a disagreement, they can still make contact by an alternative route, sending a message to *B* via *C* and *D*. Given the crucial role of networks in sustaining social and economic activity, and the vulnerability

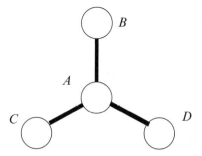

Figure 5.1.3   Hub network

of individual linkages, a degree of redundancy is always useful, despite the cost of the additional link. Trading-off cost and reliability of performance determines the optimal degree of redundancy in a network.

Hubs

Hubs are points at which three or more linkages converge: they act as consolidation centres and distribution centres for the traffic over the network. Hubs are often connected to other hubs by trunk connections which carry high-volume traffic (Watts, 2003).

A simple hub configuration comprises just a single hub, such as the element *A* in Figure 5.1.3. Unlike a ring, where all elements are connected to two other elements, the ordinary members of a simple hub system are connected only to the hub. The great advantage of a simple hub configuration is that each element is not only connected directly to the hub element, but is indirectly connected to every other element by a path comprising just one intermediate element – the hub itself. This advantage increases with the number of elements in the network. Whilst with a line or ring, the average number of intermediate elements on any path increases directly with the number of elements, the number of intermediate elements remains constant in a hub.

The power of a hub can be measured by the proportion of through traffic that it handles in proportion to the amount of traffic originating or terminating at the hub itself. When every linkage in a network carries the same amount of traffic, the power of a hub is proportional to the number of linkages it possesses. With n elements, including a solitary hub, and two-way flow of traffic x between each pair of elements, the total traffic through the hub will be $(n-1)(n-2)x/2$. The traffic originating from, or destined for the hub will be $(n-1)x$, and so the power of the hub will be the ratio of the first term to the second – namely $(n-2)/2$.

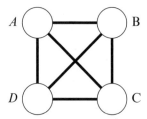

Figure 5.1.4   Web network

Webs

A weakness of the hub configuration is that there is no redundancy. A failure in any link will completely disconnect one of the elements from the network and a failure of the hub itself is fatal. A natural solution is to use more than one hub. In the limiting case, every element becomes a hub. This creates a web configuration, in which every element is directly connected to every other.

This situation is illustrated in Figure 5.1.4. Each element *A*, *B*, *C* and *D* acts as a hub, which can carry traffic between any other pair of elements. This provides a high level of redundancy, but at significant cost.

It is often said that networks afford significant economies of scale, but these economies are in fact attributable to hubs. In a web, where every element is directly connected to every other, the number of linkages, $n(n-1)/2$, is equal to the number of connections achieved, and so there is no saving in linkages as the number of elements in the network increases. On the other hand, the number of linkages in a corresponding hub is only $n-1$, and so network economies increase without limit when a hub configuration is adopted. The difference between the hub and the web becomes more pronounced as the number of elements increases, as moving from a hub to a web increases the number of linkages by a factor $n/2$.

Branch Configurations

Hubs are prone to congestion. Where traffic from many different linkages flows into the same hub, the different flows can interfere with each other. There is both a physical burden of handling the traffic, and an information burden created because each consignment coming in from any direction has to be switched onto the correct outward route.

To reduce the burden, satellite hubs can be created. This leads to a pyramid (or 'branch') configuration. Figure 5.2.1 shows a system of three hubs, *A*, *B* and *C*, handling traffic between seven elements, *A*, *B*, *C*, *D*, *E*,

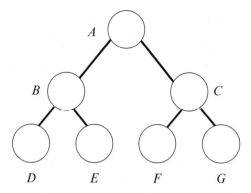

Figure 5.2.1 Satellite hubs

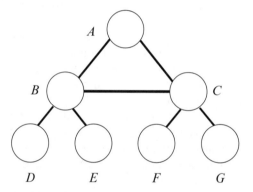

Figure 5.2.2 By-pass

F and *G*. Traffic between *D* and *E* is handled at hub *B*, traffic between *F* and *G* is handled at hub *C*, and all the other traffic between *D, E, F* and *G* is routed via *A*. If most of the traffic in the network flows within the groups *B, D, E* and *C, F, G,* then the satellites *B* and *C* may relieve much of the burden from the centre, *A*. If, on the other hand, every element consigns roughly the same amount of traffic to every other element, then only a relatively small amount of traffic will be diverted from *A* unless there is a direct connection between *B* and *C*.

Congestion and the 'By-pass' Principle

Figure 5.2.2. shows a modified configuration with a direct link from *B* to *C*. This 'bypass' diverts all through traffic from *A*. This arrangement is particularly useful if *A* is the origin and destination of much of the traffic on the network, because then it is free to concentrate on its role as a terminus instead. This principle is reflected in the way that most large cities are by-passed by roads which carry through traffic, leaving the city roads free to accommodate the substantial amount of traffic originating or terminating there.

5.9   SIZE

The importance of size has been recognized much more by geographers than by historians. Large networks have distinctive features that are not found in small networks. They are more likely, for example, to employ specialized infrastructure that channels traffic through major hubs. A large network tends to be qualitatively different from a small network, and not merely a scaled-up version of it.

A major feature of the transport revolution that began with turnpike roads in the eighteenth century is the consolidation of traffic along trunk routes capable of carrying large volumes of traffic at relatively high speed. This not only improved the transport of high-value goods but facilitated faster communication by letter and newspaper.

A trunk connection, such as a railway line, turnpike road or motorway, is created when long-distance traffic from various localities is funnelled into a high capacity linkage at various access points. These points may be terminals at either end of the line, or intermediate points such as railway stations or motorway junctions.

The access point to a trunk linkage acts as a local hub; it is not only a collection and dispersal point for trunk traffic, but may also attract local traffic that uses facilities established nearby. It is distinct from a trunk hub, which is where trunk lines meet to transfer traffic. The number of linkages converging on a local hub may be very large compared with a trunk hub, where the number of converging lines is often relatively small. However, trunk hubs have large amounts of traffic to sort for onward despatch, whereas local hubs are mainly concerned with the despatch or receipt of traffic to or from the local area.

5.10   MIXTURES OF DIFFERENT TYPES OF ELEMENT

Having considered the size and configuration of a network, it is now appropriate to consider the *types* of element that belong to it. Members of different networks command different amounts of resource. Thus the

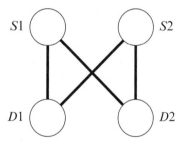

Figure 5.3   Simple market

information exchanged in an elite social network comprising bankers and entrepreneurs may be of much greater economic significance than the information exchanged by a group of friends who meet in a café. Poor people are often excluded from networks of wealthy people; social stratification means that different networks have members of different status.

Social stratification is not the only influence on network membership, however; occupational specialization is important too. Networks which help to coordinate a division of labour will comprise people who occupy different roles. These roles exert a crucial influence on network structure (Doreian and Stokman, 1997).

Buyers and sellers need to meet to make a market, for example. Buyers shop around between sellers to find the best price. This is illustrated in Figure 5.3, in which buyers *D*1, *D*2 each visit suppliers *S*1, *S*2 to obtain a quote. The structure resembles a web (see Figure 5.1.4), except for the crucial difference that neither the buyers nor the sellers communicate with each other.

Figure 5.3 illustrates a number of important points. It shows that markets have a network structure, and therefore supports the view that 'everything is a network', as set out above. It allows for the fact that market-related networks may be socially segmented, with high-status people trading in high-priced quality products and low-status people trading in discounted low-quality products. But it also shows that a market only works because it connects people who play different roles. Finally, it shows that the interplay of roles exerts a significant influence on configuration.

5.11   DIFFERENT TYPES OF RELATIONSHIP

If a market is a network, it may be asked, what prevents every network from being a market? The simple answer lies in the type of relationship involved. Market relationships, as explained above, tend to be transitory and impersonal, whilst the classic 'network' relationships are long-lived and personal.

There are many different types of relationship that can connect networks. Failure to distinguish different types of relationship can cause serious confusion in the analysis of networks. Social relationships play a prominent part in institutional theory (North, 1990; Williamson, 1985), but they are usually discussed in terms of deviations from the market norm rather than as subjects in their own right. Granovetter (1985) provides the most sophisticated discussion of social relations in a network context, and the remarks below may be construed as a development and extension of his work.

It is sometimes assumed that relationships within social networks are symmetrical, but this is far from being the case (Knight, 1935). Social networks inside firms, for example, are often based on authority: the employment contract stipulates that a worker takes orders from a manager and that a manager takes orders from the owners of the firm. Authority relationships may also be informal; as between a parent and child, for example. Formal and informal relationships may coexist, as when a formal contract of employment is supplemented by a mutual understanding between employer and employee.

Social relationships involve reciprocal obligations between the parties. The obligations may be strictly mutual, so that the relationship is symmetrical, but even if the relationship is asymmetric the obligations need to be compatible, for example, if an employee has an obligation to carry out orders then the employer has an obligation to give orders which the employee is able to implement.

Obligations are often specific rather than general, for example, they apply only to family and friends. Members of an 'inward-looking' network recognize only obligations to fellow members of the group, whilst members of an 'outward-looking' network accept obligations to the public at large.

Some networks emphasize uniformity, so that all members incur the same set of obligations. Uniformity is normally required in an outward-looking network that seeks to maintain the value of its external reputation; as with a professional association, where the public can be assured that any member of the association will maintain certain standards of behaviour. Members of reputable outward-looking networks are well-placed to intermediate in trade, because customers from any other network can be confident that they will not be cheated.

An inward-looking group that lacks external reputation is likely to be more tolerant of diversity, but personal knowledge of other members then becomes important, in order to predict how they will behave. Such groups are good at providing mutual support for members, but not for developing people who can play a prominent role in trade.

Gossip and scandal are important features of social networks. In outward-looking groups they help to identify deviants who need to be punished (possibly by expulsion) whilst in inward-looking groups they help members to predict how their fellow members will behave.

For one person to know whether they can trust another person with whom they plan to trade, it is useful to know the social networks to which they belong. It is prudent for them to trade with someone who either belongs to a reputable outward-looking group, or to the same inward-looking group as themselves.

It is also useful to belong to a network whose members have contacts with many other networks, so that network resources can be used to check up on other people. This is particularly important for entrepreneurs. Products entering international trade are often bought and resold several times before they reach the consumer, and this requires extensive trade between entrepreneurs. Given the large value of wholesale transactions, and the difficulty of enforcing international contracts through law, trust is a crucial factor in international trade. Elite networks operating at the international level are therefore extremely useful in allowing entrepreneurs to facilitate international trade. Their success depends on the fact that each of the members has an extensive range of contacts to place at the disposal of other members.

5.12 ENTREPRENEURIAL INTERMEDIATION AND THE COORDINATION OF TRADE

To illustrate the application of network analysis to entrepreneurship it is useful to set out an example which has widespread relevance, and which exemplifies many of the general points made above. The contribution of entrepreneurship to the evolution of trade is a suitable example: trade is a generic feature of economic development, and demonstrates very clearly the importance of studying all the aspects of network structure – size, diversity, relationships and configurations – rather than just a single one of them.

As indicated earlier, social networks are used to coordinate physical networks. Trade in manufactures, raw materials or agricultural products involves networks of physical flows which are coordinated by information flows mediated by social networks. Long-distance trade is generated by a physical division of labour in which producers at one location serve consumers at another location.

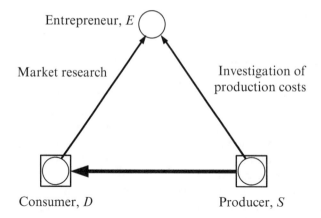

*Figure 5.4.1   Intermediation as information synthesis: role of the
entrepreneur in promoting coordination*

An accurate representation of a trade network calls for a clear distinction between the flow of resources that needs to be coordinated and the flow of information that effects the coordination. Figure 5.4.1 introduces the convention, used in subsequent figures, that physical flows are indicated by thick lines and flows of information by thin lines. The thick black line in the figure illustrates the flow of product which results when one person – the supplier S – decides to specialize in the production of a good which customer D consumes.

The physical activities that generate the physical flows are denoted by square boxes whilst the people who control the activities, and coordinate the flows, are denoted by circles. Thus the embedding of a circle within a square denotes that the individual concerned not only communicates with other individuals, but controls physical activities too (for a more complete discussion of these conventions see Casson, 1997, 2000).

Connections in networks can be either one-way or two-way. The direction of the arrow from right to left illustrates the one-way flow of the product from S to D. In economic and social networks most flows are two-way, but the flows in each direction are different. For example, when product flows from S to D, there is a reverse flow of payment from D to S, but in the interests of simplicity this is not shown.

It is assumed that trade is intermediated by an entrepreneur, E. The entrepreneur is the first to recognize the opportunity for S to specialize in production, because S is not aware of D's latent demand. Information flow is illustrated by a thin line. The left-hand line DE illustrates the entrepreneur's market research, which identifies D's demand, whilst the

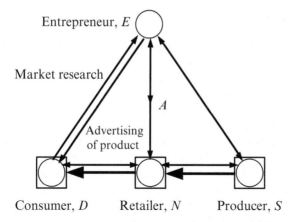

Figure 5.4.2   The market-making entrepreneur: establishing a distribution channel

right-hand line *SE* indicates the entrepreneur's investigation of production possibilities, which identifies *S* as a source of supply. The arrows indicate the direction of information flow.

To understand relationships properly, however, it is necessary to examine how the entrepreneur extracts profit from the opportunity. The answer is that the entrepreneur will block direct communication between *D* and *S* by interposing a retailer, *N*, in the product flow. The entrepreneur may also set up as a retailer himself; buying from the producer, and then marking up the price for resale to the consumer. Alternatively, the entrepreneur may use an independent retailer, in this case, acting instead as a wholesaler, buying from the producer and reselling to the retailer.

The simple case, where the entrepreneur acts as retailer, is illustrated in Figure 5.4.2. The entrepreneur negotiates with the producer over the price of the good, as indicated by the two-way flow of information *ES*. As a retailer, the entrepreneur negotiates with the customer, as indicated by the two-way flow of information *ND*, and places orders with the producer in order to maintain sufficient stock to service demand. The producer invoices the entrepreneur in return. This two-way information flow is represented by the line *NS*. The entrepreneur continues to observe the customer, as indicated by the one-way flow of information *DE*, and in addition uses the media to advertise the product to the customer. These are two distinct information flows that go in opposite directions. They are not a form of dialogue, unlike the other information flows, and therefore they are represented by two separate lines.

The relationship between the entrepreneur and the manager of the retail facility involves authority. It is fundamentally different from the other relations, connecting E and N to S and D, which involve negotiation instead. While communication between entrepreneur and manager is two-way, it is asymmetric because the entrepreneur gives orders and the manager reports back when they have been carried out. In Figure 5.4.2 the authority relation is indicated by a letter A placed next to an arrow in the middle of the connecting line. The arrow indicates the direction in which orders are given.

Entrepreneurship is normally viable only when market size is sufficient to cover the fixed costs of creating the market – that is, making contact with customers and suppliers, and establishing a retail facility. It follows that D indicates a representative consumer rather than a solitary consumer. Representing each consumer individually would make the figure impossibly complicated. There may be several producers too, particularly if the demand is large and production plants are small-scale.

5.13   COMPETITION AND COLLUSION BETWEEN ENTREPRENEURS

Competition

The analysis of product flows needs to be integrated back into the earlier analysis of markets. The essence of a market is that a customer can choose between alternative sources of supply. While an entrepreneur may have a temporary monopoly when setting up a new market, as assumed above, competitors will soon appear, who either imitate the product or market a variant of it instead. A mature market therefore features competition between rival entrepreneurs. This is illustrated in Figure 5.5.1, which portrays two rival entrepreneurs, $E1$, $E2$, drawing on distinct sources of supply $S1$, $S2$. Each entrepreneur acts as a retailer. Two representative consumers are shown, $D1$, $D2$, to emphasize the possibility that the two entrepreneurs can divide the market between them. Prior to contract, each consumer solicits price quotations from each entrepreneur, along the lines indicated in Figure 5.3. Having compared the prices, $D1$ decides to buy from $E1$ and $D2$ from $E2$; this is illustrated by the pattern of thick lines representing the product flows. It should be noted that under competition the network of information flows is far more dense than the network of product flows. This is because product only flows when a contract has been agreed, whilst information flows every time a potential contact is investigated.

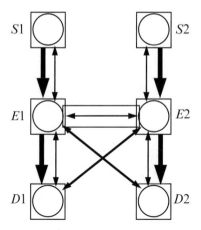

Figure 5.5.1   *Vertical and horizontal communication in a market with secret collusion between entrepreneurs*

Confidentiality

Most writers on networks assume that, if considerations of cost are ignored, then more linkages are always better, because this will shorten the paths between some pairs of elements, and thereby reduce overall communication costs. But in practice, many people devote a lot of effort to avoiding communication with others. One reason is simply that communication is time-consuming and therefore costly. There is no point in wasting time talking to someone who has nothing to offer.

There are numerous people that we walk past every day who we do not stop and talk to because we are hurrying to meetings with people to whom we do wish to talk. Although a link has already been created by chance, which has placed us at the same location at the same time, we do not wish to take advantage of the opportunity; on the contrary, we actively decline it. Even people we already know may be avoided if we do not trust them; for there is no point in talking to someone who you do not trust, since you would not wish to trade with them, and in any case you cannot believe what they say.

Other people are positively dangerous. This is not just a question of physical danger, but of economic danger. An entrepreneur will not want to communicate with a competitor for fear that the competitor will learn the price of his product; if he did, then the competitor could steal the entrepreneur's customers away by quoting a marginally lower price.

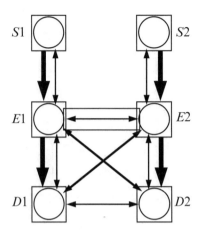

*Figure 5.5.2   Vertical and horizontal communication in a market with
            secret collusion between entrepreneurs and learning between
            consumers*

Collusion

It is possible, though, that some entrepreneurs can trust each other not
to steal customers. In this case they can profit from collusion by raising
prices. By raising prices above the competitive level, suppliers can redis-
tribute income from customers. Because higher prices will also restrict
demand, the customers will lose more than the suppliers gain, which is one
reason why collusion is regarded as anti-social. To avoid complaints from
consumers, the entrepreneurs may disguise their collusion. They therefore
communicate in secret rather than in public, in the hope that customers
will not realize what is going on. Thus if there is a link between *E*1 and
*E*2, it will normally be secret. This is illustrated in Figure 5.5.1, where a
link between *E*1 and *E*2 is shown in a box to indicate that it is hidden from
other parties.

   Consumers can also communicate with each other, as illustrated by
the link between *D*1 and *D*2 in Figure 5.5.2. In most product markets,
however, consumers lack market power because there are far more consumers than producers and therefore it is too costly for them to coordinate
their purchasing strategies. Consumers can, however, compare the prices
they have paid through normal social channels, such as gossip. This tends
to strengthen consumer market power in a different way. Each consumer
can 'free-ride' on the shopping experiences of other consumers, and
therefore economise on the amount of shopping that they do themselves.
Furthermore, any entrepreneur who reduces the price of a product can

expect to gain a larger share of the market when consumers pool their information since the entrepreneur's reputation will spread more quickly. Thus even when consumers are unable to coordinate their purchasing decisions formally, they can still improve their position by harnessing social networks to distribute price information within the group.

It should be noted that issues relating to confidentiality vary according to the type of product traded in the market. Thus in labour markets, trade unions openly organize collusion amongst the workers in order to maximize their strike-threat power, whilst employers similarly organize their labour purchasing to maximize their lock-out power, creating a system of collective bargaining underpinned by 'countervailing power'.

A set of linkages between consumers and producers exemplifies a 'vertical' network in which the flow of communication follows the same path as the flow of the product, while a network of producers and a network of consumers both exemplify a 'horizontal' network between people operating at the same stage of product flow. It is often claimed that vertical linkages strengthen competition and improve trade, whilst horizontal linkages are anti-competitive and damage trade, but this is not always the case, as the example of consumer learning makes clear. More generally, within any network composed of different types of element, it is useful to distinguish linkages between elements of the same type from linkages between elements of a different type. Once again, links between elements of different types may be presumed to be pro-competitive, and links between elements of the same type to be anti-competitive, although these presumptions will not always be correct as the competitive implications depend not only on the configuration but also the type of relationship involved.

5.14 THE DEMAND FOR PERSONAL TRANSPORT DERIVED FROM SOCIAL NETWORKING

The above analysis has emphasized the close links between social networks and physical networks, with the flow of information through the former being used to coordinate the flow of resources through the latter. The links between social and physical networks become even closer when the spatial dimension of economic activity is examined in more detail.

There is an obvious stock/flow connection between product flow and physical transport infrastructure, and between information flow and physical communications infrastructure. It is not so obvious, however, that there is also an important connection between information flow and physical transport infrastructure. This connection arises because there is a crucial difference between remote communication and face-to-face communication: while the former creates a demand for communications infrastructure, the latter creates a demand for transport infrastructure. Everyone cannot live 'next door' to everyone else, and so face-to-face communication creates a demand for travel to meetings.

When just two or three people plan to meet, people may take it in turn to act as host, but when a significant number of people need to meet a central location will normally be used. A specialized central location reduces overall travelling distance, whilst large meetings economize on the use of time as it is possible to meet lots of people by making just one trip.

Attending large meetings is also an efficient way of obtaining introductions: each person can not only be introduced, but can also introduce others. The structure of the meeting is important in this respect. People need to be able to circulate so that they can be paired up with appropriate people. Break-out areas in which people can hold confidential one-to-one discussions are also useful when the function of a meeting is to help broker business deals.

Efficiency of communication is increased if different meetings take place at the same central place, so that people can attend several meetings on the same trip. Different meetings of interest to the same groups of people can be scheduled to run in sequence, as with the annual conferences of related professional associations.

Other meetings are in continuous operation. A shopping centre, for example, may be construed as a continuous open meeting where people can come and go as they please. People who are attending scheduled meetings can 'pop out to the shops' at their convenience. Retailing is a prominent activity at many of the hubs where people meet. Historically, abbeys and castles attracted retailers, especially on saints' days, while many of today's major retail centres originally developed around ports or centres of government.

5.15 EMERGENCE OF PERSONAL TRANSPORT HUBS

Economies of Agglomeration

Retailing affords economies of agglomeration to consumers. Where different retailers stock different types of product, the consumer can collect an entire 'basket' of different goods on a single trip. Where different retailers stock different varieties of the same product, the customer can assess the design and quality of different varieties on the spot. Where different retailers stock the same product, customers can compare prices. In each case the agglomeration of retailers reduces the marginal cost of a customer's search.

Retailers supplying complementary goods have a direct incentive to locate close together. If one shop is already selling outerwear, for example, then a shop that sets up next door selling underwear can anticipate a substantial 'passing trade'.

It is not so clear, though, why competing retailers would locate together. One reason is that customers refuse to buy from a local monopolist because they believe that they will be cheated. This reflects a lack of trust in society. Thus retailers who locate together gain credibility: they acquire a small share of a large market instead of the entire share of the very small market that they would otherwise enjoy.

Another explanation relates to innovation. An effective way to advertise a new product is to display it adjacent to its closest competitor. Customers can be 'intercepted' on their way to their usual source of supply. The 'market test' may well put one of the suppliers out of business: if the new product is successful then the established retailer may quit, while if it fails then the innovator will quit. An established retailer defeated by an innovation may retire to a more remote location where they can monopolize a small market with their traditional product.

The link between innovation and agglomeration explains why a market may be regarded as a 'self-organizing' system. Volatility in the environment continually creates new consumer problems, and a consequent demand for new products to solve them. At the same time, the social accumulation of technological knowledge allows new types of product to be developed. But an innovation is only viable if it can find a market, and its market is to be found where its closest competitor is sold. To make as much profit as early as possible, a confident innovator will head for the largest market (possibly after 'proving' the product in a smaller market first), which is where the contest between the new product and the old product will be played out.

The continuous influx of new products increases both the novelty and the diversity of the products available at a major hub. The greater intensity of competition means that older obsolete products will be expelled from large markets before they are expelled from smaller ones. The larger the market, therefore, the greater is the diversity and the lower is the average age of the product.

On the other hand, the risks faced by the consumer are greater in a large market because a higher proportion of the products will be unproven. A large market will therefore attract buyers who are confident of their ability to judge design and quality, and who value novelty for its own sake, while smaller markets will retain the custom of less confident people, and those who prefer proven traditional designs. Optimal innovation strategy therefore explains both the capacity of the market system to renew itself continually by up-dating its product range, and also the concentration of novelty in the largest markets.

Varieties of Transport Hub

Meeting points and major markets constitute information hubs. People visit these centres specifically to meet other people. Travel to the hub both sustains the existing division of labour and also helps to effect changes in it. Shopping sustains profitable production, whilst meetings support the innovation process: researchers 'network' at conferences, entrepreneurs meet venture capitalists at elite gala events, and inter-firm alliances are planned at trade fairs.

With so many visitors to the hub, accommodation, catering and entertainment facilities are required. Infrastructure may be built to facilitate mass transit to the hub. The ease of access and the variety of services available at the destination attracts tourists. A *visitor hub* of this type is, in principle, quite distinct from the *transit hub*, such as a railway junction or airport hub, at which people change from one trunk route, or transport mode, to another. People travel *through* a transit hub in a particular direction, whereas they travel *to and from* a visitor hub as part of a return journey (see Chapter 11).

The essence of a transit hub is that a number of connecting trunk lines all converge on the same point. Through traffic is switched from the incoming link to the outgoing link. Some traffic can be switched from one route to another without stopping – for example, express trains at country railway junctions and car traffic at motorway intersections – but in other cases a stop is required so that a connection can be made with another route. It is when traffic has to stop that it may 'stop over' rather than proceeding on its way at the first available opportunity.

There is little point in stopping over at a pure transit hub, as there are no major services to attract the visitor. A visitor hub, on the other hand, can attract stop-overs if it can also be used as a transit hub. In order to act as a transit hub, however, it needs to occupy an appropriate location on the transport network, at the intersection of important routes. A transport hub without visitor potential is exemplified by the railway town of Crewe, which is an important junction that provides few visitor services. By contrast nineteenth-century London became a great metropolis by combining the roles of transit hub and visitor hub. Many railway trunk routes converged on London from different points of the compass, but each had its own terminal, so through travellers were obliged to change terminals as well as trains. However, the railway companies provided massive station hotels which not only allowed travellers to break their journey with an overnight stop, but encouraged them to spend several days in the capital, consulting with doctors, bankers and solicitors and attending theatres and museums.

Combining the role of transit hub and visitor hub can lead to congestion, however. In the late twentieth century visitor attractions have tended to concentrate in the centres of the cities whilst transit hubs have moved to airports and motorway junctions on the periphery. London has strengthened its visitor appeal by excluding through traffic from the centre using a congestion charge, whilst Birmingham has acquired visitor appeal by building shopping centres and exhibition halls close to its motorway transit hubs. In the global economy of the twenty-first century, competition between 'world cities' is based on finding an efficient way of combining the roles of transit hub and visitor hub.

5.16   CONCLUSION

Networks have stimulated a lot of interest in many disciplines. In the social sciences networks have even acquired an ideological significance: 'network organizations' have been hailed as an alternative to large impersonal organizations such as a rigidly hierarchical multinational firm or the state. Indeed, it has been suggested that the modern capitalist system took a 'wrong turning' about a century ago when the large managerial corporation superseded the networks of flexible specialization that prevailed in the industrial districts of the time (Piore and Sabel, 1978). This focus on ideology, however, has diverted attention away from the purely analytical significance of networks. This chapter has sought to re-focus the discussion of networks on analytical issues, and in particular on their role in refining and extending entrepreneurship theory.

Networks are inherently complex, but this does not mean that they cannot be properly understood. The structure of a network is governed by four main factors.

- *The size of the network, as measured by the number of elements*   Size is an important determinant of both the type of relationship and the configuration of flows. Large size encourages network members to opt for a multiplicity of impersonal relationships rather than a small number of personal relationships. It also calls for the consolidation of network flows along trunk connections, and the emergence of specialist trunk hubs where trunk traffic is sorted and sent on.

- *The membership of the network, as reflected in the types of element that belong to it, and the extent to which different types are mixed* A typical trade network, for example, will contain at least three types of element: a consumer, a producer and an intermediator such as an entrepreneur.
- *The types of relationship between members, which reflect the roles that they play* Social relationships, for example, vary from highly impersonal relationships sustained by remote communication, which are characteristic of commercial networks, to highly personal relationships, sustained face-to-face, which are characteristic of smaller and more localized bonding networks.
- *The configuration of the network, which describes the pattern in which the different elements are connected up* Intermediators often act as hubs in networks. Multiple hubs stimulate competition within the network, and provide redundancy which makes the network resilient to shocks.

Recent analysis of social networks has been dominated by the study of relationships, and in particular by the issue of trust (see Chapter 6). This has distracted attention from the issue of configuration. Configuration is an important influence on the cost of operating a network. Configuration is the major focus of graph theory, and has received much attention in research on physical networks, but most writers on entrepreneurship have ignored it.

This chapter has outlined the structure of a positive theory of networks which explains why certain types of network are particularly common in certain situations. A simple approach is to identify the function that a network exists to perform. The division of labour provides the rationale for many physical networks. It creates a wide variety of industries whose products are distributed to millions of individual consumers. The division of labour needs to be coordinated, and a social network is well adapted to this task. Some networks coordinate long-distance trade, whilst others coordinate production processes; others regulate access to public goods, such as heritage sites, or facilitate mutual support between individuals.

Specialized intermediators emerge within networks, acting as communications hubs. If these intermediators work for profit then they normally re-sell products to the members, and if this is not possible then they charge a brokerage fee. Intermediation for profit is a classic example of entrepreneurial activity. Entrepreneurship is often presented as a highly individualistic activity, but in fact it depends heavily on the use of networks. Successful entrepreneurs will identify the key networks that they need to join. This requires a good understanding of the relationships that exist within the various networks, and their implications for the ways in which the members of those networks behave.

Many intermediators do not work for a profit, however. They may be charismatic idealists seeking to improve society; operating for profit would be incompatible with their moral principles. Alternatively they may be high-status individuals who are rewarded by deference and respect. In some cases non-profit intermediators can cover their costs from voluntary donations to their organization, or by charging membership fees.

Different coordination requirements are best satisfied by different network structures. Hence the nature of the division of labour determines the pattern of coordination required, which in turn determines the most appropriate network structure. If coordination is efficiently organized then the most efficient network structure will be the one that is used.

Long-distance trade, for example, is usually coordinated by for-profit entrepreneurs through inter-firm contracts, whilst the delivery of local social services is usually coordinated by non-profit leaders who establish schools, hospitals, churches, sports clubs, and community associations for this purpose.

The leader of a non-profit group has a significant advantage over an entrepreneur who runs a for-profit firm in establishing a reputation for integrity. The selection of non-profit activity suggests altruistic motives, whilst the absence of charges for services eliminates the incentive to offer services that the non-profit leader does not intend to supply. This in turn is a significant advantage in establishing the external reputation of the network to which the leader belongs.

Any given person will belong to a substantial number of networks: family, church, sports club, work group, political party, professional association and so on. The fact that many non-profit networks recruit part-time volunteers and rotate tasks gives people ample opportunity to join many networks and to get acquainted with a high proportion of the membership of each. It is therefore quite probable that, by chance, they encounter someone with whom they are able to trade; for example, a distant family member may become a business partner, or a fellow member of a sports club may become a customer or employee.

Because each person in the economy belongs to so many different networks, the networks to which people belong are intertwined. Every network is connected, directly or indirectly, to every other network by multiple links. Thus every network is a sub-set of a single giant network that encompasses the entire global economy.

To cut through this complexity, it is necessary to analyse any given network phenomenon by concentrating on just one part of the global system. Research must proceed by abstracting the network under scrutiny from the system as a whole, in order to examine its internal structure in full detail. It must not be overlooked, however, that the network under scrutiny is connected to the rest of the system at numerous points – it is an 'open system', in other words. Disturbances originating elsewhere in the economy can impinge on the network at any point, and sometimes at several points at once.

This methodology of examining the part in relation to the whole is common to all social science, however, and so in this respect the study of networks merely conforms to general research practice. What has been missing from the study of networks so far is not so much an awareness of this interdependence, as a reluctance to examine the structure of individual networks in adequate detail. It is hoped that the survey of network structure presented in this chapter, and the analysis of its economic significance, will encourage entrepreneurship scholars to pay more attention to network structure in future.

ACKNOWLEDGEMENTS

I am grateful to Paloma Fernandez Perez and the Organizing Committee for the invitation to present an early version of this chapter to the 10th Symposium of Economic History at the Universitat Autonoma de Barcelona in January 2005. Some preliminary ideas contained in the chapter were presented to a Workshop on Social Capital at the Institute of Entrepreneurship, University of Lancaster, organized by Mary Rose and her colleagues, where I received valuable comments from Bob Jessop and others. I have also benefited greatly from discussions with my colleagues Marina Della Giusta and Zella King.

REFERENCES

Armstrong, Harvey and Jim Taylor (2000), *Regional Economics and Policy*, 3rd edn, Oxford: Blackwell.
Biggs, Norman L., E. Keith Lloyd and Robert Wilson (1986), *Graph Theory, 1736–1936*, Oxford: Oxford University Press.
Burt, Ronald S. (1992), *Structural Holes: The Social Structure of Competition*, Cambridge, MA: Harvard University Press.
Casson, Mark (1997), *Information and Organization*, Oxford: Clarendon Press.
Casson, Mark (2000), *Entrepreneurship and Leadership*, Cheltenham, UK and Northampton, MA, USA: Edward Elgar.
Diestel, Reinhard (1997), *Graph Theory*, New York: Springer.

Doreian, Patrick and Frans N. Stokman (1997), *Evolution of Social Networks*, Amsterdam: Gordon and Breach.

Foreman-Peck, James S. and Robert Millward (1994), *Public and Private Ownership of Industry in Britain, 1820–1980*, Oxford: Clarendon Press.

Granovetter, Mark (1985), 'Economic action and social structure: the problem of embeddedness', *American Journal of Sociology*, **91** (3), 481–510.

Haggett, Peter and Richard J. Chorley (1969), *Network Analysis in Geography*, London: Arnold.

Isard, W., E.W. Schooler and T. Vietorisz (1959), *Industrial Complex Analysis and Regional Development*, London: Chapman & Hall.

Jones, Geoffrey G. (2000), *Merchants to Multinationals: British Trading Companies in the Nineteenth and Twentieth Centuries*, Oxford: Oxford University Press.

Jones, Geoffrey G. and Franco Amatori (2003), *Business History around the World*, Cambridge: Cambridge University Press.

Knight, Frank H. (1935), *The Ethics of Competition and Other Essays*, London: Allen and Unwin.

Leibenstein, Harvey (1978), *General X-efficiency Theory and Economic Development*, New York: Oxford University Press.

North, Douglass C. (1981), *Structure and Change in Economic History*, New York: W.W. Norton.

North, Douglass C. (1990), *Institutions, Institutional Change and Economic Performance*, Cambridge: Cambridge University Press.

Piore, Michael J. and Charles F. Sabel (1978), *The Second Industrial Divide: Possibilities for Prosperity*, New York: Basic Books.

Putterman, Louis (1990), *The Division of Labour and Economic Welfare*, Oxford: Oxford University Press.

Thompson, Grahame F. (2003), *Between Hierarchies and Markets: The Logic and Limits of Network Firms*, Oxford: Oxford University Press.

Wasserman, S. and K. Faust (1994), *Social Network Analysis: Methods and Applications*, Cambridge: Cambridge University Press.

Watts, Duncan J. (2003), *Six Degrees: The Science of a Connected Age*, London: William Heineman.

Williamson, Oliver E. (1985), *Economic Institutions of Capitalism*, New York: Free Press.

6. Entrepreneurial networks as social capital

With Marina Della Giusta

Successful entrepreneurship relies heavily on access to social networks, which provide both information and trust. Membership of a network not only provides useful contacts that can be trusted – it can also enhance an entrepreneur's own reputation for trustworthiness. Trust is important to entrepreneurs because they need to know that the information they obtain from others is reliable, in order to manage risk. Access to networks is sometimes restricted, however, and this may impair the generation of trust. Governments have invested heavily in building local and regional social networks in order to stimulate entrepreneurship, in the expectation that this will improve economic performance and facilitate regeneration. However, there are many types of network; some are most useful in the early stages of entrepreneurial activity and others at later stages. Careful definitions are necessary in order to analyse the role of networks in generating interpersonal and inter-organizational trust, and hence in augmenting the stock of social capital. Effective networks are normally intermediated by reputable trust-brokers. The reputation of government gives it a significant role as a trust-broker, but there is a danger that its reputation may be undermined when it extends its activities into areas where it lacks the competence to intervene effectively.

6.1 INTRODUCTION

Although the popular perception of entrepreneurship is very much that of an individualist, there is ample evidence that entrepreneurship is, in fact, socially embedded in network structures (Aldrich, 1987; Aldrich and Zimmer, 1986; Johannison, 1988). The precise nature of this embeddedness is not always clear, however. Just as the concept of entrepreneurship requires careful definition (see Chapter 1), so related concepts such as social capital and trust also require careful definition if the nature of embeddedness is to be properly understood. This chapter builds upon the previous discussion of networks in Chapter 5, which provided a rigorous definition of a network and an associated typology. The focus of the present chapter is on social networks, and on the role of trust in promoting their efficiency. Special attention is paid to the role of trust in enhancing entrepreneurial performance.

6.2 THE CONCEPT OF SOCIAL CAPITAL

The concept of social capital is widely agreed to be ambiguous. It has many different connotations, and so the scope for confusion is considerable (Anderson and Jack, 2002). There are tensions between the way the concept is used in sociology and political science on the one hand (for example, Putnam, 1993, 2001; Portes and Landolt, 1996) and economics on the other (for example, Dasgupta and Serageldin, 2000). One way of resolving this tension is to apply the rational action modelling of economics to the processes of social interaction studied by sociologists. This approach was pioneered by Coleman (1988) and has been followed up both theoretically (Della Giusta, 1999; Casson and Della Giusta, 2004) and empirically (Knack and Keefer, 1997).

The question arises as to how social interaction between rational actors is to be modelled when there is a large number of actors to be considered. The economic analysis of social networks offers a way forward in this respect (Casson and Rose, 1997). Networks facilitate social interactions between their members through investments in high-trust channels of communication. 'Networking' is often regarded as a manifestation of social capital, and many of the insights of social capital theory can be found, quite independently, in the network literature (Brown and Duguid, 2002; Himanen and Castells, 2004). Indeed, scholars familiar with the social network literature might well regard some of what is written on social capital as a 'reinvention of the wheel'.

Network analysis is not the only way of analysing social relations between a large number of actors. An analysis based on social class offers an alternative way forward, but this is rejected here because it imposes a structure on relationships between network members that is too restrictive for the purposes of this chapter.

Economists and sociologists tend to use the concept of capital in different ways. Sociologists typically regard capital as a stock that is accumulated steadily over time, whilst economists tend to adopt a forward-looking approach in which capital is valued in terms of the benefits derived from its future use. In accounting terms, sociologists tend to value capital in terms of its 'historic cost', whilst economists use the 'market value'. This market value is reflected in the expected net present value of the future stream of benefits generated by the asset. The market value approach is the one which is best adapted to the requirements of this chapter.

It has been noted that certain forms of social capital – such as capital embedded in the personal loyalties between members of a drugs cartel – may have a negative impact on society. It must therefore be recognized that in certain contexts social capital may have a negative value (Bowles and Gintis, 2002).

The network literature suggests that social capital can be defined in terms of the creation of high-trust social networks, and this is the approach adopted here. Specifically, social capital is defined as *the capitalized value of improvements in economic performance that can be attributed to high-trust social networks*. Emphasizing networks highlights the 'social' aspect of social capital, whilst emphasizing the value of future improvements highlights the 'capital' aspect.

Given the social emphasis, it is appropriate to construe economic performance broadly; to include not just the usual range of goods and services included in the national accounts, but a range of un-priced factors, such as visual amenity, which enter into *quality of life*. Placing too much emphasis on qualitative factors can, however, lead to the trivial conclusion that networks are useful simply because people enjoy belonging to them. The focus of this chapter is therefore on the *instrumental* benefits of network membership, such as the promotion of productivity and trade, rather than *intrinsic* benefits, such as personal recognition and emotional support.

A rational actor will pursue both intrinsic and instrumental benefits, perhaps advertising one and concealing the other according to the particular situation. Thus when working for a private firm a rational actor may emphasize the instrumentality of any actions to the pursuit of profit, whilst at home the emphasis might be on intrinsic domestic pleasures, playing down the instrumental side of family life. As we shall see, this ambivalence about objectives permeates social capital, where the overt pursuit of one type of benefit may be associated with the concealed pursuit of another.

The impact of social networks can be explored at either the local, regional, national or global level. The unit of analysis is quite important. Where face-to-face contact is important, it is natural to focus on the local level. Where the utilization of specific resource endowments is concerned, the regional level is often the most appropriate, since it is at this level that the impact of networking on specific sectors such as mining and tourism, and on specific activities, such as university spin-out, can be discerned. The national level is important for the formulation of government policy initiatives, whilst the global level is the most appropriate level at which to study the role of networks in international trade and capital movements.

The main focus in this chapter is on the local and regional level, but the analytical approach is valid for any geographical unit of analysis.

Social networks can affect economic performance through a number of channels. For example, a strong extended family may promote entrepreneurship by providing inter-generational capital flows that can compensate for a lack of bank finance for the family business, and may also provide flexible child-care which allows family members to increase family income by taking part-time work. In the first case the network helps to overcome deficiencies in the provision of bank finance, whilst in the second case it compensates for a missing child-care system, which could have been provided by the state. The analysis in this chapter aims to capture a range of network effects. Furthermore, the generality of the approach means that it can be extended to incorporate other effects as well.

6.3   DEFINING SOCIAL NETWORKS

The defining feature of a network is *connection* (see Chapter 5). A set of elements that are connected to each other form a network. In a local business network, for example, the elements may be business owners who live in the area. The relationship is that they are in regular contact with each other. Every member does not necessarily know every other member personally, but every member knows some other member who knows some other member, and so on, so that every member can in principle be put in touch with every other member using the resources of the network.

A popular impression of a social network is that it is a collection of people who meet fairly regularly on a casual basis in order to share their experiences. Networks are often described as 'self-organizing', because no one appears to be in charge: people show up at meetings simply because they expect others to show up, and provided others do indeed show up, a spontaneous equilibrium is maintained.

In fact, social networks take a variety of forms (Wasserman and Faust, 1994) and relationships between members differ widely (Doreian and Stokman, 1997) – for example, parentage creates family networks, trading relations create commercial networks and so on.

Some social networks are purely transitory – they may be a group of people attending a party who then disperse to go their separate ways. Such networks can be useful for making contacts, but their individual importance is low. Since there are many such meetings, however, their combined effect can be significant. Most networks, though, persist for a considerable time. Long-term persistence requires that the network renew itself by recruiting new members to replace those who have died, retired or moved away. Families, for example, persist through the recruitment of spouses and the production (or adoption) of children. Persistence is usually associated with high levels of commitment between members (Granovetter, 1985).

Some networks are unstructured: there is no internal differentiation of roles. A group of commuters travelling together on a train exemplifies an unstructured network. No one is in charge, and if one or two members leave, the network may disintegrate.

The larger the network, the greater the advantage of structure. A leadership role may emerge, occupied by someone who exerts influence over the other members and represents them in negotiations with outside groups. With the emergence of a leader, a network may acquire an identity, represented by a collective name, and possibly symbolised by a logo, crest or flag. A structured social network may be described as a social group.

A group can be structured either formally or informally. An informal structure may be based on a personality cult around the leader, whilst a formal structure is more likely to involve a codified constitution. A formally structured group may be termed an *organization*. An organization has an authority system, which determines who is authorized to take what decisions. Authority is normally conferred on offices or roles, rather than on particular individuals, and the constitution then determines how people are allocated to a role.

A formal group may develop into a corporate *institution*. It acts as a fictitious person, making contracts with other institutions as well as with individual people. All the well-known forms of institution – including firms, markets, governments and clubs – may be regarded as highly-structured highly-formalized social groups. A firm is a for-profit organization, while a club or charity is a non-profit organization, Both firms and clubs operate on the voluntary principle whereby people decide whether they wish to become members or not; by contrast, government is a compulsory organization which conscripts its members and coerces a subscription through taxation. A market economy is a distinctive kind of institution with a highly decentralized authority system in which control over resources can be traded between individual members without the specific consent of the group as a whole. From a network perspective all these forms of organization merge into each other: there is a continuum of organizational forms, and careful definition is required to determine which organizations are of which particular type.

It is possible to have networks composed of networks, creating a hierarchical structure in which low-level networks belong to higher-level networks. The high-level networks coordinate relations between the lower-level networks. Where the lower-level networks are organizations or institutions, this leads to inter-organizational and inter-institutional networks.

The interpersonal aspect of a social network is always fundamental, however, because inter-organization networks are maintained in practice by interpersonal communication between representatives or leaders of the respective organizations. Turnover of personnel can undermine inter-organizational relationships if successors are not properly briefed when they take over. Indeed, many inter-organizational relationships are often little more than impersonal formalizations of highly personal relationships, and therefore dissolve as soon as one of the key people dies, retires or moves on. The discussion which follows therefore focuses on the role of interpersonal networks, on the grounds that inter-organizational networks are usually based on interpersonal networks linking the representatives involved.

A significant feature of any network is its configuration, and in particular the structure of its hubs. Most writers on social networks tend to assume one of two configurations. For an unstructured network, they assume a web configuration, whilst for a structured network they assume a single-hub configuration. In the web every member is directly connected to every other member, whereas in the hub only the central person is directly connected to everyone else and other people are only indirectly connected through the centre. Allied to this, it is usually assumed that the web involves symmetrical relationships between people of equal status, whilst the hub involves an asymmetrical relationship of influence or authority, directed from a high-status person at the centre towards ordinary lower-status members around the periphery. In practice, however, networks can take a wide variety of different configurations (see Chapter 5), with the chosen configuration reflecting the specific purposes for which the network was formed.

6.4   THE CONCEPT OF TRUST

The connectivity provided by a social network can reduce 'social distance' between its members. There are two main determinants of social distance: the ease of communication and the degree of trust. Ease of communication is facilitated by a common language, common culture and effective channels of information flow. Common culture avoids misunderstandings that are caused when differences in basic values and beliefs lead to information being interpreted in an unintended way. The risk of misunderstandings is further reduced when a message is conveyed using a variety of media, such as speaking, writing and gesture, so that a misleading impression given in one medium can be corrected through the others. Until fairly recently, speaking and gestures were characteristic of face-to-face communication, but not any more: telephones facilitate speaking and TV communicates gestures.

In business networks ease of communication is not normally a critical issue. Trust is absolutely essential however. Unfortunately, however, trust is also a potentially ambiguous concept, and it is therefore crucial to define it carefully (Casson and Della Giusta, 2005).

If an entrepreneur with a bad reputation reneges on a deal, a previous victim of that entrepreneur might exclaim 'Trust him not to deliver!' This does not mean, of course, that he considers him trustworthy – it simply means that he considers that his dishonesty is predictable. *Predictability* is the first meaning of trust.

If a reputable person were introducing an entrepreneur to a banker at a reception, he might say 'You can certainly trust him.' This would have the more usual meaning: that he can be relied upon to honour his obligations. A *propensity to honour obligations* is the second meaning of trust.

To be trusted is not the same thing as to be trustworthy (Gambetta, 1988). Trustworthiness is an objective characteristic of an individual in a given type of situation, but it cannot be directly observed. Trust is the belief that the other person holds about them (Hardin, 1993). This belief may or may not be correct. This leads to an important distinction between naive trust and warranted trust. Naive trust signifies a misplaced belief in the character of the other party whereas, by contrast, warranted trust signifies a belief that is correct. In economic terms, warranted trust is an equilibrium concept, since expectations are fulfilled, and so there is no reason to change them. On the other hand, naive trust is a disequilibrium concept because the expectations are not fulfilled and so need to be revised.

Some business transactions require mutual trust, whilst others depend only on unilateral trust. In mutual trust each party trusts the other, whereas in unilateral trust one party trusts the other, but the feeling is not necessarily reciprocated. For example, if an entrepreneur supplies a customer though mail order and the customer pays in advance, the entrepreneur does not need to trust the customer, but the customer needs to trust the entrepreneur. Conversely, if the customer only pays when he/she receives the goods then the entrepreneur needs to trust the customer, but the customer no longer needs to trust the entrepreneur. But if the goods and the payment are liable to cross in the post then they both need to trust each other.

Taking all these factors into account, trust is most usefully defined as a *confident and warranted belief that the other party will honour their obligations*. Confidence gives predictability, whilst the warranted nature of the trust ensures that the predictions are broadly correct. Mutuality is not required by this definition, as it is not always necessary.

6.5   NATURE OF OBLIGATION

The definition of trust in terms of obligation raises the issue of why anyone would accept an obligation in the first place. The simple answer is that they get something in return. If they recognize an obligation to another party then the other party will recognize a reciprocal obligation to them. This is the basis on which social groups are formed. All the members of a group accept an obligation to respect the rights of the other members in return for respect from others. Trust therefore normally develops within the context of a social group.

Different types of social group emphasize different types of obligation.

Contractual obligations   In business dealings, keeping promises is regarded as being of paramount importance. A contract is a reciprocal set of promises in which the seller agrees to deliver in return for the buyer agreeing to pay. An entrepreneur promises to repay a loan to a bank; an employee promises to work hard and obey orders; a supplier promises to deliver quality products on time, and so on. Defaulting on a contract is a very serious matter.

Customary obligations   When people do not have a contract, obligations may still apply. Customary obligations allow people to behave towards each other in a predictable fashion even though there has been no prior communication between them. People are expected to reply to business correspondence, and to compromise in negotiations, even though they have not specifically promised to do so. People therefore have a common obligation to observe business customs although they have not made a contract. Indeed, without respect for custom, contracts would be difficult to negotiate.

Considerate obligations   Entrepreneurs may feel obliged to consider the wider implications of their actions. They do not confine their obliga-tions to respecting customs and honouring contracts. The paternalistic employer, for example, accepts an obligation to care for his workers, and even their dependants, in times of sickness or stress. A philanthropic banker might extend a loan against his better judgement because if the borrower went bankrupt many people would lose their jobs. Business people who accept considerate obligations can be trusted to take account of the wider implications of the impacts of their decisions in a way that those merely entering into contractual obligations cannot.

Philanthropic obligations   Some entrepreneurs may even accept a duty to society which extends beyond the parochial boundaries of their firm. They move beyond paternalism to philanthropy. They sponsor hospitals or holiday homes for the use of everyone and not just their own employees. In modern jargon, they take corporate social responsibility seriously.

For any given type of obligation, trust is greater the larger the value of resources involved. An individual who can be trusted to repay a debt of £1000 cannot necessarily be trusted to repay a debt of £1 million. When people commit themselves to honouring obligations, there is an implicit restriction on the size of the obligation that they are willing to accept. The significance of this restriction may not be appreciated until unusual circumstances arise. People can often train themselves to be honest in regular dealings but can be caught out by temptations they cannot resist when they are confronted with a type of situation they have not encountered before. Thus unanticipated circumstances are more likely than anticipated circumstances to precipitate dishonest behaviour.

6.6   APPLICATIONS OF NETWORK ANALYSIS TO SOCIAL CAPITAL AND ENTREPRENEURSHIP

Social networks influence several different aspects of entrepreneurship. It is useful at the outset to distinguish three aspects of entrepreneurship: opportunity-seeking, resource acquisition and project implementation. From the standpoint of network analysis, the organization of a new market is the most important aspect of project implementation, and so this is the focus of discussion below.

Opportunity-Seeking

Opportunity-seeking is mainly about gathering information. Coordination failures provide opportunities for entrepreneurs to correct them. In a simple case, an entrepreneur might spot an opportunity for arbitrage – for example, a brownfield industrial site that could be converted to residential use. The entrepreneur might use networks to discover the existence of the site, to assess the potential local demand for housing, and obtain an estimate of local construction costs. In practice, a combination of direct personal observation, social networking, private publications and official information sources will be used.

In opportunity-seeking, much of the information gathered will be 'spillover' information acquired from people who cannot use the information themselves. The entrepreneur is not looking for commercial secrets acquired by eavesdropping on business rivals, but rather information obtained from non-competing sources which is surplus to their requirements. Information about a prospective brownfield site could come from a conversation with a manufacturer who is planning to close his factory, whilst information about the demand for housing could come from a recent arrival to the area who has found it difficult to buy a particular type of home.

This type of information can be acquired at social events such as receptions, club meetings, or even through conversation at the school gates. People barter surplus information through their contributions to general discussion. An entrepreneur can influence the information that they acquire by turning the conversation in particular directions. Normally there is no reason to believe that the other party is lying, because they have no hidden agenda, and so trust is not a crucial issue.

It is, however, important for entrepreneurs that the people to whom they are talking have relevant information to contribute to the conversation. This suggests that the people invited to a reception, or accepted for club membership, should be suitably influential or wealthy. A diversity of members' interests is also useful, as entrepreneurs will learn little that is new by talking to people from exactly the same backgrounds.

Resource Acquisition

Once an opportunity has been identified, the entrepreneur must decide how best to implement it. This will require mobilizing resources of labour and capital. At this point trust becomes a major issue. The entrepreneur needs to trust the financier to reach a quick decision and deliver the funds, and to trust employees to work hard and remain loyal. Social networks help the entrepreneur to make contact with reliable people. Suitable people can be met face-to-face outside the formal environment of the office interview, their behaviour in a more relaxed environment can be accessed, and the information used to predict how they might react to an unexpected problem. Depending on the trust that develops, the entrepreneur may decide to make a deal on the basis of a handshake, to make a deal on the basis of a formal contract, or not to make any deal at all.

Trust is also important because of the confidentiality issue. The entrepreneur requires at least a temporary monopoly of exploitation in order to recover the sunk costs involved in seeking out the opportunity – including the time spent networking. This monopoly would be undermined if a prospective financial backer or prospective employee set up in competition. Fear of imitation means that the entrepreneur cannot afford to disclose the opportunity to people of doubtful trustworthiness. Meeting people socially allows the entrepreneur to assess how far they are discreet.

The entrepreneur can also check people out with other members of the network. It may be possible to talk to customers of the bank from which he/she plans to borrow, and to former employers of the people he/she plans to hire. It is therefore useful if the network contains a mixture of people who have already made contracts with each other or who are about to do so. It is also useful if there are some experienced people present – perhaps as chairpersons or speakers – who can advise the entrepreneur on the criteria that would be best for assessing the most suitable business partner.

A useful type of network for building trust is a church, charity, sports club or hobby club. There is an opportunity for regular meetings and for the discussion of important issues which will reveal the fundamental values and beliefs of the person involved. Religious commitment, degree of compassion, team spirit and single-mindedness can all be assessed from organizations of this type. In general, non-profit voluntary organizations are extremely useful in building trust because the role that a person plays in such an organization, and the way that they play it, signals the degree of commitment that can be expected from them in other situations too. These organizations also provide a safe environment for open discussion because they are not being run in the interests of a profit-seeking owner who could make strategic use of the information being shared.

Resource acquisition therefore calls for a different type of network from that required for the discovery of opportunities.

Market Organization

Market organization is a key aspect of most large-scale entrepreneurial activity. If the entrepreneurial opportunity relates to the innovation of a new product, or a better or cheaper variant of an existing product, then the entrepreneur will need to establish an organization to sell the product. Even if this involves simply setting up a wholesale operation to hold a better range of stock, or a new retail operation to serve a growing residential area, there will be a need to invest in market organization. The entrepreneur appropriates a reward by altering the network of trade in the product concerned. Trade is diverted away from existing channels into new channels that have been set up for this purpose.

To implement the diversion of trade the entrepreneur needs to win customer support. In terms of social networks, this necessitates encouraging potential buyers to join the entrepreneur's customer club. To attract interest the product must be advertised and displayed at a convenient location – typically close to existing outlets where the target customers normally go shopping. They are lured in with introductory offers and then locked in, as far as possible, through a loyalty scheme.

Innovative entrepreneurs marketing consumer products will join the established agglomerations at major retail centres. By locating next to established rivals, they can intercept customers before they make their usual purchases. If successful, they will take market share from their rivals and may even drive some of them out of business; but they may in turn be replaced by other innovators following in their footsteps. In this way agglomerations renew themselves by attracting successive waves of innovators.

Innovation, therefore, alters the configuration of trade in markets. The geography of trade may be unaffected, in the sense that agglomerations at strategic centres such as river estuaries and the feet of mountain passes continue to be the major hubs, but the control of trade will change. New firms, created by innovative entrepreneurs, and dealing in novel products, now own the products from the point at which they leave the factory (or before) to the point at which they are placed in the customers' hands. Entrepreneurship, therefore, provides a dynamic to networks – it exploits networks to discover and implement opportunities, but the implementation of the opportunities feeds back to change the network structures on which the next generation of entrepreneurs depends.

This discussion suggests that each stage of entrepreneurship benefits from membership of a particular type of network

The opportunity-seekers' network involves a regular programme of social events which provides plenty of opportunity for people to circulate. Conversation may be primed by a short lecture or debate, after which there is a reception which affords opportunity for discussion. Members barter surplus information, so there is no particular need for confidentiality. People can circulate freely, and leave as early or as late as they wish. However, participants have to have interesting and important information to 'trade', and so attendance is by invitation only. The guest list is designed to ensure a variety of people from different areas. The event may be tailored to a particular sector, but beyond this, it is pointless to target particular categories of people because no one can predict exactly where opportunities are likely to occur.

The resource acquisition network engages key people in activities which reveal how far they can be trusted. It involves highly-structured social groups, usually with non-profit objectives. These groups have a dual role:

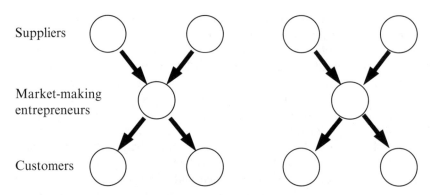

Figure 6.1   Segmented market-making

they support society through good works, and also act as a marketplace where people can meet prospective business partners, and check up on them at the same time. Networks of this type are particularly valuable to bankers looking for businesses in which to invest, and owners of growing businesses looking for additional funds.

The market organization network is essentially a customer club. It may consist of a database of regular customers who receive mail-shots about new products, together with their credit ratings. The club exists to strengthen the firm's reputation and to boost its brand. Celebrities may be paid to 'join the club' and endorse the brand. The firm's product may even become a fashion icon which identifies the consumer as a member of the club. A supplier club may also be useful, based, for example, on a list of suppliers who can be invited to bid for various types of work.

6.7   SCHEMATIC REPRESENTATION

Because networks are inherently complex, it is useful to employ a schematic approach to summarize the arguments (Casson, 1997). Consider an entrepreneur who believes that there may be an opportunity to enter an established market with a new product. The initial state of the market is represented in Figure 6.1. Upstream from the entrepreneur's proposed point of entry are suppliers, represented by the top row of circles, whilst downstream are potential customers for the product, represented by the bottom row of circles. The lines indicate the flows of information that coordinate trade. In the interests of simplicity, the physical flows of resources that result from the trades are not shown in the figure.

At the outset the entrepreneur faces two established rivals which divide

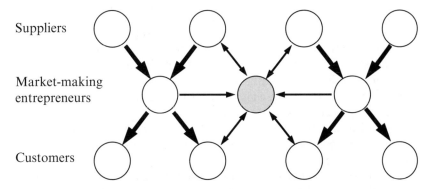

Suppliers

Market-making
entrepreneurs

Customers

Figure 6.2   Integrated market-making

the market between them; these firms intermediate between the suppliers and the customers, and are therefore positioned in the middle row of the figure. Two of the suppliers work for one of the intermediators and two for the other. The figure illustrates the flow of information from the suppliers to the intermediators, and from the intermediators to the customers. Each intermediator serves several customers and acts as a hub.

The intermediators serve two separate segments of the market which initially do not overlap. However, some customers in each segment may be able to switch to the new product. Each customer base therefore contains two groups, one of which is able to switch and one of which is not. The first group is represented by the two circles towards the centre of the diagram on the bottom row and the second by the circles at the left-hand and right-hand sides of the bottom row.

To identify such an opportunity and confirm its existence the entrepreneur needs to make contact with suppliers and customers to discover whether they would indeed be willing to switch. The entrepreneur needs to talk to dissatisfied customers of the established firms who constitute the group that may be prepared to switch, and to suppliers who either have excess capacity or are dissatisfied with the terms they receive from the established intermediators who buy from them. Both customers and suppliers have an incentive to negotiate once the entrepreneur has made contact with them. It is also necessary to obtain information about the established intermediators, but since they will be unwilling to talk to a potential rival this has to be achieved simply by observing their activities.

The entry strategy is summarized schematically in Figure 6.2. The entrant is represented by the shaded circle in the centre of the middle row. Initial information requirements are represented by the thin black lines. These indicate the need for market research through dialogue with representative customers who may be prepared to switch, and discussion with representative suppliers to assess the terms on which they would be willing to supply. Dialogue/discussion involves two-way flows of information and is indicated by arrows which point in both directions. Observation of established rivals, by contrast, involves a one-way flow of information from the rival to the entrepreneur, and so a single arrow is shown.

The entrepreneur may find it difficult to make direct contact with suppliers and customers. However, a social network can provide the opportunity for this. A trade fair might provide the chance to meet suppliers, while if the potential customers are local businesses contacts might be established through the Chamber of Commerce or Rotary Club. If there is a shortage of suitable networks, then government-sponsored events may help.

Just as the entrepreneur intermediates between suppliers and customers, so a social network can intermediate between the entrepreneur and the people he/she wishes to meet. The situation is illustrated in Figure 6.3. Two contact-brokers are shown, each of whom is in touch with both the entrepreneur and a group of people that the entrepreneur wishes to meet. The customer contact-broker provides a forum where the entrepreneur can make contact with potential customers, whilst the supplier contact-broker provides a forum where the entrepreneur can make contact with potential suppliers. While, in principle, a single broker could introduce the entrepreneur to both groups, this is unlikely, since if the two groups found it easy to make contact with each other then there would be no demand for entrepreneurial intermediation, and hence no profit in the activity.

The supplier contact-broker is more than a mere contact-broker, however; as shown in the figure, the role also encompasses that of a reputation-broker. This allows provision of an independent assessment of whether the suppliers whom the entrepreneur has met can be trusted or not. While entrepreneurs are interested in the trustworthiness of both customers and suppliers, an entrepreneur entering a mass market is normally more concerned about quality assurance in the supply chain than in customers' ability to pay. Personal customers who lack reputation generally pay at the time they receive their goods, and specialized intermediaries already exist to manage credit risks relating to customers who pay in arrears.

While the reputation-broker's judgement may be based on personal business experience, it is also possible to utilize information about the clubs and societies to which the suppliers belong. If the supplier belongs to a group that is noted for its strong business morals then the broker can factor this information into the assessment. The use of this information is illustrated in Figure 6.3 by the link between the reputation-broker and the leader of a representative social group to which a supplier belongs.

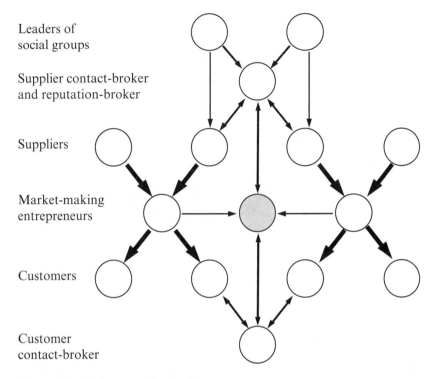

Leaders of
social groups

Supplier contact-broker
and reputation-broker

Suppliers

Market-making
entrepreneurs

Customers

Customer
contact-broker

Figure 6.3   Influence of leadership

The link between the supplier and the leader is shown by the vertical line, whilst the link between the leader and the reputation-broker is shown by the angled line. The link between the leader and the supplier involves the leader influencing the moral obligations of the supplier, and is indicated by the flow of values from the leader to the supplier. Using the link between the leader and the broker, the leader confirms to the broker that the supplier is a member of his/her group and provides a 'reference' for him/her. The broker then passes on this information to the entrepreneur through the vertical link which appears in the middle of the figure.

Having checked out potential customers and suppliers, the entrepreneur can move into the implementation phase. This involves setting up a personal network, as shown in Figure 6.4. The most important step is to make contact with potential customers. The entrepreneur therefore advertises the product. Since it is difficult to target advertising precisely, the messages may also be directed to customers who have little interest in the product. In any case, the entrepreneur may be unsure who exactly falls into the group which is likely to switch as opposed to the group which is not. This

Leaders of
social groups

Suppliers

Market-making
entrepreneurs

Customers

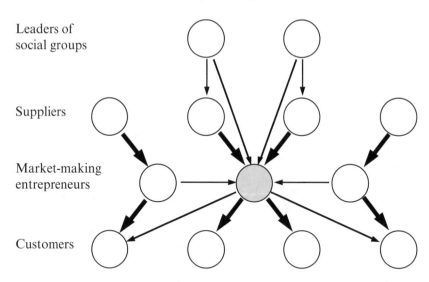

Figure 6.4   Emergence of a major hub

is captured in the diagram by the way in which communication fans out
from the entrepreneur to all the customers in the market.

The entrepreneur may also wish to strengthen relationships with his
suppliers. Despite knowing that they belong to reputable groups, the
entrepreneur might believe that their sense of obligation is even stronger
towards fellow members of their group. It might seem reasonable, therefore, to attempt to join the structured groups to which they belong in order
to reduce potential risk. This strategy will vary according to the type of
group: it could involve studying for a suitable professional qualification,
changing religion or marrying into a supplier's family. The entrepreneur's
affiliation to the suppliers' groups is illustrated by the lines which connect
the entrepreneur directly to the leaders of the relevant groups.

6.8   HORIZONTAL AND VERTICAL NETWORKS

The example above focused on *vertical* relations within a market. Contacts
were made, and trust developed, in order to support a flow of product
from customers to suppliers through an intermediator. The emphasis was
on flows of information between people at different stages of the market
process or involved in different types of activity.

In some contexts, however, flows between people at the same stage
of the market process or involved in the same activity are required for

coordination. Within a team, for example, members doing similar jobs need to communicate with each other in order to coordinate production. Similarly, funding a business may require different investors to team up together. Networks which connect people at similar stages or doing similar work are known as *horizontal* networks.

It is often suggested, with good reason, that vertical networks contribute more to the economy than horizontal ones. The danger with horizontal networks is that they promote collusion: one of the more spectacular examples are drugs cartels as mentioned in the introduction. Buyers may collude to exploit monopsony power, or sellers collude to promote monopoly power. The exercise of market power not only redistributes income but leads to a wasteful restriction of trade, independently of whether the collusion is legal or not.

One form of collusion encourages the other. Buyers who believe they are victims of monopoly may collude to exert countervailing monopsony power – for example, through a consumer cooperative – whilst sellers who believe they are victims of monopsony may seek countervailing monopoly power through a trade association – for example, defence contractors who believe they are exploited by government. In the labour market, the monopsony of the employers' association may confront the monopoly power of the trade union, resulting in collective bargaining over the wage rate. It is for this reason that horizontal networks are often studied in the context of industrial relations and class conflict more generally.

Horizontal networks can also improve economic performance, however – in appropriate circumstances. A group of local producers in a particular industry may benefit from local resources which can only be supplied on a scale too large for any individual producer to support. Specialized transport infrastructure may be required, or a training facility tailored to industry needs. Standards may need to be set to facilitate the interchangeability of components and to reassure the buyers of durable goods that they will not be locked in to any one supplier of replacement parts. Basic R&D may generate new sector-specific know-how that different firms can commercialize in different ways.

In a sense, however, these productive uses of horizontal networks are related to the existence of a vertical network reaching back to a previous stage of production. The firms collaborate in setting up organizations or facilities to supply better transport services, better training, greater standardization and more technological opportunities. Each of the firms is networked to the supplier of the relevant input which is shared by all the user firms. In so far as it is the horizontal initiative that establishes the vertical structure, however, it is remains the case that horizontal networking can be said to promote economic performance.

6.9 POLICY INTERVENTIONS

The argument that networks promote economic performance is often used to justify political interventions which subsidize networking. Most developed economies now promote entrepreneurial networks through fostering partnerships between academic institutions, businesses, venture capitalists and government. It is, however, quite difficult to appraise policy interventions based on 'soft' activities such as networking. Performance measurement indicators can be used to estimate the impact of policies on the productivity and profitability of supported firms relative to the public expenditure involved. But it is an 'act of faith' to interpret the measured outcomes as pure 'networking' effects.

The analysis of social capital developed in this chapter suggests an alternative approach to evaluation, in which impact of policy is measured by the increase in the value of social capital attributable to government support. An initial estimate is obtained by interviewing the participants in the networking activity. The social interactions between members of the network are then mapped out using the schematic technique set out above. The mapping is used to assess how far the effects identified by participants can be safely attributed to the network investments funded by government.

Government interventions involving any kind of business support are typically justified by appeal to market failure. In the absence of public subsidies, market failures may cause private firms to under-invest in networks, leading to a sub-optimal level of communication within the economy. In this context, the 'null hypothesis' used in an evaluation is that the economy already supports an optimal number of business networks, so that there is no need for any subsidy. Network affiliation is time consuming, and a successful entrepreneur will be well aware that 'time is money'. As a result, it can be argued, encouraging business managers to network may simply mean that they spend too much time networking, and too little time attending to their ordinary business affairs.

A straightforward argument for additional networks is that existing ones are simply not good enough. The fact that there is a shortage of really effective networks does not, however, mean that more should be created. Effective networks require effective leadership, and leadership, like any other resource, is scarce. If new networks are created without effective leaders then they are likely to perform worse, not better, than existing ones. There is no way of overcoming the basic problem that scarcity of resources affects both the quantity and quality of the services that can be supplied.

It could be argued that while potential leaders exist, there are inadequate rewards for leadership. It has already been noted that many structured networks are based on non-profit principles. It is usually assumed that leaders derive non-pecuniary rewards from their roles; they may be committed to charitable causes supported by the network, or value the status they achieve, or appreciate the respect they receive from their members and their peers. In a selfish and materialistic culture, however, people may place the pursuit of profit ahead of more traditional non-profit objectives. As a result, potential leaders in the non-profit networks may be diverted into concentrating purely on maximizing the performance of for-profit businesses instead. The solution to this problem lies more in cultural change than in the creation of additional networks, however. Government may be able to improve the supply of leadership by increased public recognition of non-profit leaders. Unfortunately, the promotion of enterprise culture is usually associated with the public recognition of successful businessmen and celebrity entertainers instead.

A variant of this argument is that leaders are frustrated and demoralized by the difficulty of recruiting members – especially active members who will share the effort of running the network. This is consistent with the recent experience of many churches and charities, and public bodies that rely on unpaid volunteers to join parish councils, school management boards and so on. The basic problem is still the same, however; it lies in the way in which people prioritize competing demands on their time. The 'long hours' culture – particularly evident in the US and UK – leaves people little time for non-work activities. This explanation suggests that voluntary networks will be dominated by people who are either in retirement or are working part-time. Ironically, the UK government itself is widely seen as endorsing such trends, through the deregulation of shopping hours, the liberalization of the media, and its opposition to the limitation of working hours (Bunting, 2004). An unintended byproduct of its policies may therefore be the erosion of the social infrastructure on which entrepreneurial activity depends.

Social exclusion is sometimes invoked as a reason why more networks are needed (Andall, 2000; Pang and Lau, 1998). However, networks focused on the socially excluded may not appeal to other people. A network of excluded people may well prove successful in tackling local social problems such as vandalism on a housing estate. But a network of this type is unlikely to promote enterprise unless the excluded people have sufficient business experience and financial resources to benefit from contacts established between themselves. While some networks, such as immigrant ethnic networks, may well contain people of considerable entrepreneurial ability who generate significant benefits for other members (Basu, 2004), a network composed entirely of people who have failed in business may well develop a 'victim' mentality which actually discourages them from making a fresh start. Although public sector professionals may facilitate such groups in order to encourage positive thinking, they may not possess the experience, or the credibility, to promote an entrepreneurial outlook.

If special groups cannot address exclusion, then, it could be suggested that excluded people should be admitted to established groups. The difficulty here is that it can be dangerous to meddle in the operation of established groups. If exclusion is based on ignorance and prejudice then, when the new members join, they will be welcomed once they are recognized as an asset to the group. But if the people who were excluded disrupt a group when they join then its performance will be impaired; bad members will drive out good, and the group will go into decline. New groups will be set up by the former members, and the previous discrimination by type of member will be reproduced. Indeed, the division may be even worse as the new groups become even more exclusive in the light of previous experience.

There is insufficient evidence at present to say whether or not the limitations of networking policies outlined above are significant or not. While the network approach to social capital set out in this chapter raises a number of potential concerns, this does not mean that these concerns represent significant constraints in practice.

6.10 CONCLUSION

This chapter has examined in detail the key concepts of networks, trust and social capital. Each of these concepts links in to a large literature which connects the discussion of social capital to a bewildering variety of topics. Concepts such as 'network' and 'trust' have different meanings in different contexts, but equally, there are certain core ideas that are independent of context. Connectivity, for example, features in all the applications of these concepts.

This chapter has focused on the issue of building entrepreneurial networks which will improve the performance of the economy. It has argued that different types of social network are required for different purposes. Some types of networks are most useful in the early stages of entrepreneurial activity and others at later stages.

Policy interventions need to be precisely targeted in order to maximize their impact, but targeting cannot be effective if the underlying analysis is fuzzy. Effective networks are created around reputable people. In the long run, reputable institutions sustain their reputations through the calibre of the people they employ. It is important that government does not overestimate its own reputation, and assume that any network that it sponsors will 'leverage' its reputation successfully.

Government reputation, like any form of reputation, is specific, and 'extending the brand' to encompass new forms of business support may take government into areas where its reputation carries little weight. There are already many different social groups which support business activity, either directly or indirectly, and it is possible that government might achieve better results by strengthening the activities of these groups, rather than by subsidizing the establishment of new groups that compete with them. Rigorous evaluation is needed to inform decisions on the appropriate types of network to support.

REFERENCES

Aldrich, Howard E. (1987), 'The impact of social networks on business founding and profit: a longtitudinal approach', in Neil Churchill et al. (eds), *Frontiers of Entrepreneurship Research*, Wellesley, MA: Babson College, pp. 154–68.

Aldrich, Howard E. and C. Zimmer (1986), 'Entrepreneurship through social networks', in D.L. Sexton and R. Smilor (eds), *The Art and Science of Entrepreneurship*, Cambridge, MA: Ballinger, pp. 3–23.

Anderson, A.R. and S.L. Jack (2002), 'The articulation of social capital in entrepreneurial networks: a glue or lubricant?', *Entrepreneurship and Regional Development*, **14**, 193–210.

Andall, J. (2000), *Gender, Migration and Domestic Service: The Politics of Black Women in Italy*, Aldershot: Ashgate.

Basu, Anuradha (2004), 'Entrepreneurial aspirations amongst family business owners: an analysis of ethnic business owners in the United Kingdom', *International Journal of Entrepreneurial Behaviour and Research*, **10** (1), 12–33.

Bowles, Samuel and H. Gintis (2002), 'Social capital and community governance', *Economic Journal*, **112** (483), F419–F436.

Brown, John Seeley and Paul Duguid (2002), 'Local knowledge: innovation in the network age', *Management Learning*, **33** (4), 427–38.

Bunting, Madeleine (2004), *Willing Slaves: How the Overwork Culture is Ruling Our Lives*, London: HarperCollins.

Casson, Mark (1997), *Information and Organization*, Oxford: Clarendon Press.

Casson, Mark and Marina Della Giusta (2004), 'The costly business of trust', *Development Policy Review*, **22** (3), 321–42.

Casson, Mark and Marina Della Giusta (2005), 'Economics of trust', in Aks Zaheer and Reinhard Bachmann (eds), *Handbook of Trust Research*, Cheltenham, UK and Northampton, MA, USA: Edward Elgar, pp. 332–54.

Casson, Mark and Mary Rose (1997), 'Introduction to the special issue on Institutions and the Evolution of Modern Business', *Business History*, **39** (4), 1–8.

Coleman, James S. (1988), 'Social capital in the creation of human capital', *American Journal of Sociology*, **94** (Supplement), 95–120.

Dasgupta, P. and I. Serageldin (2000), *Social Capital: A Multi-faceted Perspective*, Washington, DC: The World Bank.

Della Giusta, Marina (1999), 'A model of social capital and access to productive resources', *Journal of International Development*, **11**, 921–34.

Doreian, Patrick and Frans N. Stokman (1997), *Evolution of Social Networks*, Amsterdam: Gordon and Breach.

Gambetta, Diego (ed.) (1988), *Trust: Making and Breaking Cooperative Relationships*, Oxford: Blackwell.

Granovetter, M. (1985), 'Economic action and social structure: the problem of embeddedness', *American Journal of Sociology*, **91**, 481–510.

Hardin, R. (1993), 'The street-level epistemology of trust', *Politics and Society*, **21** (4), 505–29.

Himanen, Pekka and Manuel Castells (2004), 'Institutional models of the network society: Silicon Valley and Finland', in M. Castells (ed.), *The Network Society: A Cross-cultural Perspective*, Cheltenham, UK and Northampton, MA, USA: Edward Elgar, pp. 49–83.

Johannison, B. (1988), 'Business formation: a network approach', *Scandinavian Journal of Management*, **4** (3/4), 83–99.

Knack, S. and P. Keefer (1997), 'Does social capital have an economic pay-off? A cross-country investigation', *Quarterly Journal of Economics*, **112** (4), 1251–88.

Pang, M. and A. Lau (1998), 'The Chinese in Britain: working towards success?' *International Journal of Human Resource Management*, **9** (5), 862–74.

Portes, Alejandro and Patricia Landolt (1996), 'The downside of social capital', *American Prospect*, **26** (May–June), 18–21.

Putnam, Robert (1993), *Making Democracy Work: Civic Tradition in Modern Italy*, Princeton, NJ: Princeton University Press.

Putnam, Robert (2001), *Bowling Alone: The Collapse and Revival of American Community*, New York: Simon & Schuster.

Wasserman, S. and K. Faust (1994), *Social Network Analysis: Methods and Applications*, Cambridge: Cambridge University Press.

7. Co-operatives as entrepreneurial institutions

With Marina Della Giusta

This chapter examines the circumstances under which an entrepreneur would choose to establish a co-operative rather than a conventional firm. The modern institutional theory of the firm analyses a variety of institutional forms, including firms, markets, networks and governments, but fails to take account of the role of the entrepreneur in establishing these institutions and influencing their operations. A standard argument about the benefits of co-operation is that it can improve efficiency by building trust, thereby reducing transaction costs. Participation in the ownership or governance of an institution can raise members' status and reputation, enhance their non-pecuniary rewards, and strengthen peer-group pressures to perform well. However, performance could be undermined if participation also reduces internal specialization. Different patterns of participation are distinguished, including a neglected form of co-operation involving job rotation. It is argued that co-operation is likely to be under-supplied in a competitive market economy because some of the benefits are external to the co-operative itself. This provides a case for subsidizing co-operatives in order to improve the overall performance of the economy.

7.1 INTRODUCTION

Co-operative organization is popularly perceived as an alternative to entrepreneurial organization. The entrepreneur is regarded as the personification of profit-seeking in a private enterprise economy. The entrepreneur's profits are extracted from the firm at the expense of the employees, critics allege, and the appropriation of profit is therefore a form of exploitation. Historically, this critique of entrepreneurial capitalism was an important motive for early co-operators, such as the Rochdale Pioneers of Victorian Britain.

There is an alternative view, however. Following the earlier chapters, entrepreneurship can be defined, not in terms of private profit-seeking, but in terms of the quality of judgement in decision-making. On this view, it is the competence of the entrepreneur, rather than the motivation, that is the distinguishing feature of entrepreneurship. This alternative approach leaves open the possibility that an entrepreneur could be driven by altruism as well as by purely selfish motives.

An entrepreneur who sought to discover projects that would benefit society as a whole might well, under certain circumstances, decide to establish a co-operative rather than a conventional private firm. In Britain, the retailer John Lewis and the architect Ove Arup are iconic examples of entrepreneurs who did exactly this. By giving employees a financial stake in the firm, and a right to be consulted, co-operative entrepreneurs may encourage their members to devote more effort to their work than they would if they were ordinary wage-earners.

Sceptics doubt the possibility of altruistic motivation, and argue that altruistic motivations can always be reduced to some form of enlightened self-interest. It is certainly true that the behaviour of rational individuals always reflects their preferences, but if someone prefers to sacrifice their material interests to those of others then there is nothing inherently irrational in doing so. In this sense an altruistic entrepreneur can serve the material interests of others in order to further their own moral interests. An altruistic entrepreneur may become happy when making other people better off; by making others better off they make themselves happier too.

7.2   KEY ISSUES IN COOPERATION

Modern institutional economics identifies a variety of institutional forms, including firms, markets, networks and governments (Williamson, 1985; Casson, 1997). It is therefore appropriate to ask 'What is gained by introducing co-operatives into this framework?' The answer is that co-operatives are an efficient solution to certain types of coordination problem. Co-operation can improve efficiency by building trust and thereby reducing transaction costs, but it may also reduce efficiency by reducing specialization.

Section 7.3 examines the relationship between co-operatives and other institutions. It identifies six main dimensions along which institutions differ, and positions co-operatives relative to the other forms along these dimensions. It is argued that a co-operative is a distinctive type of institution, and not merely a combination of existing types recognized by the theory.

Section 7.4 considers how best to define a co-operative. A definition is sought which has good theoretical credentials. Previous writers on co-operatives have identified a number of characteristics which they claim are key, including non-profit objectives, a strong egalitarian ideology and a preference for collective self-sufficiency. These criteria are all rejected, however, in favour of defining a co-operative as an institution whose members are expected to fulfil two or more distinct roles, and in particular to participate actively in management. By requiring people to take on two or more roles, a co-operative institution deliberately constrains the application of the principle of specialization. So far as their role as managers is concerned, members may either take personal responsibility for some specific area of management, or merely share collective responsibility for supervising a salaried manager with specialized skills.

There is little point in constraining the scope for specialization unless there is some corresponding benefit. Section 7.5 identifies this benefit with the principle of mutuality. Mutuality reinforces incentives to honesty, hard work and loyalty to the institution, and thereby affords potential efficiency gains. Mutuality is related to concepts of empathy and reciprocity, but has a distinctive logic of its own. A co-operative maximizes the potential for obtaining gains from mutuality.

Section 7.6 examines the various forms that co-operative institutions can take in practice. It shows that a wide variety of seemingly unrelated institutions are in fact related by their embodiment of co-operative principles. This insight is a direct consequence of defining co-operatives in accordance with theoretical principles, rather than simply assuming that any institution that calls itself a co-operative is truly co-operative, and that an institution that does not call itself a co-operative is not.

Sections 7.7 and 7.8 consider two issues raised by the collective nature of management within a co-operative. Section 7.7 considers whether factions could develop within a co-operative, which could paralyse collective decision-making. If there were a high degree of specialization within the workforce, or amongst the customer base, then vested interests could develop which sought to influence management decisions in opposite directions. One way of tackling this is to extend the principle of mutuality to relations between one worker and another, or between one customer and other, by reducing the degree of specialization amongst them. So far as workers are concerned, organized job rotation, and encouragement for workers to be flexible, will give workers' experience of each others' jobs and thereby reduce the potential for conflict. Industries and activities that facilitate job rotation are therefore particularly suitable for co-operative organization.

Section 7.8 considers whether the collective style of management within a co-operative leaves any room for the creative activity of the entrepreneur. It is argued that while entrepreneurship is more difficult within a co-operative, as the entrepreneur cannot acquire personal ownership of the institution, it is not impossible, provided that the entrepreneur has the leadership skills necessary to influence opinion amongst the membership in order to legitimate his/her competitive strategies in terms of the ideological principles of the institution.

Section 7.9 argues that the benefits of mutuality conferred by a co-operative spillover outside the institution into society as a whole, reducing transaction costs more generally and thereby boosting the performance of the private sector too. There is therefore a case for selective and carefully targeted subsidies to co-operative enterprises. The propensity of states to support co-operative enterprises in the past is nowhere near as misguided as it may appear, and selective subsidies to co-operatives may well prove an enlightened policy for the future.

7.3   CO-OPERATION AND THE INSTITUTIONAL THEORY OF THE FIRM

The modern institutional theory of the firm begins with the question raised by Coase (1937): if markets coordinate the allocation of resources, and firms also coordinate the allocation of resources, why do we need both institutions? If markets are best then all coordination can be effected by legal contracts negotiated in competitive markets; if firms are best then all coordination can be effected by a single giant enterprise. The answer, of course, lies in the fact that coordination is a costly process. Different forms of coordination incur different costs, and economic efficiency requires that the lowest cost method of coordination is chosen in any given case.

The basic notion that the coordination of resource use is a costly process, and that different institutional arrangements incur different co-ordination costs, is a very general insight with wide-ranging implications. It is therefore unduly restrictive to apply it simply to a comparison of firms and markets. There are various ways in which its application can be extended (Casson, 1995, Chapter 3).

Intermediate institutions: inter-firm networks   Firm and market can be regarded as the two extremes, with another type of institution being located in the middle. This institution is often described as a network (see Chapter 5). Typically, writers on networks are concerned with high-trust inter-firm relationships, often localized in industrial districts. These networks can be regarded as markets based on informal open-ended or long-term contracts, rather than on the formal short-term contracts found in the typical market. In addition, contracts are typically enforced through peer-group pressure exerted by network members, rather than by appeal to the law as an external force.

Coercive institutions: government Firms, markets and networks all rely on the voluntary principle to some degree, but government relies on coercion. Obligations include paying taxes, military conscription, and obedience to the law, and default on any count can lead to imprisonment. By contrast, no one is forced to participate in a market, though in a highly specialized economy people would find it hard to avoid markets altogether and become entirely self-sufficient. Similarly, people do not have to join a firm if they do not wish to follow orders, and are free to quit on giving the agreed amount of notice, although people in certain occupations may find it difficult to practise their craft without joining a firm of some description, and people living in remote areas may have little alternative to working for the dominant employer unless they are willing to emigrate.

From an institutional perspective, government coercion is justified by appeal to the free-rider problem in the provision of public goods. If people were simply invited to contribute to the costs of providing defence, or merely exhorted to respect the rights of fellow citizens, then purely selfish people would leave others to make the sacrifice involved. Public services would be under-provided, and the burden would fall unfairly on those with the strongest sense of moral obligation.

Clubs and associations Clubs supply public goods on a voluntary basis. They operate by excluding non-members from benefits (Olson, 1965). Unlike an ordinary market, members pay a subscription, rather than a separate charge for each service. Clubs are normally non-profit institutions: surpluses are carried forward, and invested in promoting the corporate objectives of the club. As a non-profit organization, a club is therefore like a government, but without the element of coercion. Social activity plays an important role in most clubs, and relations between members are expected to be cordial. In this respect the club resembles a network, although its structure is more formal. Some clubs, such as churches and sports clubs, correspond to interpersonal networks, whilst others – such as trade associations – resemble the inter-firm networks described above.

Given that there are all these different coordinating mechanisms, what is there left for co-operatives to do? In terms of Coase's original question, what do co-operatives add once markets, firms, networks, government and clubs have all performed their respective roles? Some might argue that there is no longer anything for them to do – that co-operatives are only useful when the market system is immature, and that as the market system matures, the scope for co-operation is reduced. While there may still be scope for co-operatives in some developing countries where market institutions remain weak, it could be claimed, it is only a matter of time before this problem is resolved.

This chapter rejects this negative view. It argues that co-operation has positive benefits, although it also incurs certain costs. Institutional theory suggests that when co-operatives play to their strengths, they will concentrate on the coordination of particular types of activity, and leave others to be coordinated by other modes. Co-operation is not an ideological antidote to other forms of coordination, but rather a useful complement to them – a mechanism that can address situations in which other mechanisms are relatively weak.

Understanding cooperation is also particularly relevant as it constitutes the core coordinating mechanism in the social economy or third sector – that is, among those socio-economic activities which are neither pure business nor public sector – which has recently become the focus of academic enquiry particularly in relation to social enterprises in their various forms (from businesses with social aims to charities engaging in profitable trading) (Defourny, 2001).

Table 7.1 suggests how co-operation compares with other coordinating mechanisms. The table examines six dimensions along which coordinating mechanisms differ, and indicates the position of each mechanism along each dimension using a particular letter. Where a mechanism spans an entire dimension, two letters are given.

Government and market appear as the two most distinctive modes. Markets are the only institution to promote short-term relationships at the expense of long-term relationships. This is what gives markets their extreme flexibility. People belonging to other institutions can always opt into the market at short notice, and the fact that so many people do so regularly increases market liquidity. Government is the only institution committed to coercion: anyone who resides in its territory is subject to its power.

None of the four dimensions uniquely differentiates one type of institution from another. For example, both markets and government involve relatively impersonal relations between parties – an impersonality that is often valued as an assurance of impartiality. By contrast, both networks, clubs and households involve personal relations. Firms cannot be classified easily according to this dimension, because some – such as small family firms – rely mainly on personal relationships, whilst others – such as large managerial firms – rely mainly on impersonal relationships. Co-operatives are similar to networks, clubs and households, in that their relations tend to be personal.

Table 7.1   A classification of seven coordinating mechanisms according to six criteria

	Market	Firm	Network	Govern-ment	Club	Co-operative	Households
Voluntary (V)/ Coercive (C)	V	V	V	C	V	V	C
Short-term (S) / Long-term (L) relations	S	L	L	L	L	L	L
Personal (P)/ Impersonal (I) relations	I	I/P	P	I	P	P	P
Pay-as-you-go charging (C) / Subscription (S)	C	C	C	S	S	C	S
Egalitarian (E) / Authoritarian relations (A)	E	A	E	A	E	E/A	A
Motivation: Self-interest (S) / Multi-interests (M)	S	S	S/M	M	M	M	M

Firms, markets and networks all charge people for specific services on a 'pay-as-you-go' basis. By contrast, clubs normally charge subscriptions, whilst government demands a compulsory 'subscription' in the form of general taxation. Subscriptions are charged because clubs and governments supply public goods which are shared by the members, so that members cannot negotiate for something that others do not want. Co-operatives generally provide specific services, and therefore operate on a pay-as-you go basis – for example, the goods supplied by a purchasing co-operative are paid for according to the quantity that each member takes.

In a market, network or club, relationships are generally egalitarian – the parties involved are all of roughly equal status. In a market, for example, a large firm may have more financial and political influence than the individual consumers it supplies, but a consumer – as a customer – still has considerable power, especially if they can choose whether or not to recommend the firm to their friends. Similarly, the senior members of a club may be more influential than the junior ones, but they still need to canvass the support of the junior members in order to get elected to office. Within a firm or government, working relationships are normally based on authority. A co-operative is an interesting intermediate case. The daily work of the co-operative may be coordinated through a line of authority involving, perhaps, a salaried manager, but the members who carry out the orders may also determine collectively, through a meeting, the policy that the manager is implementing. In one sense, therefore, they are sub-ordinates within an authority system, yet in another sense they constitute a governing elite.

7.4   DEFINING COOPERATION

The preceding analysis suffers from the deficiency that the key concept – the co-operative – has been discussed without first being defined. There are surprisingly few definitions of co-operatives offered by economists. To say that co-operatives are institutions whose members co-operate – or attempt to do so – does not advance matters very far because the concept of co-operation itself remains ambiguous in the literature (see, for example, Potter, 1907; Kropotkin, 1915; Thomas and Logan, 1982; Bradley and Gelb, 1983).

A satisfactory definition must appeal to theory. The main function of a co-operative, according to this chapter, is to facilitate coordination. Its value derives from the fact that it can improve upon alternative methods of coordination in certain cases. It is necessary, however, to establish that a co-operative is more than just a variant of some other type of institution, such as a firm or a club. What qualities are unique to a co-operative, and how exactly do they promote coordination?

The lack of an agreed theory-based definition of co-operatives has led many writers to adopt a purely descriptive approach: an institution is a co-operative if it calls itself a co-operative, or refers in its name to the principle of mutuality. As a result, a very diverse collection of institutions have been defined as co-operatives. All they appear to have in common is that their founders have believed it to be advantageous to use the term 'co-operative' in their name, or to associate themselves with an established national or international co-operative movement. Conversely, there may be many 'co-operative' institutions – such as inter-firm joint ventures – which are excluded from the discussion. It is quite possible that some types of excluded institution may have more in common with some types of included institution than one included institution has with another.

Co-operation is often contrasted with competition. Under competition, ownership of different resources is assigned to different people, who nego-tiate to buy the resources they desire but do not own, and sell the resources they own but do not need for themselves. In the negotiations, buyers play sellers off against each other, whilst the sellers play off the buyers. With many buyers and many sellers, none of whom owns a dominant share of any given resource, negotiation leads to a situation of competitive equilibrium in which no resource owner can expect to improve their own situation further.

Under co-operation, the ownership of resources may be vested collectively in the members of some institution, each of whom has a vote. The members debate the allocation of resources and come up with a collective decision. A consensus will normally emerge, however, only if all the owners share a common objective and possess a shared perception of the constraints under which the objective must be pursued. If consensus is unlikely, then some other decision-making principle, such as majority rule, may be used instead.

It is also possible to apply the notion of co-operation to a system of individual ownership. Indeed, it is one of the main principles of institutional economics that ordinary competitive markets require a degree of co-operation, because unless there is mutual respect amongst transactors, they will cheat. Indeed, it is possible to go further, and to argue that the entire market process is just a 'game', with traders acting as players, and negotiating with each other according to the rules of this game. On this view, even the competitive process of negotiation involves co-operation, as there needs to be a common language and a common set of conventions for the communication and recording of offers and bids.

Since it is difficult to sustain the notion that co-operation is the opposite of competition, it is necessary to consider alternative approaches. Early writers on co-operation often contrasted co-operation with private monopoly rather than with competition. It was alleged, for example, that local retailers – the corner shops or village stores – often possessed a degree of local monopoly power, because customers faced a long walk to an alternative shop. Other critics of capitalism argued that in an industrial society, economies of scale in production turn competition into an unstable process which normally finishes up with a monopoly. Thus even if the local store were run by the community it would still have to buy its products wholesale from private monopolies. This explains why local co-operatives often federated together – they perceived a need to exploit similar economies of scale if they were to compete with the private monopolies. Thus retail co-operatives integrated backwards to form wholesale co-operatives, in order to escape from monopoly at the upstream stage of production.

The same line of argument can be applied to other sources of monopoly power. A national or international co-operative could disseminate a technology to local co-operatives which would allow them to compete with a proprietary technology controlled by a multinational firm. This strategy has been employed to help farmers avoid becoming dependent on proprietary seed strains developed by multinational agribusinesses. Alternatively, a co-operative could establish a brand – perhaps embodying the values of social responsibility – to compete with a private brand that instead fostered a spirit of competitive individualism. An interesting feature of this approach is that it leads to a simple testable proposition: that co-operatives will be most common in sectors where the private sector has a significant degree of monopoly power.

The difficulty with this approach, however, is that it classifies as a co-operative any non-profit institution that competes against a private monopoly. It says nothing about the way that the institution is organized, and could therefore be applied to any state-owned producer or a charity engaged in trade (such as Oxfam Trading – a high street retail operation – or the National Trust – which is a major supplier of leisure and tourism services in the UK).

In this context, it is interesting to note that in the business strategy literature, some private ventures have been described as 'co-operative' even though they operate on a for-profit basis. Joint ventures have always been a prominent feature of international business activity, but until the early 1980s most joint venture partnerships involved a private foreign investor and a local firm – often a state-owned firm – in the host economy. In many cases the joint venture was the consequence of a requirement imposed by a suspicious host government that wished to monitor the foreign investor, and to appropriate a share of the profit. In the early 1980s, however, there was a remarkable growth in joint ventures between private firms themselves, and this raised the question of whether joint ventures could be viewed as a 'co-operative' form of business.

Buckley and Casson (1988) argued that the aim of a co-operative joint venture is to engineer trust between the partner firms. A minimum degree of trust is necessary to start a joint venture, because of the initial commitment involved. The venture would develop successfully if trust evolved, because the level of commitment could then increase. Not all joint ventures would be co-operative, however, for the reasons given above.

The mere fact that an activity is jointly owned does not make it co-operative, however. By definition, joint-stock companies, which are the backbone of modern capitalism, are jointly owned by different shareholders. A joint venture, from this perspective, is simply a special application of the joint-stock principle in which there are a very small number of owners who are not individuals but other firms.

A major consideration when identifying a joint venture as co-operative was that the owners would also be contributing key resources, such as know-how, and participating in the management of the firm. The owners were not therefore merely passive 'portfolio' investors, but stakeholders who played a variety of roles. They regarded these roles as interdependent: thus the partners not only shared the equity and contributed know-how, but used their influence as owners to negotiate the uses to which their know-how was put.

The number of partners in a joint venture is an important influence on the extent to which the partners can actively participate in management. Where an institution has many joint owners, it is difficult for individual owners to have much say in its long-term strategy, but where there are relatively few, individual owners are likely to be more influential. The annual general meeting of a large joint-stock company with a diversified group of shareholders is unlikely to challenge the decisions of senior managers, but the regular monthly meeting of joint venture partners or the members of a club may provide a genuine opportunity for an individual owner or member to put forward their personal point of view. From this perspective, it is the level of involvement in management that is the key feature of the co-operative. Owners exercise their rights to manage rather than just delegating these powers to salaried professional managers.

Just because people are able to influence the management of a venture does not mean that they will necessarily wish to do so, however. Participation in management is time-consuming, and can be frustrating if agreement on decisions is difficult to reach. There are several factors that may encourage a person to seek influence over management.

A person is likely to want a say in management if they are not being directly paid for their contribution, but depend for their reward on the kind of work they are required to do. A volunteer working for a charity, for example, is, by definition, not paid for their work, but may derive non-pecuniary rewards from certain types of job that they are asked to perform. Some jobs may be more rewarding than others, however. This gives them an interest is acquiring some influence over the jobs to which they are assigned. A participatory approach to management in which people can volunteer for jobs they enjoy doing can help to retain the loyalty of productive members who have strong preferences for what kind of work they do.

Even where people are paid, though, they may still be concerned about the size of their non-pecuniary rewards. Some of the most able and energetic people in an institution may be those who are committed to certain moral or ideological goals. The value of the rewards they derive from working for the institution may depend upon the institution remaining committed to these goals. To reduce the risk that their efforts are nullified, they need to have an influence on the overall strategy of the institution.

Where teamwork is involved, committed individuals will be aware that their own efforts could be undermined by the apathy or laziness of others. If they have a substantial stake in the institution, either as owners or as recipients of substantial non-pecuniary rewards, then they have an incentive to ensure that other members of the team are well-motivated too. If participation in management improves motivation, then they have an incentive for others to participate in management as well. Furthermore, management meetings provide an opportunity for them to share their ideological commitments with their colleagues.

One reason why participation in management improves motivation is that people feel more responsibility for implementing strategies when they have approved the strategies themselves, and may even have helped to develop them. They may well feel much guiltier about shirking if they know that they endorsed the job they are expected to do, rather than having had it imposed upon them. Similarly, the sense of shame will be greater if they are caught shirking by their colleagues. Participation may not improve the facility for monitoring, but it does increase the potential sanctions against a shirker. It removes the excuse that they are only shirking because they are working under duress; it also means that there may be an opportunity at a management meeting for more highly committed members to 'name and shame' them in front of their colleagues.

From this perspective, therefore, the key feature of a co-operative is that people who are involved as workers, suppliers or customers are also actively involved as managers. They may either occupy executive positions, or belong to a non-executive board. In the latter case, they will normally be the joint owners of the institution.

The most comprehensive definition of a co-operative is the one supplied by the International Co-operative Alliance (2005), which is exhibited in Table 7.2. Whilst this definition is very useful for certain purposes, it is difficult to integrate it into the framework of the institutional theory of the firm. The definition refers to a co-operative as a 'jointly-owned and democratically-controlled enterprise' – a description that could equally well be applied, according to proponents of market capitalism, to a joint-stock company. It cannot really be said that a joint-stock company is undemocratic, since it has a system of representation of shareholder interests by elected directors who report back at an annual meeting.

The difference between a joint-stock company and a co-operative lies in the fact that the owners have additional responsibilities. In a producer co-operative they may be expected to work for the co-operative, in a purchasing co-operative they may be expected to buy from the co-operative, and so on. The converse also applies: if they work for the co-operative, or purchase from it, they are expected to share in the ownership too. There may be further conditions: for example, some health-food co-operatives expect members not only to buy from the co-operative but also to serve as volunteer shop-workers.

An important feature of the ICA definition is the emphasis on non-

Table 7.2   Statement of co-operative principles by the International Co-operative Alliance

---

Definition

A co-operative is an autonomous association of persons united voluntarily to meet their common economic, social, and cultural needs and aspirations through a jointly-owned and democratically-controlled enterprise.

Values

Co-operatives are based on the values of self-help, self-responsibility, democracy, equality, equity and solidarity. In the tradition of their founders, co-operative members believe in the ethical values of honesty, openness, social responsibility and caring for others.

Principles

The co-operative principles are guidelines by which co-operatives put their values into practice.

1st Principle: Voluntary and Open Membership

Co-operatives are voluntary organisations, open to all persons able to use their services and willing to accept the responsibilities of membership, without gender, social, racial, political or religious discrimination.

2nd Principle: Democratic Member Control

Co-operatives are democratic organisations controlled by their members, who actively participate in setting their policies and making decisions. Men and women serving as elected representatives are accountable to the membership. In primary co-operatives members have equal voting rights (one member, one vote) and co-operatives at other levels are also organised in a democratic manner.

3rd Principle: Member Economic Participation

Members contribute equitably to, and democratically control, the capital of their co-operative. At least part of that capital is usually the common property of the co-operative. Members usually receive limited compensation, if any, on capital subscribed as a condition of membership. Members allocate surpluses for any or all of the following purposes: developing their co-operative, possibly by setting up reserves, part of which at least would be indivisible; benefiting members in proportion to their transactions with the co-operative; and supporting other activities approved by the membership.

4th Principle: Autonomy and Independence

Co-operatives are autonomous, self-help organisations controlled by their members. If they enter to agreements with other organisations, including governments, or raise capital from external sources, they do so on terms that ensure democratic control by their members and maintain their co-operative autonomy.

Table 7.2   (continued)

5th Principle: Education, Training and Information
Co-operatives provide education and training for their members, elected
representatives, managers, and employees so they can contribute effectively
to the development of their co-operatives. They inform the general public -
particularly young people and opinion leaders - about the nature and benefits of
co-operation.

6th Principle: Co-operation among Co-operatives
Co-operatives serve their members most effectively and strengthen the co-
operative movement by working together through local, national, regional and
international structures.

7th Principle: Concern for Community
Co-operatives work for the sustainable development of their communities
through policies approved by their members.

Source: International Co-operative Alliance (2005).

profit orientation. The ICA expects co-operatives, in common with other
non-profit institutions, to re-invest surpluses rather than to distribute
them as dividends to members. This implies that when members subscribe
capital in order to become owners, they do not do so in expectation of
financial return. In this respect, the purchase of capital represents a joining
fee. In practice, of course, some retail co-operatives declare dividends,
and it is quite possible for members to receive substantial pay-offs when a
co-operative is wound up, or demutualized and sold off to a private firm.
Since networks, clubs and government are also non-profit institutions,
the non-profit nature of a co-operative emphasized by the ICA does not
differentiate the co-operative from other institutions recognized by the
institutional theory of the firm, and so it is not considered an essential
characteristic of a co-operative for the purposes of this chapter.

   The ICA's rejection of profit-orientation is linked to its endorsement
of other values. These include 'self-help' and 'self-responsibility' – values
which could be interpreted, in a different context as an expression of High
Victorian individualism rather than as co-operation. The solution to this
apparent paradox appears to be that the 'self' referred to in these terms is
the corporate body rather than an individual member of it. It is a statement that the co-operative seeks to be independent of outside agency, and
in particular to avoid dependence on private institutions. This notion is
reinforced by the seventh principle set out in Table 7.2, which recommends
that co-operatives establish ties with other co-operatives, rather than with
private institutions. The ICA definition suggests, therefore, that the co-

operative movement as a whole should be largely self-sufficient, or even autarkic, and should avoid embedding itself within the market system.

The difficulty with this autarkic view, however, is that it seems to reject on principle any gains from trade that might arise from relations between the co-operative sector and the private sector. This principle would make it very difficult to implement the underlying notion of the institutional theory of the firm that co-operatives are efficient in some contexts but inefficient in others, and that co-operatives should therefore be encouraged to flourish within a market environment whenever the particular function they perform will benefit from co-operative organization. The autarkic view suggests, instead, an ideological polarization between an economic system based on co-operation on the one hand and a system based on private profit on the other, which coexist, each with their own membership, in each country. In practice, though, most co-operatives purchase specialized services from the private sector, rather than going to the trouble of providing them for themselves – for example, co-operatives not only purchase stationery and energy supplies, and rent premises, but employ specialist managers and accountants, as described below. In view of its limited practical relevance, this autarkic view of the co-operative is therefore rejected in this chapter.

The values of 'equality, equity and solidarity', also referred to by the ICA, have a closer bearing on institutional economics. They can be understood as principles of internal organization which will stimulate trust between members. Equality suggests that no member has more authority than others, and equity suggests that all members receive similar pecuniary or material rewards. This implies that there will be no dominant shareholder amongst the owners. If it is taken literally, it also suggests that there will be no chief executive, because such a position would dominate the management team. In practice, however, many so-called co-operatives have a chief executive, who is often a salaried manager, hired as an ordinary employee, and who possesses professional skills that ordinary members lack. The manager may not be a full member of the institution, however, but might report to a management board comprising the ordinary members, or their elected representatives, who have powers of dismissal if the manager does not perform well. By ensuring that the supplier of a specialist input is not a full member, the co-operative can prevent any member exerting a greater influence than others. In the context of ownership, this means that no member has a dominant shareholding, and in the context of management it means that management is shared, or supplied by an independent specialist who reports to the membership as a whole.

The defining characteristic of a co-operative is therefore that suppliers of inputs, or users of outputs, also have a role as either owners or managers of the institution. Those who join the institution are expected to play an active part in ownership or management, or both, in order to prevent any other individual from acquiring a dominant position in this respect. Conversely, the owners or managers act as either suppliers of inputs or users of outputs, or possibly both. Owners are not allowed to increase their shareholding beyond a certain limit, and managers are not allowed to exercise disproportionate power unless they forgo the right to be members and become salaried employees instead.

From this perspective, the key feature of a co-operative is that functional specialization is limited. Individuals do not specialize in particular roles, as is the case in an ordinary firm where shareholders bear the risk, managers take executive decisions, workers supply effort and follow instructions, and customers buy the product. In a typical co-operative, the workers or the customers also act as owners, and as owners, participate in management, either sharing out the management tasks between them or hiring a salaried manager who reports to them as a group.

7.5 MUTUALITY

Since specialization affords economic gains by allowing resources to be concentrated on those activities in which they have a comparative advantage, there must be some corresponding benefit to co-operation to offset this loss. The main benefit is a lower cost of coordination, arising from greater trust between the parties involved. The enhanced level of trust arises from a sense of mutual obligation within the institution. The nature of this mutual obligation is considered further in this section.

The simplest form of mutuality is where a person is effectively working for themselves. This is a powerful motivator in a small business where the owner carries out the work for themselves, or in a family business, where the family members work for the benefit of the family as a whole. In a co-operative, the entire membership represents a kind of extended family; although individuals do not manage their own work, they collectively plan the programme of work that determines the nature of the work that each individual does.

A more subtle form of mutuality arises when a person works for someone who occupies a role which that person has themselves performed before, and may expect to perform again. Although they do not currently perform the other role themselves, they can readily empathize with that person. In a co-operative bank, for example, a borrower may appreciate the importance of repayment better if they have been a depositor themselves, whilst a depositor will appreciate the importance of not being panicked into a withdrawal of their funds if they have been a borrower themselves. While people may not have the imagination to understand what another person's role involves, practical experience can provide the understanding that would otherwise be missing. As a result, they are better able to predict how the other person will behave, because they appreciate the constraints under which they are acting. This implies, for example, that they are less likely to misinterpret helpful actions as aggressive actions simply because they turn out differently from what the other person intended. Thus a consumer who also works as a producer is likely to appreciate better that poor quality can arise from ordinary human error rather than deliberate misrepresentation, whilst a worker who is also a consumer will appreciate the importance of ensuring that quality is high in the first place. Both parties will therefore behave in a more responsible and trustworthy manner.

Mutuality not only improves understanding, but enhances emotional rewards for good behaviour. By identifying with the other party, it is possible to obtain vicarious pleasure from their pleasure, and vicarious pain from their discomfort. Honest people therefore feel a 'warm glow', whilst dishonest people experience guilt, as well as shame if their bad behaviour becomes public knowledge. In general, mutuality means that agreements are easier to negotiate and to enforce, and that potential disputes are easier to resolve in a friendly manner.

Mutuality can emerge either naturally or by design. In a small rural community, for example, a farmer may sell part of his/her spring crop to another farmer for consumption, and later purchase from that farmer an autumn crop for his/her own consumption. While the prospect of repeated trade may encourage honesty if each farmer believes that the other could switch their source of supply, if alternative supplies are difficult to obtain then the threat of switching loses its force. Mutuality then becomes an important factor in sustaining honest trade, because it encourages each farmer to take account of the effect of his/her actions on the other. Mutuality reduces transaction costs when people are locked in to trading with each other.

Co-operative institutions do not leave mutuality to chance, however. It would be at variance with common usage to describe as a co-operative a local market in which, quite spontaneously, a degree of mutuality had emerged. In this chapter, therefore, a co-operative has been defined as a formal institution into which mutuality has been designed. This is effected by requiring all full members of the co-operative to participate in two or more roles, as explained above.

Two interesting illustrations of the interaction between mutuality and organizational form are provided in Cook et al. (2002), who analyse the effects of demutualization in building societies, and Arthur et al. (2004), who illustrate the opposite process, that is the effects of the transformation of a publicly-owned mine into a workers' cooperative. Cook et al. suggest that corporate managers and speculators reaped the benefits from demutualization in the form of earnings and status and windfall gains, whereas borrowers and communities lost out through higher-cost loans and the closure of local branches. Arthur et al. (2004) argue that worker co-operatives are significantly different from other work organizations, constituting social movements capable of creating an alternative space in which capitalist relations of production are at once challenged and reaffirmed. Their research at Tower Colliery, a co-operatively owned mine, shows that in spite of the need to compete in the marketplace and the historical legacy of workers' relations with management, there has been ample room for innovative and more participatory worker relations through a social process which they define as 'deviant mainstreaming'.

7.6   A TYPOLOGY OF CO-OPERATIVES

Definitions are often somewhat abstract, because they need to be general and context-free. A good definition of a concept will, however, lead naturally to a typology in which different manifestations of the concept can be identified. These manifestation should map into commonly occurring forms which can readily be recognized in practice.

The definition of a co-operative presented above leads naturally to a typology constructed from the various combinations of roles that members of the co-operative may perform. The main possibilities are listed in Table 7.3.

The most comprehensive application of the co-operative principle generates a self-sufficient utopian community, described in the first line of the table, in which everyone shares in ownership, management, consumption and work. Such communities were not uncommon in the USA in the nineteenth century, but none of them survived for long. The period 1815–48 was a time of significant political and economic upheaval throughout the West, which stimulated utopian thought and action, and visionaries such as Robert Owen (1813, 1815) were an important influence on these communities.

A major problem faced by utopian communities was the irruption of internal ideological conflicts over management issues. The obvious way to resolve these is to confine the membership to setting broad policy objectives and long-term strategy, and hire a salaried manager to determine tactics on a day-to-day basis. This is the strategy followed by many modern community self-help organizations. Services are provided by the community

Table 7.3   Typology of co-operatives

Type of co-operative	Owner	Manager	Worker	Customer
Self-sufficient utopian community	x	x	x	x
Community self-help organization run by a hired manager (including micro-finance institutions) Support group (e.g. mutual counselling)	x		x	x
State-run local collective meeting subsistence needs		x	x	x
Worker's co-operative selling to the public (employing a professional manager)	x		x	
Self-managed firm, usually state-owned		x	x	
Charity giving away funds raised, and services provided, by volunteers	x	x	x	
Club or professional association that employs salaried support staff	x	x		x
Purchasing co-operative or financial mutual employing professional managers (also a club that employs both managers and workers)	x			x
Professional partnership employing salaried support staff	x	x		
State-funded self-governing institute employing waged assistants (e.g. institute for basic scientific research)		x	x	

for the community. Finance may be raised by a membership subscription, which can be maintained at a fairly modest level when members are willing to provide support in kind, for example, by helping with building work.

Support groups such as Alcoholics Anonymous are particularly interesting as examples of the principle of mutuality. Members take it in turn to share their experiences with others, and to counsel others on their problems. Thus each person alternates between the role of worker (counsellor) and customer (client).

Another solution to the problem of the utopian community is for the state to intervene. In communist countries the state has sometimes encouraged local party members to set up collective farms and other co-operative enterprises to meet subsistence needs. In this case the state provides the capital and exercises ideological control over the party members who manage the enterprise.

Economists have devoted most attention to the analysis of workers' co-operatives, in which workers manage the firm themselves. These co-operatives typically sell their output to customers in competition with private firms. Workers' co-operatives have enjoyed some significant successes in the retail sector, where the capital requirements for start-up are relatively modest. Co-operative chains have been able to grow from small beginnings through the reinvestment of profit.

Where capital-intensive heavy industry is concerned, however, it is usually the state, rather than the workers, that supplies the capital to the co-operative. Private shareholders will generally not support a firm where the workforce intends to take responsibility for management, because the workers do not have a sufficiently strong incentive to maximize profit. Thus the workers manage the co-operative, but they do not own it.

State-owned workers' co-operatives are sometimes described as participatory or self-managing enterprises, although they do not involve any new principles of self-management or participation – they simply apply the general principles of co-operation described above to the special case of workers' control. Incidentally, the term 'workers' control' is often used in a different context, in which workers occupy a plant that a private firm intends to close down and attempt to operate it using the remaining stocks of materials.

The most authentic case of worker-ownership and worker-management is a charity, in which the workers are unpaid volunteers, and the output is given away. The volunteers raise capital funds by soliciting donations. Donors do not generally become heavily involved in managing a charity, but rather allocate their skills to deciding which charities to support. While some charities employ professional managers, such managers are normally accountable to a management board which is dominated by working volunteers.

In a club or professional association it is the customers rather than the workers who take responsibility for ownership and management. Indeed, the club members may well employ waged labour to carry out the manual and clerical work required to service the club's facilities.

One of the most common forms of co-operative observed in modern market economies is the purchasing co-operative – particularly in the agricultural sector. The co-operative is owned by its customers, and frequently employs both managers and workers. Managers need to have specialist knowledge and commercial acumen to negotiate with suppliers and anticipate market trends, whilst waged casual labour is an efficient response to the seasonal nature of transport and storage requirements.

Finally, there are two interesting forms of co-operative which are not normally recognized because they do not overtly promote the values of co-operation. The first is the business partnership – particularly common in professions such as law, accountancy and general medical practice – in which the partners manage the business in a collegial manner. In many cases the partners also do much of the work as well, but in other cases they act more like account managers, developing new business and maintaining the custom of existing clients, whilst junior professionals, hired at market rates, or employed as apprentices, do most of the work.

Another example of collegiality is the self-governing institute – again, usually managed by professionals, such as academics, researchers, librarians or curators. Although they may be amateurs in management, they prefer to manage their own affairs rather than to employ a professional manager to do it for them. Whilst private investors would normally be unwilling to back such a management team, the state may well be willing to do so.

7.7 JOB ROTATION

The collective nature of decision-making is not unique to a co-operative. Any joint-stock company requires shareholders to collaborate in taking collective decisions by voting at general meetings. However, because the owners of a self-financing co-operative are actively involved in the institution as workers or customers, factions could develop based on the vested interests of different groups of workers or different groups of customers. Whilst shareholders in a private enterprise may have little concern for the welfare of workers or customers, they may still be united by their selfish concern to maximize overall profit, and so be unanimous in the decisions that they take. By contrast, the parochial concerns of co-operative members for the welfare of their particular group could create conflicts instead.

Job rotation affords a possible way of addressing this issue so far as workers are concerned (Cosgel and Miceli, 1998). If workers do not specialize in particular jobs, but take on different jobs in turn, then the principle of mutuality can build solidarity amongst the members. Although economies of learning through repetition are reduced when people move between jobs, innovation may be stimulated when everyone receives a varied experience as part of their career in the institution (Babbage, 1832; Ure, 1861 [1835]; Meek and Skinner, 1973). The demands of learning several jobs at once may increase stress, but the variety and interest of the work may eliminate monotony and so reduce stress at the same time. If more able and enterprising people benefit in deriving the greatest non-pecuniary benefits from the variety of work then the co-operative may succeed in attracting and retaining the most able people.

Under different systems of job rotation members change jobs with varying regularities and with different frequencies. Rotation may be planned using a daily or weekly rota, or improvised as events unfold. Planning has the advantage that people can prepare for their next task in advance, thereby maximizing what they learn, whereas improvisation provides both excitement and flexibility. In a volatile sector of the economy, a major advantage of job rotation is that colleagues can cover for each other very easily. They can help each other out when fluctuations in demand or supply generate pressure on one particular task, as well as providing cover in case of accident or illness. Theory therefore suggests that job rotation will be used most widely in co-operative institutions operating under volatile conditions.

7.8   ENTREPRENEURSHIP AND LEADERSHIP

The growth of successful private firms is often driven by a particular individual, such as a charismatic entrepreneur. In a small business this entrepreneur may also be the owner, but in a large company he/she is likely to be a salaried chief executive. To align the motives of such an individual with those of the profit-seeking owners, share options might be provided, or profit targets established that must be met if the job is to be retained (see Chapter 1). The collective nature of decision-making in a co-operative does not inhibit entrepreneurship, but it may transform the objectives that the entrepreneur pursues. Whilst it is possible that the members of the co-operative behave like ordinary profit-maximizing shareholders, they may well have an ideological agenda instead. Whereas private shareholders are united by a common interest in maximizing profit, as noted above, members of the co-operative may be held together by a shared ideology linked to a radical, or even utopian, view of society in which co-operation and mutuality play fundamental roles.

There are charismatic individuals, such as the founders of charities, political pressure groups and religious movements, who establish new co-operatives in much the same way as a classic entrepreneur founds a new for-profit firm (see Chapters 8 and 13). Unlike a private company, members of a co-operative are not normally allowed to acquire personal control of the institution by accumulating a dominant holding of shares. Thus the authority of the founder does not stem from power, but rather from influence, which in an ideologically-driven co-operative stems from moral rather than legal authority. The founder of a co-operative who wishes to retain control of the institution therefore faces a more difficult problem than the ordinary entrepreneur. He/she requires skills of leadership as well as entrepreneurship. He/she needs to legitimate strategies in terms of the ideology of the institution. Where morality severely constrains the range of options, it may be difficult for the leader to define a viable competitive strategy which is also morally acceptable. Given these constraints, a morally committed individual might prefer to adopt a conventional corporate form in which money buys power, simply in order to retain control of strategy. This allows determination of the trade-off between moral compromise and survival without need to surrender key decisions to the members of the organization.

7.9   CONCLUSION AND POLICY IMPLICATIONS

This chapter has examined the consequences of introducing co-operatives into the modern institutional theory of the firm. The theory of the firm already recognizes a variety of institutional arrangements for coordinating the use of resources, including firms, markets, networks, governments and clubs. Some of these institutions, such as networks and clubs, exhibit co-operative forms of behaviour, and this raises the question as to whether a co-operative is a distinct form of institution, or merely a variant of an existing form.

The chapter has suggested that the co-operative is a distinctive form, although one that has affinities with others. Whilst it is similar to networks and clubs in some respects, it differs from them in other ways. Unlike a network, it normally involves authority relations, although the managers who exercise authority over workers may do so with the permission of the workers, acting collectively as a management board. Unlike a club, a co-operative is not primarily concerned with the provision of public goods, but with the sale of ordinary private goods, either to members of the co-operative or to the public as a whole.

The defining characteristic of a co-operative, it has been proposed, is that all full members of the co-operative are obliged to fulfil two or more distinct roles. A key feature of co-operation, therefore, is that the extent of specialization is limited.

Since specialization affords economic gains by allowing resources to be concentrated on those activities in which they have a comparative advantage, there must be some corresponding benefit to co-operation to offset this loss. It has been argued that the main benefit is a lower cost of co-ordination, arising from greater commitment and trust between the parties involved. The enhanced level of trust arises from a sense of mutual obligation between the owners of the resources.

The definition does not require each member to participate in all roles. There are a variety of possibilities, according to which particular roles the members share. For example, a group of workers who also supply capital to their business could employ a professional manager to allocate them to their individual jobs on a day-to-day basis. The workers would jointly own the business, and would collectively determine its overall strategy. As workers, they would be working for the owners – namely themselves. But on a daily basis they would be accepting orders from a salaried manager; this manager would be a specialist, and would not be a full member of the co-operative.

The roles that are shared by the members of a co-operative must include either ownership or management, but not necessarily both. In a self-managing co-operative, for example, long-term management strategy may be set collectively by members who either supply effort (as in a worker's co-operative) or use the output (as in a purchasing co-operative). However, the capital may be supplied either by the members themselves, or by the state.

Self-management can provide intrinsic emotional rewards from the enhanced status and responsibility that members acquire in their management role. These differ from the emotional rewards of independence, as enjoyed by a self-employed person, because in a co-operative management decisions are not taken individually but collectively. Nevertheless, participation in management legitimates authority so far as members are concerned, which means that orders are more likely to be carried out with enthusiasm and in accordance with the spirit as much as with the letter of the instruction.

Participation in management can also strengthen peer-group monitoring systems. When members perceive themselves as managers they are more likely to intervene if they observe a colleague behaving in an irresponsible manner. This effect is particularly useful where complex team-work is involved, because in this case it can be difficult for an individual supervisor simultaneously to monitor all the team members involved (Vanek, 1970).

Despite these advantages, however, private investors are unlikely to take the risk of funding a self-managing co-operative. Since the members are not management specialists, there is a risk that its long-term strategy may be unsound; furthermore, the members will have separate interests as customers or suppliers which could conflict with the private owner's objective of making a profit. For these reasons, self-managing co-operatives are normally owned and funded either by their individual members (a self-financing co-operative) or, in the case where substantial capital is required, by the state (a state-owned co-operative).

A number of predictions have been given concerning the types of activity that co-operatives are best equipped to coordinate. A full analysis of the relative advantage of co-operatives over other institutional forms cannot be attempted in this chapter, but nevertheless it can be suggested that co-operatives are most likely to survive and prosper in activities where:

- Expensive capital equipment is utilized intensively, so that the strike threat power of labour is likely to be high, and therefore the principle of mutuality is helpful in maintaining good industrial relations.
- Labour does not involve different craft or professional skills, so that vested occupational interests are not likely to undermine the mutuality required for participative management.
- Management does not require a large number of highly-specialized skills which have to be hired in, and which the ordinary members lack the ability to assess.
- Flexible working is advantageous, and job rotation is easy to implement.
- Co-operative values of honesty and equity are reasonably well aligned with the needs of the market place, so that the ideology of the co-operative does not rule out the strategies needed to meet private-sector competition.
- The activity attracts entrepreneurial individuals with a social conscience who are prepared to accept a smaller pecuniary reward than they could obtain in the private sector in return for the non-pecuniary benefit of running an ethical business.
- These 'social entrepreneurs' possess the leadership skills necessary to set a strategy that ordinary members are prepared to follow.

The benefits of mutuality, versatility and breadth of experience conferred by a co-operative suggest that co-operatives form an excellent device for educating and training responsible and useful citizens (Hahnel and Albert, 1990; Klein, 2002). Michie and Blay (2005) argue that the stronger the co-operative and mutual presence in the market, the less other companies are able to raise prices. At the same time, the rewards to those who establish a co-operative may be rather small. Thus the benefits conferred by leaders who found co-operatives may systematically exceed their personal rewards. Although a leader may derive substantial non-pecuniary benefits from the establishment of a co-operative that furthers his personal ideology, the financial and other sacrifices involved may be so great that co-operation remains under-supplied. This creates a *prima facie* case for government to subsidize the use of the co-operative institutional form. Subsidy could be effected through tax concessions on income generated by co-operative activity. It is important not to create perverse incentives for the foundation of bogus co-operatives – avoiding, for example, soft start-up loans whose repayment is independent of whether the co-operative achieves its stated aims.

Overall, this chapter has shown that the inclusion of co-operatives considerably enriches the modern theory of the firm. Integrating the theory of co-operatives within the theory of the firm allows a number of important general economic insights to be brought to bear upon the subject, whilst the results of applying these insights to co-operatives generates important new results that can be fed back into the theory of the firm.

REFERENCES

Arthur, Len, Tom Keenoy, Russell Smith, Molly Scott Cato and Peter Anthony (2004), 'Cooperative production: a contentious social space?', paper presented at the Annual International Labour Process Conference, Amsterdam, 5–7 April.
Babbage, Charles (1832), *On the Economy of Machinery and Manufactures*, London: Charles Knight.
Bradley, K. and A. Gelb (1983), *Co-operation at Work: The Mondragon Experience*, London: Heinemann.
Buckley, Peter J. and Mark Casson (1988), 'A theory of co-operation in international business', in Farok J. Contractor and Peter Lorange (eds), *Co-operative Strategies in International Business*, Lexington, MA: Lexington Books, pp. 31–54.
Casson, Mark (1995), *The Organisation of International Business*, Aldershot, UK and Brookfield, US: Edward Elgar.
Casson, Mark (1997), *Information and Organization*, Oxford: Clarendon Press.
Coase, Ronald H. (1937), 'The nature of the firm', *Economica*, New Series, **4**, 387–405.
Cook, Jacqueline, Simon Deakin and Alan Hughes (2002), 'Mutuality and corporate governance: The evolution of UK building societies following deregulation', *Journal of Corporate Law Studies*, **2** (1), 110–38.
Cosgel, Metin M. and Thomas J. Miceli (1998), 'On job rotation', working paper, University of Connecticut, Department of Economics, Storrs, CT.
Defourny, Jacques (2001), 'From third sector to social enterprise', in Carlo Borzaga and Jacques Defourny (eds)', *The Emergence of Social Enterprise*, London: Routledge.
Hahnel, R. and M. Albert (1990), *Quiet Revolution in Welfare Economics*, Princeton, NJ: Princeton University Press.

International Co-operative Alliance (2005), 'Statement on the co-operative identity', www.ica.coop/ica/info/enprinciples, 28 June 2005.

Klein, Naomi (2002), *Fences and Windows: Dispatches from the Front Lines of the Globalisation Debate*, London: Flamingo.

Kropotkin, Peter (1915), *Mutual Aid: A Factor of Evolution*, New York: Alfred A. Knopf.

Meek, Robert L. and Andrew Skinner (1973), 'The development of Adam Smith's ideas on the division of labour', *Economic Journal*, **83**, 1094–116.

Michie, Jonathan and Jonathan Blay (2005), *Mutuals and their Communities,* London: Mutuo.

Olson, Mancur (1965), *The Logic of Collective Action*, Cambridge, MA: Harvard University Press.

Owen, Robert (1813), *A New View of Society: Essays on the Formation of Human Character*, London.

Owen, Robert (1815), *Observations on the Effect of the Manufacturing System*, 2nd edn, London.

Potter, B. (1907), *The Co-operative Movement in Great Britain*, London: Swan Sonnenschein.

Thomas, H.B. and C. Logan (1982), *Mondragon: An Economic Analysis*, London: Allen & Unwin.

Ure, Andrew (1861 [1835]), *The Philosophy of Manufactures*, 3rd edn, London: H.G. Bohn.

Vanek, Jaroslav (1970), *The General Theory of Labour-Managed Market Economies*, Ithaca, NY: Cornell University Press.

Williamson, Oliver E. (1985), *The Economic Institutions of Capitalism*, New York: Free Press.

8. The cultural embeddedness of entrepreneurship

Culture, defined as shared values and beliefs, can influence the performance of an economy in many ways. The culture of a group, whether
national, regional or ethnic, may be regarded as a particular type of intangible public good. This chapter summarizes and critiques a positive theory
of intercultural competition. According to this theory, culture is created
by leaders who specialize in the production of culture, and is shared by
their followers. Successful leaders require entrepreneurial judgement,
but they employ this judgement in different fields to entrepreneurs. They
innovate values and beliefs rather than ordinary types of product, and
to exploit their innovations they establish social groups and non-profit
organizations rather than conventional firms.

Leaders compete for followers in order to increase the rents that they
can extract from their groups. Whilst some of these rents may be pecuniary, most are non-pecuniary, such as the enjoyment of pursuing a public
project that glorifies the leader and the group. There are four main
dimensions of culture that influence performance, and there are trade-offs
between them which are governed by the environment of the social group.
The positive theory is useful in interpreting historical evidence and the rise
and decline of societies, institutions and organizations of various kinds.

8.1 INTRODUCTION

It is popularly believed that culture has a significant effect on economic
performance (Buruna, 1999). Whilst some economic historians are sym-
pathetic to this hypothesis (Landes, 1998), most economists are sceptical.
They question the intellectual rigour of the underlying theory, and the
objectivity of the evidence. In *The Wealth of Nations*, Adam Smith down-
graded cultural factors from the prominent position they had occupied in
his previous work, and subsequent economists have largely followed his
lead (Macfie, 1967). Recently, however, theoretical interest in the economics of culture has revived (Olson, 2000). This chapter reviews attempts to
bring greater rigour to the subject. It is argued that models of rational

action, on which conventional neoclassical economics is based, can be extended to allow for cultural influences. Such models suggest that some cultures promote economic performance better than others.

Culture may be regarded as an economic asset – a form of cultural capital. It is an intangible public good, shared by the members of a social group. The analysis below identifies four major dimensions of culture which influence the performance of a group:

- individualism versus collectivism,
- pragmatism versus proceduralism,
- the degree of trust, and
- the level of tension.

Individualism emphasizes personal autonomy, and echoes the former UK Prime Minister Mrs Thatcher's dictum that 'there is no such thing as society', whilst collectivism asserts that it is natural for people to be socially embedded in a larger group. Pragmatism favours improvisation and flair in taking decisions, whilst proceduralism emphasizes reliance on rules. High trust reflects a belief that other people are honest and hard-working, whether they are supervised or not, whilst low-trust reflects a belief that people will take every profitable opportunity to shirk and cheat. The level of tension reflects the level of achievement to which people aspire and their determination to succeed.

The analysis distinguishes between economic performance in a material sense and overall quality of life. Quality of life depends on emotional as well as material rewards. Culture is not merely instrumental in the pursuit of material rewards; it is also a direct source of emotional rewards. Boosting emotional rewards can also boost material rewards – as in highly-motivated teams – but there are trade-offs too: for example, a religion that encourages prayer and fasting may reduce material performance even though it improves quality of life. Bias in the measurement of material living standards adds a further complication. A market economy may appear to outperform a non-market economy in material terms simply because a higher proportion of its output is recorded in the national income statistics.

It is relatively easy to show that culture can have a positive effect on quality of life. Quality of life depends heavily on the provision of intangible public goods such as visual amenity, safety on the streets and so on. Culture is not only a public good itself, but is instrumental in creating popular support for investment in other public goods. It is more challenging, however, to show that culture can improve the material output of private goods, and it is this challenge that is therefore the focus of attention in this chapter. Furthermore, since material performance is easier to measure than quality of life, hypotheses linking culture to material performance are in principle easier to test.

Modern neoclassical economics implicitly endorses a Western culture of 'competitive individualism', which is individualistic and low trust. The collapse of Soviet communism and the 'triumph of the market' was widely interpreted as demonstrating the advantages of an individualistic culture over a collectivist culture. However it said nothing about the advantages or disadvantages of high trust. Until the 1970s, the justification for markets was seen mainly in their ability to adjust to incremental change. Globalization, however, precipitated major changes, and led to the growth of 'enterprise culture', which emphasized the value of pragmatic improvisation over routine procedure when taking key decisions (see Chapters 1 and 3). At the same time, Soviet communism remained wedded to procedural decision-making. Thus Western capitalism was not only individualistic but pragmatic, whilst Soviet communism was both collective and procedural. It is therefore unclear whether the superiority of individualism over collectivism, or pragmatism over proceduralism, was mainly responsible for the revealed superiority of the West.

The success of many newly industrializing countries in pursuing state-led export programmes suggests that where government has been pragmatic rather than procedural it has sometimes been able to achieve remarkable results. It may therefore be that excessive reliance on procedure, rather than collectivism per se, caused the collapse of communism.

Western capitalism and Soviet communism were both high-tension cultures, whilst developing countries, on the whole, exhibit low-tension cultures. In the third world, high-trust culture seems to perform better than low-trust culture (Sherman, 1997). Combining the lessons from these various comparisons suggests that the most promising culture is individualistic, pragmatic, high-trust and high-tension. This is entrepreneurial associationism – a culture which encourages people to freely commit themselves to ambitious pragmatic team-based projects. It differs from competitive individualism in having a high level of trust. No country has been able to sustain associationism for very long, however, and so competitive individualism has emerged as a 'second-best' solution.

High tension stimulates competition, which tends to undermine trust. It is sometimes suggested that trust arises naturally, through repeated interaction, but it remains the case that selfish individuals have a strong incentive to cheat in the final play of any 'repeated game'. If trust is to prevail generally, it cannot be regarded as natural, but must be engineered (Casson, 1991). This is achieved by moral leadership, as explained below. From this perspective, lack of trust reflects a scarcity of leadership – indeed, there are grounds for believing that there is a systematic shortage of suitable leaders in most countries. An unfortunate legacy of inter-war Fascism is that the very concept of moral leadership has fallen into disrepute. This has discouraged the systematic production of moral leaders through education. Families and local communities have under-invested in the supply of leaders for future generations. Furthermore, as is argued below, the growth of mass media has distorted competition between potential leaders, favouring those who appeal to narrow self-interest. It is suggested that ineffective moral leadership has impaired the performance of Western economies over the last twenty years. Individualism and high tension have been pursued to the point where they undermine trust, creating a consumer society marred by crime and anti-social behaviour. Undermining trust has raised the costs of coordination, eroded material performance, and caused serious detriment to quality of life.

If this economic theory of culture is correct and its diagnosis of events is sound, then the policy implication is that nations must improve the supply of moral leadership. Intellectual leaders such as priests, politicians, philosophers and artists all have an important role to play in stimulating the imagination of political and business leaders; in a successful society such intellectual leaders will tend to embrace a high-trust high-tension culture.

The chapter is organized in four parts. Sections 8.2–8.6 introduce basic concepts and definitions; sections 8.7 and 8.8 outline an economic theory of culture, concerned with competition between groups; sections 8.9–8.11 discusses the key dimensions of culture; and sections 8.12–8.14 examine broader methodological and historical issues. Section 8.14 concludes the discussion.

8.2 THE DEFINITION OF CULTURE: CULTURE AS A PUBLIC GOOD

There are many important contemporary economic issues in which culture is a significant factor, for example:

- Is a common European currency a symbol of political unification?
- Will contracting-out public services such as health to private firms undermine the public service ethic?
- What exactly is 'consumerism'? Do heavily advertised 'lifestyle' consumer brands delude consumers with false hopes, and does it matter if they do?

It is necessary to define culture in a way that captures the common elements in these questions. For the purposes of this chapter, therefore, culture is defined as *shared values and beliefs* relating *to fundamental issues*, together with the *forms in which they are expressed*. This suggests that there are three main aspects to culture:

- values, which represent the moral aspect of culture,
- beliefs, which represent the technical aspects, and
- forms of expression, which represent the symbolic and artistic aspects.

These values, beliefs and forms of expression are shared within a social group.

It can be seen that this approach to culture is more general than that employed in the economics of the arts. Arts tend to be identified with 'high culture', involving the expression of emotion through artefacts (for example, paintings, books) and performances (for example, drama, ritual). Culture, as defined above, relates not only to emotional responses, but also to more detached views connected, for example, with scientific topics. Furthermore, it encompasses more than just expression – it includes the formation and dissemination of views as well.

Culture is an intangible good. Cultural values and beliefs can be shared, which indicates that culture, like knowledge, has the property of a public good (Reisman, 1990). The fact that one person holds certain beliefs, for example, does not preclude another person from holding these same beliefs too. Thus there is no rivalry in the consumption of culture. Culture may be a good because it has intrinsic value, or because it is instrumental towards some other purpose. People may value certain beliefs because holding these beliefs makes them happy (Layard, 1980; Easterlin, 1998, 2001). They may value other beliefs because they are purely instrumental – for example, holding correct beliefs eliminates mistakes and so reduces waste, thereby improving the material standard of living. It follows that culture can also be a 'bad'. Some beliefs make people unhappy – for example, the belief that nobody likes them. Other beliefs may be damaging because they are wrong – mistakes are made when acting on these beliefs, and resources are wasted as a result. From an economic perspective, therefore, the elimination of cultural bads is just as important as investment in cultural goods.

8.3   CULTURAL DIVERSITY

Cultural diversity is a topic that generates considerable controversy. Conventional economic theory suggests that culture is simply a set of beliefs which will ultimately converge on correct beliefs as a result of learning. According to this theory there is a unique set of correct beliefs on which everyone will eventually agree; groups that refuse to learn will fail to survive. The only cultural guarantor of economic success is a correct economic theory and the implementation of policies derived from it. Some economists seem to believe that convergence on the correct theory is almost instantaneous. Adherents of rational expectations theory, for example, maintain that everyone holds correct beliefs because they already know the true model of the economy (Lucas, 1981). Others allow the process of adjustment to take a little longer; they concede, for example, that the final collapse of authoritarian socialism in the 1990s occurred only after a century of institutional experimentation.

Simple economic models, such as rational expectations, assume that information is costless to collect and communicate and easy to verify. These assumptions about costless information are critical to the prediction that incorrect beliefs will be eliminated and only correct beliefs will survive. The rational expectations approach to economics is a recent innovation which is very much at odds with traditional mainstream writing, even in the Chicago School (see, for example, Leacock, 1998; and Viner, 1972, 1978). However, any plausible economic theory of culture must recognize the significance of information costs. Whilst knowledge is a public good, it is costly to share. No one has complete access to all available knowledge. Costs of collecting information mean that everyone bases their beliefs on only a limited amount of information. Optimal search theory shows that once a certain amount of information has been collected, it is no longer cost-effective for an individual to refine their beliefs by collecting more. Beliefs are therefore based on a very limited amount of information. Indeed, it is interesting to note that recent research has introduced costs of rationality into rational expectations modelling, which has aligned the approach more closely with that set out in this chapter (see, for example, Ginsburgh and Michel, 1997).

Access to information can be improved by pooling information, but this requires communication between people, which is costly too. It is often more efficient to leave someone to discover something for themselves rather than to incur the costs of telling them about it. Information sources are typically localized, which means that when people rely upon their own resources, different groups of people in different localities have different sets of information. Each group generates beliefs on fundamental issues by generalizing from its own experience. This leads to different sets of beliefs, and so to cultural diversity.

Cultural diversity is likely to diminish over time. Much information is a byproduct of action – it is acquired through 'learning by doing' – and so accumulates over time. Additional information can be captured through scientific experiment. As a result, the information available to each group is likely to become more and more the same. Groups can also compare beliefs, and refine them through a process of criticism. In this way the accumulation of knowledge, combined with critical debate, encourages the emergence of consensus. Diversity cannot be eliminated, however, because there is a lack of decisive information on certain crucial issues. Evidence is decisive when it convinces not only believers but also sceptics. Much of the evidence used in social science is difficult to replicate because it cannot be collected under fully controlled conditions. It therefore lacks the 'objectivity' that would convince a sceptic. Lack of objectivity is particularly problematic in the investigation of fundamental issues such as the origin of consciousness, inequality of intelligence, and the relative importance of 'nature' and 'nurture'. Lack of objectivity allows people to remain attached to beliefs which explain their own experience but not the experiences of others.

Disagreements are even more difficult to resolve in the field of values. Some value systems can be criticized for lack of consistency, although not everyone would accept that logical consistency is a requirement of a value system. Religious value systems often appeal to revelation and sacred texts as a source of authority, but secular critics deny their validity. Diversity in values therefore tends to be not only greater, but also more enduring, than diversity in beliefs (for further discussion of the influence of diversity in values see Baxter, 1988; Hahnel and Albert, 1990; and O'Brien, 1988).

Overall therefore, fundamental problems in assuring the quality of information mean that despite the increased quantity of information flowing within the world economy, cultural convergence on a true model is unlikely to be attained. The spread of the internet, for example, may well promote convergence on relatively superficial issues, such as the consumption of heavily advertised brands, but it is unlikely to promote convergence on more fundamental issues. Indeed, the proliferation of special issue lobbies such as anti-globalization protest groups coordinated through the internet suggests that increasing scepticism about the quality and integrity of 'official' information is generating new sources of cultural diversity. Thus while cultural diversity in international consumption patterns may be reduced through greater quantities of information flow, the limitations on information quality mean that intra-national diversity in political and religious beliefs may well increase.

8.4   STEREOTYPES

There is considerable popular awareness of differences between the cultures of particular groups. These differences are usually expressed in terms of stereotypes. A stereotype is an oversimplified characterization of a social group that ignores diversity within the group. It is a form of group reputation.

The members of a group generally view their own group more favourably than do outsiders (which partly explains why they are happy to remain within the group). Indeed, competing groups often adopt negative stereotypes of each other in order to justify their antagonism. For this reason stereotypes are often condemned for promoting distrust between groups. However, different outside groups often hold rather similar views of any given group, which lends support to the idea that there is an objective kernel to the outsider's view. Thus although stereotypes ignore internal diversity and are often hostile, they are still useful because they usually contain significant insights too; for the use of national stereotypes to analyse economic performance see Casson (1990, Chapter 4).

8.5 CULTURE AS AN ASSET

Culture is a durable asset: values and beliefs are memorized by individuals, and are transmitted to the next generation through parenting and education. Education is strengthened when culture is recorded in books, embodied in art and artefacts, and embedded in rituals and routines. The durability of culture has encouraged some writers to see it as the 'dead hand of the past'. Culture is acquired from early childhood when critical faculties are undeveloped. People become very attached to their early beliefs for emotional reasons – loyalty to parents, a concern for their 'roots', or fear of change. Beliefs are not revised in the light of new circumstances and hence there develops a disjunction between culture and the real world. This view ignores the fact that people often review their beliefs in adolescence or when they come of age. It also has the misleading implication that a very old culture is likely to be less appropriate than a newer one.

An alternative view is that culture adapts to changing circumstances, but with a lag. It is sometimes suggested that a traumatic set-back such as a military defeat is necessary to undermine confidence in a culture. Defeated groups may sometime adopt their conqueror's culture (or selected aspects of it). On this view cultures which survive do so not because of mere inertia but because the beliefs they embody are more correct or more successful than those they replace.

The most efficient way for a culture to cope with change is to adapt its beliefs in an incremental fashion, updating them in response to significant events and new discoveries. Monitoring the environment and updating

Table 8.1   Typology of social groups

Type of group	Membership system
Nation-state	Citizen by birth or naturalization. Tax-payer by residence
Market	All buyers and sellers of a product are members of the relevant market – especially competing sellers who locate close to each other
Network	Member by regular contact with other members – often met through introductions arranged by existing members
For-profit association: firm	Member by negotiation. Core members supply services on a regular basis: e.g. shareholders and employees. Customers may be regular, casual, or one-off purchasers
Non-profit associations: co-operative, profession, club, church, charity, political party, etc.	Member by application, invitation, qualification or election
Local community: friends, school etc.	Member by residential location
Family	Member by birth or adoption

beliefs is a complex task, however, and benefits from specialization. It is impossible for everyone within a group to find the time continually to re-examine their beliefs for themselves. To understand how culture changes, therefore, it is necessary to understand the division of labour within social groups.

8.6   A TYPOLOGY OF SOCIAL GROUPS

The basic unit of cultural analysis is the social group: it is the unit within which culture is shared (Newman, 1983; Pryor, 1977). The most significant types of group from a cultural perspective are listed in Table 8.1. People are born into families and the local community where they live. They also acquire nationality at birth. When they come of age they can take decisions for themselves. They can choose the firm for which they work, the profession (if any) they wish to follow, and the clubs and societies they wish to join. They can also decide whether they wish to be active members of a church or a political party. In taking these decisions they affirm some values and beliefs acquired from family and friends and reject others.

In a high-tension society, belonging to a group involves significant commitments; furthermore, in a high-trust society there are significant emotional penalties for breaking such commitments – disloyalty and lack of perseverance bring guilt and shame. Within a group there are distinctive roles. Roles with greater responsibility generally carry higher status. High-status people can demand deference from other members of the group. In addition, there are differences in status between different groups. Some groups are task-oriented (like the firm) whilst others are support-oriented (like the family), although most types of group combine elements of the two. In a task-oriented group the clients or customers who consume the output are usually different from the workers who produce the output, whereas in a support group the consumers and producers are often the same. In a charity for example, the donors who supply the funds are quite distinct from the beneficiaries or clients who receive them, whereas in a support group like Alcoholics Anonymous the members support each other (Bolnick, 1975).

Clients usually have low attachment to a task-oriented group. Customers may have only casual contact with a firm, for example, whereas workers are heavily involved on a daily basis. Those who provide finance usually have less attachment than those who provide labour. Shareholders in a large firm can easily sell out for speculative gain whereas employees may serve for life; similarly, donors to a charity are usually less involved than the volunteers. There are also differences amongst workers; whilst some may be permanent full-time staff, others may be casual part-time staff. In a high-trust society commitment from workers and volunteers may be readily forthcoming, but in a low-trust society people will prefer low-commitment involvement instead. People may prefer to give money rather than time to a charity and to take only casual work, while shareholders may be very concerned that their holdings are liquid.

Some groups have formal structures: these are typically large and long-lived groups. Formal structures institutionalize the division of labour, creating posts or offices to which people are appointed; some posts may be filled on a rotating basis, often by election. Other groups are informal. For example, a market consists of all the people who turn up in the mar-ketplace to trade – whether the market is a physical location, a commercial publication or a web-site. Although access to the market may be free, traders must abide by the rules for enforcing contracts. A network is even more informal – it is simply a group of people who are in regular contact with each other (Putnam, 1993). Networks are typically governed by customs that are enforced through reputation effects. A low-trust culture requires formal rules and procedures, whereas a high-trust culture is more versatile: both formal and informal systems can be used. Networks are useful for sharing information, particularly between entrepreneurs. In a high-tension culture networks can foster innovation, but in a low-tension culture they may simply foster collusion.

8.7   AN ECONOMIC THEORY OF CULTURE BASED ON COMPETITION BETWEEN LEADERS

Up to this point, the discussion has simply taken existing insights from sociology and social anthropology and reformulated them in economic terms. Further development of an economic approach to culture requires specific analysis of competition between cultures, leading to an explanation of the competitive strategies employed by social groups. This section outlines a set of assumptions on which a formal model of cultural competition can be developed.

Leadership

Leadership is the most important role within a group. The leader typically manages the external relations of a group. 'Take me to your leader' say outsiders who need to negotiate a commitment from a group. The leader demands loyalty from the members in order to guarantee the delivery of commitments and to maintain the reputation of the group. The leader has the power to discipline or expel disloyal people.

The logic of leadership is very simple. In a highly complex and uncertain world, people cannot resolve every issue for themselves. In particular, fundamental questions about the future of the world and the destiny of the individual cannot be easily answered; the costs of collecting and processing all the relevant information would be prohibitively high. Specialist leaders such as priests and politicians are required. Even then their answers cannot be definitive. Different leaders give different answers to the same questions, based on different information, and so different cultures prevail.

Leaders also provide answers to more specific questions; thus the leader of a firm decides what type of product is most in demand, and the leader of a charity decides what kind of people are most in need of help. The leader is the person deemed to have a comparative advantage in processing the relevant information. He/she may also claim to have privileged access to information, perhaps through external contacts. Alternatively, a leader might claim to be able to interpret information in a better way than others (Casson, 2000).

Leadership styles vary. Some charismatic leaders seek publicity, whereas others are self-effacing. Some leaders even seek to disguise their identity – such as an agitator leading a demonstration or the 'brain' at the centre of a spy-ring. The common notion that groups can achieve 'spontaneous order' without a leader is a myth. It is simply a consequence of failing to identify where leadership really lies.

Leadership requires very scarce talents and as a result many leaders lack appropriate qualifications for the job. Successful leaders must justify the trust that their followers place in them. A leader who has lost the trust of his or her followers is of little value to the group, since members no longer feel secure in following their orders or advice. An alternative leader may emerge 'from the ranks' of ordinary members and constitute a rival source of authority – the militant British shop-steward, for example. The rival leader may organize a revolution to depose the incumbent if the incumbent cannot appoint a successor first.

Competition between groups

In a free society people can choose which leaders they follow. At any given time rival leaders will disagree about fundamental issues and people will have to decide who they agree with. In particular, different political parties promote different ideologies, based on different theories of the economy and different views of human nature. In principle, only one of the rival leaders can be right. Indeed, the most likely scenario is that none of the leaders is right, since each is promoting an oversimplified and somewhat distorted view of the situation. Disagreements may persist because it is impossible to find any decisive evidence for or against a particular view. In practice most leaders do not debate on an abstract level, but rather in terms of strategy and policy. They promote specific projects which embody the values they support and which, it is claimed, will work because the theory on which they are based is sound. For example, a political leader may promote a project to create a welfare state, based on the optimistic view that new technology makes 'welfare for all' an affordable proposition. A business leader may motivate their workforce by claiming that their product is the best in the world, and a great benefit to all who consume it.

An articulate leader offers to followers a vision of what the project can achieve. The leader's rhetorical skill in creating 'sound-bites' and 'buzz-words' may be supported symbolically – perhaps by a launch at a prestigious location. The vision typically ignores the short-run constraints under which the project operates and emphasizes its long-run potential. A vision will often be deliberately vague. It may be expressed in an artistic form which conveys an overall impression without revealing much key detail. The rationale for this ambiguity lies in the fact that much can change

before the project achieves its goal, so that it would be potentially misleading to be too specific about the final outcome. Indeed, the more ambitious
the project, the longer it is likely to take to complete and so the vaguer the
final outcome will be at the initial stage.

Competition may also induce leaders to scorn their rival's visions –
arguing that they represent unworkable delusions. In Western democ-
racies, debate between party leaders sometimes degenerates into mutual
scorn. The emergence of negative stereotypes, promoted by leaders who
wish to discourage their members from defecting to rival groups, can
be explained in similar terms. This negative strategy has its limitations,
however – too much emphasis on another leader's faults may suggest to
honest followers that a leader is simply diverting attention from their own
shortcomings.

A key feature of a vision is that it arouses an emotional response in the
follower. Such emotions are often described as 'beauty' (in the discovery of
a simple theory, for example), 'glory' (as in winning a great team victory)
or 'awe' (as in creating a monumental piece of architecture or engineering). The follower is enthused by contemplating the vision; by assessing
their own emotional response to the vision, the follower can assess the
magnitude of the emotional rewards that they will obtain through participation in the project.

Participation in each project involves a contract – usually an implicit
contract assured through trust, but sometimes also a formal contract
backed by law. There is an important psychological dimension to this contract. The leader emphasizes that the reward obtained by contemplating
the vision will be strongest for those who make the greatest effort. Each
follower will know how much effort they have committed to the project;
the greater the sacrifices they have made, the greater the rewards they
will obtain. These rewards come from two main sources. The first is the
satisfaction of being absorbed in a worthwhile project to the point where
the worker is unaware of their surroundings or of the passage of time. The
second is a sense of pride and contentment when they rest from their work
and reflect not only on what they have already achieved but also on what
will be achieved when the project is complete. Followers who know they
have made little effort will experience little reward, whilst those who have
deliberately shirked will experience guilt and wish that they had never
joined.

An effective leader will show appreciation of followers' efforts. But the
leader cannot always monitor individual effort with great accuracy. In
certain types of work this agency problem may be overcome by basing
rewards on measured output. But output may be only weakly correlated
with individual effort, particularly in large teams. The 'psychological

contract' is particularly valuable, therefore, in motivating effort in teams. However, team-work is not just a matter of effort. Loyalty is important in any project, and particularly so in teams, where the loss of a member can be very disruptive. Every new member has to learn their role, and the cost of training usually falls on the leader. Loyalty is thus an important element in the psychological contract. The stronger a person's emotional attachment to the project at the outset, the greater their sense of guilt when quitting.

When an individual is deciding whether to follow a particular leader, therefore, they will need to know both how they are likely to respond to the vision, and how they will actually perform. They therefore need to know their own competencies and their own emotional characteristics. If these characteristics are incorrectly assessed then a mis-match will occur between the individual and the project, and thus between the individual and the group. This will in turn lead to a waste of resources, in both material and emotional terms. It is typically assumed in economics that individuals possess full information on their own personal characteristics. In practice, however, it can be argued that they do not. In neoclassical economic theory, asymmetric information is usually construed as meaning that an individual knows their own characteristics, but others do not. It is possible, however, to construe the concept differently, and to suppose that other people know a person's characteristics better than they do themselves. Focusing on emotional characteristics highlights this point. Most parents have a better understanding of their children's emotions than the children do themselves. Many people remain 'child-like' (or even 'childish') in their emotions when grown up, and so not only family but also friends may be better aware of a person's emotional characteristics than the person themselves. Indeed, using biological evidence Frank (1985) has argued that people signal their own emotions to others unselfconsciously through facial expression and posture, and that their inability to control these emotional signals gives a credibility to their statements that they would otherwise lack. In a similar vein Freudian psychoanalysts have argued that people sublimate their emotions in order to disguise their feelings from themselves. People not only lack self-knowledge and self-awareness – they also systematically deny the existence of certain emotions.

It is unnecessary to accept all of these claims in order to agree that many followers may be unaware of their emotional characteristics at the time they take a decision to join a group. Joining a group is therefore not only risky because of uncertainty about the leader and about the behaviour of other members of the group, but also because of uncertainty about one's own characteristics. People's uncertainties about their own characteristics provide a significant opportunity for plausible leaders who are a good judge of character. The leader can invite people who in their judgement have the correct characteristics to join their group. People who feel very uncertain about their own characteristics are likely to respond in a positive fashion to such an invitation. Trusting people are also likely to respond, as they are more likely to accept the leader's judgement. An honest leader pursuing a socially worthwhile project can turn such mechanisms to good advantage, but it is equally obvious that an unscrupulous leader can take advantage of vulnerable followers. The most vulnerable people are those who are unaware that their own uncertainties and trusting nature are very obvious to others. Those whose competencies are obviously limited are particularly vulnerable, because it is obvious that they will receive few offers from other leaders. They may however receive some offers from honest but highly altruistic leaders, who wish to save them from falling under the influence of unscrupulous leaders.

8.8   THE CHANGING NATURE OF COMPETITION BETWEEN LEADERS

The nature of competition between leaders has been changed fundamentally by the growth of the communications and media industries – from the growth of print journalism in the eighteenth century to the spread of cinema, radio and television in the twentieth. The lower cost of mass communication has intensified competition between the leaders of high-level groups, especially political parties. Most significantly, the technologies of photography, film and video have reduced the cost of pictures relative to words, giving pictorial images an increasing role in propaganda and persuasion. Images liberate arguments from the requirement of a literate readership. They make use of a natural visual language which transcends any specific written language and reaches a mass multilingual audience (the links between culture and language are explored further from an economic perspective in Jones, 2000).

Certain images elicit strong emotional reactions. These reactions are almost instantaneous and are therefore invaluable to leaders in gaining attention for their messages. Indeed these reactions are so strong that the image itself may become the argument. Pictures of starving children or police brutality, for example, make their own political points without any need for verbal interpretation. Competition between leaders for visual attention encourages the pursuit of the outrageous. In any collection of competing images the most outrageous is likely to win. People may be attracted by beauty but shock and horror have an even greater fascination.

The abstract nature of competition between ideologies does not lend itself readily to visual expression. The loss of media space to more visual subjects may be one reason why vigorous political debate appears to have declined as consumption of media services has increased. Social projects are easier to promote, as visions of better houses, schools and hospitals are easy to project. This encourages politicians to argue less about ideology and more about specific projects – a strategy recently adopted by New Labour in the UK (Protherough and Pick, 2002).

Consumer products are remarkably easy to promote by picturing the consumer as relaxed and self-assured; this works particularly well for simple products which provide emotional benefits of a social nature – cosmetics and alcoholic beverages, for example (see Chapter 10). The multilingual nature of a visual proposition benefits multinational consumer brands. Faces attract attention – particularly faces that are instantly recognized. This favours the promotion of ideas through celebrity endorsement. Since sportsmen and entertainers are not generally noted for their political wisdom, celebrity endorsement works best in product promotion, although it has been used with some success in politics too.

Commercial advertisers are unlikely to increase their sales if consumers give money to good causes instead of spending it on themselves. The implicit message of a typical product advertisement is therefore that low trust is the norm. Similarly, many products are advertised as impulse purchases that allow the consumer to show off in a social setting. This promotes a low-tension spontaneous lifestyle as the norm, rather than a single-minded high-tension lifestyle which would produce better long-term results.

The optimization of visual images for persuasive purposes requires very scarce skills. Creative workers in advertising and public relations can command substantial economic rents. The financial requirements of major promotional campaigns constitute a significant barrier to entry for many types of leader. A highly visual political campaign may require powerful industry backers who expect rewards if their candidate is elected to office. Thus leadership becomes more like commercial entrepreneurship as the economic requirements converge on the funding of media campaigns.

In most modern societies newspapers, magazines, radio and television rely heavily on advertising revenues rather than sales and subscriptions. They have a strong financial incentive to attract an audience that is susceptible to advertisers' messages. This can induce the 'dumbing down' of content in order to attract the people most likely to be influenced by the visual message that the advertiser plans to use. Some messages are easier to dumb down than others – for example a blatant appeal to short-term self-interest is easier to communicate than a sophisticated appeal to long-term social concerns.

To summarize, there are many reasons why in a modern society characterized by competitive individualism the role of moral leadership is difficult to carry out. Whilst the power of visual imagery favours the promotion of

Table 8.2   Four dimensions of culture

Limit of dimension corresponding to competitive individualism	Limit of dimension corresponding to utopian solidarity	Corresponding dimension in Hofstede	Optimal combination
Individualism	Collectivism	Individualism–collectivism	Voluntarism
Pragmatism	Proceduralism	Low–high uncertainty avoidance	Good judgement
Low-trust	High-trust		Warranted trust
High-tension	Low-tension	Femininity–masculinity	Warranted self-confidence

Note: Only three of the four dimensions identified by Hofstede (1980) appear in the table. The missing power–distance dimension in the Hofstede classification may be loosely construed as a hybrid which combines elements of individualism–collectivism with elements of low-trust–high-trust.

certain types of charitable project such as child poverty or animal welfare, it discriminates against the promotion of high-trust high-tension political values. Competition for attention in the visual media is on average biased against the promotion of high-trust cultural values.

8.9   FOUR MAIN DIMENSIONS OF CULTURAL VARIATION

There are many fundamental issues which cultures must address. Some are very general, such as 'What are people really like?', whilst others are more specific such as 'Who can you trust?' and 'How do you motivate people?' Other issues include 'What forms of organization are natural?' and 'How far can technological progress advance?' Describing a culture in full can therefore be a very complex task.

A parsimonious theory of culture must identify just a small number of dimensions along which cultures vary. By focusing on those aspects of culture which are likely to influence economic performance, four main dimensions of culture can be derived. These dimensions were introduced at the outset, and are summarized in the first two columns of Table 8.2. The first column of the table identifies the end of the dimension which is found in a typical Western competitive individualistic society, whilst the second column indicates the end of the dimension which corresponds to 'utopian solidarity' – the kind of culture that would be found in an idyllic closed society of the kind visualized by Rousseau. This four-way classification is a refinement of a classification proposed in Casson (1993).

Individualism versus collectivism   An *individualist* believes that people are autonomous. Everyone is different and each person values personal 'lifestyle' projects above others (Earl, 1986). The information required for coordination is widely distributed – shocks are individual-specific. Ownership and control of resources should be vested in individuals, since only individuals have the information required to take decisions that affect themselves. A *collectivist* believes that we are all part of the community into which we were born. Even as adults we remain dependent on others for our survival. A collectivist also believes in uniformity – everyone is the same, and everyone values large awesome projects. Information required for coordination is centralized – shocks have collective impact. Collectivists believe that ownership and control of resources should be vested in the group (Ekelund and Tollison, 1997).

Pragmatism versus proceduralism   *Pragmatists* believe that intuitive judgements based on wide personal experience hold the key to successful decisions. Hunches can also be tested through informal conversation with other people. The best decisions are made promptly. A single individual should be ultimately responsible for each decision. *Proceduralists* believe that good decisions are generated by closely following formal procedures whose design is underpinned by theory and which involve the systematic collection of objective information. The use of committees may delay decisions, but it is better to 'get it right' than to do it too quickly.

Low trust versus high trust   *High-trust* individuals believe that others will be honest, work hard, be loyal, and generally keep their promises even when they have little material incentive to do so. *Low-trust* individuals believe that others are guided by material incentives, and will therefore often lie, cheat or shirk. High trust is particularly important in an individualistic society, because individuals do not have the same power of enforcement as a collective body (Holmes and Sunstein, 1999).

High tension versus low tension   A *high-tension* person is attracted to ambitious projects, while low-tension people prefer easy projects. The high-tension person is stressed because they are aiming high, and will be ashamed of failure (for an excellent discussion of high tension in the context of fundamentalist religious sects see Stark and Bainbridge, 1987). Conversely, a *low-tension* person is relaxed, because they are aiming low, and they will blame any failure on factors outside their control. Low-tension people like to behave in a spontaneous manner, which often has anti-social consequences (Casson, 2002), although it is a manner of which some economists approve (Scitovsky, 1976).

There are many other classifications of culture which have been devised for a variety of purposes, but there is one particular classification, due to Hofstede, which has been particularly influential in management and organizational studies and is particularly relevant to performance issues (Hofstede, 1980; Graham, 2001). Hofstede's classification was arrived at empirically by applying factor analysis to a large-scale cross-national study of the employees of a multinational firm. Unlike the classification used here, Hofstede did not deduce his classification from first principles, but nevertheless a comparison is useful. It is interesting that he also focused on four dimensions, some (though not all) of which correspond to the theoretical classification as noted in the third column of Table 8.2.

Taking the two limits of each of the four key dimensions described above identifies 16 ideal types of culture which are presented in Table 8.3. Some of these are particularly interesting, especially the high-trust analogues of competitive individualism. These embody the principle of voluntary association for the purpose of pursuing ambitious projects but add the notion that the aims of the project may be altruistic, that competition between the projects is orderly rather than aggressive, and that co-ordination of projects relies heavy on trust between members of a team. It is known as associationism.

To keep the theory really simple it would be nice to identify just one of these 16 cultures as the best from a performance point of view. It would then be possible to compare the actual culture of any social group with the ideal culture, and measure how many dimensions were in agreement: the closer the actual culture to the ideal culture, the better the economy would perform. Given the advantages of a high-trust culture in reducing agency costs and transaction costs, some form of associationism would be a natural choice. The form that is closest to classic Western individualism is entrepreneurial associationism, and so this appears to be the natural choice as the ideal.

8.10   TRADE-OFFS INVOLVED IN A HIGH-PERFORMANCE CULTURE

However, there are three difficulties connected with identifying entrepreneurial associationism as the unique high-performance culture, however.

Table 8.3 Typology of cultures

	HG High-tension pragmatic (judgemental)	HD High-tension procedural (administrative)	LG Low-tension pragmatic (spontaneous)	LD Low-tension procedural (bureaucratic)
IS Individualistic low-trust (competitive individualism)	*Enterprise culture* Aggressive competition between highly entrepreneurial selfish people	*Big business culture* Aggressive competition between selfish, ambitious but unimaginative people controlling formal organizations	*Libertarianism* Social anarchy constrained only by legal enforcement of market contracts.	*Play-the-system culture* Unprincipled competition between formal organizations regulated unsuccessfully by weak and corrupt bureaucracy
IH Individualistic high-trust (associationism)	*Entrepreneurial associationism* Orderly markets allocate resources between ambitious altruistic projects	*Administrative Associationism* Orderly competition between ambitious altruistic people running professional organizations	*Good neighbour culture* Social ambitions are limited to relief of current problems such as poverty. Individuals act on impulse to help the needy who are known to them	*Charity culture* Compassionate leaders set up formal organizations to help the needy, and recruit volunteers

Table 8.3 (continued)

	HG High-tension pragmatic (judgemental)	HD High-tension procedural (administrative)	LG Low-tension pragmatic (spontaneous)	LD Low-tension procedural (bureaucratic)
CS Collectivistic low-trust (coercive collectivism)	*Revolutionary state* Totalitarian dictator personally promotes prestige projects in which people are forced to participate	*Soviet-style planning* Professional government planners implement ambitious projects using conscripted workers	*Arbitrary dictatorship* Dictator with ambition simply to survive in power improvises strategies to defeat rival bids for power	*Conformist culture* Coercive bureaucracy resists change and demands conformity from apathetic people
CT Collectivistic high-trust (paternalism)	*Charismatic leadership* Paternalistic leader with utopian vision enthuses population	*Welfare state* Ambitious altruistic programmes are devised by a paternalistic leader and administered using public service ethic	*Familism* Paternalistic leader presides over low-productivity economy where socialisation is more important than work	*Utopian solidarity* Low-productivity economy is coordinated through compulsory participation in traditional rituals presided over by leader

The first is that a combination of four extreme values is rarely an optimal choice in any problem. There are strong grounds for believing that along each of the four dimensions there is scope for a trade-off. The importance of trade-offs in culture is recognized by many writers (see, for example, Hampden-Turner and Trompenaars, 1997). Typical results of the trade-offs are listed in the right-hand column of Table 8.2. They may be summarized as follows, taking each dimension in turn:

- *Voluntarism* Individuals are encouraged to transfer their resources to institutions on a voluntary basis. They are encouraged to identify opportunities for projects that these institutions can carry out. Individuals like group projects, but prefer to choose the type of project with which they are involved
- *Good judgement* Procedures work well in dealing with frequent minor shocks of a transitory nature. Improvisation is required in dealing with intermittent major shocks of a persistent nature. Successful improvisation requires good judgement, which is based on wide experience.
- *Selective warranted trust* Whilst trust reduces coordination costs, naive trust is of little value, since naive people provide easy pickings for cheats. A high-trust equilibrium is what counts, in which the majority of people (who are trustworthy) can identify each other and transact with each other, whilst the minority of people (who are untrustworthy) cannot transact at all. Trust is engineered through moral leadership. Leaders demand loyalty and hard work from those who join their teams.
- *Warranted self-confidence* High tension delivers results in task-oriented projects. But high tension cannot be sustained indefinitely. A high-tension person relaxes in a secure environment where they reflect on their performance and learn from their mistakes. The low-tension person likes to mess around at work, and have lots of fun when relaxing.

A combination of voluntarism, good judgement, selective warranted trust and warranted self-confidence may be termed refined associationism, and may be taken as the most accurate characterization of optimal culture from a performance point of view.

The second difficulty with this choice is that none of the forms of associationism discussed above correspond to the cultures of the most successful Western economies. These tend to be much lower trust than associationism would imply. It could therefore be argued that the entire theory is a predictive failure. This leads on to the third point, however, which is that the exact position of the trade-off will reflect the local circumstances with which a culture has to contend. Thus a very large, transient and widely-dispersed group may have to reconcile itself to lower levels of trust than a small, stable and compact group. It is therefore unrealistic to expect every group to conform to the same ideal. In another case, one group may have an outstanding moral leader – a 'man of the moment', say – who intervenes at a critical moment when change is required, whereas other groups may have to cope without such a leader. Drawing upon a larger number of less able and less trustworthy individuals to do the same job, they may institute a division of powers between the leaders and even endeavour to promote a degree of competition between them.

It is in fact possible to explain the current predominance of competitive individualism in successful Western countries such as the USA in terms of adaptation to changing global conditions in the period since World War II. Volatility has increased as a result of accelerated technological change and the globalisation of trade, driven by lower transport costs and tariffs. An increase in volatility favours a switch from collectivism to individualism, and from proceduralism to pragmatism, because of the need for greater flexibility (for earlier examples of such switching see Hirschman, 1982).

Globalization has also reduced trust between trading partners, as local networks of trade have been disrupted by the emergence of foreign competition; social trust has been eroded too, as migration has disrupted the customs of local communities. The globalization of communications has encouraged a switch from low-tension to high-tension culture as people in low-productivity economies have become aware of the opportunities presented by innovation and export-led growth. Countries across the world have therefore switched towards a specific type of competitive individualism, namely an individualistic, pragmatic, low-trust, high-tension 'enterprise culture', as indicated in the top left-hand cell of Table 8.3.

The economic theory of culture therefore predicts that culture will adapt to the environment, both across space and over time. This accords with basic economic intuition that despite all the qualifications noted above, a successful culture must correspond closely to the realities of a situation facing a group. As circumstances change, so the optimal culture changes too, and forces of adaptation, driven by competition between rival leaders, come into play.

8.11   REFINING THE DIMENSIONS OF CULTURE

Sociological writers on culture have between them identified over a hundred different dimensions of culture. Furthermore, cultural analysis of

Table 8.4   Sub-dimensions of culture

Characteristic favouring competitive individualism	Characteristic favouring utopian solidarity
Individualistic (I)	*Collectivistic* (C)
Atomistic	Organic
Dynamic	Static
Incremental	Radical
Democratic	Elitist
Market-based	Planning-based
Efficiency-oriented	Equity-oriented
Consumer-oriented	Producer-oriented
Pragmatic (G)	*Procedural* (D)
Empirical	Theoretical
Outcome-based	Process-based
Risk-taking	Risk-averse
Artistic	Scientific
Personal	Impersonal
Low-trust (S)	*High-trust* (T)
Unprincipled (moral scepticism)	Principled (morally committed)
Secular	Religious
Selfish	Altruistic
Autocratic	Consultative
Aggressive	Orderly
High-tension (H)	*Low-tension* (L)
Aspirational	Complacent
Deliberative	Spontaneous
Optimistic	Pessimistic
Confident	Unsure
Progressive	Conservative

cross-country differences in industrial policy has identified other dimensions besides those mentioned above (Foreman-Peck and Federico, 1999). Almost all of these additional dimensions can however be subsumed under the four key dimensions; indeed, these key dimensions were developed in part as composite dimensions under which various other dimensions could be subsumed. Table 8.4 lists 22 sub-dimensions of culture, including many of the most frequently cited sub-dimensions, and attributes each of them to one of the four key categories.

Where issues relating to political constitutions and national economic policy are concerned, the sub-dimensions associated with the first dimension – individualism versus collectivism – are most important. Where issues of organizational structure and management style are concerned, the sub-dimensions associated with pragmatism versus proceduralism are most important. The quality of personal relationships within organizations, the intensity of competition between organizations, and the general quality of social life are governed by the sub-divisions of the third dimension – the degree of trust. The extent to which people are energized and inspired by visions of a better life, either for themselves or others, is governed by the sub-divisions of the fourth dimension – the degree of tension. Since there is insufficient space to examine each of these sub-dimensions in detail, their principal features are summarized in Tables 8.5 to 8.8. The middle columns of these tables explain the nature of the variation along the dimension concerned, whilst the right-hand column considers the point along the spectrum on which the best results are likely to be obtained. This is described as the 'high-performance mix'. It is important when studying culture to remember that the dimensions of cultural variation do not normally run from 'good' to 'bad' or vice versa but, like ordinary economic variables, express a trade-off in which the optimum is usually at an interior point. Just as in conventional economics, extremes are rarely efficient in cultural life.

An optimum in this context represents a cultural mix that is likely to prove efficient in the long run. In modern parlance, it is 'sustainable'. However, the optimum along any one dimension cannot be determined without reference to the other dimensions of culture. Thus a culture that promotes a distrustful attitude to other people may have an optimal degree of competitiveness that is quite high, whilst a culture which encourages people to trust each other may have an optimal degree of competitiveness that is much lower. In the long run there will be a tendency for competition between cultures to select the culture that is most efficient in overall terms. The characteristics of an optimal culture are summarized in general terms in the next section. However, as noted above, the optimal culture varies according to environmental constraints, and this means that the optimum is difficult to specify in terms of all the 22 sub-dimensions discussed in Tables 8.5 to 8.8. Furthermore, the process of competition between cultures is so slow and disjointed that for the foreseeable future the detailed predictions of the theory merely identify a sub-set of viable cultures which are likely to remain in competition with each other for a considerable time to come.

Some of the dimensions described in Tables 8.5 to 8.8 are much more relevant at one level of leadership than another. Individualism versus collectivism and the sub-dimensions associated with it are particularly important for high-level leaders of large groups such as the nation-state. They influence attitudes to the decentralization of power. A high-level

Table 8.5   Detailed analysis of individualism versus collectivism

Characteristic: individualist/ collectivist	Commentary	High-performance mix
Atomistic/organic	An atomist believes that individuals are autonomous and independent of society. Their personal rewards derive from their own activities and their attitude to others is purely instrumental. Atomists play down emotions as a source of utility and emphasize pleasure from material consumption instead. Organicists believe that the most important rewards are emotional and derive from participation in social activity. Activities devoted to improving and strengthening society generate especially large rewards. The more sacrificial effort people put in, the greater the emotional rewards they get out.	Atomism is bad psychology since it underestimates the importance of emotional rewards, particularly those derived from harmonious social interaction. The atomist is correct, however, that ultimately it is individuals that take decisions. A high-performance culture recognizes that economic performance depends on the interaction of numerous individual decisions – decisions taken by people with real concerns about the society in which they live.
Dynamic/static	A dynamic culture regards the environment as highly volatile. Change is endemic and it is necessary to adapt and evolve in order to survive. Change is exciting and people can thrive on it. A static culture believes that the environment is stable. Change can be neutralized in order to preserve the status quo. Homeostasis provides much-needed security.	The environment is volatile. Major changes usually require adaptation but minor changes can sometimes be neutralized by an appropriate response. People can only stand so much excitement from change.

Table 8.5 (continued)

Characteristic: individualist/ collectivist	Commentary	High-performance mix
Incremental/radical	An incrementalist believes that changes are typically small and localized. They relate to particular products or places. The people close to the changes are in the best position to respond. A decentralized system that empowers individual decision-making produces the most effective responses. A radical believes that changes affect the entire economy. Radical actions are required to take advantage of new opportunities or respond to emergent threats. This requires a centralization of power.	Volatility in the environment takes different forms. Minor changes occur all the time, whilst major changes occur only intermittently. Minor changes can easily be delegated to individuals to handle; indeed, standard procedures can be developed to deal with the most common types of change. Major changes can take many different forms and require a more consultative and collective response. Leaders have an important role in building consensus where radical change is required.
Democratic/elitist	A democrat believes that everyone has unique life experiences, which make them worth consulting on how to respond to major changes. So far as minor changes are concerned, they can be left to handle them themselves. An elitist believes that only a select group of people of high intelligence, 'good breeding' or the like, have the ability to form correct opinions and to carry out the appropriate calculations.	Leaders are specialists in taking complex decisions. Leaders constitute an elite – but they should be an 'open elite' which anyone can attempt to join. Leaders should consult their followers, but ultimately they must act on their own judgement. Ineffective leaders should be replaced – followers should be able to replace a bad leader, or quit a badly-performing group. Leadership roles require people of exceptional ability, but this ability is difficult to identify in advance.

Market-based/ planning-based	The atomist recognizes that markets provide the flexibility that allows different people to respond in different ways to similar events. Market-making middlemen adjust prices to match long-run supply and demand; they also hold inventories to buffer short-run fluctuations. From an organic perspective, planning is the most direct means of achieving consistency between individual responses since it uses a single directing mind. A planner may administer prices or ration quantities.	Planning and markets need to be combined. Firms are planning units which coordinate tightly-coupled systems. Households also plan, but on a smaller scale. Markets link these different planning systems in a loosely-coupled way. Factor markets price the labour and capital employed by firms. Firms which attempt to plan activities which are better coordinated by a market will fail to break even. By allocating scarce factor supplies to the most viable firms, the factor markets determine which activities are planned and which are not.
Efficiency-based/ Status-based	The atomist exploits market competition to eliminate waste. An inefficient producer cannot match the price of an efficient producer, and so customer switching eliminates wasteful production methods. Consumers who value products most out-bid those who value them least, so outputs are not wasted by consumers who do not value them. The organicist notes that a consumer's ability to pay depends on income. Consumption should reflect basic needs and social status. Since basic needs are similar, necessities should be allocated fairly. Luxuries should reward service to society as a whole and not just wealth derived from scarce factors of production.	People care both about their own consumption and about the kind of society in which they live. Market-based incentives to eliminate wealth can make everyone better off, but only if those who make the savings are prepared to share them with others. If they are forced to share them, then the incentive to make the effort to drive out waste is reduced. An ethic of community solidarity, which provides emotional rewards to those who reduce waste for the benefit of others is the best solution. Thus a market system can usefully be supplemented by an 'honours system', provided that honours are awarded for sacrificial effort and not simply sold to the highest bidder.

Table 8.5 (continued)

Characteristic: individualist/ collectivist	Commentary	High-performance mix
Consumer-oriented/ producer-oriented	The atomist believes that people derive rewards mainly from material consumption. Novelty and fashion, packaging and presentation are not trivial matters, but sources of serious satisfaction. The proliferation of different product varieties made possible by technology and trade is to be welcomed. So too are the efficiency gains generated by specialization, even though work becomes monotonous. Services are also valuable, even though no tangible artefact is produced. Organicists believe that people derive rewards mainly from producing goods. They value product variation only when it arises from the use of local materials, and from the personal style of the worker. They value tangible products over intangible services, and craft-work over mass production. Producer motivation is strengthened by a long-term relationship with the customer which allows the producer to witness the product in use.	Consumer culture promotes the development of new technology. It exploits advances in technology and communication to significantly improve the material living standards of the poor. However, workers 'alienated' by mass production will produce poor quality, so 'job enrichment', which limits specialization, may actually improve overall efficiency. They may also seek enrichment through trade union activism. Not all workers may require job satisfaction, however. Satisfactions can also be obtained from hobbies and recreations. Boring jobs may indirectly enrich cultural life by encouraging people to seek satisfaction in community activity instead.

Table 8.6   Detailed analysis of pragmatism versus proceduralism

Characteristic: pragmatic/ proceduralist	Commentary	High-performance mix
Empirical/ theoretical	A pragmatist believes that the response to change should be based on evidence rather than theory – it should be improvised on the basis of previous experience. Everyone has unique life experiences which help to prepare them for taking decisions. Belief in the uniqueness of personal experience links pragmatism to atomism. A proceduralist believes that decisions should be explicitly rational, in the sense of being grounded in some theory. Without the correct theory, evidence cannot be properly interpreted. Decisions should be based on calculation rather than improvisation. Since the mastery of theory often requires intellectual ability, theoretical orientation is often linked to elitism.	Theory and experience need to be combined. Neither evidence without theory, nor theory without evidence, will produce good decisions on how to respond to change. In some situations there is no relevant theory, whereas in other cases there are multiple theories, and hence confusion. Theories invariably abstract from certain factors, and may therefore distort a decision if the omitted factor is important. On the other hand, ignoring relevant theory can mean that the significance of key evidence is not appreciated.
Outcome-based/ process-based	Proceduralists believe that a correct theory can suggest a rational procedure which will guarantee a correct decision. A group of people (e.g. a committee) may be involved in taking the decision. Pragmatists believe that procedures normally delay a decision, and make the outcome	Rational procedures may be useful in dealing with transitory volatility, e.g. in recording reservations or managing inventory. But there are few cases where theory is good enough to identify an optimal procedure. Procedures can also be useful in encouraging autocratic individuals to consult with

Table 8.6   (continued)

Characteristic: pragmatic/ proceduralist	Commentary	High-performance mix
	worse. Disagreements in committees can add to delays; it is better to make one person clearly responsible for a decision, and let them 'get on with it' right away.	knowledgeable people. Otherwise it is individual experience that is crucial. Selecting the right individual is more important than optimizing the procedure they employ.
Risk-taking/ risk-averse	A proceduralist believes that risk can be reduced through rational decision-making processes, whereas a pragmatist denies this. The proceduralist worries that correct procedures have not been properly followed, whereas the pragmatist, having improvised their decision, simply sits back and waits for events to unfold.	Large intermittent shocks cannot easily be addressed by routine procedures, and so risk is inescapable. Frequent minor shocks can often be addressed by rational procedures which involve collecting and processing information before a decision is made. The collection of information allows risk to be managed, although it cannot be eliminated altogether. People who are responsible for dealing with large intermittent shocks must be willing to take substantial risks.
Artistic/scientific	Science analyses local situations in terms of timeless universal laws, whereas the artist often expresses surprise and wonder at a situation. The scientist typically values uniformity whereas the artist values diversity. A scientific approach supports the development of a theory and the collection of evidence in a systematic way. It therefore underpins	Economic theory has employed social scientific principles, such as the division of labour, specialization according to comparative advantage and global competition, with considerable success. Decision-makers who do not understand these principles are at a major disadvantage in business life. Economics has proved much less successful, however, in analysing the emotional

Table 8.6 (continued)

Characteristic: pragmatic/ proceduralist	Commentary	High-performance mix
	a procedural approach. Art tends to emphasize an emotional or even mystical response to a situation that is not fully understood. It focuses on situations that are difficult, or impossible, to understand in purely scientific terms. It therefore supports a pragmatic approach to decision-making.	rewards that people derive from work and social activity. A combination of scientific understanding of the laws of markets on the one hand, and an artistic appreciation of emotional factors on the other, is therefore the appropriate combination for successful decision-making.
Personal/ impersonal	Pragmatists believe that people know a great deal more than they realize, and so it pays to converse with them rather than wait for them to tell what they know. People can also say more than they can write, because tone and gesture can aid expression. Pragmatists try out their ideas in conversation with other people, provoking others into revealing what they think. This helps them to arrive at a decision quickly. Proceduralists believe that written communication is superior to the spoken word because it is more precise. There is less scope for ambiguity and reason is unlikely to be clouded by emotion. Proceduralists prefer to consult through memoranda, which they	Complex arguments benefit from being set out formally, but simple powerful ideas can often be expressed most vividly in conversation. Highly original ideas are difficult to articulate in a formal way. Original solutions to problems are therefore more likely to be generated through personal interaction.

Table 8.6   (continued)

Characteristic: pragmatic/ proceduralist	Commentary	High-performance mix
	study carefully before arriving at their decision.	
Unprincipled/ principled	A principled person believes that they are under moral obligation to a higher authority. They are called to play a particular role in society. They can only achieve peace of mind by doing their duty. Their higher nature (conscience, or spirit) recognizes that they need to control their lower nature (body, or passions). Self-control can be exercised through positive emotions, e.g. enthusiasm for a cause, or negative emotions, such as guilt and shame. Principles need to be based on functionally useful moral values: honesty, loyalty, hard work, and so on. These support teamwork on projects and facilitate coordination between different teams. An unprincipled person believes in satiating their biological needs. The only source of authority is their body; their objective is pleasure rather than peace of mind.	People need to respect their bodily requirements for physical survival, but over-indulgence can damage health. People have emotional as well as material needs, and those who realize this will be happier than those who do not. A moral framework enhances emotional rewards derived from participation in socially beneficial projects. Traditional moral principles such as honesty, loyalty and hard work facilitate coordination in complex economies by reducing transaction costs, encouraging investment, and promoting hard work. An effective leader will therefore promote traditional moral principles, even if their ambitions are purely materialistic.
Secular/religious	The secular moralist expects to derive emotional benefits as part of an	Rivalry between religious groups can promote distrust as well as trust. Religious

Table 8.6   (continued)

Characteristic: pragmatic/ proceduralist	Commentary	High-performance mix
	enhanced quality of life, whereas the religious person expects a dividend in the after-life. Religious people are therefore motivated by deferred rather than immediate emotional rewards. Their moral conduct is therefore more robust to disappointments. On the other hand, their beliefs in the after-life can prove vulnerable to attack from sceptics.	commitment can make religious conflict very intense. On the other hand, religious commitment can also promote extreme forms of self-sacrifice and heroism, such as those involved in fighting in defence of a country. While both secular morality and religious belief can generate emotional satisfactions (for people of good conduct), religion adds a further dimension to motivation which secularism lacks.

leader must decide how far his or her followers should be allowed to form lower-level groups on their own initiative. Should the emergence of lower leaders be encouraged, as a welcome display of initiative, or discouraged as a potential threat to the leader's power? Other dimensions apply at every level. The issue of trust, for example, is fundamental at every level. A high-level leader who does not trust lower-level leaders will either discourage the formation of low-level groups or will promote aggressive competition with them, whereas a trusting leader may encourage low-level groups and promote cooperation and orderly competition between them (Knight, 1935). At the same time leaders of lower-level groups must decide whether to monitor their members and offer material rewards for good behaviour, or whether to trust the members to monitor themselves and to reward themselves emotionally for good behaviour.

8.12   METHODOLOGICAL ISSUES IN MODELLING CULTURE

This final part of the chapter attempts to draw together the threads of the preceding discussion. It begins by summarizing the principal differences between conventional neoclassical economics and the economic theory

Table 8.7   Detailed analysis of degree of trust

Characteristic: low-trust/ high-trust	Commentary	High-performance mix
Selfish/ altruistic	Selfish people cannot empathize with others. Their concerns are focused on their own consumption, work and leisure. They may be concerned with status, but only in an instrumental way – as a means of gaining privileged access to resources. They are concerned with the state of society only in so far as it impacts on their own material interests. Altruistic people empathize with others – either personally, e.g. friends, or impersonally, e.g. concern for the poor. They can derive vicarious pleasure from other people's happiness, and share their suffering too. Degrees of altruism differ depending on the weight that people place on other people's interests.	Altruism is important in channelling high-tension people into providing support for others. Self-interested ambition can stimulate high-tension but generates external diseconomies, and leads to under-provision of emotional support. It does nothing to address the income inequality generated by competition between self-interested people, or to support the losers from the competitive process and their dependants.
Autocratic/ consultative	When other people are selfish and cannot be trusted, their opinions will reflect where their own interests lie. Consultation creates a risk of distorting decisions through lobbying from vested interests. If you cannot believe what other people say, there is no point in asking their opinion. If other people are honest and their preferences are aligned with those of the decision-maker, their opinions may be valuable since they are likely to have been thinking about	Consultation is useful not only in improving a decision but in motivating people to implement a decision through participation in the decision process. Opinions received need to be critically examined, however. Where vested interests are important, conflicting opinions from the different interests will reveal that a problem exists.

Table 8.7 (continued)

Characteristic: low-trust/ high-trust	Commentary	High-performance mix
	similar issues for themselves. Hence consultation is worthwhile.	
Aggressive/ orderly	People naturally respond aggressively when they feel frustrated or threatened. Unanticipated conflicts in congested public spaces often provoke displays of aggression. A low-trust society sees aggression as natural, and may rationalize reprisals as a useful form of deterrence. Aggression is also believed to be useful in strengthening competition. It discourages collusion and stimulates competitive entry into profitable industries. A high-trust society believes that aggression destroys harmony. Provocations often stem from misunderstandings. Disputes should be resolved, not through hasty reprisals, but in a more considered way through intermediaries such as law courts. People must avoid reprisals by exercising self-control. A high-trust society believes in orderly competition, conducted according to 'rules of the game' which maximize benefits such as innovation, and reduce costs from, e.g. dishonest advertising.	The high-trust view is correct. An advanced society is highly complex and the 'law of the jungle', which usually rewards aggression, does not work well. Reprisals can lead to feuds which originate with a simple misunderstanding. Competition is not just about challenging monopoly but about stimulating and diffusing socially useful innovations. Competitors who sabotage each other's activities do not benefit society and so 'rules of the game' are required. Competition works best when rivals can be trusted to abide by the rules. While aggression may sometimes motivate innovation, other motivators such as public recognition are available too. Channelling aggression into competition may be a useful way of controlling a potentially disruptive biological urge, but it still needs to be moderated through self-control.

Table 8.8   Detailed analysis of the Degree of Tension

Characteristic: high-tension/ low-tension	Commentary	High-performance mix
Aspirational/ complacent	Aspirational people have high norms. These norms may correspond to ideals deduced from moral or theoretical principles. Alternatively, people with wide horizons may know that higher standards are being achieved elsewhere. They are dissatisfied with the status quo. They believe that it can and must be changed. Complacent people have low norms. They have narrow horizons due to a parochial outlook. They are satisfied with the status quo, and their chief ambition is to maintain it.	The high norms of the aspirational person are indispensable to a high-performance culture.
Deliberative/ spontaneous	A deliberative person concentrates single-mindedly on achieving their objective. He/she remains focused on it until it has either been achieved or has irretrievably failed. Success is quietly satisfying but failure is mortifying. A spontaneous person focuses on whatever has caught their attention most recently. It is not necessary to finish one task before starting another. Success is a cause for celebration, however minor it may be. Failure is attributed to bad luck or blamed on others.	Deliberation prevents people with high norms from giving up too easily. Spontaneity undermines the value of aspirations, since the aspirations are merely fantasies.

Table 8.8   (continued)

Characteristic: high-tension/ low-tension	Commentary	High-performance mix
Optimistic/ pessimistic	An optimist believes that the environment is favourable for the successful completion of a project whereas a pessimist believes that it is unfavourable. An optimistic culture promotes general optimism through notions such as 'the time is right' and 'it's all up for grabs'. A pessimistic culture promotes the idea that if something was really a good idea then someone else would already have done it.	Optimism reduces perceived risks and thereby encourages investment and innovation. However, unwarranted optimism can lead to wasteful projects being undertaken. Where the private benefits of investment are less than its public benefits, optimism may induce investors to risk losses for the public good. If private and social benefits are aligned, realism is better than either optimism or pessimism, as it leads to better investment decisions.
Confident/ unsure	When an optimist is confronted by a group of pessimists they may decide that they must be wrong. They need self-confidence to believe that they can be right when everyone else is wrong. A confident culture sustains the idea that people in the group are always right, at least compared with people in other groups. It may be based on a notion of innate superiority. People who are unsure usually adapt their opinions to conform with the majority view.	Most leaders require self-confidence to take the initiative in setting up groups, and take the responsibility if things should go wrong. A combination of optimism and self-confidence is a hallmark of an entrepreneurial culture.
Progressive/ conservative	Progressives regard change as largely benign. They believe it provides opportunities rather	A high-performance culture requires a combination of science-driven innovation with the maintenance of

Table 8.8   (continued)

Characteristic: high-tension/ low-tension	Commentary	High-performance mix
	than threats, whereas conservatives take the opposite view. Progressives are continually raising their norms in line with new possibilities whereas conservatives are more concerned with ensuring that existing norms are maintained. Being progressive involves innovation rather than conservatism. Both are demanding, but innovation tends to be more demanding because the element of novelty increases the risks.	functionally-useful traditional morals. It therefore requires both a progressive technical agenda and a conservative moral agenda.

of culture outlined above. Five main differences have been identified. Contrary to conventional neoclassical economics, the economic theory of culture put forward above asserts that:

- Information is costly, both to collect and communicate. Where fundamental issues are concerned it is often impossible to collect objective evidence that will discriminate between alternative theories: thus different systems of belief can coexist almost indefinitely. Conflicts between rival value systems are even more difficult to resolve; their authority often derives from tradition or from spiritual experiences whose authenticity it is impossible to assess. Information costs help to explain uncertainty – uncertainty exists because it is prohibitively costly to collect all the relevant information before taking a decision. Many uncertainties are radical and existential, because fundamental issues are peculiarly difficult to resolve. It is not just 'facts' that are uncertain – theories are uncertain too.
- The economic environment is volatile. Factual information is therefore continually obsolescing. A steady flow of new information is required to permit the economy to adapt appropriately to changing

circumstances. Information sources are localized, so different people have access to different information. Furthermore, since different people use different theories to interpret this information, individuals will react to similar events in very different ways. An important advantage of decentralization is that it empowers people to act immediately on their judgement of a situation. Where opinions differ about the advisability of change, competition permits the optimists to bid resources away from the pessimists, and so the weight of opinion as expressed in the market determines whether and how much change takes place.

- Because information is a public good, it is inefficient to replicate its collection unless communication costs are high. Furthermore, it is better to concentrate information processing on people with a comparative advantage in interpretation – that is, on those whose beliefs are closest to the truth. These will tend to be the people with a track record of successful decisions. Intermediaries therefore emerge who specialize in processing information of particular kinds. Entrepreneurs intermediate by setting up new firms to sell new products, whilst social leaders intermediate by setting up new clubs and charities.

- Each person's utility depends upon emotional as well as material rewards. Change often elicits a powerful emotional response; some people thrive on the excitement of change, while others fear its consequences. Leaders need to be calm when taking decisions – they have to be confident in their judgements. They also need to understand the anxieties of their followers and provide them with reassurance if they can.

- Emotions are morally framed. Pride and self-esteem on the one hand, and guilt and shame on the other, are powerful emotions. Leaders can associate positive emotions with actions that promote coordination and negative emotions with actions that undermine coordination. This engineers trust and so reduces agency costs and transactions costs. Improved coordination enhances the performance of the group. The leader can recover costs from this enhanced performance by various means – taxes, membership fees, voluntary donations – depending upon the type of group involved.

These assumptions are perfectly compatible with a rational action approach to modelling. However, the detailed specification of a model is rendered difficult by the fact that both theories and facts are uncertain. Nevertheless, the basic structure of the model can be set out using three propositions:

- Leadership operates at different levels. High-level leaders control nation-states, organized religions and international pressure groups. Middle-level leaders manage firms, clubs and charities, whilst low-level leaders manage families and local communities. High-level leaders set a high-level culture within which the other leaders must operate. Lower-level leaders can 'free-ride' on useful values and beliefs inculcated by the high-level leader, but if they disagree with the values promoted at the higher level they must invest in counteracting them. This issue separates people into those who prefer to assimilate and conform, and those who oppose or resist (Jones, 1984).
- Followers have a choice of leader. In a democracy they are free to vote for a political party and to practise their preferred religion; they can also decide which firm to work for, which clubs to join, and which charities to support. People recognize that when they decide to follow the leader of a particular group they must adopt the leader's values and beliefs. Many key decisions regarding choice of leader are made around the time a person comes of age. Using the prior beliefs inculcated in their childhood by their family and community, people decide which leaders they will follow in their adult life. They evaluate the risk that a given leader's values and beliefs will turn out to be wrong. They take account of their own personal characteristics, as they perceive them, because these will determine their emotional responses later on. The final choice that an individual makes will reflect not only their beliefs but also their preferences – selfish or altruistic, material or emotional and so on.
- Leaders seek to optimize the values and beliefs they promote in order to fulfil their own objectives. Honest leaders will promote their true beliefs – acting on conviction – but dishonest leaders may adapt their values in order to maximize their following. Culture change will occur both through leaders modifying their values to maintain market share, and by followers switching between committed leaders who are unwilling on principle to adjust their values for the sake of expediency.

These propositions show how the basic economic principles of choice and competition can be applied to culture. The economic theory of culture subsumes standard neoclassical economics as a special case. In a simple neoclassical economic model, there is just a single culture which corresponds to the 'true' model of the economy. This 'true' model assumes that people are selfish and materialistic. It is therefore a model of a low-trust society. The high-trust alternative is excluded by assumption. It is also a model of an individualistic society, since people care nothing about the welfare of others and take a purely instrumental view of the kind of society in which they live (for a comprehensive critique along these lines see Roberts and Holden, 1972; Schoeffer, 1955).

8.13 HISTORICAL PERSPECTIVES

The empirical and historical literature linking culture to economic performance is extremely diffuse. It is possible, however, to identify three specific issues which have had a significant impact on the economic analysis of culture: the Weber thesis, obstacles to development and the role of freedom.

Economic historians have long debated the Weber thesis that the Protestant ethic promoted the growth of capitalism (Weber, 1930). There is broad agreement that the spread of international commerce in Europe coincided with the Reformation (although pre-Reformation origins in Italian city-states must not be overlooked). However causality has been questioned. The Protestant ethic can also be understood as accommodating Christian beliefs to the requirements of an emerging mercantile middle-class (Schlicht, 1995). Behind the theological revolution, therefore, a vested business interest may be detected. Protestantism 'dis-intermediated' the papacy and gave people a direct relationship with God through prayer. It undermined the case for paying the church for indulgences and the upkeep of chantries, and for obeying prohibitions on usury – and thereby reduced the economic burdens on the middle-class.

The theological content had real effects, however. The Protestant convert accepted grace through personal salvation. The sign of grace was not monastic seclusion, as before, but spreading the Gospel through engagement with the world. Business was a 'calling' which could promote missionary work. It supported the expansion of commercial empires into the 'darker corners' of the world. Whilst the origins of Protestantism may be questioned, therefore, its effects appear to be those which Weber predicted. Protestantism replaced the collectivist and procedural culture of the Roman Catholic church with a more individualistic and pragmatic culture, which formed the foundations of the competitive individualism that characterizes the West today.

Jones (1981, 1988) examines the 'take off' of commercialism in Western Europe from a different perspective and arrives at rather similar conclusions. Jones regards entrepreneurship as a natural human behaviour which supports survival by encouraging people to show initiative in meeting their material needs. However entrepreneurship can be stifled by political tyrannies, in which collectivism and proceduralism are imposed (Rosenberg and Birdzell, 1986). The motive is to monopolize the tax-base and use its revenues to support a leisured lifestyle for the elite. From this perspective the Reformation is a protest movement which, by overthrowing a parasitic religious elite, liberated people to follow their natural entrepreneurial inclinations. China and other Asian powers have never liberated themselves in this way; when one elite is deposed, another simply takes its place. Once again, however, the explanation may be cultural – perhaps Western society is intolerant of political oppression in the way that some Asian societies are not.

Development economists have addressed similar issues but from a more secular perspective (Bardhan, 2000). A drive to 'modernize' post-colonial societies is typically advocated (McClelland and Winter, 1969). In the 1960s, modernization became the secular equivalent of the Protestant ethic. The object was to engineer a high-tension society driven by a desire to catch up with the West in place of a low-tension society where people are content with low living standards and high mortality. Individualism was a secondary consideration; in the 1960s, planned industrialization behind protective tariffs was the recommended strategy, and it was only in the 1990s that privatization and liberalization took over.

A major obstacle to economic development in the poorest countries is weak internal communications which perpetuate a cellular social structure based on local family and tribal loyalties. High levels of local trust are combined with low levels of trust at the national level. National government is too corrupt to intermediate the flow of funds between international agencies and local people. The engineering of trust at the national level has been accomplished in a number of Asian economies but with one or two notable exceptions there has been little success in Africa. As noted earlier, creating a high-tension high-trust society has proved difficult even in prosperous Western countries.

The disintegration of Soviet communism has led to a resurgence in research dedicated to showing that 'freedom' holds the key to economic performance (Gwartney and Lawson, 2003). The guarantor of freedom is usually said to be a US-style constitution (Scully, 1992). A range of freedom indicators has been developed, and cross-country statistical regressions have been reported which confirm the impact of freedom on living standards and economic growth. On the whole these regressions simply confirm that, other things being equal, Western-style competitive individualism promotes economic growth. The point is not difficult to make if a sufficient number of poor African dictatorships is included in the sample of countries. As in any cross-section regression, there are omitted variables, and much of the sample variation remains unexplained. The apparent significance of some of the variables may be due to the presence of omitted cultural variables, including the legacy of traditional religion (Kohut et al., 2000). Whilst these regressions are a significant advance on anecdotal evidence, the range of explanatory variables is too narrow to offer a full account of cultural factors in economic performance.

Advocates of freedom as the critical factor are usually unsympathetic to a cultural interpretation of their findings and this biases the way in which they interpret their results. They typically believe that laws, not morals, reduce agency costs and transaction costs. They believe that a written constitution enforced through impartial courts is better than an unwritten constitution enforced through social sanctions. They believe that the biological drives such as greed and aggression are better guarantors of competition than a genuine desire to benefit the customer. They therefore ignore crucial issues such as why greedy judges do not accept bribes, and how the basic needs of people with low incomes are met.

The historical significance of culture is related to the historical significance of other intangible public goods, such as technological know-how. It is therefore not surprising that modern writers on convergence of national economic growth rates have begun to develop an interest in cultural issues. The traditional way of analysing the convergence of growth rates focuses on technological diffusion, but there is no reason why the analysis should not include cultural diffusion too. The rapid spread of free-market ideology in the 1990s, with many governments reducing tariffs and privatizing and deregulating their utilities, is a clear example of cultural diffusion. Such cultural diffusion can lead to convergence in institutions as well as in rates of growth. A particularly interesting development has been the incorporation of religion in the convergence model (for a significant step in this direction see Barro and McCleary, 2003).

Whilst the European empires of the nineteenth century are often credited with the spread of Christianity, the US-led Western 'empire' of the late twentieth century is noted chiefly for the spread of secularism. This raises the issue of whether religion or secularism is best for economic growth. If religion is best then the spread of secularism could lead to convergence on a sub-optimal level of growth. The analysis in this chapter suggests that it is the specific content of religious belief that is crucial in this respect, because it is the specific beliefs that determine the emotional incentive structure that motivates people. A simple distinction between religion and secularism is therefore too crude to properly identify the link between religious belief and economic performance. The impact of the spread of religion and culture on the convergence of growth rates is clearly an important topic that warrants further research.

8.14   CONCLUSION

This chapter has shown that the influence of culture on the economy extends well beyond the production and consumption of cultural goods in the fields of media and the arts. Culture is concerned with the production and distribution of values and beliefs relating to fundamental issues. Cultural products are simply one of the means through which these values and beliefs are expressed. Identifying the fundamental issues addressed by culture is the key to analysing its impact on economic performance. Values and beliefs of a suitable kind can improve economic performance – both materially, and by enhancing quality of life. Culture is therefore an economic asset. Culture is shared by communication between the members of a social group. It is, in fact, an intangible durable public good. Significant investment is required to create and maintain this public good. Competition between cultures, in terms of relative economic performance, is essentially competition between social groups in investing in appropriate public goods of this type.

By modifying five key assumptions of conventional neoclassical economics, and introducing a theory of leadership, it is possible not only to explain how culture influences performance but also to explain how cultures will adapt to changing local conditions. There are different levels of leadership, corresponding roughly to the size of the group that the leader controls. At any given level the nature of competition is strongly influenced by the media that leaders employ to recruit and retain their followers. The development of mass media disseminating visual images has had a profound effect on ideological competition between political leaders. Changes in the media have made the promotion of high-trust cultures extremely difficult, whilst a sceptical attitude towards leadership in general has diminished the supply of able leaders. Distorted incentives in the market for leadership mean that the most effective culture does not always prevail.

The ideal culture from an economic point of view is individualistic, pragmatic, high-trust and high-tension, though each of these attributes must be moderated to some degree by the need to adapt the culture to local requirements. A simple way of summarizing the advantages of this culture is to note that it is both entrepreneurial and moral. It is entrepreneurial because it encourages innovation and risk-taking, and it is moral because it discourages innovations or risky ventures that cause disproportionate damage to the interests of others. It is moral because it encourages honesty and loyalty, but it is entrepreneurial because it does so without stipulating rigid conformity to specific practices.

The high-performance culture also encourages both freedom and responsibility. Freedom allows diversity of behaviour and thereby facilitates innovation. It also decentralizes power: it allows decisions to be taken by people who have immediate access to relevant information, and so avoids the expense and delay of referring straightforward decisions to higher authority. However, responsibility requires people to show consideration for others (Ellickson, 1991). In respecting other people's freedoms, they accept constraints on their own. They consult with other people before acting in an unexpected way. Consultation is effected both formally and informally. A high-trust culture encourages people to honour informal agreements. A legalistic culture sets out rights and responsibilities, records them and enforces them. People are obliged to negotiate with others who hold the relevant rights before they act. Informal methods work well with members of a tightly-knit social group – friends, relatives and neighbours – whilst formal methods are more appropriate for more impersonal groups. A moral culture will rely on trust as much as possible but will underpin trust by the rule of law.

The high-performance culture respects both tradition and modernity. Embracing modernity promotes scientific research and the practical application of science in engineering and medicine. It also encourages economy through the systematic elimination of waste. Tradition, on the other hand, underpins many core moral values. Conflict can ensue when scientific discoveries appear to undermine traditional religious beliefs on which conventional morality is based. Some religions are more vulnerable than others on this score, however. An entrepreneurial culture is not devoid of religion, but rather involves religious beliefs which coexist with a scientific view of the world.

REFERENCES

Bardhan, P. (2000), 'The nature of institutional impediments to economic development', in M. Olson and S. Kahkonen (eds), *A Not-so-Dismal Science: A Broader View of Economies and Societies*, Oxford: Oxford University Press, pp. 245–68.

Barro, Robert and Rachel M. McCleary (2003), 'Religion and political economy in an international panel', discussion paper, Harvard University, Cambridge, MA.

Baxter, J.L. (1988), *Social and Psychological Foundations of Economic Analysis*, Brighton: Harvester Wheatsheaf.

Bolnick, B.R. (1975), 'Towards a behavioural theory of philanthropic activity', in E.S. Phelps (ed.), *Altruism, Morality and Economic Theory*, New York: Russell Sage, pp. 197–224.

Buruna, I. (1999), *Voltaire's Coconuts, or Anglomania in Europe*, London: Weidenfeld and Nicolson.

Casson, Mark (1990), *Enterprise and Competition*, Oxford: Oxford University Press.

Casson, Mark (1991), *Economics of Business Culture: Game Theory, Transactions Costs and Economic Performance*, Oxford: Clarendon Press.

Casson, Mark (1993), 'Cultural determinants of economic performance', *Journal of Comparative Economics*, **17**, 418–42.

Casson, Mark (2000), *Enterprise and Leadership: Studies on Firms, Markets and Networks*, Cheltenham, UK and Northampton, MA, USA: Edward Elgar.

Casson, Mark (2002), 'Leadership and cultural change: an economic analysis', *De Ekonomist*, **150** (4), 409–38.

Earl, Peter E. (1986), *Lifestyle Economics: Consumer Behaviour in a Turbulent World*, Brighton: Wheatsheaf.

Easterlin, R.A. (1998), *Growth Triumphant*, Ann Arbor, MI: University of Michigan Press.

Easterlin, R.A. (2001), 'Income and happiness: towards a unified theory', *Economic Journal*, **111**, 465–84.

Ekelund, Robert B. Jr and R.D. Tollison (1997), *Politicized Economies: Monarchy, Monopoly and Mercantilism*, College Station, TX: Texas A&M University Press.

Ellickson, R.C. (1991), *Order without Law: How Neighbours Settle Disputes*, Cambridge MA: Harvard University Press.

Foreman-Peck, J. and G. Federico (eds) (1999), *European Industrial Policy: The Twentieth Century Experience*, Oxford: Oxford University Press.

Frank, R.H. (1985), *Choosing the Right Pond*, Oxford: Oxford University Press.

Ginsburgh, V. and P. Michel (1997), 'Optimal policy business cycles', *Journal of Economic Dynamics and Control*, **22**, 503–18.

Graham, J.L. (2001), 'Culture and human resources management', in Alan M. Rugman and Thomas L. Brewer (eds), *Oxford Handbook of International Business*, Oxford: Oxford University Press, pp. 503–36.

Gwartney, J. and R. Lawson (2003), *Economic Freedom of the World: 2003 Annual Report*, Vancouver, BC: Fraser Institute.

Hahnel, R. and M. Albert (1990), *Quiet Revolution in Welfare Economics*, Princeton, NJ: Princeton University Press.

Hampden-Turner, C. and F. Trompenaars (1997), *Mastering the Infinite Game*, Oxford: Capstone.

Hirschman, Albert O. (1982), *Shifting Involvements: Private Interests and Public Action*, Oxford: Martin Robertson.

Hofstede, Geert (1980), *Culture's Consequences*, Beverly Hills, CA: Sage.

Holmes, S. and C.R. Sunstein (1999), *The Cost of Rights: Why Liberty Depends on Taxes*, New York: W.W. Norton.

Jones, Eric L. (1981), *The European Miracle*, Cambridge: Cambridge University Press.

Jones, Eric L. (1988), *Growth Recurring: Economic Change in World History*, Oxford: Oxford University Press.

Jones, Eric L. (2000), 'The case for a shared world language', in M. Casson and A. Godley (eds), *Cultural Factors in Economic Growth*, Berlin: Springer, pp. 210–35.

Jones, Stephen R.G. (1984), *The Economics of Conformism*, Oxford: Blackwell.

Knight, Frank H. (1935), *The Ethics of Competition and Other Essays*, London: Allen & Unwin.

Kohut, A., J.C. Green, S. Keeter and R.C. Tuth (2000), *The Diminishing Divide: Religion's Changing Role in American Politics*, Washington, DC: Brookings Institution.

Landes, D.S. (1998), *The Wealth and Poverty of Nations*, New York: W.W. Norton.

Layard, R. (1980), 'Human satisfactions and public policy', *Economic Journal*, **90**, 737–50.

Leacock, S. (1998), *My Recollection of Chicago and the Doctrine of Laissez Faire*, ed. C. Spadini, Toronto: University of Toronto Press.

Lucas, Robert E. (1981), *Studies in Business Cycle Theory*, Cambridge MA: MIT Press.

Macfie, A.L. (1967), *The Individual in Society: Papers on Adam Smith*, London: Allen & Unwin.

McClelland, D.C. and D.G. Winter (1969), *Motivating Economic Achievement*, New York: Free Press.

Newman, K.S (1983), *Law and Economic Organization: A Comparative Study of Pre-industrial Societies*, Cambridge: Cambridge University Press.

O'Brien, G.E. (1988), 'Work and leisure', in W.F. Van Raaj, G.M. Van Veldhoven and K.E. Warnweryd (eds), *Handbook of Economic Psychology*, Dordrecht: Kluwer, pp. 538–69.

Olson, Mancur (2000), 'Big bills left on the sidewalk: why some nations are rich and others poor', in M. Olson and S. Kahkonen (eds), *A Not-so-Dismal Science: A Broader View of Economies and Societies*, Oxford: Oxford University Press, pp. 37–60.

Protherough, R. and J. Pick (2002), *Managing Britannia: Culture and Management in Modern Britain*, Denton: Brynmill Press.

Pryor, Frederic L. (1977), *The Origins of the Economy: A Comparative Study of Distribution in Primitive and Peasant Economies*, New York: Academic Press.

Putnam, Robert D. (1993), *Making Democracy Work: Civic Traditions in Modern Italy*, Princeton, NJ: Princeton University Press.

Reisman, David (1990), *Theories of Collective Action: Downs, Olson and Hirsch*, London: Macmillan.

Roberts, B. and B.R. Holden (1972), *Theory of Social Process: An Economic Analysis*, Ames, IA: Iowa State University Press.

Rosenberg, Nathaniel and L.E. Birdzell (1986), *How the West Grew Rich: The Transformation of the Industrial World*, London: I.B. Tauris.

Schlicht, Ekerhart (1995), 'Economic analysis and organized religion', in E. Jones and V. Reynolds (eds), *Survival and Religion: Biological Evolution and Cultural Change*, Chichester: John Wiley, pp. 111–62.

Schoeffer, S. (1955), *The Failures of Economics: A Diagnostic Study*, Cambridge, MA: Harvard University Press.

Scitovsky, Tibor (1976), *The Joyless Economy: An Inquiry into Human Satisfaction and Consumer Dissatisfaction*, Oxford: Oxford University Press.

Scully, G.W. (1992), *Constitutional Environments and Economic Growth*, Princeton, NJ: Princeton University Press.

Sherman, A.L. (1997), *The Soul of Development: Biblical Christianity and Economic Transformation in Guatemala*, Oxford: Oxford University Press.

Stark, R. and W.S. Bainbridge (1987), *A Theory of Religion*, New York: Peter Lang.

Viner, Jacob (1972), *The Role of Providence in the Social Order: An Essay in Intellectual History*, Philadelphia: American Philosophical Society.

Viner, Jacob (1978), *Religious Thought and Economic Society: Four Chapters of an Unfinished Work*, ed. J. Melitz and D. Winch, Durham, NC: Duke University Press.

Weber, Max (1930), *The Protestant Ethic and the Spirit of Capitalism*, (trans. T. Parsons), London: Allen & Unwin.

PART III

History

9. Entrepreneurship and vertical integration: the origins of the Singer global distribution system

With Andrew Godley

The emergence of the modern industrial enterprise towards the end of the nineteenth century was associated with the innovation of new managerial methods. It also involved a significant extension of the boundaries of the firm through horizontal and vertical integration. As Schumpeter (1934, 1939) emphasized, such institutional innovations are essentially entrepreneurial. Unfortunately, however, these changes are often analysed as if they were largely routine. They are seen as a consequence of managerialism rather than of entrepreneurialism, and their origins have consequently been misunderstood. This chapter uses the theory developed in the previous chapters to put the historical record straight. It reinterprets the rise of the modern corporation by focusing on the case study of vertical integration *par excellence*, Singer sewing machines.

9.1 INTRODUCTION

The dramatic changes in technology and the global spread of market activity during the second half of the twentieth century were associated with equally dramatic changes in the structure of firms. The dominant corporations that emerged during this 'second industrial revolution' were giant, multidivisional, bureaucratic organizations. While powerful for many decades, their structures were later revealed to be inefficient and uncompetitive in what the renowned business historian, Lou Galambos, has called the 'third industrial revolution' at the turn of the twenty-first century (Galambos, 2005). Rather it is flexible and dynamic entrepreneurial firms that are competitive today.

This transformation of firms and industries is, in historical terms, indeed revolutionary. It has been simplified as a paradigm shift from the big, bureaucratic firms dominant in the second industrial revolution to the entrepreneurial firms of today. And it is a transformation that must necessarily prompt reinvestigation of the underlying premises of the dominant account of the second industrial revolution, business historian A.D. Chandler's explanation of what he called 'the emergence of the modern business enterprise' (Chandler, 1977).

This began in the last quarter of the nineteenth century, in particular in the United States, and especially in sectors like steel production and railroad transportation. It also appeared in the emerging sectors of oil, food and tobacco production, automobiles, sewing machines, chemicals and electrical engineering. It was in this second group of sectors, most iconically in automobiles, that the emergence of the modern corporation was also associated with breakthrough innovations in the technology and organization of production, typically known as mass production and scientific management.

The emergence of giant multidivisional firms in the latter part of the nineteenth century was a frequently noted phenomenon among contemporaries. Of course they did not describe it as vertical integration, indeed they most frequently personalized the entire process, focusing on the roles of key individuals. At a time of great social inequality, these individuals were given the pejorative epithet of 'Robber Barons'. Exactly how they were described is less important for the purposes of this chapter than the recognition that, to contemporaries, the emergence of the modern business enterprise in the years from around 1880 up to the 1920s was explicitly framed in terms of an entrepreneurial process. Indeed the theoretical contributions of Frank Knight (1921) and Joseph Schumpeter (1934, 1939) focused on what was then the new corporate form. And yet in the more recent scholarly literature on the rise and decline of the large bureaucratic corporation, the role of the entrepreneur appears to be missing.

9.2.　DISTRIBUTION, DIVISION AND THE EMERGENCE OF THE MODERN CORPORATION

The modern vertically-integrated corporation emerged at a time of great volatility; according to Chandler, this took place in three phases. First (1790 to 1840) was the initial period of market expansion, followed (1840 to 1880) by the necessary developments in transport to allow mass markets to emerge. The 'most transformative' phase, according to Richard John (1997, p. 158), was the third, from 1880 to 1920. This saw the integration of mass production and mass distribution among a few pioneering manufacturers, who 'could sell in volume only if they created a massive, multiunit marketing organization . . . It was the decade of the 1880s when enterprises in these industries began to build or rationalize their national and global sales forces' (Chandler, 1977, pp. 308–9). It was this group of successful experiments in forward integration that in turn prompted the creation of managerial hierarchies to monitor the different divisions, these hierarchies enabled professional managers to apply their expertise and begin to build industry-specific and technology-specific capabilities, and so pursue paths of high innovation throughout the twentieth century (Klepper, 2002).

The dominant theoretical explanation of this creation of managerial hierarchies remains Williamson's transaction cost economizing approach, where, under behavioural norms of bounded rationality and opportunism, the presence of asset specificity and other 'market failures' may prompt Coasian internalization of multi-stage production and distribution systems (Coase, 1937; Williamson 1981, 1985; Chandler 1992). The popularity of Williamson's interpretation means that the historical emergence of vertically-integrated firms is no longer understood, as it was by contemporary observers, like Knight and Schumpeter, as the result of great acts of entrepreneurial endeavour, but rather as the linear outcome of incremental cost-minimizing decisions by a far-seeing professional management pursuing sequential 'make-or-buy' decisions. Vertical integration became viewed as a managerial process focused on contractual change, rather than entrepreneurial innovation (Lamoreux et al., 2003, 2004). But reducing this key organizational innovation to a set of contractual amendments trivializes the degree of uncertainty faced by key actors and reduces the significance of their improvised solutions.

It is a mistake to suppose that the transition from one set of routine management practices to another set of routine management practices is itself a routine procedure. Changing routines requires judgement and improvisation, based on experiments with alternative methods. It also requires considerable leadership to motivate staff to change their ways. Changing routines, in other words, is a significant entrepreneurial endeavour.

In addition, there are two specific difficulties with the orthodox Chandler-Williamson interpretation of vertical integration. First, the evidence mostly fails to support the claims made, and second, in the one genuine case of a firm creating a 'massive, multiunit marketing organization' – that of Singer – the best explanation for its success is actually one that emphasizes superior entrepreneurial judgment rather than the routine reduction of transaction costs.

From the pioneers of expansive marketing divisions, clustered in the food and machinery industries, Chandler selected four illustrative cases: Singer, Armour, McCormack Reaper and American Tobacco (Chandler, 1977). While evidence on the exact size of the marketing organizations of Armour and American Tobacco remains elusive, they were similar to equivalent pioneers in branded, packaged, processed food, such as Heinz, which employed 450 sales agents by 1904, rising to 952 by 1915. Coca Cola, another pioneer in food and drink, employed 543 sales agents in 1910, rising to 950 by 1914. In machinery McCormack Reaper employed 140 sales agents in 1905. This was in fact less than other marketing-led machinery producers. For example, NCR, the office machinery producer with its near monopoly, employed 750 sales agents in 1910 (Chandler 1977; Friedman 2004; Godley 2006; Tedlow, 1990).

There were, of course, much larger marketing organizations: railways, banks, civil services and military organizations were used to managing far larger bureaucracies. Bureaucratic organizations of up to one thousand people were far from unusual at the time. The Chandlerian logic of firms needing to invest in central managerial organizations to oversee the activities of expanding marketing organizations is difficult to sustain in the face of what was in reality the creation of only relatively small such organizations before 1920. Singer, however, employed a global sales force of 61,444 in 1905. It was the seventh largest firm in the world, and it is the only firm that could remotely be described as having created a 'massive, multiunit marketing organization' before 1920 (Hannah, 1999; Schmitz, 1995).

The case of Singer must therefore be the crucial piece of evidence for the Chandler-Williamson interpretation of the rise of the modern business enterprise. But while it did indeed make the requisite scale of investment in marketing to trigger centralized managerial hierarchies, the scale of this investment means that it has to be understood as an exceptional entrepreneurial decision.

In fact the Chandler-Williamson interpretation of Singer is not the only one of Chandler's key four case studies to be subject to severe revision. As Les Hannah has recently shown, his account of the marketing-led growth of American Tobacco is also flawed (Hannah, 2006). Indeed, despite the popularity of his interpretation, the truth is that the least well-understood element of Chandler's account of the rise of the modern business enterprise is the move into mass distribution (Galambos, 2005). To better understand this and its association with the more recent emergence of entrepreneurial firms, the myth and reality of the Singer case need to be clearly differentiated.

9.3   THE EMERGENCE OF SINGER'S GLOBAL DISTRIBUTION SYSTEM: MYTH AND REALITY

The fable of Singer follows a simple, linear narrative. An 1850 partnership between the reprobate mechanical genius Isaac Singer and the shrewd lawyer, Edward Clark, led to the formation of the company I.M. Singer. The firm's key assets were two of the nine or ten patents essential to the successful manufacture of a sewing machine. Clark (Singer's president from 1876 to 1882) was the leading force behind the creation of the Albany patent pool. This was critical to the development of the early industry, for the holders of these key patents agreed to forgo litigation and to license their technology to other members of the patent pool, thereby creating an informal oligopolistic cartel. Along with Grover and Baker and Wheeler and Wilson (two other members of the patent pool), Singer experimented in retail investment, opening fourteen luxurious retail branches in the United States by 1859. By then Singer was perhaps the third largest American producer, with around a 20 per cent share of this infant industry, somewhat smaller than the market leaders Howe and Wheeler and Wilson (Bourne, 1895).

Chandler (1977) describes Singer's backward integration into timberlands, iron-mills and transportation as evidence of an expansionist strategy to pursue complete integration, which further stimulated investment in managerial hierarchies. Williamson (1985) actually ascribes this strategy as mistaken. But in fact the company rarely pursued backward integration at this time and was rarely concerned by potential opportunistic behaviour among suppliers. Indeed, Singer was happy to deal with only one supplier of its iron castings at its largest factory for many years, and without even a written contract (Singer Manufacturing Company, 1882). The actual acquisitions were in fact dwarfed by other investments of its surplus cash in bonds and other securities. Indeed, the few related investments that it made cannot be explained by any potential 'hold-up' of their key raw materials supplies, which at the time were only wood and steel.

The fable uses the limited experiment in forward integration among a few sewing machine producers in the USA as an explanation for subsequent global success. This interpretation is best illustrated by Williamson's summary statement that between 1856 and 1859 'Only three [patent holders] attempted to integrate forward, however, and only they remained major factors in the industry' (Williamson, 1985, p. 109). The inference is that it was this initial integration into marketing, and not the earlier technological innovation, that became the key to long-term survival in this industry. Chandler linked the innovation in American retailing to dominance in overseas markets. 'After 1860 Singer moved more aggressively than the other two in replacing [independent] regional distributors with [company-owned] branch stores supervised by full-time salaried regional agents' (Chandler, 1977, p. 303). And then 'in 1876 . . . [it was] decided to eliminate the independent agencies altogether, at home and abroad' (p. 304). As Figure 9.1 shows, Singer became remarkably successful,

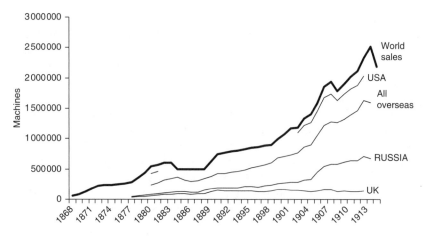

Source: Godley (2006).

Figure 9.1 *Singer's global sales, 1868–1914 (total sewing machines sold and share in major markets)*

especially overseas. But in fact this mythical story of an apparently purposeful and deliberate expansion of the US retail system, the key features
of which were then successfully internationalized, is wholly inconsistent
with the reality of the historical record.

The focus on forward integration into US retailing in the 1850s
and early 1860s misses the fundamental point that demand for sewing
machines then came almost entirely from domestic clothing manufacturers, who either bought direct or via specialist industry agents. Very few
US households could afford a machine. Those who could typically bought
bespoke clothing. There were no patterns available for home-produced,
machine-stitched clothing. Three-quarters of all sales were to the clothing
industry in the early 1860s. With industry demand dominant, the total
market remained subdued: only 20,000 machines in 1858, rising to a still
meagre 40,000 from 1859 to 1864 (Bourne, 1895; Godley, 2001).

It was the household market and not the clothing industry demand
which nevertheless represented the serious growth prospects for American
sewing machine manufacturers. Along with other sewing machine industry
entrepreneurs, Clark targeted the family market with investments in advertising and instalment purchasing, as well as those renowned company-
controlled sales outlets in the late 1850s. But before the American Civil
War (1860–65) these were all relative failures: demand from consumers
was simply not there.

Chandler's (1977) account glosses over the period from 1860 to the late

1870s, and subsequently historians have simply presumed that there was a linear pattern of growth from Singer's early development; from a small-time mechanical engineering company experimenting with owning some retail outlets, into what became perhaps the most significant vertically-integrated multinational enterprise in the world by 1900. Lamoreux et al. (2004), for instance, state that Singer had to integrate vertically to take on demonstration and repair functions for US consumers from the late 1850s, going on to assert that, 'These investments in distribution paid off in a growing stream of orders' (p. 418). In fact, after a short-lived boom, Singer's investment in its American distribution channel was an abject failure.

Initial consumer reluctance to purchase sewing machines disappeared after 1865 and Singer rode a post-Civil War boom in domestic demand. US real wages rose by two-thirds from 1864 to 1876 (Williamson, 1995), and total sewing machine industry sales increased almost twenty-fold, from 40,000 per annum during the war to almost 800,000 at peak in 1873. But thereafter sales stagnated, perhaps because, with two-thirds of US households already owning a machine, saturation was already being approached in the US market. Singer enjoyed the boom. But no more nor less than its American rivals, most of whom had forgone forward integration into retailing and its associated investment in instalment purchasing. In 1872 Singer remained third in rank order of US sales, with a market share probably somewhat less than 20 per cent; smaller than before its experiment in forward integration. (Because of the persistent aggregation of global sewing machine sales by US producers in this period, it is difficult to do more than estimate the companies' US market shares – see Godley 2001, 2006 for a discussion.) Singer sold far more overseas than its US rivals, so its share of the US market has been persistently overestimated.

Like the other manufacturers, Singer's domestic sales suffered after 1873. But in 1877 worse was to happen. The final patent expired and oligopolistic control of the industry ceased. Sewing machine prices in the United States halved within a week. In an industry already suffering stagnant consumer demand, revenues plummeted. By the end of the 1870s Singer's domestic retail network was losing vast amounts, $250,000 in 1879 alone.

Retrenchment of this high-cost, elaborate retail network ought to have begun. New low-cost entrants were looking to become the market leaders. But a vast cross-subsidy from Singer's booming European sales division kept the parent company afloat in the late 1870s and early 1880s and allowed its American retail network to restructure and survive. This overseas windfall emerged because in Europe Singer had already begun a

second experiment in vertical integration, this time successfully, which was
to lead to its unparalleled global supremacy.

9.4   WOODRUFF'S ORGANIZATIONAL INNOVATION

Singer's principal European sales office was based in London, and the
London agent, William Woodruff, recognized that the high population
density in England created an ideal environment for a direct selling organization. In 1876 Woodruff developed the 'canvasser-collector' system,
which overcame the main agency problems by separating out the opening
of an account (the 'canvassing' for business) from the collection of instalment payments. Woodruff's solution borrowed from Clark's original distribution system in that retail outlets were also used as local branch offices
and depots, but the emphasis on direct selling and the scale of instalment
sales were both novel.

Outside the protection of the patent pool, Singer's British agent had
been operating under near-complete autonomy, and had conceived of
the idea of direct selling as a method of distribution in highly urbanized
Britain. But the British market was in its infancy in 1875, and real wages
were only about half those in the United States (Williamson, 1995). The
dilemma for the experienced Woodruff was in knowing whether the British
market in 1875 was about to behave more like the American market
during the fast growth years of 1865 to 1872 or during the slow growth
era of 1850 to 1865. In his letters to Clark, Woodruff repeatedly claimed
that he was convinced that his innovation would be successful in Britain,
but there was no attempt to provide evidence. Indeed it is unlikely that
any evidence existed. He was simply exercising entrepreneurial judgement
in a very uncertain environment. Singer's mostly American competitors
in Britain were just as well placed to develop a novel distribution system
there, but they did not. At least not until after Singer had moved first.

From 1878 Clark began to extend Woodruff's organizational innovation
to other national markets and the direct selling system quickly assumed a
far greater significance than any other aspect of the company's activities.
Figure 9.1 shows this sales growth outside the domestic American market.
By the late 1870s and early 1880s well over half of Singer's machines were
sold overseas. Such rapid expansion meant that by 1882 Singer employed
6,000 people in its overseas selling organizations, over half in direct selling.
No other company in the world had remotely similar numbers of sales
agents at that time. With refinements Singer continued to expand its global
selling organization, employing (as already noted) well over 60,000 in its

sales force all around the world by 1905, cornering an astonishing 80–90 per cent share of the rapidly growing world market. By 1912, US sales were a mere 12 per cent of the total, outstripped by sales in markets such as Russia. Singer's eventual global dominance came from the decision to extend the British selling model to all markets throughout the world.

Williamson and Chandler both correctly identified the fact that Singer's remarkable success was associated with the high transaction costs in purchasing this complex consumer good. As durable goods, sewing machines were rarely repeat purchases, so consumers had to rely on third-party sources for product information. Independent retailers may not have had the specialist knowledge properly to inform consumers, and so company reputation became a substitute for consumers' own testing. Furthermore, as relatively sophisticated products, sewing machines required pre-sales demonstration and after-sales service to overcome the information asymmetries between seller and consumer (Langlois, 2003, 2004). Singer's pervasive direct-selling organisation, knocking on doors and collecting instalment payments, therefore gave consumers many opportunities to inspect in their own homes before purchasing, ensured that they would have ready access to after-sales service for at least the two-year repayment period, and presented a physical manifestation of the reliability and omnipresence that the company came to stand for. Singer's global distribution system was a successful transaction cost economizing solution, and so prompted the large investment by the company in its marketing organization, and the emergence of a large, bureaucratic corporation.

But the innovation of the direct-selling method was not the result of a continuous process of incremental adjustments to an existing distribution system. Neither was it the consequence of the professionalization of management or personal belief in the efficiency of centralized bureaucracy. This managerial perspective is simply an attempt to make the facts fit the fable – the fable that innovation is a product of professional management in a large firm rather than the product of entrepreneurial flair. Although Singer was a large firm at the time of the crucial innovation, it was to some extent a failing firm. The crucial innovation did not emerge from the failing management team, but from an independent agent who was a classic example of an imaginative and self-confident entrepreneur. Finally, the innovation did not emerge in the USA – the alleged home of mass marketing – but in the UK. The entrepreneurial UK agent had so much confidence in his innovation that he persuaded the US management to support his new system at a time when evidence in support of it was still very scarce.

Clark was surprised how quickly the new distribution system created such a strong competitive advantage. As they witnessed Singer's strong sales growth, competitors such as Wheeler and Wilson copied and invested in direct selling organizations, but they were unable to generate sufficient returns and so quickly withdrew. Wheeler and Wilson left the British market in 1882. Woodruff's innovation, while much less costly than the original American distribution system, still required substantial sunk costs. In particular in markets where income levels were so much lower than in the USA, 80–90 per cent of sales were on credit, placing enormous demands on working capital as sales grew. But by expanding the market, Singer was well-placed to reap first-mover advantages and so sustain what was still a high-cost direct-selling organization. Second-movers were simply unable to match their investment.

The contribution of Clark, the dominant stockholder based in the USA, was to recognize Woodruff's success and to appreciate that his innovation could be codified and 'rolled out' to other national markets. This too was an entrepreneurial judgement, although less radical than Woodruff's, because Clark already had evidence of the UK success at the time the rollout began. Nevertheless, risk was involved, for no one knew for sure whether other overseas markets would respond to the Singer distribution system in the same way as the UK. In fact, the impact was enormous. Singer's reward as an entrepreneurial first-mover offering consumers in emerging markets around the world a transaction cost economizing solution to the distribution of sewing machines was to capture an 80–90 per cent share of these markets as the sewing machine diffused through the fast growth phase of its product life-cycle. Global sewing machine sales peaked in 1913, never again to reach their previous level.

9.5   CONCLUSION

The Chandler-Williamson fable of Singer has misunderstood the sequence of events in the company's history – in particular, that its initial US experiment in forward integration was in fact an abject failure. Given Singer's centrality to the Chandler-Williamson paradigm, had the evidence been available then, the view of the emergence of the modern business enterprise as a linear and incremental extension from marketing divisions to managerial hierarchies would surely have been severely qualified. The simplistic interpretation of senior management extending the boundaries of the firm through deliberate transaction cost economizing simply misrepresents the sheer complexity and confusion facing Singer's senior management as they operated in 'uncharted strategic space' (Hannah 2006, p. 45).

The benefit of this revision to the Singer case is that the role of entrepreneurship once again returns to the story of the creation of the modern corporation, just as contemporary observers insisted. The identification of key decisions being made by a small number of key actors and under conditions of very great uncertainty, suggests that the actual historical experience was at considerable variance from the orthodox view. Because the information required to proceed with transaction cost economizing decision rules was simply either partial or absent in such a volatile environment, it is unsurprising that the sequence of events was characterized by successive experiments in different locations. These were sometimes failures, sometimes successful: in the case of Woodruff's solution, the experiment was far more successful than ever anticipated.

The invention of the domestic sewing machine was a technological breakthrough of the first order, one that was poised to introduce major change into world markets. But the obstacle to sales was how to minimize the transaction costs associated with consumer purchase. While the American experience of the 1860s had provided some relevant information, conditions elsewhere in the world were very different; above all living standards were much lower. Singer's London agent improvised a solution, creating a direct sales distribution system, which reduced transaction costs and required lower sunk costs than the original American model. This key investment transformed the sewing machine market, rendering previous assumptions about likely demand invalid. Competitors were unable to match Singer's first-mover advantages and withdrew. While successful in highly urbanized Britain, Singer's senior management further experimented and extended the model elsewhere, devising routine procedures and introducing a bureaucratic organization to manage sales. The Singer case of integration into marketing, the key case in the most transformative phase of the emergence of the modern business enterprise, is therefore much better understood as an exercise in entrepreneurial judgement in a volatile environment.

By changing our understanding of these events, this chapter suggests that a more complete understanding of how and why entrepreneurial firms exist would stress the continuities of the entrepreneurial function over time, in contrast to the obvious changes in the environment. This conclusion frees scholars from the shackles of a false paradigm – a view that characterizes the leading firms of the second industrial revolution as firms dominated by bureaucratic organizations and contrasts them artificially with the entrepreneurial firms of the third industrial revolution. Instead, entrepreneurial judgement has prompted, and continues to prompt, different organizational responses to differing economic conditions at different points in time. There remains ample scope, therefore, for entrepreneurship scholars to embrace historical evidence with productive results.

REFERENCES

Bourne, F. (1895), 'American sewing machines', in C. M. Depew (ed.), *One Hundred Years of American Commerce*, reprinted by Greenwood Press, New York, 1968, pp. 525–39.

Chandler, Alfred D., Jr (1977), *The Visible Hand*, Cambridge, MA: Harvard University Press.

Chandler, Alfred D., Jr (1992), 'Organizational capabilities and the economic history of the industrial enterprise', *Journal of Economic Perspectives*, **6** (Summer), 79–100.

Coase, Ronald (1937), 'The nature of the firm', *Economica* (New series), **4**, 386–405.

Friedman, Walter (2004), *Birth of a Salesman: The Transformation of Selling in America*, Cambridge, MA: Harvard University Press.

Galambos, Lou (2005), 'Recasting the organizational synthesis: structure and process in the twentieth and twenty-first centuries', *Business History Review*, **79** (Spring), 1–38.

Godley, Andrew (2001), 'The global diffusion of the sewing machine, 1850–1914', *Research in Economic History*, **20** (November), 1–45.

Godley, Andrew (2006), 'Selling the sewing machine around the world: Singer's international marketing strategies, 1850–1920', *Enterprise and Society*, **7** (June), 266–314.

Hannah, Leslie (1999), 'Marshall's "trees" and the global "forest": were "giant redwoods" different?' in N. R. Lamoreux, D. Raff and P. Temin (eds), *Learning by Doing in Markets, Firms and Countries*, Chicago: University of Chicago Press, pp. 253–93.

Hannah, Leslie (2006), 'The Whig fable of American Tobacco, 1895–1913', *Journal of Economic History*, **66** (March), 42–73.

John, Richard (1997), 'Elaborations, revisions, dissents: Alfred D. Chandler, Jr.'s, *The Visible Hand* after twenty years', *Business History Review*, **71**, 151–200.

Klepper, Steve (2002), 'The capabilities of new firms and the evolution of the US auto industry', *Industrial and Corporate Change*, **11** (4), 645–66.

Knight, Frank H. (1921), *Risk, Uncertainty and Profit*, Boston, MA: Houghton Mifflin.

Lamoreux, Naomi, Dan Raff and Peter Temin (2003), 'Beyond markets and hierarchies: toward a new synthesis of American business history', *American Historical Review*, **108**, 404–33.

Lamoreux, Naomi, Dan Raff and Peter Temin (2004), 'Against Whig history', *Enterprise and Society*, **5**, 376–87.

Langlois, Richard (2003), 'The vanishing hand: the changing dynamics of industrial capitalism', *Industrial and Corporate Change*, **12**, 351–85.

Langlois, Richard (2004), 'Chandler in a larger frame: markets, transaction costs and organisational form in history', *Enterprise and Society*, **5**, 355–75.

Schmitz, Christopher (1995), 'The world's largest industrial companies of 1912', *Business History*, **37**, 85–98.

Schumpeter, Joseph A. (1934), *The Theory of Economic Development*, trans. R. Opie, Cambridge, MA: Harvard University Press.

Schumpeter, Joseph A. (1939), *Business Cycles: A Theoretical, Historical and Statistical Analysis of the Capitalist Process*, New York: McGraw-Hill.

Singer Manufacturing Company (1882), *Report of the Proceedings on the Occasion of Breaking Ground for the Singer Manufacturing Company's New Factory (at Kilbowie, near Glasgow, Scotland), May 18th, 1882*, Glasgow: Singer.

Tedlow, Richard (1990), *New and Improved: The Story of Mass Marketing in America*, New York: Basic Books.

Williamson, Jeffrey (1995), 'The evolution of global labour markets since 1830: background evidence and hypotheses', *Explorations in Economic History*, **32**, 141–96.

Williamson, Oliver E. (1981), 'The modern corporation: origins, evolution, attributes', *Journal of Economic Literature*, **19**, 1537–68.

Williamson, Oliver E. (1985), *The Economic Institutions of Capitalism*, New York: Free Press.

10. Entrepreneurship and the development of global brands

With Teresa da Silva Lopes

This chapter explains how entrepreneurs have contributed to the development of successful global brands in consumer goods industries in the twentieth century. It also explains why so few independent brands survived the merger waves of the 1980s. The industries analysed are ones in which the success of products is determined mainly by advertising rather than by the technology embodied in the product. Drawing on cross-industry and cross-country comparisons of branded consumer goods, the chapter highlights the entrepreneurial and innovative strategies pursued in developing brands. It shows that successful brands usually outlive the firms that create them. Successful local brands are transformed into national and even global brands through a process of continuous development and rejuvenation. It is not only the origination of a brand that is entrepreneurial, but rejuvenation too. Whilst origination is often effected by entrepreneurs who own small family businesses, rejuvenation is usually undertaken by internal entrepreneurs working for large multi-brand firms, who are assisted by marketing professionals. Small-firm entrepreneurs and large-firm entrepreneurs therefore combine to exploit the potential of successful brands by drawing on different types of knowledge. At each stage in the life of the brand, the type of firm that possesses the most relevant knowledge becomes the owner of the brand.

10.1 INTRODUCTION

Studies of entrepreneurship in business history tend to focus on a single entrepreneur, usually the founder and owner-manager of a firm, and creator of a single successful product and brand with distinctive characteristics. This study follows the example of earlier chapters by defining the entrepreneur more broadly, including entrepreneurs working for large firms as well as small ones, and operating not only as owners but also as salaried managers. Furthermore, while researchers such as Schumpeter (1934, 1939) tend to associate the role of the entrepreneur with invention and innovation in technology-based industries, here the analysis focuses on marketing-based industries, where innovation relies on other activities, such as branding. Marketing knowledge is defined as the intelligence and skills that exist within firms concerning the management of brands and distribution channels.

This chapter examines the lives of successful brands in global marketing-based industries and traces their trajectories, from the time they were created until the present day. It analyses the roles of the entrepreneurs and entrepreneurial managers who helped to develop those brands. Successful brands are defined as those that became leading (measured in terms of market share) in their product categories in the relevant markets (domestic or global). Global brands are those sold in multiple markets using similar marketing strategies, even if in practice only a small number of such markets account for most of the sales (Aaker and Joachimsthaler, 1999). A brand evolves from international to global when there is almost total standardization in the marketing strategy of that brand across different markets.

The industries analysed are those where the promotion of the brand relies principally on advertising (brand image and other intangible assets) rather than on product performance (attributable to tangible assets such as high quality production plant) (Blaszczyk, 2006). Specifically, the focus is on industries in which the number of patents registered per year is low relative to the size of the industry (USPTO, 2003). Relevant industries include food and drink, fashion and cosmetics. The global brands studied include Smirnoff vodka, Carlsberg beer, Perrier water, Lancôme beauty products, Gucci fashion, Nescafé coffee, and KitKat chocolate (for a ranking of these brands see Interbrand, 2006). Some of them are long-established brands, going back to the nineteenth century, whilst others are more recent. The key finding is that the long-run success of a global brand depends not just on the entrepreneurial flair of the individual founder but on the subsequent refinement and rejuvenation of the brand by entrepreneurial marketing managers in multi-product multinational firms.

The choice of a group of successful brands in particular industries leads naturally to the selection of firms to be analysed. These are the firms which owned the brands at particular points in time. Some are leading multinationals, whilst others are small firms. As the chapter will show, the small-firm entrepreneurs who created the brands are frequently distinct from the large-firm entrepreneurs who, from managerial positions, adapted the brands to changing supply and demand conditions by turning them into successful global brands.

Most of the brands analysed changed ownership during their lives. Many of the brands have outlived the firms that first developed them. To some extent this is a consequence of the method of sampling used in this chapter, but it also reflects a basic feature of the lives of brands in consumer goods industries. Only a few global brands have remained in the ownership of the same firm throughout their lives. Most of the firms concerned are controlled by families, trusts, or a small group of major shareholders. They have been relatively immune to pressure from independent shareholders to maximize short-term payment of dividends. They also tend to be headquartered in a country in which larger firms can rely on long-term support from banks rather than being obliged to issue equity to finance expansions, as is the norm in some countries; examples are Carlsberg from Denmark, Asahi Brewery from Japan and Nestlé from Switzerland.

10.2   THE LIFE OF A BRAND

The concept of a life-cycle is used in many areas of research. So far as people are concerned, the cycle begins with birth and progresses through adolescence, maturity and old age to death. Industries too have life-cycles, beginning with an innovation, which is followed by imitation. A period of intensive competition may then ensue, followed by a 'shake out' as the industry matures. Maturity is often associated with an oligopolistic market structure, which may encourage cartelization, and possibly rationalization, before terminal decline sets in. Within the industry life-cycles are the life-cycles of individual firms. Few firms last as long as the industry to which they belong. Studies of new firm formation show that 'infant mortality' is high amongst small firms (Storey, 1994). The long-term survivors in any industry tend to be those that take over their rivals or diversify early out of declining segments of the market into growing ones. Such firms are the exception, however, rather than the rule.

Just as industries outlive firms, successful firms can outlive individuals. Indeed, the rationale for establishing a firm is partly that the firm as a legal entity can outlive the entrepreneur who founded it (as noted in Chapter 1). In similar fashion, this study shows that successful brands can outlive the firms that establish them. Successful brands may be sold by a declining firm to a growing firm, which can then rejuvenate the brand. Alternatively the growth potential of the brand may be so great that it exceeds the limited resources available to the firm that created it.

The typical life-cycle of a brand begins with its creation by a small firm that uses it to serve a local market. This brand may be based on a trademark registered by the owner of the small firm. In some cases the trademark may be based on the owner's family name, although in other cases a special name may be created that is easily memorized and captures the 'unique selling point' of the product. Many of the brands discussed below originated with, or were initially developed by, family firms, but few of the families had the financial and managerial resources to exploit the global potential of their brands (Rose, 1995).

The initial success of a brand is often difficult to sustain. Successful brands may well attract imitators, and as brands proliferate so consumers become increasingly confused. Eventually a small number of popular brands may emerge. They are the 'survivors'. They may be brands that meet the needs of several different segments of the market and are widely available in different locations – this allows them to exploit economies of scale. Alternatively they may be perceived as the most exclusive and luxurious brands, and therefore able to command a high price.

To endow a brand with general popularity, or to give it an exclusive image, the original brand may have to be changed. Whilst retaining the core qualities on which its initial success was based, it may need to become somewhat blander and multicultural (for mass market appeal) or to be endorsed by the rich and famous (to warrant a premium price). This refreshment or rejuvenation of the brand may require a different type of entrepreneurial ability from the initial launch of the brand.

Whilst the initial launch of a brand may well be based upon improvisation and intuition, the rejuvenation of a brand is likely to benefit from a more systematic approach. Inspiration rather than information may hold the key to initial success, but information will be more important later on. Rejuvenation requires a detailed understanding of different market segments and different locations in which the product is consumed. Whilst the informal judgement of the small-firm entrepreneur is well-adapted to the initial launch, a formal process of judgement, supported by careful analysis of information, is appropriate at the later stage. This later stage may therefore benefit from being carried out by entrepreneurial marketing professionals working for a large firm.

This chapter applies the concept of the 'life of a brand' to explain why and how, in different industries, brands emerge, evolve and become global, staying 'forever young'. It traces the lives of selected brands from their creation until the present day. Particular focus is placed on the period from the 1980s, when liberalization of markets took place, world trade and foreign direct investment increased and the global merger waves accelerated. In this process only a small number of successful brands survived independently without changing hands.

10.3   A REVIEW OF THE EVIDENCE

Brands are recognized by consumers as a signal that the product satisfies basic requirements for consistency and quality (so-called vertical differentiation) and that it embodies a unique combination of characteristics that differentiates it from other brands (so-called horizontal differentiation) (Keller, 1998; Chernatony and McWilliam, 1989; Michel and Ambler, 1999). Brands are seen as an important mechanism by which firms communicate with consumers and cultivate their loyalty. They add value to the firm by sustaining a continuing revenue stream because of the consumer propensity for long-term brand loyalty. Brands also create 'personalities' for products or services. These personalities usually combine performance or tangible characteristics of products with imagery or intangible characteristics. In some cases, such as in the automotive industry, the performance aspects outweigh other characteristics of the personality of the brand. In others, imagery predominates. This is the case with alcoholic beverage brands for example, as production technologies tend to be standardized in either wines, spirits or beer (Cavanagh and Clairmonte, 1985; Church and Clark, 2001; Gourvish and Wilson, 1994; Jones, 2005). The account provided here of the evolution of firms and brands in the beauty industry, bottled water, chocolate and fashion, where technological innovation is not in itself a condition for competitive advantages of the firm and success of the brand, also aims to show the importance of imagery in marketing.

The research into these brands was carried out in the archives of major firms. The findings were then synthesized with information from secondary literature. The largest archives examined were those of Diageo, Nestlé and Cadbury-Schweppes. In 1998 Cadbury and Schweppes de-merged in order to re-focus their activities on specific sectors, but this de-merger did not have a direct bearing on the research for this chapter.

During the period covered by this study trademark legislation was in force in the major economies and brands and trademarks were legally defensible proprietary names. Table 10.1 lists the lives of the brands analysed in this study. It shows the relevant industry, when the brands were launched and the different owners they have had. It also shows the countries of origin of these owners, down to the present day. Ownership is divided between the small firms who created and developed the brands and the larger firms whose entrepreneurial managers transformed them into successful global brands.

Table 10.1 indicates four key patterns in the lives of brands, irrespective of industry.

Table 10.1   The life of brands

Industry/ brand	Date of origin	Ownership	Country
Alcoholic beverages			
Smirnoff	1864	Vladimir Smirnoff	Russia
	1933	Kunnett	USA
	1939	Heublein	USA
	1987	Grand Metropolitan	UK
	1997	Diageo	UK
Arthur Bells	1825	Thomas Sandeman	UK/ Scotland
	1985	Guinness	UK
	1997	Diageo	UK
Carlsberg	1847	Carlsberg	Denmark
Bombay	1980s	Grand Metropolitan	UK
Sapphire	1997	Bacardi	Bermuda
Corona	1925	Modelo	Mexico
	1998	Modelo – 50% investment by Anheuser Busch	Mexico/USA
Asahi Super Dry	1987	Asahi Brewery	Japan
Bottled water			
Perrier	1888	Louis Perrier	France
	1903	Sir John Harmsworth	UK
	1947	Gustave Leven	France
	1990	Exor	France
	1992	Nestlé	Switzerland
Evian	1789	Marquis de Lessert	France
	n/a	Société Anonyme des Eaux Minérales d'Evian-les-Bains	France
	1969	BSN	France
	1971	Danone (merger: BSN/ Gervais Danone)	France
Fashion			
Dior	1946	Christian Dior and Marcel Boussac	France
	1972	Sold trademark for perfume and cosmetics to MH	UK
	1978	Agache-Willot	France
	1984	Financière Agache	Switzerland
	1988	LVMH (Bernard Arnault)	France
Gucci	1881/1921	Guccio Gucci	Italy
	1987	50% Gucci Family, 50% InvestCorp	Italy/Bahrain
	1993		Bahrain

Table 10.1 (continued)

Industry/ brand	Date of origin	Ownership	Country
	1996	100% InvestCorp	–
	1999	Fully publicly quoted Pinault-Printemps-Redoute	France
Fragrances and up-market cosmetics			
Lâncome	1935	Lâncome	France
	1965	L'Oréal	France
Helena	1902	Helena Rubinstein	Australia
Rubinstein	1979	Colgate	USA
	1980	Albi Enterprises	USA
	1984	Palac (51%) + L'Oréal (49%)	USA/France
	1987	L'Oréal (100%)	France
Hugo Boss	1923	Hugo Boss	Germany
	1994	Procter & Gamble – licensing agreement	UK/Netherlands
Calvin Klein	1968	Barry Schawtz and Calvin Klein	USA
	1989	Unilever – licensing agreement	UK/Netherlands
	1995	Coty Inc. – licensing agreement	USA
Coffee			
Nescafé	1938	Nestlé	Switzerland
Starbucks	1971	Starbucks (Bowker and Baldwin)	USA
	1987	Il Giornale (Howard Schultz)	USA
Chocolate			
KitKat	1935	Rowntree	UK
	1969	Rowntree merger with Mackintosh	UK
	1988	Nestlé	Switzerland
Cadbury	1824	Cadbury	UK
	1919	Merger Cadbury and J. S. Fry and Son	UK
	1969	Cadbury merger with Schweppes	UK

Sources: Various companies' archives, histories, newspaper articles, and annual reports and accounts.

- Very few brands (Carlsberg, Nescafé and Asahi Super Dry) remained successful and became global under the single ownership and management of the entrepreneurs who created them or their descendants.
- Brands may change ownership in various ways. They may be traded together with the firms that own them through mergers and

acquisitions; they may be transferred independently from one firm to another; or ownership might be transferred though licensing agreements.

- Ownership of modern brands is concentrated in a relatively small number of countries. The high levels of investment necessary to manage global branded products and the complex networks required to distribute them worldwide explain why these global brands are based in Western countries such as the UK, USA, France and Switzerland or Japan, in which large-firm entrepreneurs have opportunities to prove their worth and receive recognition for their success. These are also countries where the nature of the educational system (in particular the specialization of degrees), the relative status of entrepreneurial careers, the regulatory environment, religious beliefs and the entrepreneurial culture in general are all favourable to the development of entrepreneurship.

- The timing of changes in brand ownership is clustered. There was a high turnover in the ownership of brands during the 1980s, when the accelerating globalization of leading economies had a significant effect on the structure of global consumer goods industries. The marketing and logistical strategies of leading firms began to converge as they switched from a regional to a global focus. Multi-market competition emerged between a small group of large multinational firms with high levels of marketing knowledge.

A key aspect of this corporate globalization strategy in the alcoholic beverage industry was to acquire existing regional brands which were believed to have the potential to become global, so that the acquiring firm could rapidly obtain market share in new geographic regions, while maintaining high levels of control over implementation in terms of costs and time. During the 1980s, for example, new opportunities appeared in some emerging markets in Africa, Latin America and Asia where rising incomes stimulated an interest in Western lifestyles and brands.

This route to expansion had both advantages and disadvantages, however. On the one hand, firms could acquire large portfolios of complementary brands, but on the other hand, problems of brand rationalization arose when newly-acquired brands competed with existing brands already in the firms' portfolios.

The net result of all these changes is that ownership of brands in food, drink and cosmetics is now highly concentrated in a small group of multinationals: Bacardi, Diageo, Danone, Louis Vuitton Moët-Hennessy (LVMH), Pinault-Printemps-Redoute, L'Oréal, Procter & Gamble (P&G),

Unilever and Nestlé. Amongst the many products owned by these firms are the world's most valuable brands.

10.4   STRATEGIES FOR GLOBAL SUCCESS: SINGLE-FIRM BRANDS

Some brands have become globally successful while remaining under the management of the small-firm entrepreneurs who created them, or under their descendants. Other brands only become successful when ownership changes and they are managed by large-firm entrepreneurs distinct from their creators.

Brands Created and Retained by Small High-Growth Firms

Examples of brands which became successful on a global scale under the management of their original entrepreneurs or their descendants are the Danish beer Carlsberg and the fashion brand Gucci. But there are differences in the ways these brands developed. Carlsberg achieved international success soon after it was created, while Gucci had to wait several years for success. Both became global brands only after their original entrepreneurs had died.

Carlsberg beer was produced for the first time in 1847 after J.C. Jacobsen created a new lager beer that was stronger and of better quality than its competitors in Denmark. One of those competitors was Jacobsen's son, Carl Jacobsen, who established a production unit in an annexe of the J.C. Jacobsen plant in 1871, producing a beer branded as Ny Carlsberg. The use of a similar brand name led J.C. Jacobsen to sue his son. The breweries were united under the same ownership – a foundation – in 1902, after the death of both father and son (Glamann, 1991).

The early success of the brand Carlsberg is not only associated with the domestic market, but also with its exports. The firm started exporting to the UK in 1868. By the end of the twentieth century Carlsberg was one of the most widely distributed beer brands in the world. Currently around 95 per cent of Carlsberg sales are generated outside the home market. After World War II the firm started intense marketing campaigns to sell more beer abroad. Between 1958 and 1972 exports tripled, and Carlsberg established breweries in Europe and Asia. In 1968 it made its first investment in a foreign market by setting up brewing operations in Malawi, and in 1969 it created its first licensing agreement in Cyprus. An important step in its internationalization strategy was the joint venture created with Grand Metropolitan in 1974 to sell Carlsberg in the UK, in a period when tastes were moving towards lighter beers. In 1969 Carlsberg merged with its major Danish competitor Tuborg. Slogans such as 'Carlsberg: probably the best lager in the world' were launched in the 1970s. The advertising still emphasizes the international prestige image of the brand and also the original values of the founder – namely heritage and high quality.

The fashion brand Gucci also achieved initial success while its creator was alive – although late in his life. The House of Gucci was founded as a saddlery shop in Florence in 1881. But it was only in the 1920s that Guccio Gucci started producing luxury luggage. He learned that his clients were gradually replacing equine transportation with horseless carriages and that luggage functioned as a symbol of affluence and taste. In the 1950s Guccio Gucci diversified into other luxury items such as ties, shoes and handbags sporting a bamboo handle. He died in 1953 and his family took the successful company to new heights by opening stores in fashionable locations such as Paris, Beverly Hills, London, Palm Beach and Tokyo (Forden, 2001; McKnight, 1987; Trimarco, 2001).

During the 1980s the brand suffered some erosion due to family dis-agreements and over-licensing, and was sold out to InvestCorp in Bahrain, which failed to improve its global image. In the 1990s, under new owner-ship, Gucci was brought back to the centre of chic. In the late 1990s the threat of its acquisition by Bernard Arnauld, the owner of Louis Vuitton Moët-Hennessy (LVMH), led the management of the firm to sell it to another French multinational Pinault-Printemps-Redoute, which invested heavily in Gucci's global image.

Brands Created by Large Multi-Brand Firms

Carlsberg and Gucci represent brands that were created by small firms that focussed on a single brand in which they retained ownership, over time delegating the control of the brand to professional teams. The family successfully grew from small-firm entrepreneurs to large-firm entrepre-neurs over several generations (although the Gucci family finally sold out). Other brands, however were created by large firms which already had one or more existing brands under their control. In this case it was the entre-preneurial managers – or 'intrapreneurs' – who innovated the brands.

It might be expected, however, that the brands created by large-firm intrapreneurs would not represent such radical innovations as those effected by small-firm entrepreneurs, and the evidence suggests that this is indeed the case. The new brands created were often closely related to existing brands possessed by the firm, and may, for certain purposes, be seen as natural extensions of them. This is illustrated by the case of Asahi Super Dry discussed below. By contrast, Nescafé and KitKat were radical innovations which bore little relationship to their creators' existing portfolio of brands. In these cases, however, external researchers and consultants played a significant role.

An entrepreneurial CEO of a large firm may authorize his marketing department to carry out market research designed to identify emerging product niches which remain to be filled. The newly discovered niches can then be filled either by the extension of an existing brand (as in the case of Asahi Super Dry), or the creation of a new brand, or some compromise between the two (as in the case of Nescafé). The firm may also hire new managers and consultants in order to temporarily boost the creative resources at the firm's disposal (as in the case of KitKat). A more permanent solution may be obtained by changing the firm's recruitment policies and hiring new managers with strong entrepreneurial capabilities.

The Japanese beer Asahi Super Dry was launched in 1987 by Asahi Brewery as an extension of Asahi Draft beer. It exploited a revolutionary innovation based on new ingredients and a new production process. In the late 1980s the Japanese beer industry was suffering a variety of demographic, dietary, social, economic and distribution changes that affected the demand for beer (Craig, 1996). Whereas Japanese consumers traditionally exhibited strong brand loyalty and conservative tastes, modern drinkers were eager to try new types of beer. This was also a difficult period for the firm, which was on the edge of bankruptcy and was therefore sufficiently desperate to risk a frontal attack on the industry leader, Kirin. Asahi Super Dry targeted an unexploited niche of the Japanese market – *koku-kire* – 'rich in taste and yet also sharp and refreshing'. The level of sales not only surpassed those of any other brand owned by the firm but led Asahi Brewery in 2002 to become Japan's top beer brand.

Nescafé soluble coffee is another illustration of a global brand that was launched by a team of managers in a large multi-brand multinational. Since the late nineteenth century, with the development of modern consumer society, entrepreneurs had been attempting to produce a soluble coffee. World War I, due to increased demand from troops, raised prospective profits. But the products offered did not correspond to the aroma of coffee from freshly roasted beans, they were not durable, were too expensive and were not satisfactorily soluble (Pfiffner, 2002).

Henri Nestlé started producing formula milk in 1843 in Switzerland. He tried to convince doctors, pharmacists and hospitals of the value of his product, but it was mothers that started using his formula milk after evidence that he had saved a premature baby. In 1905 Nestlé merged with the Anglo-Swiss Condensed Milk Company, and throughout the 1920s and 1930s continued growing through acquisitions. After World War II Nestlé diversified by first creating an alliance (later merging) with the chocolate producer Vevey. In 1947 it merged with Maggi (a large Swiss multi-national famous for its sauces and soups), which opened Nestlé's business to world markets (Heer, 1991).

Nescafé was created in 1938. The new brand resulted from a combination of internal motivation within the firm and external opportunities. Nestlé was heading for an economic crisis as a result of its high reliance on two major market segments – mothers and babies. Nestlé's management felt it was important to find a product to target men. The company had had investments in the Brazilian market since the 1920s, and in the early 1930s the board of directors of the Banque Française et Italienne pour l'Amérique approached Nestlé's management for help in increasing the consumption of coffee on account of the excess stocks they had in Brazil. Nestlé's laboratories started research to try to find a dry coffee extract which could be prepared instantaneously. The company appointed two research chemists – Bakke and Morgenthaler – but after four years of unsuccessful research Nestlé management decided to abandon the project. Morgenthaler, however, continued the experiments on his own account and in 1936 he found an adequate formula for instant coffee. After Nestlé's management had seen his findings, the company decided to launch the product (Morgenthaler, 1944, 1988). After its launch in 1938, Nescafé instant coffee quickly became very popular.

KitKat is another good illustration of a brand launched by a firm in a difficult period. The firm overcame its internal problems by hiring new managers and consultants. The aim was to create a product that would avoid direct competition with Cadbury chocolate. The product was created by Rowntree in 1935 and was initially branded as 'Chocolate Crisp'. In 1937 the name was changed to KitKat – a name first registered by Rowntree as early as 1911, but not used at that time. Rowntree was almost bankrupt in the 1930s, and in desperation the firm hired new professional managers, among whom was George Harris, who married into the Rowntree family. Harris emulated the successful strategy for the penetration of Mars in the British market. Aided by the new technique of market research and the flair of the J. Walter Thompson advertising agency, a stream of winning products such as Aero, Smarties and Black Magic chocolates were launched (Fitzgerald, 1995). By the outbreak of World War II, Rowntree had undergone a marketing revolution and recouped much of the ground lost to its rivals.

Rowntree's internationalization started after 1945, not only through exports but also through foreign direct investment in markets such as Australia, Canada, South Africa and Ireland. By the early 1950s the growth of the firm meant that it had created separate product divisions, each with a different marketing manager (confectionery, grocery and chocolate), and also marketing strategy committees. However, Rowntree failed to diversify successfully in the 1960s, the same decade in which the confectionery market stagnated and international competition intensified. This led to the merger in 1969 with Mackintosh, another confectioner, with brands such as Rolo and Quality Street. Like the merger between Cadbury and Schweppes, the new firm looked forward to combining two strongly marketing-oriented companies in confectionery and grocery, and to obtaining scale economies in marketing, distribution and production. Rowntree-Macintosh was acquired by Nestlé in 1988 in a hostile take-over. Despite its very respectable financial performance and its innovative record, Rowntree was perceived as an underperformer in stock market terms. The high price that Nestlé paid for Rowntree's shares reflected the company's powerful brands and their potential for profitable expansion into world markets. This acquisition by a leading multinational in chocolate allowed the brand KitKat to become global.

Small Firms that Grow a Brand under the Umbrella of a Larger Firm

A small firm that lacks the large-firm capabilities to develop a brand it has created may find it more convenient to operate under a 'big firm umbrella' than to attempt to go it alone. An experienced large firm may inject capital into the small firm through long-term trade credit, a loan or a minority equity stake. It gives the small firm access to its international marketing and distribution network in return for interest payments and a share of the profit. An interesting example of this strategy concerns the Mexican beer Corona, produced since 1925 by Modelo, which enjoyed rapid international growth, beginning in the 1980s when it started forming alliances with the US brewer Anheuser Busch. In 1998 this leading multinational acquired a 50 per cent non-voting stake in Corona's Grupo Modelo which owned the leading beer brand in Mexico. Through Anheuser Busch, which distributes the brand in most of the states, Corona became the leading imported beer brand in the USA.

10.5   STRATEGIES FOR GLOBAL SUCCESS: MULTI-FIRM BRANDS

The brands in Table 10.1 tend to change ownership in one of two main ways: by merger and acquisition or by arm's length contract involving either the sale or the licensing of the brand. Mergers and acquisitions have been the most common form through which brands have changed ownership. Acquisitions have been more important than mergers in the food, drink and cosmetics industries.

Acquisitions by Large-Firm Entrepreneurs

Starbucks coffee, Perrier water, Evian water, Lâncome and Helena Rubinstein are all examples of brands which only became globally successful after changing ownership and coming under the management of entrepreneurs who acquired them from their creators (or their successors).

Starbucks is a relatively young coffee brand created in 1971 by two entrepreneurs, Bowker and Baldwin, who started selling high-quality coffee in Seattle. Another entrepreneur, Howard Schultz, who at the time worked in a different business, realized that the baby-boomers in the USA were starting to reject pre-packaged food in favour of more natural and higher quality products. In 1981 Schultz contacted the Seattle company about the possibility of transforming their business into a high-quality national business, re-creating the Italian bar-culture in their home market. The management of Starbucks hired Schultz in 1981, but in 1983 he left to start his own coffee chain called Il Giornale. In 1987 Starbucks came up for sale, and Schultz's chain bought it, from which time Schultz began to internationalize the brand. It was his understanding of changing social trends that led him to promote premium coffee sold in a relaxed and informal retail environment. The powerful brand was a key factor in helping to create a mass market for speciality coffee (Schulz and Yang, 1997)

In 1898, Dr Perrier, a medical researcher and proponent of the virtues of thermal water, applied for a variety of patents and established the Société des Eaux Minérales, Boissons et Produits Hygiéniques de Vergèze. Using English capital from 1903, the firm first sold Perrier in England and the British Empire. Only in 1933 did it turn to the French market, merging in 1936 with Eaux Minérales de Vergèze. In 1947 it was acquired by Gustave Leven, who through mergers and acquisitions of other water springs and mass advertising revolutionized the bottled water business and caught up with his main competitors, Evian and Vittel (Simmons, 1983; Bure, 2001).

In the mid-1970s Leven took the brand to the USA, despite being advised by several consulting firms that it would be foolish to try to sell sparkling water in the land of Coca Cola and 'gin and tonic' drinkers. The saturation of the French market and campaigns against soft drinks with added sugar served as strong incentives for this investment decision. Its immediate success created a substantial market in the USA for bottled water. The marketing of Perrier positioned it as a status drink for the fashionable and affluent.

The global potential of the brand, coupled with the high cost of transporting and distributing a bulky low-value product like water, created a strategic need to establish local production facilities overseas. Perrier therefore began to acquire other water firms which held dominant positions in foreign markets. In 1980 it acquired several US bottled water firms with a strong regional presence, such as Poland Spring and Calistoga Mineral Water, in order to reduce shipping costs. Leven also continued investing heavily in advertising. In 1992 Perrier was acquired by Nestlé, after Leven had retired and the brand started suffering some erosion. During this decade Nestlé turned Perrier into a truly global brand and invested more in the bottled water business by acquiring sources such as San Pellegrino mineral water. In 1999 Nestlé started rolling out its Nestlé Pure Life bottled water and in 2003 acquired Hutchison Wham Powwow and also Clear Water, a bottled water home and office delivery company located in Russia.

Evian bottled water provides another case in which the brand was developed after the firm was purchased. Evian water is differentiated from most other bottled water brands in that the product is not filtered or processed in any way. Source Cachet, the spring from which Evian is obtained, was discovered in 1789 near Mont Blanc in France. Soon after this discovery a health resort was constructed at the site. The beverage was first bottled in 1826 and sourced from the Chablais foothills in the Haute Savoie region of France. Until the mid-twentieth century Evian was sold in pharmacies and could only be bought with medical prescription. It was only in the 1960s in France, and in the mid-1970s in other countries, that bottled water experienced a sudden surge in popularity and the brand became famous internationally.

By 1969 Evian was suffering from a depressed equity market in France and from price controls imposed on mineral waters. It was acquired by Boussois-Soucho-Neuvesel (BSN) whose management had major marketing capabilities. At the time BSN produced glass bottles, industrial containers, flagons and glass tableware. However, the management of BSN felt that it was losing its competitiveness in the glass bottle industry, and so it decided to diversify into products that it could bottle, such as water and beer. In 1973 BSN merged with Danone, which started to develop the water business globally. Since then Evian's management has invested in globalizing the brand, being very innovative in the way they have bottled the water. They were the first to develop plastic bottles in 1978; to switch to plastic screw-tops in 1984; and to introduce handles on the packages in 1988. These and other innovations allowed Evian to grow even in periods of stagnation of consumption. By 2005 Evian was the top-selling brand of non-carbonated bottled water in the world.

Lancôme is another example of a brand that became global only after it changed ownership. The cosmetics brand was created in 1935 by a French entrepreneur Arman Petitjean, who had studied with François

Coty, the 'father of twentieth century luxury perfumes' (Monsen, 2001). He launched his first five fragrances in 1935 at the universal exhibition in Brussels and immediately captured popular interest. Building upon this initial success, Petitjean soon expanded beyond his perfume line to offer a complete range of products, including make-up and skincare products. During the years that followed, Lancôme continued to establish its prestigious reputation throughout the world and internationalized to the US in the 1950s, answering a growing need for quality products. However, it was only from 1964, when the brand was acquired by L'Oréal, that it developed into a global brand. This was achieved through sophisticated and careful segmentation strategies in which Lancôme was sold through selected channels of distribution, in France and abroad (Bonin et al., 2001; Dalle, 2001; Jones, 2005).

Helena Rubinstein started in Australia at the turn of the twentieth century when she opened her first beauty salon in Melbourne. She was always concerned with internationalizing the brand and with innovation. Her innovations had a very strong impact in the cosmetics industry in the twentieth century. She was the first to sell cosmetics in large department stores through mini beauty institutes; she was the first to create a waterproof mascara (in 1939); and was also the first to include vitamins in cosmetics (vitamin C, vitamin A and phosphorus). In the 1950s Helena Rubinstein was, along with Elizabeth Arden, one of the most popular luxury beauty product suppliers in the USA. However, by the early 1980s the brand was being sold in US drugstores at very low prices and was not receiving much merchandising support (Peiss, 1999; Woodhead, 2003). It had a much better position in Europe, Japan and Asia, however, where it was still considered upmarket. Its various owners throughout the 1980s, such as Colgate Palmolive and Albi International, did not invest in the elitist image of the brand. The acquisition of Helena Rubinstein by L'Oréal in 1987, as part of its strategy to cover all the different segments of the beauty market, transformed the brand into a truly global upmarket brand. In the 1960s only 3 per cent of its sales were in foreign markets, but by 2000 over 50 per cent of its sales were outside Europe. The L'Oréal process of transformation of local brands into global brands had two stages which overall took about ten years: the first consisted of choosing the brands that had the potential to become global, and the second was to achieve a critical mass of sales in the target markets.

Merger of Large Firms

The merger between Cadbury and Schweppes is an illustration of the advantages to brands of combining resources. Cadbury was set up as a shop in the centre of Birmingham in 1824, and sold tea, coffee, cocoa, patent hoops and mustard (Williams, 1931). In 1831 John Cadbury decided to concentrate on the manufacture and marketing of cocoa, so he sold the shop to a relative. The firm became Cadbury Brothers in 1847, and the first major breakthrough came in 1866 when the second generation of Cadbury Brothers introduced an improved cocoa to Britain. Cadbury built up a large export trade in chocolate and confectionery before 1914 and after World War I invested in overseas manufacturing in the British Empire and the Commonwealth (Jones, 1984). In 1919 Cadbury merged with J.S. Fry & Son, a family firm dating back to 1728, which had been the leading company in the industry. The first directors who were not family members were appointed in 1943, even though the firm was only floated on the stock market in 1962. By 1960 low product growth and intense competition from rivals compelled the management of Cadbury to diversify into sugar confectionery, cakes and convenience foods. Unable to generate sufficient product diversity internally, Adrian Cadbury merged his company with Schweppes in 1969 (Corley, 1994). This merger allowed the combined firm to achieve economies in distribution and product development.

Brands Sold as Pieces of Intellectual Property

The gin Bombay Sapphire is an example of a brand that was sold by one firm to another, with the original owner continuing to trade independently. The brand was launched in 1987 by International Distillers and Vintners (IDV) which became a subsidiary of Grand Metropolitan, who used attractive ingredients, innovative design (blue bottle) and a new recipe (more spicy and more lemon than competitor brands such as Gordon) to capture market share. The brand changed ownership, not because its new owners failed to exploit it successfully, but because they merged with another firm. This merger between two leading British multinationals in alcoholic beverages – Guinness and Grant Metropolitan – formed Diageo, whose dominance of the market led to anti-trust concerns in the USA. To avoid a confrontation with the US Federal Trade Commission, Diageo's management decided to sell Bombay. The brand was sold to Bacardi in 1998, the year after the merger.

The sale mainly involved the intellectual property represented by the name of the brand, although some stocks and the recipe were traded too. Bacardi retained the essential components of the brand: the distinctive bottle, the recipe and the ingredients. However, major changes were introduced elsewhere to speed up the distribution process, and to enhance the premium image through heavy advertising and higher prices. Following its acquisition, the global sales of Bombay grew from 0.5 million bottles in

1998 to 1.4 million bottles in 2004. By moving to a smaller multinational the brand became relatively more important in the firm's overall portfolio, and so received more attention from the top management of the firm.

Transfer through Licensing Agreements

The fragrances Calvin Klein, Hugo Boss and Dior exemplify the transfer of control of a brand through a licensing agreement which gives one firm the rights to produce and distribute a product originated by another for a given number of years and in a given set of countries.

Calvin Klein is known for its designer jeans, and for its wholesome all-American look. Over the years Calvin Klein diversified into other related business such as underwear, fragrances, swimwear, home décor and cosmetics. It entered the fragrances market with the launch of fragrances for men: Obsession in 1981 and Eternity in 1988. This was a period when the perfume industry caught on to the ideal of the sensitive, successful 1980s man, and decided that they were ready for their own fragrances. In 1989 Unilever signed a licensing agreement to produce Calvin Klein fragrances under the Calvin Klein brand. Even though this business appeared to present international growth opportunities, in 2005 Unilever disposed of these licences, as part of its strategy to withdraw from premium cosmetics (Elizabeth Arden had been sold in 2001). While under the ownership of Unilever the brand became global. The licence was acquired by Coty, a large US cosmetics family firm, which became the world's largest manufacturer of mass-market fragrances (Jones, 2005).

Hugo Boss has been a globally successful brand name in men's apparel since 1923. In the light of the general trend towards greater use of fragrances by men, Hugo Boss entered into a licensing agreement with the American consumer products giant Procter & Gamble in 1993 for the production of fragrances with the Hugo Boss brand name. This was the first investment of Procter & Gamble in the fragrances business, and with that investment they were able to achieve global leadership in men's fragrances (Dyer et al., 2004).

The perfume Dior provides a similar story. Dior is a brand created after World War II. It became very fashionable soon after it was launched, symbolizing luxury rather than comfort. During the 1970s the brand suffered some erosion when the firm started licensing its trademark, Dior, for the production of items such as household products, towels and sheets and fragrances. Parfums Christian Dior was sold to Moët & Chandon in 1971 – the year Moët & Chandon merged with Hennessy. When Bernard Arnauld became senior manager of the fashion and retail company Financière Agache in 1984 he terminated all the Dior licences that were harmful to its image, and in the process purchased LVMH which had the Dior fragrances and cosmetics business. Under the ownership of this global multinational in luxury products the brand became more avant garde.

10.6   REJUVENATION

It was noted at the outset that large firms acquire brands from small firms because they have the entrepreneurial skills and financial resources to rejuvenate brands on a regular basis. If rejuvenation were simply a matter of 'tweaking' the brand image to appeal to a new generation of consumers then it is quite possible that a small family firm would have sufficient resources for this purpose – if the brand were profitable then the rejuvenation could be funded out of retained profits. It would only be if the ageing founder, or his/her successors, had lost touch with recent social trends that were influencing their consumers that they might need to relinquish control of the brand in order that it could be rejuvenated.

In practice, however, there is often more to rejuvenation than this. Rejuvenation of the brand may require the development of a global image rather than a local or national image. Increased mobility of consumers, and their demand for a product that is always available wherever they happen to be, may require a global image to be supported by a global marketing and distribution system.

The traditional market for a brand may stagnate without disappearing altogether. At the same time, the traditional product may not be acceptable to a newly emerging market for the brand. If the firm cannot afford to ignore either of these markets then it will need two variants of the same brand. The brand therefore needs to be extended to create an additional product adapted to the requirements of the new market.

Global marketing and distribution channels incur substantial fixed costs and need to handle a large volume of product – much more than any single product line may supply. This provides an additional cost-based motive for brand extension – namely the need to develop a comprehensive range of products sold through similar types of retail outlets whose total volume will keep a global marketing and distribution centre fully utilized.

Smirnoff, the world's top-selling spirit, is an illustration of a brand which has successfully rejuvenated through globalization and line extension. Smirnoff was created in 1864 in Russia and was drunk by the Russian royal family. In 1933 a former US supplier of the brand bought the US rights to produce it. In 1939 Heublein, a large US firm, bought the brand. In 1987 Heublein was in financial difficulty and was unable to continue investing in the brand. Grand Metropolitan, which had the right to distribute Smirnoff in Europe, saw its potential as a global brand, and acquired Heublein. In 1997, after Grand Metropolitan merged with Guinness to form Diageo, the brand came into the hands of the world's largest multinational in the drinks industry. Smirnoff is now part of a limited number of global priority brands from which Diageo derives most of its profit in several countries.

In 1992, when the sales of Smirnoff were maturing in the British market, Grand Metropolitan launched a line extension called Smirnoff Mule. It was a ready-mixed beverage that reconstituted a cocktail prepared in the 1940s by bartenders in the USA, who mixed the vodka brand with imported ginger ale and lime. This cocktail was called 'Moscow Mule' and greatly contributed to the establishment of Smirnoff as a vodka brand on the US West Coast. The idea was that of the managing director of Heublein, who thought that he could teach Americans to use vodka in mixed drinks. Moscow Mule eventually became a very popular beverage throughout the USA.

The launch in 1992 of Smirnoff Mule in the UK as a ready-to-drink beverage was a response to the problems that cocktails raised by taking preparation time at the bar and by varying in quality according to the capacities of the bartender. This frequently led consumers to drink beer instead. However, Smirnoff Mule was unsuccessful. It did not have sufficient appeal to the target market, and the bottle, which was too sophisticated, did not correspond to the content of the beverage. This was in fact International Distiller and Vintners' second unsuccessful attempt to enter the ready-mixed market. It had previously launched Saint Leger, a California Wine Cooler, an alternative to wine and beer. The product failed because the company had not transferred the knowledge from its wine and spirits business to the beer market, and had not done sufficient consumer research.

These unsuccessful ventures were, nonetheless, very useful as learning experiences for the subsequent launch in 2002 of Smirnoff Ice, which turned out to be very successful. Smirnoff Ice's imagery was very different from that of Smirnoff Mule, being much less sophisticated and more connected with the spirit brand. The success of Smirnoff Ice was such that it regenerated consumer interest in the core brand.

10.7 CONCLUSIONS

This chapter has looked at the role of entrepreneurship in the growth and survival of global brands in food and drink and also the cosmetics and fashion industries. Inter-industry, international and inter-firm comparisons have highlighted several interesting patterns.

Successful brands usually change ownership several times during their lives. Typically the original owner lacks the resources to take the next step in the life of the brand, to globalize it, or to create new line or brand extensions. It is the recognition of this lack of capacity to exploit the brand to its full potential that may lead to its sale (on its own or together with the firm that owns it). The owner may lack tangible resources, such as physical assets or capital, or intangible resources such as knowledge of global markets. Often it is a combination of these that leads to changes in ownership.

Successful brands are often old, dating back to the eighteenth and nine-teenth centuries. For cultural reasons, tradition is important in the food and drink industries. It suggests authentic ingredients rather than artificial flavours created by synthetic chemicals. But while tradition may be useful in the context of quality assurance, products still require a modern image, especially when they are targeted at young consumers. Their image needs to be updated regularly to keep the product attractive to new generations of potential purchasers.

Firms that sell brands that they have originated often go into decline once they have disposed of their major asset. In many cases they disappear altogether as they are absorbed by an acquiring firm. Whilst this firm retains the identity of the brand it does not normally retain the identity of the firm that owned it. Thus brands often outlive the firms that originally developed them.

The firms that acquire brands normally do so in order to rejuvenate the brand, globalize it, and in some cases extend it to other products. This process is generally undertaken by 'intrapreneurs' – typically entrepreneurial marketing professionals working for large firms.

The most important wave of brand acquisition and globalization occurred in the 1980s. It resulted in the ownership of a high proportion of leading global brands becoming concentrated in the hands of a small number of large firms.

The firms that rejuvenate and globalize brands tend to be based in a relatively small number of highly-developed economies. These countries afford a good supply of marketing professionals. Their legal institutions provide an effective mechanism for defending intellectual property rights, including patents, brand names and trade marks. Their financial institutions supply capital with which to finance takeovers, acquisitions or arm's length purchases of brands. Not all such firms rely on external sources of funds; some are family firms that finance their expansion from retained profit or from bank loans and who combine their professionalism with entrepreneurial flair.

The knowledge exploited by these firms derives from the social habits of a target group of consumers. They also employ sophisticated logistics to manage the distribution of their products to retail outlets patronised by their target market – in the case of alcoholic drinks these include bars and clubs, as well as off-licences, liquor stores and supermarkets.

The owners of global brands typically own a portfolio of such brands, rather than just a single brand. They are large not only because their brands are global and successful, but also because they own several such brands. This allows them to exploit economies of scope in knowledge. Where a target consumer purchases different types of product on different occasions, knowledge of their social habits can inform entrepreneurial decisions not just about a single product but about an entire family of products consumed by the same social group. In addition, different products may be distributed through the same retail outlets. Economies of scale may therefore be available through distributing different products through the same distribution channel. Finally, owning several brands generates a continuous flow of work in rejuvenating brands to meet the needs of the next generation of consumers. Multi-brand firms can therefore offer steady employment to the marketing professionals who oversee the rejuvenation process.

Overall, therefore, the emergence of a market for the purchase and sale of brands has served to extend the life of brands. Brands can new remain 'forever young'. Cosmetics may give the appearance of eternal youth, alcohol may create the delusion of eternal youth, but ordinary consumers are doomed to lose their youthful looks eventually. Popular global brands are ageless, however. While the firms that own the brands will probably outlive the consumers, the brands will in turn outlive the firms. The 'magic of the market' has made brands immortal, it would seem.

REFERENCES

Aaker, D.A. and E. Joachimsthaler (1999), 'The lure of global branding', *Harvard Business Review*, November–December, 137–44.

Blaszczyk, Regina Lee (2006), 'Styling synthetics: DuPont's marketing of fabrics and fashions in postwar America', *Business History Review*, **8** (3), 485–528.

Bonin, Hubert, Caroline Pailhe and Nadine Polakowski (2001), 'The French touch: international beauty and health care at L'Oréal (since 1907)', in H. Bonin et al. (eds), *Transnational Companies*, Paris: PLAGE.

Bure, Giles de (2001), *Perrier by Perrier*, Barcelona: Agence Kreo Cavanagh.

Cavanagh, John and Frederick F. Clairmonte (1985), *Alcoholic Beverages: Dimensions of Power*, London: Croom Helm.

Chernatory, Leslie de and G. McWilliam (1989), 'The varying nature of brands as assets', *International Journal of Advertising*, **8**, 339–49.

Church, Roy and Christine Clark (2001), 'Product development of branded packaged household goods in Britain, 1870–1914: Colman's, Reckitt's and Lever Brothers', *Enterprise and Society*, **2**, 503–42.

Craig, Tim (1996), 'The Japanese bar wars: initiating and responding to hyper-competition in new product development', *Organization Science*, **7** (3), 302–21.

Corley, T.A.B. (1994), 'Best practice marketing of food and health drinks in Britain, 1930–70', in G.G. Jones and N.J. Morgan (eds), *Adding Value: Brands and Marketing in Food and Drink*, London: Routledge, pp. 215–36.

Dalle, Francois, (2001), *L'Aventure L'Oréal*, Paris: Odile.

Dyer, Davis, Frederick Dalzell and Rowena Olegario (2004), *Rising Tide: Lessons from 165 Years of Brand Building at Procter & Gamble*, Boston, MA: Harvard Business School Press.

Fitzgerald, Robert (1995), *Rowntree and the Marketing Revolution, 1862–1969*, Cambridge: Cambridge University Press.

Forden, Sara G. (2001), *The House of Gucci: A Sensational Story of Murder, Madness, Glamour and Greed*, New York: Harper Collins.

Glamann, Christof (1991), *Jacobsen of Carlsberg – Brewer and Philanthropist*, Copenhagen: Gyldendal.

Gourvish, Terry and Richard G. Wilson (1994), *The British Brewing Industry*, Cambridge: Cambridge University Press.

Heer, Jean (1991), *Nestlé – 125 Years*, Vevey: Nestlé.

Interbrand (2006), *The 2006 Best Global Brands Report*.

Jones, Geoffrey G. (1984), 'Multinational chocolate: Cadbury overseas, 1918–1939', *Business History*, **26**, 59–76.

Jones, Geoffrey G. (2005), *Renewing Unilever: Transformation and Tradition*, Oxford: Oxford University Press.

Keller, Kevin Lane (1998), *Strategic Brand Management*, London: Prentice-Hall International.

McKnight, Gerard (1987), *Gucci: A House Divided*, London: Sidgwick & Jackson.

Michel, G. and Tim Ambler (1999), 'Establishing brand essence across borders', *Journal of Brand Management*, **6** (5), 333–45.

Monsen, Randall Bruce (2001), *A Century of Perfume: The Perfumes of Coty*, Atlanta: Mosen & Baer.

Morgenthaler, M. (1944), 'La naissance du Nescafé', *Bulletin Nestlé*, No.2.

Morgenthaler, M. (1988), 'Cinquante ans du Nescafé!', *Nestlé Gazette*, April, No. 2.

Peiss, Kathy (1999), *Hope in a Jar: The Making of America's Beauty Culture*, Kinlough: Owl Books.

Pfiffner, Albert (2002), 'A real winner one day: the development of Nescafé in the 1930s', in Roman Rossfeld (ed.), *Genuss und Nuchternheir: Geschichte des Kaffees in der Scwheiz*, Baden.

Rose, Mary B. (ed.) (1995), *Family Business*, Aldershot, UK and Brookfield, US: Edward Elgar.

Schulz, Howard and Dori Jones Yang (1997), *Pour Your Heart into it: How Starbucks built a Company one Cup at a Time*, New York: Hyperion.

Schumpeter, Joseph A. (1934), *The Theory of Economic Development*, trans. R. Opie, Cambridge, MA: Harvard University Press.

Schumpeter, Joseph A. (1939), *Business Cycles*, New York: Wiley.

Simmons, Douglas A. (1983), *Schweppes: The First 200 Years*, Ascot: Springwood Books.

Storey, David (1994), *Understanding the Small Business Sector*, London: Routledge.
Trimarco, Paola (2001), *Gucci: Business in Fashion*, Harlow: Pearson.
USPTO (2003), *Patent Counts by Class by Year, 1917–2001*, Washington DC: United States Patent and Trademark Office.
Williams, I.A. (1931), *The Firm of Cadbury: 1831–1931*, London: Constable.
Woodhead, Lindy (2003), *War Paint: Madame Helena Rubinstein and Miss Elizabeth Arden: their Lives, their Times, their Rivalry*, Chichester: Virago.

11. Entrepreneurship in Victorian Britain

With Andrew Godley

There are two common misunderstandings about the economy in Victorian Britain, which this chapter attempts to correct. The first is that economic growth was driven by the expansion of manufacturing industry – and in particular by the textile industries of the north – and the second is that the quality of entrepreneurship declined after the mid-nineteenth century. The two misunderstandings are related, and they have a common cause in a lack of proper appreciation of the economic role of the entrepreneur. Victorian entrepreneurship became increasingly specialized in the finance and management of large-scale projects – first in Britain itself, and then in the empire. These projects related to railways, shipping, mining and agriculture rather than to manufacturing. Within manufacturing it was the engineering trades that provided mechanical equipment for these projects that prospered most. More so than the textile industry itself, which, because it was based on the import and re-export of cotton, was always potentially vulnerable to overseas competition. Project promotion was supported by a growing range of specialized service industries, linked to professions such as law and accountancy, and centred on the imperial metropolis – London. The most profitable way to exploit these professional skills was by exporting capital and labour to settler economies, where large-scale projects could generate cheap supplies of minerals for industry, and food for the urban population back home. It was only after 1900 that the grand 'Project of Empire' began to encounter serious problems and that domestic economic growth began to suffer as a result.

11.1 INTRODUCTION

This chapter examines the role of entrepreneurship in the growth of the Victorian economy over a seventy-year period, beginning at a time when the Industrial Revolution was approaching maturity and ending when the overseas British empire was approaching its zenith.

While the factory system was the major technological innovation of the Industrial Revolution (1760–1830), the introduction of railways and the switch from sail to steam in ocean-going shipping were the major technological innovations of the Victorian period (1837–1901). It was not so much in manufacturing, but rather in infrastructure, and most particularly in transport and communications systems, that Victorian Britons made their mark.

It is therefore a mistake to suppose that technological innovation in the manufacturing sector was the driving force in the economy of Victorian Britain. There was certainly a good deal of incremental innovation in manufacturing, concerned with the fine-tuning of product design, but relatively little radical innovation. Steam power was the principle moving force at the end of the Victorian period, just as it was at the beginning, and horses still provided the major motive power on the roads. Although the principles of electro-magnetism were discovered in Britain before the Victorian period, it was only after 1900 that large-scale urban electrification – let alone rural electrification – got under way. Apart from the electric tram, little systematic use was made of electrical power until the very end of the nineteenth century.

It was not only technological innovation that was important in the Victorian era, however: institutional innovations were important too. Entrepreneurial attitudes were not confined to the private business sector; they were also evident in far-sighted political leadership, and in the rapidly-growing professional civil service.

The Victorians were immensely proud of Britain's (unwritten) political constitution. They created an empire which exported British institutions to many parts of the world – most notably the Indian subcontinent and the large settler economies of Canada and Australia. Having 'learned their lesson' from the American Revolution of 1776, when their principal colonial foundation declared independence, successive British governments administered their empire in a relatively decentralized manner. Although access to imperial markets was restricted, trade within the empire was largely based on the principles of free trade enunciated by Adam Smith. The empire therefore constituted an enormous captive export market for British manufacturing firms, which they accessed through the transport linkages provided by rail and sea. The steady growth of the imperial population, through both natural increase and territorial expansion, coupled with rising incomes in the settler economies, encouraged product innovation. By the end of the Victorian period, British firms exported an enormous range of trade-marked products, especially in sectors such as steam-powered machinery and metal household goods.

Private entrepreneurs did not enjoy particularly high status in Victorian

Britain. Indeed, the owners of small firms were often classed as 'trades-men' and looked down upon by middle-class professionals and those with inherited wealth. On the other hand, setting up a business was easy, as regulations were few. A business partnership between a wealthy investor and an enterprising artisan became a widely accepted and very successful business model (Payne, 1988). But other avenues of wealth accumulation were possible too. The ever-shifting imperial frontier provided the potential for rich pickings for soldiers and bounty-hunters. Furthermore, many young men of great ability chose to enter the church in search of spiritual rather than material rewards, with the entrepreneurial risk-takers opting for missionary work overseas.

The principle of partnership was extended during the Victorian period through a series of reforms to company law which made it much easier for large businesses to be incorporated as joint-stock companies with limited liability for their shareholders. This in turn increased liquidity in stock markets by making it easier for ordinary people to buy and sell shares in small denominations. This in turn facilitated the growth of large firms.

However, little trust was placed in the law as a means of resolving business disputes. The law had a bad reputation for being slow, complex and extremely expensive. Many businesses, including quite large businesses, therefore relied on local people to subscribe capital. The family was an important unit of business organization: it was not only the moral bedrock of Victorian society, but also a device for building trust between partners in a business. Many large businesses remained under the control of family dynasties, and 'marrying the boss's daughter' was a reliable way of securing promotion in many firms. This illustrates the general point that Victorians invested heavily not only in political institutions, but also in social and moral institutions.

While the Victorian economy is, in many respects, a success story, it certainly had its failures. Its failure to develop the economic potential of new technologies such as electricity has already been noted. While electricity was widely used to facilitate imperial communications through the electric telegraph, mundane applications such as household lighting and power supply were relatively neglected. Similar criticisms can be made in terms of Britain's failure to capitalize on chemical discoveries such as synthetic dyes, which allowed Germany to gain a major technological lead in the chemical and pharmaceutical industries. Britain was also slow to exploit the potential of the internal combustion engine. Engineers were more concerned to perfect the working of the steam engine. Their decision to ignore the new technology was reinforced by the large supply of cheap coal available in Britain, the poor state of the roads, and highway regulations that protected the interests of pedestrians and horse traffic.

The evidence on Victorian entrepreneurship is compatible with general theories of entrepreneurship which emphasize the role of entrepreneurs in making sound decisions regarding risky innovations. Victorian Britons generally made good judgements regarding infrastructure investments and their use in building an empire of free trade, but their judgements were much weaker in the manufacturing sector. Entrepreneurs appear to have been aware of their own strengths and weaknesses, and to have concentrated on investing in those areas in which their judgements were likely to prove successful. However, if entrepreneurship is understood exclusively in terms of small business formation and growth, initiated by the self-employed, then the theory does not work so well in explaining the facts of the Victorian period. The large infrastructure projects, such as railways, at which the Victorians excelled were not run by the self-employed, but by boards of directors of joint-stock companies: boards that comprised professional experts, such as engineers, bankers and lawyers, together with leading merchants and manufacturers who had already built large businesses of their own. The distinguishing feature of successful Victorian entrepreneurship was that it was based on extensive partnerships between wealthy investors and professional specialists, rather than on the efforts of thousands of small-scale self-employed businessmen. Whilst there were many such small businessmen, most successful small businesses seem to have thrived mainly because of the large size of the imperial market to which they had access. This market was not the product of technological innovation by small private enterprises, but of political initiatives backed up by large infrastructure projects, endorsed by politicians and civil servants and implemented by large joint-stock firms.

11.2 BACKGROUND: KEY FEATURES OF BRITISH ECONOMIC AND SOCIAL DEVELOPMENT, 1830–1900

The period 1830–1900 was a time of considerable political and social change. It began badly. Following the end of the Napoleonic Wars in 1815, the economy entered a serious depression. There were riots in Manchester and other cities. The Duke of Wellington, the hero of the Battle of Waterloo, soon became a most unpopular prime minister.

The political situation improved after 1832, when the Reform Act extended the franchise and removed some of the so-called rotten boroughs. But new problems emerged. In Ireland the mismanagement of the famine stimulated calls for home rule. The population grew rapidly (see Figure 11.1) and rural poverty was rife. The great industrial cities were

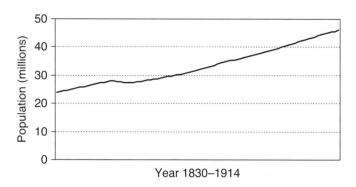

Source: Officer (2005).

Figure 11.1   Population of the United Kingdom, 1830–1914

insanitary, and as a result health became a major Victorian obsession. Millions left the land and emigrated to Australia, New Zealand, North America and elsewhere.

Nevertheless, in comparison with other European countries, the UK remained remarkably stable. Victorian paternalism encouraged local elites to be responsive to local needs, and many successful businessmen became social reformers. Religion was very important to the Victorians. It provided a bond between members of different social and economic classes, particularly in the Nonconformist churches, where artisans and small businessmen could take on responsible roles as pastors. Although there was conflict between different denominations, the Christian ethic was a potent unifying force, promoting high standards of behaviour in both public and private life.

The performance of the economy was steady, if unspectacular by modern standards. But compared to the relative stasis of medieval and early modern times, growth appears to have been remarkably high. Gross domestic product per head rose from £1672 in 1830 to £3911 in 1900 (at 2003 market prices), an average compound percentage growth of just over 1.2 per cent per year (Figure 11.2). Prices were steady throughout the period, apart from cyclical changes caused by periodic booms and slumps (Figure 11.3). The stability of prices helped to sustain relatively low rates of interest. Long-term interest rates were rarely above 3.5 per cent, and in the 1890s fell to below 2.5 per cent (Figure 11.4), although short-term rates were far more volatile, particularly at times of financial crisis, such as 1846 and 1866.

The combination of low inflation and low interest rates encouraged

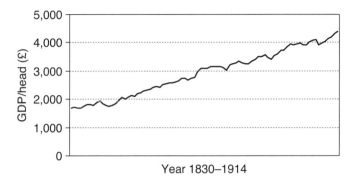

Source: Officer (2005).

Figure 11.2 *Gross domestic product per head in the United Kingdom,*
            1830–1914

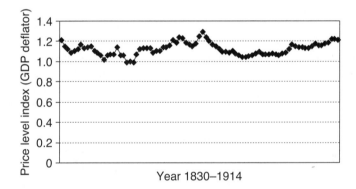

Source: Officer (2005).

Figure 11.3 *Price level in the United Kingdom, 1830–1914 (1851 = 100)*

long-term investment. The Victorians were great builders – in almost every
sense of the word. They built grand public buildings, which were symbolic
of national pride, such as the new Houses of Parliament; and at a local level
they built numerous town halls, and clock towers. They built institutions
– reforming local government and creating numerous local charities; they
built an empire, on which they believed that 'the sun would never set'; and
– most importantly – they built a massive infrastructure of ports, railways,
urban gas and water systems and so on. This infrastructure supported the
evolution of major agglomerations of factories – the specialized industrial
districts later described by Alfred Marshall (1923).

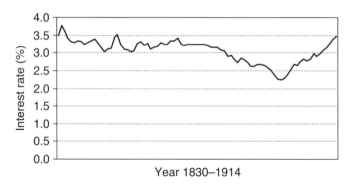

Source: Officer (2005).

Figure 11.4   Long-term interest rates in the United Kingdom, 1830–1914

In the late eighteenth century, at the start of the Industrial Revolution, infrastructure projects were often undertaken as an adjunct to factory-building. Entrepreneurship was focused on the innovation of the water-powered (and later steam-powered) factory. The building of canals, and the conversion of roads into turnpikes, was useful to entrepreneurs because it reduced transport costs and thereby widened the market for their mass-produced factory goods. Consequently, for example, many factory masters invested in canal projects (Pearson and Richardson, 2001). By the start of the Victorian period, however, the first major wave of factory-building had come to an end. After the final defeat of Napoleon in 1815, Britain was master of the seas, and there were major opportunities to extend maritime trade. This encouraged investment in ports and harbours instead.

To realize their full potential, however, ports needed to be connected to the great industrial centres, and canals were proving inadequate for this purpose; they dried up in summer and iced up in winter. Railways were the answer. But it soon turned out that railways could do much more than carry freight; they could carry mail and passengers at unbelievably high speed as well. New opportunities for tourism, commuting and the development of a national system of banking were opened up. Infrastructure projects acquired a life of their own. Cities began to develop as information hubs as well as industrial centres – a function that they had always performed, but which they could perform more easily once long-distance communication had been speeded up.

The social tensions alluded to earlier led to difficult industrial relations in many factory-based industries. British workers valued autonomy – a status very much associated with the skilled artisan – and resented the military-style discipline of the factory. If labour had been cheap then factory owners could simply have ignored the wishes of their workers, but their workers had alternatives to factory employment; not only emigration, but employment in service industries such as transport, retailing and banking. Factory production became steadily less economic as a result.

Infrastructure, on the other hand, prospered (Millward, 1991). The British Empire was growing fast, and everywhere there were new opportunities for development. Ports, railways, telegraphs and urban investments were the key. It was not so much the factory as the engineering workshop that became the hub of British manufacturing. While the factory remained dominant in the textile trades, engineering workshops and 'yards' were responsible for producing most of the sophisticated machinery that was exported overseas; in particular, ships and steam locomotives, and the prefabricated bridges and pipework that were exported for use in overseas projects. By the end of the century the Victorian economy was economically driven by – and dependent upon – the project of imperialism.

When the age of imperialism came to an abrupt end in 1914, so did much of British entrepreneurship. A whole generation of budding entrepreneurs was wiped out in the trenches of the First World War. Furthermore, the international political instability created by the post-war settlement at Versailles undermined the system of international trade on which the empire was built. It was not the fault of individual British entrepreneurs that they became locked in to such a vulnerable imperial system. If there was a failure, it was the over-optimistic belief, encouraged by Britain's political leaders, that the project of empire would continue indefinitely without disruption.

The Victorians, therefore, were basically successful entrepreneurs operating under good incentives that rewarded socially beneficial enterprise. They were not good at everything, however. As the Victorian era progressed, entrepreneurs increasingly focused their efforts on promoting large infrastructure projects. This was because factory production became less profitable and infrastructure projects more profitable.

Despite the apparently modest levels of growth in national income they attained, the Victorians left a valuable and impressive legacy. Although much of this legacy was squandered in the twentieth century in fighting two world wars and defending the empire overseas, the Victorians built so well that a significant amount of their infrastructure – both social and physical – has survived to this day.

11.3 THE CONCEPT OF THE ENTREPRENEUR IN VICTORIAN HISTORIOGRAPHY

The Victorian period in Britain has always been controversial. No sooner had Queen Victoria died in 1901 than Edwardian intellectuals began to criticize her legacy, and the debate has continued ever since. A bewildering variety of factors have been used to explain the performance of the Victorian economy. Several writers have identified entrepreneurship as an explanatory factor, but their explanations have not been developed in a systematic way.

Although the term 'entrepreneur' is widely used in histories of Victorian Britain, there is no consistency in the way that it is employed. Most writers treat the entrepreneur as a Weberian 'ideal type'. This ideal type is, in turn, often drawn from literature rather than life. Charles Dickens's description of horse traders at Howden fair in East Yorkshire is a case in point. With breath smelling of beer and stale tobacco, they talk amongst themselves in a private language, clinching deals with a shake of the hand. Every horse has it price; Dickens jokes that if the queen arrived at the horse-fair in a 'coach and four', the dealers would not be shy to offer her a price for her horses.

Dickens, as a social critic, did not portray Victorian entrepreneurs in flattering terms. Perhaps the most influential contemporary was Karl Marx, who equated the entrepreneur to a capitalist. To Marx, the fundamental feature of early Victorian capitalism was the alienation of the worker from the means of production. The artisan no longer owned his own tools, and his work had been de-skilled. Under the factory system, his tools had been replaced by large-scale machinery operated by teams of workers subject to military-style discipline. The expense of the machinery meant that the ownership of the means of production, and hence the control of the worker, had fallen into the hands of a specialized capitalist class.

Whilst Marx identified the capitalist entrepreneur with large-scale production, he also recognized the role of the petit bourgeoisie – such as the traders described by Dickens. Modern labour economists also emphasize the petit bourgeoisie in their discussion of entrepreneurship. They typically define entrepreneurship in terms of self-employment (see Chapter 1). This definition is too narrow to be of much use in analysing the Victorian economy, however. In the early nineteenth century a high proportion of the population was either wholly or partially self-employed. Even women and children gleaning in the fields after harvest were effectively self-employed. The factory revolution actually reduced self-employment, rather than increasing it, by turning self-employed out-workers into wage workers, and the subsequent growth of major transport and utility industries sustained this trend. Self-employed entrepreneurship remained vibrant in the retail trades, as 'the nation of shopkeepers' prospered, but only a small proportion of shopkeepers demonstrated significant entrepreneurial ability by introducing new retail concepts, such as the high-street chain and the department store. To identify Victorian entrepreneurship with self-employment is therefore misleading, as entrepreneurship reduced self-employment rather than increased it, and those who were self-employed were not particularly notable for their entrepreneurship.

This chapter employs a more systematic approach to the study of entrepreneur, as set out in the preceding chapters. The entrepreneur is someone who specializes in taking risky decisions about major investments. These investments involve irreversible commitments; people cannot easily get their money back if an entrepreneurial project fails. Entrepreneurs come forward to take these decisions because they believe that their judgement is better than that of other people, and if other people share that judgement then they will lend their money to the entrepreneur.

This focus on judgement is well adapted to the study of entrepreneurship in Victorian Britain. The framework of company law within which entrepreneurs operated changed significantly over the Victorian period, so that any definition of entrepreneurship in terms of the ownership or management of firms suffers from the problem that the legal nature of the firm was undergoing significant change at this time. On the other hand, the function of exercising judgement in high-risk innovative sectors remained a constant requirement.

In early Victorian Britain firms could obtain joint-stock status and limited liability only by Act of Parliament, following the precedents set by the early chartered trading companies. All canal and railway promoters, for example, had to apply to Parliament if they required these privileges (see below). These companies were typically incorporated with a large authorized capital, because additional capital could only be raised by a further act. Thus most large firms were 'born large' – they did not grow from small beginnings, as happened later. Most small firms were started as partnerships or family businesses, and although they could grow, for example, by increasing the number of partners or extending the family through marriage, there were limits to how far and how fast this could happen. By the end of the century, however, companies could incorporate as joint-stock limited liability companies through a simple act of registration. This allowed small firms to grow into large industrial enterprises without a major reconstruction of their capital.

Nevertheless, as Chandler has pointed out, many family firms remained suspicious of diluting ownership by flotation on a stock exchange. They were also reluctant to delegate entrepreneurial decisions to professional employees, especially, it would seem, when the professional specialists were better qualified than the family members themselves. The predominance of close-held family firms impeded the operation of the market in corporate control, as alluded to above. The owners of many family firms adopted a dynastic view – treating the firm as they treated their land: as an asset to be maintained under family ownership and control and held in trust for future generations.

The eldest son had a customary right to run the business, and an obligation to exercise this right, irrespective of his inclination or his competence. This created an endemic 'succession' problem (Rose, 1993), made famous as the 'Buddenbrooks syndrome' of 'rags to rags in three generations'. However, focusing heavily on the limitations of small family firms, as Chandler is inclined to do, distorts the picture of Victorian entrepreneurship, because the most important field for entrepreneurial judgement at that time was not in small manufacturing firms but in the growing number of large joint-stock companies.

11.4   THE RISE AND DECLINE OF ENTREPRENEURSHIP IN VICTORIAN BRITAIN: THE DEBATE

The historical literature on Victorian entrepreneurship has focused on a rather limited range of issues. Two of these issues are briefly considered here. The first is the role of free trade policies and laissez-faire in encouraging entrepreneurship, and the second is the apparent decline of entrepreneurship in late Victorian Britain.

Laissez-faire

Modern political writers have looked back to early Victorian Britain in an attempt to discover the roots of modern economic growth. It is often suggested that Victorian Britain was committed to a policy of laissez-faire. According to this view, there was a popular belief that the pursuit of profit, constrained only by free competition, would lead to benefits for all; consequently, state interference was rejected as meddlesome. Under this regime of laissez-faire, entrepreneurship thrived; the fetters of government regulation were discarded, and the economy took off. But then trades unions appeared, the story goes, and they began to monopolize the supply of labour. Using the political power of the Independent Labour Party, they crushed the spirit of enterprise. The economy went into decline, and the responsibility for carrying the torch of free enterprise passed to the USA.

There are a number of difficulties with this story. The first involves a question of dates. For a significant period prior to 1830 Britain was at war with Napoleonic France. During this period, government had an active role in stimulating demand for both textiles (for example, military uniforms) and engineering products (for example, guns and armour), and when this demand ceased at the end of the war a serious recession ensued. Indeed, some military historians turn the argument around, and maintain that military procurement, by setting challenging targets for entrepreneurs, stimulated investment and innovation in precision-made factory products.

Furthermore, free trade was not official government policy until the repeal of the Corn Laws in 1846, and the prime minister, Robert Peel, who pushed through this reform, split his political party in the process. Although Richard Cobden, John Bright and other members of the 'Manchester School' had been vociferous lobbyists for free trade, it was neither their free market ideology nor the prospective benefit to industry that finally swayed Peel and his followers but the potential benefits to the workers themselves. Peel was concerned that the benefit to workers of any reduction in the price of corn would be neutralized by lower wages, and it was only when he was persuaded that wages would remain high because of buoyant product demand that he agreed to the reform (Prest, 2004).

Another reason for government involvement in the economy was that many of the major industrial projects in Victorian Britain involved the compulsory acquisition of land, as explained below. Far from defending individual property rights unequivocally, government presided over a system in which large amounts of private land were acquired, subject to arbitration, on the authority of the state. It is a mistake to assume that, as in the USA, land could simply be acquired by pushing forward the frontier of settlement. By 1830 Britain was already a relatively mature and densely-populated country, and government regularly authorized the subordination of private property rights to the public interest.

Whilst it is true that Adam Smith had set out in the *Wealth of Nations*, as early as 1776, the benefits of a deregulated market economy, his ideas did not have the immediate policy impact that is sometimes alleged. As an intellectual product of the Enlightenment, Smith was interested in the roots of progress. His major contribution was to identify the division of labour and the growth of trade as the main 'drivers' of progress. His major criticism of the British government was that it had given a monopoly of the country's foreign trade to chartered trading companies, such as the East India Company. The profits of these companies were essentially a tax on trade, and Smith proposed to remove this tax by taking away the privileges of these companies and promoting competition instead. Whilst Smith believed that competition was part of the natural order, and should be employed to good effect, he did not state that competition should be given completely free reign, as suggested by the later doctrine of laissez-faire (Nicholson, 1909).

If there was a governing principle in early Victorian society, it was that advances in technology created the potential for sustained improvement in the standard of living. Unlocking this potential required good institutions, and since not all institutions were fully rational, institutional reform was required. The liberalization of markets emphasized by Smith was only one of the reforms required. It was also important to ensure that the benefits of improvement were fairly distributed among different members of society. Political reform in support of a more just distribution of the benefits of progress was an important aspect of legislation between 1830 and 1850.

There was disagreement, however, about how radical the reforms should be. Some people argued that existing institutions must already be rational, in the pragmatic sense that they had 'stood the test of time'. Others argued that they were irrational legacies from the medieval period. Radical popu-lists such as Marx and Engels (both of whom lived in England in the 1840s) argued that technological improvements, by liberating workers from the back-breaking toil of agricultural labour, should allow them to spend more time in rewarding and creative craft production. But factory work, they observed, was anything but creative and rewarding – it was repeti-tive, highly disciplined and alienating. Having escaped from the tyranny of the local squire, the worker was now tyrannized by the local industrial capitalist instead. Marx and Engels predicted a workers' revolution, but in practice the Chartist revolution of 1848 quickly fizzled out.

In the 1870s, democratic socialists promoted trades unions. The idea was that the trade union would neutralize the power of the capitalist by exercising a countervailing monopoly power through control of the labour supply. The trade union movement gained considerable support after 1880 – initially amongst skilled workers, and later amongst the unskilled as well. By 1900 several industries had become dominated by large and powerful trades unions, some of whose leaders sought to use strike action not only to improve wages and conditions of employment, but also to challenge the traditional rights of employers over their workers. In manu-facturing, mining and transport, wage rates rose, basic hours of work fell, and productivity growth stagnated (Broadberry, 1997, 2006).

Labour disputes began to polarize political opinion. Some employers turned to confrontation, locking workers out before a strike could take effect, and hiring strike-breakers, whilst others agreed to conciliation.

Some embraced novel forms of profit-sharing and part-ownership with employees, whilst others emphatically asserted their absolute rights as employers. Government began to legislate over workers' rights and trade union representation, leading to high-profile court cases which resolved the immediate issues but often left more ill-feeling between the parties than there had been before.

By 1900 many aspects of economic life were tightly regulated, and an increasing number of activities, such as education and local transport, were coming under local government control. If there was a period of laissez-faire in Britain then it was certainly a very short one – say between 1850 and 1880 – and even then the economic freedom prevailing in Britain was nowhere near as great as the freedoms that existed at this time in the USA.

The Onset of Decline

The zenith of Britain's technological leadership is commonly said to be 1851 – the year of the Great Exhibition in Hyde Park, London. The key innovators, it is said, were artisan entrepreneurs who, from the late eighteenth century, had pioneered the mechanized factory system (Deane, 1979; Mokyr, 2004). International exhibitions became popular attractions in the nineteenth century, attended by increasing numbers of the general public, but after 1851 the success of British entrepreneurs in winning prizes went into decline, whilst that of US and continental European entrepreneurs rose.

Not everyone agrees that the decline of Victorian entrepreneurship can be conveniently dated to some time in mid-century, however. An emphasis on economic performance rather than the pace of technological innovation suggests dating decline to the end of the mid-Victorian boom and the onset of the great depression in 1873 (Church, 1975; Saul, 1969).

Crafts (1985) has taken a more radical view. He argues that the impact of the Industrial Revolution on British productivity growth in the first half of the nineteenth century has been exaggerated. Mass production was mainly confined to the textile industries of the north: cottons in Lancashire and woollens in Yorkshire. More generally, Pollard (1997) has argued that throughout European history, innovations in manufacturing have been concentrated in marginal agricultural areas such as the north of England, where local families combined mixed farming with proto-industrial pursuits. Crafts suggests that there was greater continuity between the two halves of the nineteenth century than the traditional view implies, with a modest rate of productivity growth being sustained throughout.

It is possible that while entrepreneurship was sustained for longer than previously thought, its direction shifted. As suggested in the introduction, there was a major shift from developing the resources of the domestic economy into imperial development. Around mid-century, growing numbers of the 'middling sort' who aspired to fame and fortune emigrated to the 'settler economies' within the empire, such as Australia and New Zealand, whilst the more highly educated joined the growing colonial civil service. Thus, the dynamism of the late Victorian economy shifted to the 'frontier of empire'. Some aristocratic families made a smooth transition into merchant banking, helping to fund the growth of imperial trade and investment from its London hub. The rapid growth of financial services, together with artisan emigration, drew resources away from manufacturing industry. Overcrowding and insanitary conditions in the industrial cities reduced the quality of the manufacturing labour force, fuelled labour discontent and accelerated the spread of trade unionism to unskilled workers. The rapid industrialization of the USA, Germany and other continental European countries exposed the weaknesses caused by low manufacturing productivity growth in Britain.

Schumpeter's (1939) analysis of long waves in the world economy leads to similar conclusions regarding structural change, but by a different route. According to Schumpeter, Britain pioneered not one but two major innovations: first the factory system and then the railways. Since the diffusion of the railway system was a feature of the second half of the nineteenth century rather than the first, this suggests that Britain may have continued to be entrepreneurial, but switched its focus from manufacturing to transport infrastructure and utilities (Broadberry, 2006). Whilst early transport investments focused on the domestic economy, later investments were mainly concerned with supporting international trade. Railway technology pioneered in Britain was exported to the colonial frontier. Overseas rail investments were supported by investments in shipping lines, whereby steam-powered vessels provided regular communication with harbours served by local railways. The growing influence of infrastructure investment, and its international orientation, is reflected in the growth of British coal exports to overseas bunkering stations, and the declining proportion of coal output supplied to domestic heavy industry (Church, 1986).

Chandler (1990) suggests a different perspective on British decline, however, derived from different sources – business histories rather than national income accounts and business cycle data. According to Chandler, British entrepreneurs were slow to make the 'three-pronged' investments in marketing, professional management and organized research that he considered necessary for an economy to make the transition from artisan production to mass production. A conservative attachment to the institution of the family firm and a cult of amateurism in management made British firms unable to respond to US and German competition in high-technology industries in the late nineteenth century.

An alternative view, however, would suggest that British entrepreneurs neglected investment in mass production manufacturing industry because they perceived more profitable opportunities elsewhere. Economies of mass production, as exemplified by the Chicago meat-packing industry, benefited from cheap unskilled immigrant labour and abundant land – both factors that were missing from Britain, where land was scarce, towns were congested, and most workers aspired to artisan status. Because the territorial area of the UK is so much smaller than that of the USA, British entrepreneurs were more concerned to expand internationally. They needed to invest overseas in a range of relatively small colonial markets. As a result, they evolved more flexible managerial forms than the hierarchical Chandlerian enterprise. A good example of a flexible form is the 'free-standing firm', whose operations were based wholly overseas – often in a single country – but which was controlled from a small head office, usually in London (Wilkins, 1986; Wilkins and Schroter, 1998). A constellation of several free-standing firms provided greater flexibility than would a single hierarchical firm on the US model, managing overseas operations through national subsidiaries. By incorporating each major project as a separate company, financial transparency was increased, allowing shareholders rather than salaried managers to decide whether profits should be reinvested in new schemes.

Olson (1982) offers yet another perspective on the subject. He argues for the institutionalization of collusion as a general cause of economic decline in nations, and he uses Britain as an exemplary case. His focus is on two types of horizontal combination: combinations of workers – namely trades unions – and combinations of firms – namely trade associations and cartels. These combinations are designed to raise wages and prices by eliminating competition: in other words, they are generated by 'rent-seeking' rather than 'efficiency-seeking' behaviour (Baumol, 1994).

To discourage the entry of new competitors, a combination can obtain privileges from the state – such as immunity for strikers in the case of unions, and official recognition as lobbyists in case of trade associations. In addition, unions and employers can join forces to lobby for protective tariffs. This is what happened in Britain at the end of the nineteenth century, according to Olson. Lengthy apprenticeship schemes and restrictive practices reduced occupational mobility. The labour market became segmented into distinctive crafts, with particular types of job reserved for members of particular unions. A social hierarchy of crafts developed, analogous to an Indian caste system. So far as firms were concerned, the

protection of domestic and colonial markets became increasingly important as the international competitiveness of British labour declined.

One of the difficulties with the Olson thesis is that the types of combination which impeded growth in Britain have been credited with accelerating
growth in continental economies. It is said that in Germany, for example,
cartels facilitated the rationalization of industry, leading to efficiency
gains from the exploitation of economies of scale, whilst labour unions
supported the diffusion of technical knowledge through industrial training
schemes.

Indeed, Olson's own theory indicates that horizontal combinations can
generate productivity gains as well as losses. Local trade associations not
only fix prices: they can organize the provision of public goods, such as
harbour improvements, which improve productivity in industrial districts.
Indeed, shareholders in joint-stock firms combine horizontally to finance
indivisible investments; without such combinations, large firms could not
evolve to compete in international markets. Horizontal combination is
therefore not intrinsically collusive in nature.

To interpret the traditional view of nineteenth-century Britain in terms
of the Olson thesis it is necessary to suppose that 'efficiency-seeking' combinations, geared to the diffusion of knowledge and the provision of public
goods, dominated in the first half of the century, and that rent-seeking
trades unions and cartels dominated in the second half of the century. Part
of the explanation may lie in the shake out of less productive firms that
seems to have occurred in a number of manufacturing industries as they
matured through the Victorian period. In an infant industry composed
mainly of dynamic small firms, such as the early textile industry, there can
be a problem in providing industry-specific public goods; since individual
firms are too small to have much political influence, they must organize the
provision of these goods amongst themselves, perhaps by forming a trade
association for this purpose. As the industry matures, however, and price
competition intensifies, reducing costs through economies of scale can
promote industrial concentration, with small firms joining forces through
merger or takeover, or simply closing down and quitting the industry. The
few remaining large firms now have more political clout, and can easily
dominate the trade association and use it as a front for lobbying government for subsidies or for protection from foreign competition. On this
view the maturing of the manufacturing industries that were established
at the time of the Industrial Revolution could account for much of the
sclerosis which seemed to afflict British manufacturing industry in the late
Victorian period. Government failed to respond to the policy challenges of
regulating mature manufacturing industries in which firms had switched
from efficiency-seeking to rent-seeking activities.

11.5 CULTURAL EXPLANATIONS OF ENTREPRENEURIAL DECLINE

Decline in the later nineteenth century in Britain is popularly attributed to premature gentrification. In the second half of the nineteenth century, it is claimed, the social gulf between artisans and aristocrats widened. Self-employed artisans and the owners of small family firms could no longer aspire to the 'fame and fortune' which had motivated earlier generations. Wealthy industrialists no longer challenged the aristocracy for political power, but bought into it by investing in country estates.

Wiener (1981) claims that from about 1850 Victorians became increasingly concerned about the adverse moral and social consequences of rapid industrialization. Talented young men preferred to make a career in church or state rather than 'trade' – religious zeal and social reform provided them with greater emotional satisfaction than what was perceived as the venal pursuit of personal profit. The most prestigious schools and universities in England taught classical studies rather than science and technology, because a knowledge of the Greek and Roman empires was considered to be more relevant for careers in the army, church or colonial service. As private enterprise was drained of talent, so entrepreneurship declined, the rate of profit diminished and investment was reduced.

McCloskey and others have challenged the notion of entrepreneurial decline in Britain by arguing that British entrepreneurs' decisions not to invest in new technologies – for example, ring spindles in the cotton textile industry – were a fully rational response to local conditions (McCloskey, 1971; Leunig, 2001). McCloskey's criticisms were directed at Aldcroft (1964) and others, who blamed economic decline on the poor quality of British management. Like Wiener, these writers linked poor management to cultural failings.

McCloskey argues for the irrelevance of a cultural approach, claiming that entrepreneurs continued to make rational decisions. If the cumulative effect of individual entrepreneurial decisions was, say, the decline of the textile industry, then it was because entrepreneurs were pursuing an enlightened long-term 'exit strategy' in response to the decline of British comparative advantage as reflected in shifts in the international terms of trade.

Economic rationality does not have to be construed in the narrow way adopted by McCloskey, however. Rational individuals may pursue non-pecuniary advantage at the expense of pecuniary advantage, and so quit industries and trades which do not fulfil their social aspirations. Entrepreneurs from other countries, who have different preferences, and place greater weight on pecuniary rewards, may take their place in world markets. Rational action may also be contingent on the mental model used by an entrepreneur, with entrepreneurs in different cultures perceiving similar constraints in different ways. One mental model may identify only a narrow range of options, such as a narrow range of scientific techniques, whilst another mental model may reveal a wider range. The entrepreneurs who choose from a wider range of options are likely to make better decisions. Godley (2001) has argued that East European Jewish immigrants migrating to London embraced a local culture which was preoccupied with achieving social status through a professional career whereas their counterparts who settled in New York embraced the local culture of the independent small businessman instead; in this way local culture can perpetuate itself through the process of assimilation even at times when quite high rates of migration occur.

This emphasis on rational action within culturally-contingent mental models is a useful framework within which to evaluate Cain and Hopkins's (2002) thesis. Cain and Hopkins argue that 'gentlemanly capitalism' is a continuing, though evolving, theme in British trade and investment from the seventeenth to the twentieth century. They emphasize that the moral and social aspirations which govern gentlemanly behaviour impinge not only on the desirability of a career in trade, but also on the way that trade itself is conducted. The gentleman trader likes to trade with people who come from the same social class – who were educated at the same school, served in the same regiment, and whose families are related to his, if only distantly. A gentleman can enlarge his social circle by being introduced to other gentlemen by a reputable third party. This third party acts as a 'bridge' between the two social circles to which the respective gentlemen belong. High-status women are well-qualified to act as 'bridgers', as they have both the opportunity to cultivate social networks and the capacity to offer hospitality on a large scale.

There is a minimum amount of wealth (or credit) that is required to sustain a gentlemanly lifestyle, and marriage to a wealthy heiress – such as the daughter of successful gentleman trader – can augment capital within the business community. Bridgers can therefore play a useful role as marriage brokers.

Gentlemanly capitalism is related to, though not identical with, what Chandler (1990) calls 'personal capitalism'. But while Chandler emphasizes the negative aspects of personal capitalism, Cain and Hopkins emphasize the positive features of gentlemanly capitalism. Investment in social networks, they suggest, reduces transaction costs. Gentlemanly capitalism was particularly well adapted to the conduct of maritime trade, because merchants required a network of trusted agents in all the major ports with which they were connected. Whilst some cultures were forced to rely on kinship ties to sustain trust, gentlemanly capitalists could rely on regimental loyalty and the 'old school tie' (Jones, 1998, 2000). Overseas agents could be recruited not just from the extended family but from the wider expatriate community. The honesty of local agents was reinforced by peer-group monitoring within the expatriate community, based around 'the club'.

Gentlemanly capitalism had its political uses too. The values of the gentleman were useful in ensuring integrity in colonial administration. A gentleman had obligations to his social inferiors, which meant that gentlemanly administrators were more likely to pay attention to local needs than officials who saw themselves simply as bureaucrats employed by a colonial power. These values of self-restraint in the exercise of power assisted the growth of empire, allowing it to be extended (to some degree) through agreements with native leaders rather than by military conquest. The importance of empire as a link between the economic, political and cultural aspects of Victorian Britain is a theme to which we return at the end of this chapter.

11.6 A PROJECT-BASED VIEW OF THE VICTORIAN ECONOMY

To appreciate fully the impact of good judgement on economic perform-ance, it is useful to adopt a project-centred view of the economy (see Chapter 2). According to this view, the economy is a not a collection of activities – as portrayed in a standard economics textbook – but a col-lection of projects instead. Projects are much more heterogeneous than activities, because no two projects are ever alike. Projects have substantial set-up costs, which activities do not. Projects have finite lives, with a dis-tinct life-cycle of start-up, consolidation, maturity and decline. Projects are risky, because the set-up costs cannot be recovered if a project fails. Risks cannot be diversified away. Projects have a minimum efficient scale, so that risks cannot be spread over a large number of tiny projects. Whilst individuals may be able to diversify risks using share portfolios, society is still exposed to systemic risk if a major project fails.

The view of the economy as a collection of projects is extremely appro-priate where the economy of Victorian Britain is concerned. Throughout the nineteenth century the projects undertaken by British entrepreneurs became increasingly ambitious – especially in scale. Even the early railway schemes had impressive titles, such as the 'Great Western Railway' and the 'Grand Junction Railway', and architectural allusions to the Roman Empire and the Egyptian Pharaohs were exceedingly common. While the pace of technological progress in Britain may have diminished as the century progressed, the diversity of projects, and the locations in which they were based, increased dramatically as the empire expanded. Entrepreneurship became increasingly focused on managing and financing a range of projects in infrastructure, urban development, shipping and financial services. These projects involved the use, not only of British resources, but the resources of colonies, dominions, protectorates, mandates and independent countries under British influence all around the world.

These imperial projects were based on domestic blueprints. Transport systems, communications, utilities and public services developed in Britain were transferred abroad, being adapted incrementally to foreign conditions. Although these overseas projects sometimes foundered because local conditions were unexpectedly different from those in Britain, the performance of overseas projects often surpassed that achieved in Britain because lessons had been learned from mistakes made in the domestic environment. The Indian railway system, for example, was developed along lines designed to avoid the problems created in Britain by the 'railway mania', and the defective system of government regulation at that time.

Table 11.1 reports the number of Acts of Parliament authorizing large projects over the period 1800-1910. It shows the number of relevant acts – so-called 'Local and Personal Acts' – classified by type of project. The data presented consist of ten-year averages; the evidence is summarized using a bar chart in Figure 11.5. The table provides an approximate measure of the level and direction of project-centred entrepreneurial activity. No entrepreneur could compulsorily acquire land, or otherwise interfere with property rights, without such an act. Not all applications for acts were successful, as opposition from landowners and the promoters of rival schemes was often acute. The numbers should be doubled, at the very least, to allow for the number of unsuccessful applications. Nor were all the authorized projects successfully completed – many failed or were scaled down because of lack of capital.

The table indicates the flow of new projects rather than the stock of existing projects. However, since it also includes authorized amendments to schemes in progress, and changes to the capital stock of existing schemes, the flow at any one time reflects to some extent the accumulated stock. This in turn reflects the fact that entrepreneurship becomes a continuing activity when projects run into difficulties, because judgement must continue to be applied in order to rescue the project from failure.

Prior to 1830, large projects focused on the enclosure of commons and the extension of agricultural estates, together with road improvements effected by turnpike trusts and the building of canals. These reforms improved the productivity of the land, and the local transport

Table 11.1   Number of local and personal Acts of Parliament 1800–1910,
classified by type of project, ten-year averages

(a)   Projects relating to inland transport

	Railway	Tramway	Road	Canal	River	Drain	Bridge
1800–9	1.2	0	48.9	5.9	2.9	3.4	3.1
1810–19	1.5	0.1	50.6	5.3	1.9	3.5	4.8
1820–9	5.2	0	63.7	3.7	2.8	1.6	6.8
1830–9	18.4	0	41.4	3.0	2.6	2.5	5.9
1840–9	82.0	0	13.4	3.8	3.2	3.0	2.3
1850–9	73.1	0.2	18.8	1.3	4.0	2.7	2.7
1860–9	144.6	1.0	11.7	1.4	2.9	4.0	5.0
1870–9	81.7	11.7	1.2	1.8	3.4	5.9	4.2
1880–9	70.4	17.9	1.8	1.2	3.2	5.3	4.0
1890–9	64.1	13.4	0.6	4.1	3.7	3.2	2.7
1900–9	40.4	20.9	0.1	1.4	2.2	3.4	1.4
1910–14	21.8	7.6	2.2	1.4	2.6	5.6	1.0

(b)   Projects relating to external trade, urban infrastructure and social
improvement

	Harbour	Water	Gas	Electricity	Towns	Social	Other
1800–9	6.4	1.6	0.1	0	9.7	6.3	52.2
1810–19	5.3	2.3	2.2	0	15.4	8.6	55.8
1820–9	5.6	3.1	8.0	0	16.6	5.0	11.1
1830–9	8.5	4.4	3.8	0	12.1	3.9	14.2
1840–9	13.7	7.4	7.8	0	18.4	4.7	14.0
1850–9	10.3	14.7	12.0	0	17.5	2.2	10.6
1860–9	13.5	19.3	19.8	0	16.3	3.9	10.7
1870–9	15.0	19.6	22.5	0.1	21.6	12.6	18.5
1880–9	13.5	18.5	12.5	2.4	23.6	15.2	28.6
1890–9	15.0	25.0	17.5	11.3	32.6	13.0	32.0
1900–9	11.5	20.9	27.2	15.0	41.3	11.2	30.5
1910–14	10.6	16.0	24.8	9.2	34.4	8.4	29.8

Source: Compiled from UK Law Commission and Scottish Law Commission (1996),
Chronological Table of Local Legislation: Local and Personal Acts, 1797–1994, 4 vols,
London: HMSO.

infrastructure, providing increased traffic that could be fed into, or distributed by the railway system. Town improvements – such as new slaughter-
houses and cattle markets – also helped.

Railway projects took off in the 1830s, with a peak in the 1860s. The first

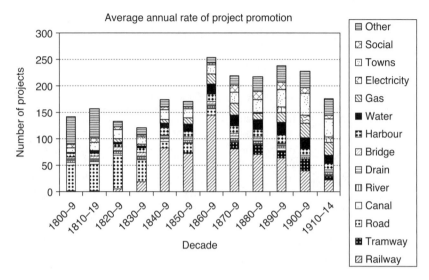

Note: For further statistical information and notes on the compilation of the data see
Casson (2009), Tables 2.1, 2.2 and Appendix 2.

Figure 11.5   *Promotion of large projects requiring statutory authorization
in the UK, 1800–1914*

'railway mania' year occurred in the period 1844–46. The railways promoted during this period were authorized with a one-year lag in the period
1845–47. There were 119 railway acts in 1845, 263 in 1846 and 187 in 1847.
Many small investors lost their life-savings in the speculation that sur-
rounded the mania. It was a while before the public regained its confidence
in railway investment, but when it did, a second – less virulent – mania
developed. It began in 1861, when 160 railway schemes were authorized.
The number rose to 251 in 1865, falling slightly to 199 in 1866. The mania
ended with the collapse in 1866 of Overend Gurney bankers in – an apparently respectable firm that had been heavily involved in railway finance.

   During the second mania, many of the schemes that had failed in the
first mania were relaunched under new names and new management.
Some of the schemes were supported by towns that had missed out on
the railway altogether, whilst other towns encouraged new schemes in the
interests of greater competition, which they believed would lead to lower
fares and freight rates.

   New canal projects were still in progress at the time that the first inter-
urban railway – the Liverpool & Manchester – was completed in 1830.
This explains the intensity of opposition from canal interests in the early

years of railway development. By 1840, however, most new schemes were either for merger and rationalization, or for the conversion of canals into railways. Canal building revived at the end of the century with the construction of the Manchester Ship Canal.

From the seventeenth century onwards, river navigations made a significant contribution to freight transport in Britain, allowing river traffic to penetrate further inland, thereby connecting the industrial heartlands to the coast. In East Anglia river navigations also assisted the drainage of the fens. The importance of maritime trade to an island such as Britain is underlined by the significant number of port and harbour improvement schemes that were promoted throughout the nineteenth century. The statistics for harbours also include piers built to develop tourism at seaside resorts.

The different transport schemes were complementary (Gourvish, 1980). Roads fed traffic to the railways, and the railways fed traffic to the ports. The rapid extension of maritime trade in the age of 'high imperialism' after 1870 allowed parts of the railway system to act as a land-bridge between the North Sea ports on the east coast, the Channel ports on the south coast and the Atlantic ports on the west coast. Even the canals, which competed most directly with the railways, could take slow-moving heavy traffic off the railway and free up capacity for higher-value loads.

The social problems of rapid urbanization had become acute by mid-century, not just in the industrial Midlands and the north, but in London too. Victorian moral revulsion, particularly at child poverty and the incidence of disease, was translated into practical action in the form of water schemes for the piping of fresh water into city centres. These were often allied to river and drainage schemes to carry sewage out to the coast. Control of crime was aided by street lighting. A ready supply of coal, facilitated by the railways, encouraged lighting by gas, both in the streets and in the home. Electrical power was slow to develop, although the switch from horse-power to electric power made the tram an important competitor to the railways so far as suburban transport was concerned.

The concept of 'town improvement' had been well established in Britain since Norman times (Chalklin, 1998). In the eighteenth century spa towns like Bath and Cheltenham, and fashionable resorts like Weymouth, were improved by large-scale property development. In the early part of the nineteenth century, the provision for the poor, the sick and elderly, through the construction of workhouses and infirmaries, became a priority. Early railway stations were often on the margins of towns, on low-value marsh-land, for example, close to cattle markets, gas-works, asylums and gaols. As stations penetrated further into the heart of cities, they became agents of slum clearance (Kellett, 1969). Some of the workers expelled from the slums were relocated to new working-class suburbs from which they commuted in special workmens' trains. Municipal socialism, which began to flourish in the 1870s, gave an added impetus to town improvement. New urban facilities, which had previously been promoted by individual acts were increasingly promoted with the framework of local government acts, as statutory orders approved by Parliament. Towns and cities extended their administrative boundaries, and often took the initiative for promoting projects away from private enterprise. Many of these towns and cities were controlled by business elites who used their influence to extend the boundaries of their town and applied the local rates to investments in public facilities which would improve the competitiveness of their town relative to its rivals.

The other category which appears near the bottom of Table 11.1 contains a diverse and changing mixture of schemes. In the first half of the nineteenth century financial institutions – particularly mutual assurance societies – predominate, whilst in the second half, investment trusts and large industrial enterprises – including several steam-shipping lines – come to the fore. Industrial patents and educational institutions are the subject of some acts. The growing amount of local government legislation described above is also included in this category when it cannot be attributed to any single sector mentioned elsewhere in the table.

The 'Local and Personal Acts' are mainly concerned with projects based wholly in Britain. Projects concerned with colonial development were authorized by the colonial governments, or the Colonial Office, and are not included except in special cases. The substantial growth of overseas projects owned and managed from Britain can be readily discerned from other sources. Wilkins (1989), for example, offers a comprehensive account of British enterprise in the nineteenth century. The global spread of UK-based entrepreneurship can also be assessed from other sources. Thus Bradshaw's Railway Manual indicates that by 1912 no fewer than 109 large overseas railway systems in 29 countries were owned and managed from Britain; 32 were in the empire, and 65 in Latin America (Bassett, 1913, Parts II–IV; a somewhat higher figure is given by Corley, 1994). Many of these companies made huge investments, although, because they often acquired control through state concession, they did not always enjoy ownership in perpetuity as with conventional manufacturing investments.

11.7   THE ROLE OF ENTREPRENEURS IN THE PROMOTION OF LARGE PROJECTS: THE CASE OF THE RAILWAY SYSTEM

The railway industry makes an excellent case study in the finance and management of large projects by British entrepreneurs. Railways were developed through visionary foresight. The vision was implemented by entrepreneurs who showed considerable perseverance under difficult conditions.

It is possible to distinguish five main visions of the railway system in early Victorian Britain.

- The notion of an integrated national network organized around a central north-south spine was set out by the artisan philosopher Thomas Gray (1825) in the 1820s. The proposed technology was not very futuristic, however, being based on the existing mineral railways of the time.
- George Stephenson – the 'father of the railways' – discovered the key combination of components which made possible the modern railway: straight routes on easy gradients, steam locomotive power, and double tracks of iron rails. As a colliery engineer, however, Stephenson always attached considerable weight to the carriage of freight rather than passengers, and the carriage of coal in particular. It was said that Stephenson always looked out for signs of coal deposits when surveying a new line of railway. His vision for the British railway system was once unkindly described as a glorified coal-distribution system.
- Brunel, the author of this remark, provided the grandest vision of the railway system: a high-speed luxury transport system for the social elite (Rolt, 1957). The elite would travel over land by rail, and overseas by steam-powered iron-built liners which would connect with the trains at the ports.
- Robert Stephenson, George Stephenson's son, believed that every part of the country should have access to a railway. He was interested in the railway as an agent of rural development, and not just as a means of serving industry and commerce (Bailey, 2003; Addyman and Haworth, 2005). Stephenson's approach was very influential in other countries, but in Britain many of his regional projects achieved only limited success.
- Finally, there was a political vision of a United Kingdom bound together by rails. Railways were seen as important in allowing Scottish and Irish Members of Parliament to take up their places in Westminster, and to carry the policies enacted there back to their provincial constituencies. Government therefore intervened to ensure that London was well connected by rail to Edinburgh and Dublin (via ferry).

In 1830 the world's first inter-urban high-speed railway opened between Liverpool and Manchester, carrying both passengers and freight on scheduled services. Between 1830 and 1860 the promotion of a railway was usually undertaken by a small group of local citizens, anxious to connect their town to a local port or industrial city, or to connect their port or city to London (Casson, 2009). They would obtain advice on the route from a reputable engineer, and consult a local solicitor about the purchase of land. They would organize a public meeting, chaired by a local dignitary, at which a motion supporting the railway scheme would be proposed. Opponents, such as local landowners, canal proprietors, turnpike trustees, or the promoters of rival schemes, would often turn up and attempt to disrupt the meeting. In this case the outcome could well hinge on a timely intervention from the engineer – a role in which showmen such as Brunel excelled.

A provisional committee would be formed with a mandate to secure an Act of Parliament, until which time the committee would act as a 'shadow' board of directors. The 10 per cent deposit paid by shareholders provided them with saleable scrip – a tradable option. Because options were so much cheaper than shares, even household servants and labourers could afford to invest their meagre savings in speculative railway stock. Once the first trunk lines to London had opened by 1840, it was clear that towns that were bypassed by a railway were destined to decline. Railway promotion now became a civic duty, and towns vied with each other to get themselves 'on the railway map'.

Although the social elites in many towns were split along religious and party lines – for example, Church of England and Nonconformist, Whigs and Tories – civic pride and collective self-interest were sufficiently strong to unite them. Most of the competition was between towns rather than within towns; where competition arose within towns it was usually because of speculators moving in from outside, as in the case of the London to Brighton line. After 1850, however, inter-firm competition became more common, with large regional companies, such as the London & North Western Railway and the Great Western Railway, seeking to invade each other's territory.

Parliament took the view that public benefit was the only reason for interfering with landowners' private property. A railway project afforded a potential 'improvement', and there was a long-standing tradition, derived from earlier forms of improvement, such as land enclosures and canal projects, that the benefits of an improvement should be distributed fairly between the different groups involved. No one should lose out. If a loss were sustained, the person concerned should be compensated. The benefits should be shared by the shareholders who financed the railway and bore the commercial risks and the local communities whose members used the railway.

In presenting a bill to Parliament, the promoters had to prove that the prospective benefits were substantial. Promoters made traffic surveys along roads and canals to establish the existence of demand, and proposed schedules of maximum fares and freight rates to ensure that much of the benefit of the railway would accrue to the public. At the same time they had to show that their construction costs were reasonable, and their estimates robust. If their scheme was financially unsound then the countryside might be dug up for nothing.

With so many lawyers sitting in Parliament as MPs or Lords it is not surprising that cross-examination by hired advocates was the preferred way of presenting evidence to a Parliamentary committee (Kostal, 1994). To ensure compliance with standing orders, Parliamentary agents were hired. Many technical 'knock-outs' were achieved, and often the knock-outs were mutual, so that both schemes failed. When a scheme failed the engineers, solicitors and Parliamentary agents would submit their claims for fees, using up all the deposits and leaving nothing for the shareholders. If the scheme succeeded, then the newly established board would call on the shares so that construction could begin. Contracts for separate sections of line would be put out to tender. Although the process was nominally competitive, some contractors might have friends on the board. In common with many construction projects, initial estimates were often too low, and so the project would either have to be scaled down, and part of the route abandoned, or additional capital would have to be raised. This could require further application to Parliament, as an act limited both the amount of capital and the time in which it could be raised.

Once a line was opened, competition for traffic would begin (Reed, 1957). In many cases, the strongest rivalry came from an alternative railway route. As the network developed, so the number of alternative routes between any two places increased (Turnock, 1998). Mergers provided an obvious solution, but from the mid-1850s Parliament became increasingly concerned about their monopolistic tendencies, and only approved them in exceptional cases. In the 1840s and early 1850s, however, major speculative gains could be made from the promotion of mergers. The 'Railway King' George Hudson, a draper from York, made his name by engineering the merger that created the Midland Railway (Arnold and McCartney, 2004). He eliminated competition between Derby and London, and between Leeds and Hull. The tradition of 'railway politics' was continued by the 'Second Railway King', Sir Edward Watkin, who coordinated the management of different companies through an interlocking chairmanship (Hodgkins, 2001). His grand design was for a through line from Manchester to Paris via a channel tunnel. He was successful in gaining financial support from shareholders and political support from government, but engineering problems and the costs they created defeated him in the end.

Popular mythology recognizes the railway engineers – men such as George and Robert Stephenson (father and son), Joseph Locke and Isambard Kingdom Brunel – as the true entrepreneurs of the railway system. Samuel Smiles's (1862) hagiography portrays Victorian engineers not only as technocrats, but as the strategic thinkers behind the new industries that they helped to create. Detailed evidence on company promotion, such as Brunel's Letterbooks (1836), suggests that this assessment is correct. It was not so much the owners of the railways as their consultant engineers who masterminded strategy in the early years. The reason is quite straightforward: the principles of railway strategy were specific to railways – a new type of network industry with a very costly infrastructure – but common across all locations. While shareholders were often endowed with good local knowledge, they had limited experience of the railway system as a whole. Consulting engineers, however, would have experience of several schemes, from which they could identify specific patterns.

Consulting engineers also socialized with each other. They met as peers at meetings of the Institution of Civil Engineers and other professional associations, and as adversaries before Parliamentary committees on railway bills. Although Brunel and Robert Stephenson could not even agree on the best gauge for a railway – Brunel favouring the broad gauge and Stephenson the modern standard gauge – they remained the best of friends. They fought an intense battle in Parliament over lines in the West Midlands, which Brunel won; yet they dined together, and even died at about the same time! Both men advised their respective companies – the Great Western and the London & North Western – on strategy, planning routes that would block rival lines, devising trunk line routes to maximize the potential for profitable branch line traffic, and helping to monopolize key ports.

By mid-century it was the company secretary who was becoming the major strategic thinker in the railway sector, together with the company chairman. In the second half of the nineteenth century the most successful railway entrepreneurs seem to have been those who combined practical experience of the industry with a wide range of general interests – such as Samuel Laing, the chairman of the London Brighton and South Coast Railway, who was a former official with the railway department of the Board of Trade and who became a popular writer on philosophical issues.

11.8 MINING AS A PROJECT-BASED INDUSTRY

Not all projects required Parliamentary authorization, of course. There were many projects that could be undertaken as soon as customers revealed a demand and a business opportunity was recognized. This was particularly true of the mining industry.

The British Isles are rich in minerals. The occupying Romans mined gold and lead in Wales. Coal was mined as a substitute for charcoal in medieval times – albeit on a small scale (Hatcher, 1993). The iron-masters of the early Industrial Revolution generated a huge demand for coal and coke, and this stimulated mining on an industrial scale. Many of the earliest mines were driven horizontally into hillsides, making it easy to bring out the minerals. Indeed, some of the key components of railway technology originated in the mining industry, where wooden tramways were used to transport minerals out of the mine and down to a river or coastal port.

Even before the Industrial Revolution, coal shipped from Newcastle in the north-east, had been widely used for brewing ale and heating the home – especially by wealthy Londoners (Nef, 1932). The discovery of iron ore nearby gave a huge boost to this industry. The Staffordshire coalfield developed as the Midlands town of Birmingham expanded its speciality metals trades.

Once mineral deposits near the surface had been exhausted, it was necessary to go further down. Shafts were sunk, and winding gear installed. Pumps were necessary once the mine went down beneath the water table. The stationary steam engine was ideal for providing power to a mine – especially in a coal mine, because the mineral extracted could be used directly as the fuel. Mounting a stationary steam engine on a colliery wagon was one of the earliest inspirations for the railway locomotive.

The aristocratic owners of large estates asserted rights to the minerals underneath their land. During the eighteenth and early nineteenth centuries the aristocracy began to exploit their mineral reserves in a highly organized way (Ashton and Sykes, 1929). Increasingly, the sinking of a coal mine became a major project. A large tract of land would be required, with not only mineral rights but also surface rights to facilitate access to the mine, to accommodate spoil heaps, and to provide washing and processing facilities for the coal. A large amount of expensive machinery would have to be installed. In remote locations, workers' housing and village facilities would also have to be provided.

There was no guarantee that the mine would be a success. In the early nineteenth century the science of geology was in its infancy, and so the volume of the deposits, as determined by the dimensions of the seams, could not be known in advance. Unexpected geological faults could always emerge, causing the mine to flood or the tunnel passages to cave in.

The mineral industry therefore required project-centred entrepreneurship of a high order. The scale of the investment required meant that coal mining was not an industry for the self-made man operating on a small scale (Mitchell, 1984). Only a wealthy aristocrat could afford to go it alone – and could still find their personal resources stretched. For this reason wealthy people often formed partnerships – sometimes with family members – creating a dynastic ownership structure. In other cases they made alliances with other families.

Since no single person could possess all the technical expertise required to operate a large mine, it was the usual practice for the owners to hire professional managers – the colliery viewers. Viewers were often self-taught, had plenty of practical experience, and needed entrepreneurial qualities. A successful viewer was someone who could improvise effective solutions to unexpected problems. Because they were so versatile, colliery viewers often moved around the country, helping to start up mines in new areas. They also transferred their skills to other industries – thus several viewers from the north-east transferred their skills to the railway industry. The most prominent example was George Stephenson. He took with him not only his familiarity with steam technology but also his ability to recognize the mineral potential of any district in which he worked. One of the skills that commended Stephenson to railway promoters was his talent for assessing the mineral potential of the district through which a railway was intended to pass.

As steam ships replaced sailing ships on the main ocean shipping routes, a demand was created for a network of bunkering stations around the world. Ships, like railway locomotives, needed top-quality steam coal, which was only available from a limited number of sources. South Wales was the main source of steam coal. Initially coal was mined in Wales to support the iron industry (centred on Merthyr Tydfil), but as iron ore deposits became exhausted, the coal was increasingly exported to bunkering stations instead. It was this development that led to the enormous expansion of Cardiff (and later Barry) as a port (Church, 1986).

In the latter part of the nineteenth century important coal deposits were identified in South Yorkshire, near the railway town of Doncaster (Buxton, 1978). A huge amount of investment went into this coalfield, including the building of several new railway lines. At a time when British manufacturing industry was losing its global market share, Britain was becoming increasingly specialized in the coal export trade. It is, to some extent, indicative of the relative decline of British manufacturing in the late Victorian period that so little of the newly discovered coal was consumed by domestic industry and so much of it was exported. Because coal of different grades is found in different parts of the world, there is no economic objection to a country exporting coal of one grade and importing coal of another. At the end of the nineteenth century, however, British coal was following British capital in leaving the country. Rather than being channelled into domestic manufacturing, it was being employed to support the country's imperial linkages.

11.9   ENTREPRENEURSHIP AND THE CULTURE OF IMPROVEMENT: SOME REFLECTIONS ON THE VICTORIAN EXPERIENCE

Examining Victorian enterprise from the perspective of infrastructure investment provides a fresh perspective on some of the historical controversies discussed above. Investment in railways was the contemporary manifestation of a more general concern with 'improvement' which took hold of British society in the eighteenth century. This concern with improvement was underpinned by a changing mind-set in which natural phenomena were increasingly interpreted as the outcome of hidden processes driven by universal physical laws. The created order was fundamentally rational, it was believed, and could therefore be comprehended by rational human beings. The cultivation of rationality required education, which in turn depended on the spread of literacy and numeracy. In Victorian Britain this demand for education and literacy was fed by the growth of schooling and local newspapers. Schooling was provided initially by 'dame schools', private grammar schools and the so-called 'public schools', but from 1870, it was provided increasingly by churches and the state.

If the entire created order was rational, then society too must be based on rational principles. For many intellectuals this had radical policy implications. Inherited aristocratic landholdings, and the privileges of monarchy, should be swept away as anachronistic in a modern rational society. The leaders of the French Revolution pursued this line of argument to its logical conclusion – and beyond.

The bloody lessons of the French Revolution were not lost on Victorian Britons, however. Populist political leaders in command of a mob were infinitely more dangerous than a traditional monarchy. Absolutist states posed a military threat to their neighbours, and absolute political power of any kind should therefore be avoided.

The British already had a Parliamentary system that addressed this issue – at least partially. The Parliamentary system was not completely democratic; only male property-owners had the vote before 1832. The monarch was not, strictly speaking, accountable to the people, but rather to the representatives of local elites – the MPs. The essence of British government was that it was local rather than national, and this was reflected in Parliamentary behaviour towards the railways, as explained above.

Improvement was not just a question of raising the material standard of living, although alleviating poverty was certainly a major concern (as demonstrated by the Poor Law Report of 1834). Improvement was a moral phenomenon (Searle, 1998). Material improvement was merely an instrument for alleviating the constraints on the moral improvement of the individual, and hence the moral improvement of society.

The importance of morality is exemplified in the career of William Gladstone, who was prime minister on no fewer than four occasions in the Victorian period (Matthew, 2004). Whilst Gladstone's responsibilities involved economic regulation and national budgeting, he spent most of his time reading theology (on which he amassed an enormous library that can still be consulted today). His political speeches focused on the application of moral principles to contentious issues, and eschewed the type of propaganda about wealth-creation so familiar today.

Gladstone and his many supporters perceived no conflict between acting morally and acting rationally. Revealed religion promised rewards for moral behaviour in the after-life. No rational individual would risk eternal damnation for the sake of a short-term gain. So promoting morals and promoting reason were essentially the same thing.

The passions were the main threat to rational action. The need to resist the most dangerous passions was emphasized by the Ten Commandments, which were liberally displayed on either side of the altar in the churches that the Victorians built or restored.

Self-discipline and self-control were therefore the hallmarks of a rational person. The greater a person's wealth or power, the greater their need to exercise self-control. Positions of great responsibility needed to be filled by people with great self-control. Team games were deemed to provide useful exercises in self-control. Team players put the performance of their team ahead of their own interests; it was commitment and effort that counted, and not just ability.

Wealth posed a moral danger, because of the temptation to use it selfishly. Wealth must be used responsibly, by putting poor people to work and supporting charitable causes. Personal reputation was not acquired by wealth alone, but by the proper use of wealth. Able people could be in particular moral danger unless they found a moral challenge that was matched to their level of ability. Not everyone might have the ability to take on a major challenge, but everyone could aspire to modest respectability.

Despite the success of the Victorian economy, and the prominent role of entrepreneurship within it, Victorian society did not have an 'enterprise culture' as that term is commonly understood today. The Victorians were supremely confident in their abilities to make improvements, and did not feel the need for government to promote an enterprise culture in order to foster change. In modern Western countries it was the economic failures of the 1970s – associated with large and bureaucratic 'national champion' firms and their inability to handle Asian competition – that led to a preoccupation with enterprise culture in the 1980s and 1990s. This switched the emphasis in Western countries from championing large firms to championing small ones instead. The Victorians experienced no such failures, and therefore saw no need to compensate for them. In the Victorian economy the direction of industrial change was the opposite to the modern West – the Victorians were involved in creating large firms; the major textile and engineering firms and – pre-eminently – the railway companies. If there is a 'lesson' for entrepreneurship from the Victorian economy, it is not that laissez-faire promotes prosperity, but rather that a sincere concern for moral and social improvement that is widely shared by all groups in society will also generate material improvements. John Stuart Mill observed, in his *Autobiography*, that happiness cannot be achieved by aiming for happiness, and the Victorian experience suggests that the same might be said about economic success – it is not achieved by aiming for economic success, but by aiming for something more fundamental that brings success in its wake.

11.10   CONCLUSION

The importance of the railways – and infrastructure in general – to the Victorian economy illustrates the danger of placing undue emphasis on manufacturing industry when evaluating entrepreneurship in Victorian Britain. Railway promotion was a highly entrepreneurial activity. A general approach to entrepreneurship, based on innovation, risk-management and judgemental decision-making, captures the full significance of the Schumpeterian railway revolution in a way that other approaches do not.

Railway companies were born large. Sales growth occurred mainly through long-term traffic growth fuelled by the gradual expansion of the economy, rather than by bidding traffic away from other companies. Growth of the capital stock occurred largely through merger and acquisition. Subsequent concentration of power was achieved by interlocking chairmanships and directorships. Shareholders took most of the risks, but specialist entrepreneurs took the strategic decisions: initially these were the consulting engineers, later they were the company secretaries and chairmen.

At the time of their construction, most railway lines were projected as civic enterprises, representing a single town, or a coalition of towns along the route. Civic enterprise was particularly notable in some of the old county towns, such as Chester, Lincoln, York and Shrewsbury, which sought to rejuvenate themselves by becoming railway hubs. A spectacular example of a coalition of towns creating a new trunk railway was the Great Northern Railway – one of the most successful of the mania schemes. This was a merger of rival schemes, based upon a common interest in serving country towns in Bedfordshire, Huntingdonshire and Lincolnshire. Because of its length, it connected London directly to York and Edinburgh, via a junction near Doncaster, and because of its breadth, achieved by a loop line, it was also able to serve the agricultural districts of Lincolnshire. The merger was organized by Edmund Dennison, MP for Doncaster, and it turned his local town into a prosperous railway hub.

The railway system was just one of the many innovations exported from Britain to the empire in the age of high imperialism. Professional governance, which had evolved steadily since Norman times, was exported through systems of colonial administration. This provided a framework of law and order within which various types of large project could also be exported. While many of these projects were first developed in Britain, others – such as river navigation, drainage and water supply systems – involved refinements of technologies developed elsewhere.

Overseas projects involved the export, not only of British technology and management, but also of British capital and labour. Much of the labour was highly skilled. Many of the civil engineers who left Britain for the colonies in the second half of the nineteenth century never returned to Britain. There were so many opportunities for engineers on the colonial frontier that there was little incentive for them to return. It was mainly the senior professionals, who ran consulting practices from London, who remained in Britain. Many of these consultants became involved in high finance and political negotiation, as foreign monarchs and ministers came to Britain to negotiate for railway schemes. The engineer Sir John Fowler, for example, received his knighthood not for his engineering expertise, but for the political assistance he rendered to the British government during the war in Sudan.

One of the key aspects of entrepreneurship is that it facilitates structural change. It is a mistake to infer that entrepreneurship declined in late Victorian Britain just because Britain failed to maintain its industrial lead over Germany and the USA. British entrepreneurs may well have been slow to recognize the magnitude of scale economies in heavy industries, and to appreciate the commercial benefits of organized industrial research in well-equipped laboratories. But in a small and increasingly crowded country, this was not where national comparative advantage lay.

The late Victorian economy is an example of what we would now call a knowledge-based economy. Its comparative advantage lay increasingly in the export of knowledge-intensive services, such as public administration, trade, shipping, finance and engineering consultancy. These services were mainly delivered in packages relating to major projects for colonial and overseas development. Each project required inputs of several of these knowledge-based services for its successful completion. The whole process depended on specialized institutions such as the London Stock Exchange, an agglomeration of scientific and professional institutions, and the 'free-standing' overseas company.

The twentieth century saw enormous geopolitical changes, most of which disadvantaged British entrepreneurship. War, followed by the collapse of international trade and global demand, more war and then the loss of empire, all reduced the scope for large complex project-based entrepreneurship coordinated through traditional British institutions such as the London Stock Exchange. The notion of an empire based on trade in agricultural products and knowledge-intensive services was replaced by the notion of an empire based on large-scale high-technology manufacturing industry. Economic logic now favoured the hierarchical multinational firm rather than the free-standing firm. It is also a mistake to suppose, however, that the loss of empire, and twentieth-century economic failure, can be blamed on the deficiencies of the Victorian entrepreneurs. Entrepreneurship was a vibrant force in Britain throughout the nineteenth century. This chapter has shown that once an appropriate concept of entrepreneurship is used as an analytical template, the persistence of entrepreneurship in Britain can clearly be discerned, right to the end of the century.

REFERENCES

Addyman, John and Victoria Haworth (2005), *Robert Stephenson: Railway Engineer*, Stretford, Manchester: North Eastern Railway Association.

Aldcroft, Derek H. (1964), 'The entrepreneur and the British economy, 1870–1914', *Economic History Review*, **17**, 113–34.

Arnold, A.J. and S. McCartney (2004), *George Hudson: The Rise and Fall of the Railway King: A Study in Victorian Entrepreneurship*, London: Hambledon & London.

Ashton, Thomas S. and Joseph Sykes (1929), *The Coal Industry of the Eigtheenth Century*, Manchester: Manchester University Press.

Bailey, Michael R. (ed.) (2003), *Robert Stephenson: The Eminent Engineer*, Aldershot: Ashgate.

Bassett, Herbert H. (ed.) (1913), *Bradshaw's Railway Manual, Shareholders' Guide and Official Directory*, London: Henry Blacklock.

Baumol, William J. (1994), *Entrepreneurship, Management and the Structure of Pay-offs*, Cambridge, MA: MIT Press.

Broadberry, Stephen (1997), *The Productivity Race: British Manufacturing in International Perspective, 1850–1990*, Cambridge: Cambridge University Press.

Broadberry, Stephen (2006), *Market Services and the Productivity Race, 1850–2000*, Cambridge: Cambridge University Press.

Brunel, Isambard K. (1836), Letterbooks, University of Bristol Library, Special Collections, DM1306.

Buxton, Neil K. (1978), *Economic Development of the British Coal Industry from the Industrial Revolution to the Present Day*, London: Batsford.

Cain, P.J. and A.G. Hopkins (2002), *British Imperialism 1688–2000*, 2nd edition, London: Longman.

Casson, Mark (2009), *Building the World's First Railway System*, Oxford: Oxford University Press.

Chalklin, Christopher W. (1998), *English Counties and Public Building, 1650–1830*, London: Hambledon Press.

Chandler, Alfred D. Jr (1990), *Scale and Scope: The Dynamics of Victorian Capitalism*, Cambridge, MA: Harvard University Press.

Church, Roy A. (1975), *The Great Victorian Boom, 1850–1873*, London: Macmillan.

Church, Roy A. (1986), *History of the British Coal Industry, Vol. 3: 1830–1913, Victorian Pre-eminence*, Oxford: Clarendon Press.

Corley, Tony A.B. (1994), 'Britain's overseas investments in 1914 revisited', *Business History*, **36**, 71–88.

Crafts, Nicholas F.R. (1985), *British Industrial Growth during the Industrial Revolution*, Oxford: Oxford University Press.

Deane, Phyllis (1979), *The First Industrial Nation*, Cambridge: Cambridge University Press.

Godley, Andrew (2001), *Jewish Immigrant Entrepreneurship in New York and London, 1880–1914*, London: Palgrave.

Gourvish, Terence R. (1980), *Railways and the British Economy, 1830–1914*, London: Macmillan.

Gray, Thomas (1825), *Observations on a General Iron Railway*, 5th edition, London: Baldwin, Cradock and Joy.

Hatcher, John (1993), *The History of the British Coal Industry, Volume 1: Before 1700: Towards the Age of Coal*, Oxford: Clarendon Press.

Hodgkins, David (2001), *The Second Railway King: The Life and Times of Sir Edward Watkin, 1819–1901*, Whitchurch, Cardiff: Merton Priory Press.

Jones, Geoffrey G. (ed.) (1998), *The Multinational Traders*, London: Routledge.

Jones, Geoffrey G. (2000), *From Merchants to Multinationals*, Oxford: Oxford University Press.

Kellett, John R. (1969), *The Impact of Railways on Victorian Cities*, London: Routledge & Kegan Paul.

Kihlstrom, R.E. and J.J. Laffont (1979), 'A general equilibrium entrepreneurial theory of firm formation based on risk aversion', *Journal of Political Economy*, **87**, 719–48.

Kostal, Rande W. (1994), *Law and English Railway Capitalism, 1825–1875*, Oxford: Clarendon Press.

Leunig, Tim (2001), 'New answers to old questions: explaining the slow adoption of ring spinning in Lancashire, 1880–1913', *Journal of Economic History*, **61** (2), 439–66.

Marshall, Alfred (1923), *Industry and Trade*, London: Macmillan.

Matthew, H.C.G. (2004), 'Gladstone, William Ewart (1809–1898)', *Oxford Dictionary of National Biography*, Oxford: Oxford University Press, article 10787.

McCloskey, Donald N. (ed.) (1971), *Essays on a Mature Economy: Britain after 1840*, Princeton, NJ: Princeton University Press

Millward, Robert (1991), 'Emergence of gas and water monopolies in nineteenth-century Britain: contested markets and public control', in James Foreman-Peck (ed.), *New Perspectives on the Late Victorian Economy*, Cambridge: Cambridge University Press, pp. 96–124.

Mitchell, Brian R. (1984), *Economic Development of the British Coal Industry*, Cambridge: Cambridge University Press.

Mokyr, Joel (2004), *The Gifts of Athena: Historical Origins of the Knowledge Economy*, Princeton, NJ: Princeton University Press.

Nef, John U. (1932), *The Rise of the British Coal Industry*, 2 vols, London: Routledge.

Nicholson, J. Shield (1909), *Project of Empire*, London: Macmillan.

Officer, Lawrence H. (2005), 'The annual real and nominal GDP for the United Kingdom, 1086–2005', Economic History Services, http://eh.net/hmit/ukgdp, 5 June 2005.

Olson, Mancur (1982), *The Rise and Decline of Nations*, New Haven, CT: Yale University Press.

Payne, Peter L. (1988), *British Entrepreneurship in the Nineteenth Century*, 2nd edition, London: Macmillan.

Pearson, Robin and David Richardson (2001), 'Business networking in the Industrial Revolution', *Economic History Review*, **54** (4), 657–79.

Pollard, Sidney (1997), *Marginal Europe: The Contribution of Marginal Lands since the Middle Ages*, Oxford: Clarendon Press.

Prest, John (2004), 'Peel, Sir Robert, Second Baronet, (1788–1850)', *Oxford Dictionary of National Biography*, article 21764.

Reed, M.C. (ed.) (1957), *Railways and the Victorian Economy*, Newton Abbot: David & Charles.

Rolt, L.T.C. (1957), *Isambard Kingdom Brunel: A Biography*, London: Longman.

Rose, Mary B. (1993), 'Beyond Buddenbrooks: the management of family business succession', in Jonathan Brown and Mary B. Rose (eds), *Entrepreneurship Networks and Modern Business*, Manchester: Manchester University Press, pp. 127–43.

Saul, S.B. (1969), *The Myth of the Great Depression, 1873–1896*, London: Macmillan.

Schumpeter, Joseph A. (1939), *Business Cycles*, New York: McGraw-Hill.

Searle, Geoffrey R. (1998), *Morality and the Market in Victorian Britain*, Oxford: Clarendon Press.

Smiles, Samuel (1862), *Lives of the Engineers*, London: John Murray.

Turnock, David (1998), *An Historical Geography of Railways in Great Britain and Ireland*, Aldershot: Ashgate.

Wiener, Martin (1981), *English Culture and the Decline of the Industrial Spirit*, Cambridge: Cambridge University Press.

Wilkins, Mira (1986), 'The free-standing company, 1870–1914: an important type of British foreign direct investment', *Economic History Review*, 2nd series, **41**, 259–82.

Wilkins, Mira (1989), *The History of Foreign Investment in the United States to 1914*, Cambridge, MA: Harvard University Press.

Wilkins, Mira and Harm Schroter (eds) (1998), *The Free-Standing Company in the World Economy, 1830–1996*, Oxford: Oxford University Press.

12. Imperialism and the entrepreneurial state

**With Ken Dark and
Mohamed Azzim Gulamhussen**

Although there have been many studies of individual empires (for example, Cain and Hopkins, 1993), the theory of imperialism has changed little since the surveys by Fieldhouse (1967) and others. Most more recent theoretical work takes a cultural history perspective (for example, Hardt and Negri, 2000). Economic research has tended to focus on the benefits generated by trade and investment flows and the costs of imperial defence (for example, O'Brien, 1988); the resultant cost–benefit evaluations shed light on decolonization and other specific issues.

However, the basic questions of why, when and where empires develop, how far they spread and how long they last have received little systematic attention. This chapter considers the contribution that the economic theory of institutions can make to the analysis of these larger questions (see, for example, Buckley and Casson, 1976; Williamson, 1985; North, 1990). It identifies six key insights that can be applied to imperialism:

1. Some states are more entrepreneurial than others because they provide strong incentives for individual discovery and innovation (for example, promoting freedom of travel, association and expression).
2. Newly-discovered knowledge is a global public good; it is therefore efficient to apply it simultaneously in all territories to which it is relevant (for example, applying the same mining technology in several different mineral-rich countries).
3. States have a role in supplying local public goods (for example, law and order, transport and communications infrastructure, and certain types of health and education); they can also establish property rights and regulations under which private goods are provided by a private sector. Newly-discovered knowledge about how to supply public goods can therefore be exploited by a state.

4. Although knowledge is a public good, there are obstacles to transferring it between locations. Foreigners may not accept the superiority of the knowledge; they may pass it on to the supplier's enemies; or they may not be able to absorb it because of limited education. A state may therefore encounter difficulty in exploiting its knowledge abroad through licensing agreements negotiated under treaty arrangements.
5. States possess military knowledge as well as civilian knowledge. The rule of law is weaker between states than it is within states. Superior military knowledge therefore permits a state to take over other territories by force. A knowledge-intensive state frustrated by barriers to knowledge transfer may therefore resort to force and take over (occupy or govern) territories controlled by other states (especially those that refuse to recognize its supremacy).
6. Knowledge obsolesces, and as it does so the strategic case for imperialism declines.

These insights suggest that imperialism is a rational response to a specific set of circumstances. They suggest that in a world where opportunities to discover new knowledge arise continuously, imperialism emerges naturally wherever these circumstances prevail. Obsolescence too is a natural process, and this explains why empires decline. The decline of one empire may generate a gap that some other rising empire may be able to fill.

The chapter concludes by reviewing a panel of empires on which the theory can be tested using case study analysis.

12.1   INTRODUCTION

It may seem unusual to discuss imperialism in a book on entrepreneurship, but the two subjects are closely linked, as this chapter will show. The fundamental idea developed in this chapter is that entrepreneurial judgement can be applied not only to projects concerned with the supply of ordinary private goods, such as household consumer goods, but also to projects for the supply of public goods such as health, education and defence. Public goods can be provided through clubs, societies and other forms of voluntary association – indeed, the use of voluntary non-profit organizations to supply a public good was illustrated in Chapter 8 in terms of the provision of culture. Voluntary organizations are not suitable for the supply of all public goods, however. Where defence is concerned, for example, not everyone may be willing to contribute to the defence of a nation even though they will benefit from it. Some people may attempt to 'free-ride' on the efforts of others in fighting the enemy or financing military supplies.

In such cases coercion, in the form of taxation or conscription, may be required. Entrepreneurial projects concerned with the provision of public goods may therefore need to be implemented through the formation, not of firms, clubs and societies, but of a state. Economists sometimes fudge this notion by assuming that a state already exists. From the perspective of entrepreneurship theory, however, institutions do not exist until someone (or some group) has taken the initiative to set them up, and this applies to any form of institution, whether a firm or a state.

It was noted in earlier chapters (for example, Chapter 1) that an ambitious project with a wide geographical scope may well be exploited through a multinational firm. If the outputs of the project are useful at many different locations, it may be advantageous to produce the outputs locally. The private production of private goods at various locations around the world thereby creates a multinational firm. Just as the supply of private goods at different locations may be implemented through a multinational firm, so the supply of public goods at different locations around the world may be implemented through an empire, because an empire is essentially a 'multinational state'.

Building upon this view of entrepreneurship, this chapter develops a theory of imperialism based on the concept of an empire as a 'multinational state'. It extends the theory of entrepreneurship to embrace the state and then reconsiders historical and archaeological evidence on imperialism in the light of this approach. In particular, it takes existing insights from one type of institution – the multinational firm – and applies them to an analogous type of institution – the imperial state. This analogy is not merely superficial: since both states and firms are institutions there is a logical isomorphism between the theory of the state and the theory of the firm (Boddewyn, 1988, 2003).

The object of this theory is not to pass judgement on imperialism, but rather to explain it. Its focus is not just on the relationship between imperialists and their subject peoples but, more importantly, on the relationships between one imperialist and another (Colley, 2006). Whilst at any given time in history there is often a single dominant empire, most empires have rivals; some of these rivals may be empires in decline, whilst others may be rising forces that are destined to take over the dominant role. This raises a number of questions about the factors governing the success and failure of empires – in particular their geographical extent, the length of time for which they survive, and the nature of their legacy. To address these questions, the chapter formulates a dynamic theory that seeks to explain not only the characteristics of an empire at any given date but also its rate of early growth and rate of subsequent decline. This theory identifies a set of key factors which govern the economic performance of an empire, as reflected in its rate of technological innovation, its institutional efficiency, the development of internal trade, and other characteristics that can be assessed from the historical record.

There are many alternative theories of imperialism, and so it might be asked why yet another theory is required. The problem is not that alternative theories are wrong so much as that they are partial. Many theories emphasize political and cultural aspects of empire and underestimate the importance of fundamental economic factors (Hardt and Negri, 2000; Passavant and Dean, 2004). Most existing 'economic' explanations of imperialism are isomorphic to highly restrictive theories of the firm. In particular, they tend to emphasize an imperial advantage derived from privileged access to capital, the managerial exploitation of labour, or institutions such as slavery (Brewer, 1990; Fieldhouse, 1967). As a result, they ignore the crucial advantage conferred by access to superior knowledge. By emphasizing economic factors governing the development and exploitation of knowledge, the theory offered here complements work on political and cultural issues.

12.2   BASIC CONCEPTS AND DEFINITIONS

Imperialism is a complex phenomenon and its study requires a synthesis of insights from a range of disciplines, including politics, economics, sociology, anthropology, geography, history and archaeology. Synthesis is difficult because these disciplines employ different conceptual frameworks, and there is plenty of scope for confusion when the same terminology is interpreted in different ways (Casson, 1997; Furubotn and Richter, 1998; Greif, 2006; North, 1990; Williamson, 1985). It is therefore important to define terms carefully at the outset.

As already explained, the object of this chapter is to explain behaviour rather than to pass judgement on it. An empire is therefore defined simply as a collection of territories controlled by a single state. There is no attempt to define an empire in terms of the subjugation and exploitation of indigenous peoples. The problem with such value-laden definitions is that they tend to assume what they seek to prove. For example, if an empire is defined in terms of exploitation, a multinational state that does not exploit people is, by definition, not an empire, whilst conversely, any institution that exploits indigenous peoples in other territories is imperialistic whether it actually governs those territories or not. There are many other definitions of empire besides the one adopted here; it is not suggested that these alternatives are wrong, but only that the chosen definition is appropriate for the purposes of this chapter. Neither is it suggested that the chosen definition is entirely value-free; it simply reflects the values of objectivity and detachment, rather than the values of subjectivity and commitment that some authors prefer.

Defining an empire in terms of territories begs the question of what is a territory. A territory is defined as an area of land, typically bounded by rivers, mountains or seas, which is to some degree economically self-sufficient. A territory is not the same thing as a nation. It is unfortunate that the term 'nation' is used rather sloppily in the economic theory of institutions; indeed, much of the literature on multinational firms uses the term 'nation' to denote what is actually a sovereign state.

A nation may be defined, for present purposes, as an ethnic group that claims the right to govern a particular territory (or group of territories). The members of this ethnic group share a belief that they possess a common culture and/or a common ancestry. Their common culture comprises shared values and beliefs relating to fundamental issues. In contrast to a nation, a state is a political and military organization that governs one or more territories. It makes laws and uses coercion to enforce them. It has rulers and citizens, can make war on other states, and make treaties with them.

At the risk of oversimplification, it could be said that nations existed before states, and that states tended to formalize the informal relations by which these early nations were coordinated. Expanding states absorbed different nations and encouraged their new citizens to adopt a common identity and culture, thereby creating the nation-state. As part of their expansion process, these nation-states made rival territorial claims, and fought with each other over disputed borders. The geographical configuration of modern nations often reflects the borders that prevailed at the time that military stalemate was reached and hostilities ceased. Such borders, enshrined in peace treaties, often lack economic logic and therefore – somewhat perversely – provide an incentive for an even more powerful state to intervene. This imperialistic state can impose more rational borders that promote trade and investment flows.

In the classic form of empire each territory is initially populated by a separate indigenous nation. Once the empire is established, the home territory, occupied by the home nation, controls foreign territories populated by different foreign nations. Matters are not always as simple as this, however. Members of the home nation may have settled in the foreign territories, helping to legitimate the home nation's claim to control. There may also have been migration between the foreign territories, so that some territories contain several different nationalities. These differences can create internal divisions that weaken local opposition to the imperial power. On the other hand, the imperial power may acquire legitimacy from its ability to deter internal factional rivalry between the separate nations. There may also be national divisions within the home territory, as discussed below. Imperialism may provide a useful project around which the national factions in the home territory can unite.

Control, as defined in this chapter, may be employed simply to occupy a territory in order to defend its borders (perhaps against rival imperialists) and to extract tax or tribute from the local people. This arrangement is compatible with the existence of a nominally independent government – even though the imperialist may influence the selection of the leader (as with a 'puppet regime'). On the other hand, control may be employed to govern a territory – establishing a bureaucracy, designing and enforcing legislation and taking key decisions. In this case the government has a choice as to how far it decentralizes decisions, and how far it encourages local people to participate in those decisions.

Where looser forms of control are used, a 'grey area' opens up in which the application of the concept of empire becomes debatable. Powerful states often make treaties with weaker states who later condemn these treaties as 'unequal' or 'unfair'; according to our definition of empire, however, the inequality or unfairness does not transform the more powerful state into an imperialist, since its treaty partners remain independent states. Using military threats to negotiate favourable treaties with weaker sovereign states is an alternative to imperialism, and not a variant of it, according to the definitions employed in this chapter.

If, however, a powerful state establishes a treaty organization which it controls through the presidency or the bureaucracy, and thereby exercises significant sanctions against other member states, then it becomes an imperialist according to our definition. Such indirect control may be termed quasi-imperialism.

A final issue concerns the level of analysis at which the definition of empire is applied. It is a general feature of the economics of institutions that insights applied at one level of analysis often work surprisingly well at other levels of analysis, and this applies to the theory of imperialism. The internal political structure of many nation-states resembles that of an empire in which the constituent units are regions or former tribal areas. Indeed, the names of certain states – such as the United Kingdom and the United States (and previously the United Netherlands) – clearly indicate a federation of previously self-governing nations. The question then becomes whether one member of the federation is so much stronger than all the others that it effectively exercises control. Thus it is often argued that England – and the City of London in particular – controls the UK. To avoid complications and needless controversies, however, this chapter concentrates only on the high-level application of the analysis to sovereign nation-states, and treats these states as unitary entities even where this is not strictly the case.

12.3   OUTLINE OF THE THEORY

The basic proposition presented in this chapter is that the expansion of a state into an empire is driven by the belief of its elite that they possess superior knowledge. Knowledge is a 'public good': it can be shared between people, and in particular it can be exploited simultaneously in different locations. An elite that recognizes this fact will seek to exploit its knowledge as widely as possible. Knowledge can, in principle, be exploited anywhere in the world where conditions are appropriate; in this sense it is not just an ordinary public good but a global public good.

A state does not have to control directly the exploitation of the superior knowledge that it possesses; it can authorize others to exploit it in return for suitable compensation. But in many cases it cannot rely on others to exploit the knowledge because they are either unwilling or unable to do so. In this case the state needs to take control of the exploitation of the knowledge itself. Given the wide geographical scope of its application, this involves taking control of territories outside its immediate boundaries. The natural way of doing this is to expand the boundaries of the state to encompass all the territories where the knowledge can be usefully exploited. The state therefore expands into an empire.

Not every state that believes it possesses superior knowledge will necessarily develop an empire, though. To appreciate the superiority of its knowledge, the state needs to be aware of the knowledge possessed by other states. Superiority is a relative concept, and can only be demonstrated using an external point of reference. The state needs to recognize that its knowledge can be applied outside its existing territory as well as within it. The state needs to understand how the knowledge can be applied in locations that differ socially and geographically from the location in which it was first developed. Typically it will first apply the knowledge at home, and then investigate conditions abroad to determine how the knowledge can be adapted for wider use.

All of this means that the state requires entrepreneurial skills. It must adopt institutions that foster innovation. It must exhibit good judgement in interpreting information. It must be outward-looking, and able to recognize practical opportunities that come its way. It must expect to make mistakes, and be willing to learn from them. It must experiment with new projects on a small scale before they are implemented on a large scale (Casson, 1982; Penrose, 1959).

Some states that believe in their own superiority may explicitly reject the imperialist option. For example, a state that believes its superiority to be based on unique local traditions may become inward-looking rather than outward-looking, as it fears the dilution of its culture by foreigners more than it values the potential to exploit its traditions elsewhere.

Much of the superior knowledge possessed by a state relates to the supply of local public goods. Five main categories of these goods may be distinguished: law and order, health and education, transport and communications, social cohesion and defence. They are all important in facilitating social intercourse and providing a sense of security. Like knowledge, they are public goods because they can be shared. But they are local public goods rather than global public goods because they need to be supplied separately to each locality. The first four involve civilian applications of knowledge, whilst the last involves military applications; knowledge employed in defence can also be used for aggressive purposes, and imperialists will often use it in this way.

There are of course many other goods that are produced and distributed within a state, including ordinary consumer goods, mineral and agricultural products and so on. However, these are private goods rather than public goods: if one person consumes one of these goods then another person cannot consume the same item, but must consume a different item instead. Within most states the supply of such goods is delegated to private firms and self-employed individuals; each item can be supplied in response to an individual need and paid for by an individual consumer; there is no need for social agreement on whether the item is supplied, as in the case of the local public goods. Thus private goods are normally supplied privately and public goods are supplied by the state. The state is still involved, however, in the provision of private goods; it must define and enforce the 'rules of the game' under which they are supplied, for example, stimulate competition and regulate the prices set by natural monopolists.

The distinction between civilian knowledge and military knowledge is very important for the theory. This is because civilian knowledge is normally exploited under a rule of law while military knowledge is not. The theory suggests that it is a combination of civilian and military knowledge that is key to imperialism, rather than civilian or military knowledge alone.

A state that possesses superior civilian knowledge can, in principle, exploit this knowledge through private contracts and treaty arrangements. Provided that other states recognize the benefits of the superior knowledge, they may be willing to pay for access to it. Equipment embodying the knowledge can be exported from the home state. Where projects need to be implemented beyond the boundaries of the home state, licensing and franchising agreements can be made, and consultancy and training contracts negotiated. Where private goods are involved, firms based in the home state may enter into agreements with foreign firms for them to implement projects on their behalf. Where local public goods are concerned, the home state may enter into agreements with foreign states to reform the local delivery of services. Provided that the foreign states recognize the value of the superior knowledge and the home state can trust these states to pay for the knowledge they receive, there is no need for the home state to occupy foreign territories or take control of their governments. There is no point in incurring the cost of government or occupation if the same benefits can be realized more cheaply by other means.

It is quite possible, however, that foreign states may resist the transfer of the superior civilian knowledge. It is also possible that the home state does not believe that the full potential of the knowledge can be unlocked unless it takes direct control. In either case, negotiations for the transfer of the knowledge will fail. If the home state believes that it possesses military superiority then it may decide to take over the territory instead. It can then insist on the transfer of the knowledge, direct it in a way that maximizes benefit, and enforce payment for it. This is the classic imperialist outcome. If, on the other hand, the home state believes that it has no military superiority then it will not attempt to take control. It knows that the foreign state will resist because it believes that it will be better off running its own affairs using its own knowledge, and this resistance is likely to succeed; thus the home state will have incurred the cost of a war for nothing.

This discussion indicates that classic imperialism based on civilian superiority occurs if and only if three conditions prevail: the imperial state correctly believes that it has civilian knowledge superiority, treaties and other contractual arrangements will not work, and the state has military superiority.

Suppose now that the state has only military superiority. Recognizing that it lacks civilian superiority, it will not attempt to reform the provision of local public goods. The focus will be on the redistribution of income through taxation or tribute. This can be effected either through raids and looting, 'unequal treaties', or occupation of the country.

If the foreign state accepts the superiority of the home state then terms can in principle be agreed. There may be a sequence of one-off agreements in which the home state threatens to invade and the foreign state offers tribute in return. This is effectively 'blackmail' or 'protection money'. Alternatively a long-term agreement may be made through a treaty. To enforce the treaty the knowledge-intensive state may occupy the country – locating military bases there – or patrol its borders or shores.

If the foreign state does not accept the superiority claimed, however, then invasion becomes the logical strategy. Once again, this may be either a transitory event in which the victor carries off booty, or a permanent situation in which an occupying force collects taxes for remittance to the home territory.

This discussion indicates that military superiority alone does not provide a sound case for taking over the government of a country. Occupation of a country by a nominally independent government is normally sufficient for this purpose. The costs of occupation may in turn be avoided by a policy of intermittent raids. The raiding strategy, however, provides an opportunity for the foreign state to strengthen its defences after a raid, whereas occupation can prevent this. In addition, raiding is a more arbitrary method of exacting rewards; uncertainty about the timing of raids (necessary for an element of surprise), coupled with uncertainty about the magnitude of the spoils that will be taken, may act as a greater deterrent to economic activity in the foreign state than would a measured and predictable system of taxation designed to minimize disincentive effects. Part of the knowledge base of a successful military imperialist lies in the ability to design appropriate fiscal systems to extract rewards from occupied countries. Another part of this knowledge base involves strategies for subverting protest movements and quashing local insurrections whilst rewarding those who dutifully pay their taxes on a regular basis.

This analysis shows that military superiority does not necessarily lead to imperialism. In any case, in the absence of civilian superiority, a military power will normally confine itself to occupation rather than control of government. If the foreign state recognizes the military superiority then it will normally prefer to accommodate the superior nation through payments under a treaty, for although the treaty may be perceived as unequal, it is likely to leave the country better off than it would be under occupation. Lacking local knowledge, an occupying force is likely to make more mistakes in the management of the economy than an independent government. Occupation will only be adopted when the foreign state does not accept the superiority of the home state and when the home state has sufficient knowledge to implement a sophisticated tax system.

The results are summarized in Table 12.1. The rows identify the three main types of knowledge superiority: civilian only, military only and a combination of the two. The columns indicate the key conditions that determine the degree of control that is exercised when exploiting these advantages. Knowledge transfer barriers are the key factors in the case of civilian knowledge: if the foreign state will not accept the superiority of the knowledge or cannot be trusted to implement it in an appropriate way then a high level of control is required. The tax system is the key factor in the case of military knowledge. Military knowledge alone leads only to

Table 12.1   *Imperialism and its alternatives: factors explaining the strategies adopted to exploit superior knowledge*

Type of knowledge superiority	Knowledge transfer barriers for civilian knowledge/ sophistication of the tax system available to exploit military knowledge	
	Low	High
Civilian only	Treaties facilitating licensing, franchising, consultancy and training	No transfer of knowledge
Military only	Raids	Occupation
Civilian and military	Unequal treaties asserting the right of the knowledge-intensive state to supply knowledge in return for taxes, fees and other payments	Government (classic imperialism)

occupation, but the combination of civilian and military knowledge leads to government. The level of control exercised in the exploitation of military superiority alone is less than in the case where it is combined with civilian superiority. All in all, six different outcomes are distinguished, ranging from no transfer of knowledge through to government of a foreign country. The intermediate outcomes are raids, treaties (equal or unequal) and occupation. This demonstrates an important feature of the theory of imperialism: it not only explains when imperialism occurs but also when it does not; and when it does not it explains what, if anything, occurs instead.

12.4   COMPETITION IN THE EXPLOITATION OF KNOWLEDGE: THE SIGNIFICANCE OF THE RULE OF LAW

The next part of this chapter examines some of the previous points in greater detail.

As noted in the introduction, the analysis in this chapter is based upon an analogy with the theory of the multinational firm (Buckley and Casson, 1976). All analogies have their limitations, however, and this one is no exception. The most important limitation is that the activities of imperialists are not governed by the rule of law in the same way as are the activities of multinational firms. This affects relations both between the imperialist and subject nations and between one imperialist and another.

According to the economic theory of institutions, superior knowledge can be used in two main ways. One is to generate new or improved goods and services that are either of superior quality or are produced in a more efficient way. The efficiency gain may be the result of using less resource, or substituting a readily available resource for a scarcer one. The advance may be achieved either by superior technology – for example, a labour-saving invention – or by superior marketing – for example, recognizing a consumer need that is poorly catered for by the existing range of products. These may be termed productive innovations. They correspond, loosely speaking, to the exploitation of civilian knowledge as discussed above.

The second use of knowledge involves obtaining control of goods or resources previously controlled by other people and offering nothing in return. This may be termed expropriation: it includes seizing land and property by deception or force. This corresponds, roughly speaking, to the exploitation of military knowledge for aggressive purposes, as discussed above.

Productive innovation generates an economic surplus but expropriation does not. The former involves a 'positive sum' game whilst the latter involves a 'zero sum' game (or a 'negative sum' game when the expropriator values the resource less than its previous user). Since productive innovation is a positive sum game, anyone who might lose from it can in principle be fully compensated in such a way that a net surplus still remains. This surplus can, in principle, be divided up so that everyone becomes better off, although in practice distribution of the surplus is often very unequal. By contrast, in a zero-sum game such as expropriation, the gains of one party are always matched by the losses of the other (Baumol, 1993).

Anyone who believes that they can accomplish a productive innovation – whether an individual, a firm or a state – will normally wish to appropriate some of this gain for themselves. If they are purely selfish then they will want it all for themselves; indeed, they may be able to appropriate even more than the surplus if they can avoid compensating those who have lost by the innovation. In any case, if they have incurred time and expense in discovering the new knowledge then they will feel fully justified in seeking a reward that compensates them for their effort.

Successful economies employ institutions that encourage the generation of new productive knowledge. One way is to reward innovators with patent rights, or allow them to exploit 'first-mover' advantages, for example, by building up a strong brand name that is associated with a registered trade mark. These rewards not only encourage people to actively seek out new opportunities for innovation, but also divert their attention away from the possibilities for mere expropriation.

Productive innovators are expected to compete with established producers by offering better deals to customers and/or suppliers. They are not
allowed to compete by damaging their rivals' interests – for example, by
burning down their factories or libelling their reputations. Competition
takes place under a rule of law. An effective rule of law encourages competitors to improve the deals they offer to others without damaging the
deals that their rivals can offer. This is the work of the 'invisible hand'
as described by Adam Smith, which, according to Mandeville, turns the
'private vice' of profit-seeking into the 'public virtue' of customer service.
The system never works perfectly, of course: resort to 'dirty tricks' may
go undetected or unpunished – for example, head-hunting a key employee
from a rival firm merely to sabotage its operations.

When analysing competition between rival empires it is important to
appreciate that the rule of law does not normally apply in the same way
that it does within a state. There is no standardized international law that
is universally applied. In the absence of a world policeman, states must
anticipate that rivals may resort to violence and to 'dirty tricks'; thus for
purely defensive reasons they may resort to such methods themselves.

This distinction is not absolute, but a matter of degree. Domestic legislation, policing and justice are all expensive processes, and the costs often
fall on the victims of crime rather than the offenders; as a result, 'transaction costs' inhibit the forces of pure competition. Conversely, states
can establish a rule of law through international treaty organizations.
Furthermore, religious commitments and political ideologies often tran-
scend state boundaries, and so provide shared moral values that constrain
international expropriation.

Nevertheless, without a rule of law the potential rewards to expropriation are much higher than they would otherwise be. Thus while the behaviour of firms can normally be analysed on the assumption that the rule
of law prevails, the behaviour of states must normally be analysed on the
assumption that it does not. As a consequence, states behave more aggressively than firms – a view that is reflected in the present theory.

Another limitation of the analogy between an empire and a multinational firm concerns economic motivation. Unlike a firm, a state acts
in the name of the citizens as a whole, and not just on behalf of a specialized group of shareholders. The objectives of citizens, and the elites who
represent and govern them, may differ from the objectives of shareholders
in a company. The latter are interested mainly in profits. The former are
not interested only in profits, but in anything that contributes to a higher
standard of living, including, for example, higher wages.

So long as the citizens and their elites are interested mainly in material
rewards, however, the state will pursue material advantage in much the

same way as would a firm. There are non-material objectives that may stimulate a different kind of behaviour, though. For example, if the elite is interested in domination and control as an end in itself, and not just as a means to a higher standard of living, then it may pursue territorial ambitions irrespective of material benefits. Indeed, if the elite seeks racial superiority by the elimination of 'inferior' races then it may drive other races out of their territories simply to populate the territory exclusively with people of its own race, or it may reduce other races to slavery or serfdom.

Non-material objectives do not necessarily lead to hostility, though. Religious conversion may have altruistic roots, although it can sometimes be pursued in a coercive way, whilst compassion may stimulate interventions to relieve famines and disease.

The theory developed in this chapter relates mainly to empires in which economic motivations normally take precedence over other motivations, such as racial domination, which might conflict with them. The analysis is not confined to empires that have purely economic motivations, however, as this would restrict its application too much.

12.5   KNOWLEDGE AS A GLOBAL PUBLIC GOOD

For the purposes of this chapter, knowledge may be defined as a belief that is subjectively certain. This does not mean that any item of knowledge is factually correct; it simply means that someone is very confident that it is true.

Knowledge is an example of a global public good (Arrow, 1962). It is a public good because it can be shared. If knowledge is passed on from one person to another then the person who passes it on does not automatically forget it; its consumption is 'non-rival' (Olson, 1965; Samuelson, 1954). As a result, it is difficult to control the spread of knowledge once it has been passed on to other people, because they can in turn share it with others; its consumption is 'non-excludable'. The strategy of internalization, described below, is designed to control the spread of knowledge by confining it within the boundaries of an organization such as a government or a firm.

Knowledge is durable – it can be memorized – although memories are lost when people die. Knowledge is also intangible – although it can be embodied in a number of tangible forms, including products and people. Although knowledge can be shared, access to knowledge can be difficult without literacy and numeracy, whilst the application of knowledge may be difficult without specialized skills. Education and training are therefore key to 'unlocking' stores of knowledge.

Knowledge has both intrinsic value and instrumental value. There is intrinsic value, for example, in satisfying personal curiosity. The main focus in this chapter, however, is on the instrumental use of knowledge in the production of goods and services. In economic terms, the focus is on knowledge as an intermediate rather then a final good.

The demand for knowledge is potentially global. Technological know-how, for example, can be applied in many different locations – wherever local conditions are favourable. Knowledge can also be spread globally – by social interaction, migration, publishing and broadcasting. Thus knowledge is not only demanded globally but supplied globally as well. These points may be summed up by saying that knowledge, as analysed in this chapter, is an intangible global durable intermediate public good.

12.6   GENERAL AND SPECIFIC KNOWLEDGE

The fact that knowledge is a global public good does not imply that every item of knowledge is valued in every part of the world. Mining know-how, for example, is of little value at locations which have no commercial mineral deposits. The scope of an empire will tend to reflect the scope of the knowledge it possesses; thus a mineral rich imperialist such as Britain is likely to develop an empire that exploits mineral deposits elsewhere – particularly once its own deposits become exhausted.

Successful practical application of knowledge typically requires both general and local knowledge. General knowledge is exemplified by mining technology, and local knowledge by geological mapping of a territory. Local knowledge often has limited value outside the area in which it is developed. General knowledge can often be developed outside the place to which it is to be applied; technology used in inaccessible areas, for example, is often developed in very accessible areas, where laboratory experiments are carried out and applications are pioneered. On the other hand, local knowledge is usually developed by collecting information on the spot.

The importance of combining general and specific knowledge is a special case of a more general proposition – namely that knowledge of practical economic value is normally developed through the synthesis of individual items of information which may be of little practical value on their own but which become extremely valuable when they are combined with complementary items of information. Nineteenth-century mining technology, for example, involved a combination of knowledge relating to civil engineering (the sinking and lining of mine shafts), mechanical engineering (the design of winding gear, the use of steam power) and basic physics (the design of ventilation systems) (see Chapter 11). At each mine location this synthesis of general knowledge was combined with a synthesis of local knowledge, regarding not only the location of mineral deposits but also the availability of transport routes and of suitable sites for miners' settlements.

In the context of empire, the synthesis of general and local knowledge has potentially important social implications, as general knowledge is most likely to originate in the imperial metropolis, or other well-established areas of the empire, whilst local knowledge may well be in the possession of indigenous people. Imperialists can gain direct knowledge of local conditions through the efforts of travellers, explorers and settlers, many of whom may be motivated by the prospect of speculative profits from land and mineral rights. But even then, such pioneers may need to enlist the help and advice of indigenous people. As the imperialist becomes established in a new territory, so opportunities may arise to educate local people with the general knowledge in order to allow settlers and expatriates to delegate more responsible work. In the long run, the talents of local people may be enlisted in the development of new general knowledge for use elsewhere in the empire, using local research laboratories or innovative local projects for the purpose.

12.7 LOCAL PUBLIC GOODS

Many of the goods produced with the aid of superior knowledge are also public goods – but they are local public goods rather than global ones. Law and order, for example, is a local public good. Like knowledge it can be shared. It is difficult, if not impossible, to supply law and order to one person in a community without supplying it to everyone else as well. But it is a local good: the fact that there is law and order in one town does not mean that there is law and order in adjacent towns.

Health and education are often described as local public goods, although in practice there are both public and private aspects to them. The eradication of infections and contagious diseases qualifies as a public good, but the treatment of an individual injury is a private good. Education in the obligations of citizenship is a public good, but on-the-job training is normally a private good.

Utility services are also local public goods. Transport infrastructure such as roads and railways are built on a scale that allows many people simultaneously to share their use. So long as they operate below full capacity, there is always scope to handle additional traffic without detriment to existing traffic. The same point applies to telecommunications systems, water and drainage systems, electricity grids and so on. Utility services are not pure public goods, however, because a private cost of connection is often incurred in gaining access to the network.

Social cohesion is also a hybrid public-private good. The quality of community life is something in which everyone can share, as is the external reputation of a social group (Gellner,1987). On the other hand, respect and admiration conferred within a social group in response to specific behaviour are confined to the individual concerned.

Defence resembles law and order in being a pure public good; it is difficult to defend one person in a community without defending everyone else as well. Successful aggression against other states may also be a public good so far as the victorious citizens are concerned.

Pure public goods such as defence and law and order tend to be supplied exclusively by government. Hybrid local goods such as health, education, utility services and social cohesion tend to be supplied by a mixture of organizations, including government, voluntary and non-profit organizations and private firms.

Overall, therefore, it may be said that imperialists use a global public good – superior knowledge – to enhance the supply of local public goods, some of which also have private aspects to them. The global public good – knowledge – is essentially an intermediate good employed in the production of final goods. The intermediate good is intangible, whilst the final goods take on a mixture of tangible and intangible forms.

12.8   KNOWLEDGE TRANSFER BARRIERS

The fact that knowledge is a global public good does not mean that it can be communicated without cost. Because it is subjective, knowledge offered by another person or another state cannot always be assumed to be true. It may not even be intelligible if it is in a foreign language, and even if it is in the same language, cultural differences may mean that it is misunderstood.

Superior knowledge that is offered to others may therefore be greeted with suspicion. A foreign state may be unable to visualize the potential benefits of knowledge offered by the home state, or it may believe that the knowledge is similar to what it knows already. If it is asked to pay for the knowledge – as will normally be the case – it may be doubly suspicious; the knowledge may have been deliberately fabricated in order to create something to sell. Supporting evidence is likely to be demanded to corroborate the knowledge. But in the process of demonstrating the value of the knowledge, the foreign state may acquire the knowledge for free. Although it becomes convinced of its value, it sees no reason to pay for what it has already learned. This is known as the 'information asymmetry' or 'buyer uncertainty' problem. The consequence is that either the knowledge cannot be supplied, or that it is supplied only on condition that the supplier retains control.

Because knowledge is a public good, anyone who acquires it can, in principle, pass it on to a third party. This means that a state that shares its knowledge is likely quickly to lose control of the exploitation process. Unless a foreign purchaser of the knowledge can be supervised, they will compete with the home state in selling the knowledge on to other states. Even worse, they might sell the knowledge to a military rival. Once again, there is a strong incentive either to control the use of the knowledge or not to supply it at all.

It was noted above that knowledge might not even be intelligible to others. This is particularly true of tacit knowledge. Tacit knowledge cannot be easily explained because it is implicit rather than explicit (it is hard to codify and quantify) and because its application is complex (success depends on a large number of factors and it requires a high degree of skill and judgement to respond appropriately to them). The problem of communicating tacit knowledge, like other knowledge-related problems, is exacerbated by cultural differences. Education and training may be required to enable the purchaser to absorb the knowledge. Taking over the government of a foreign state not only allows the home state to insist on the application of the knowledge, but can also reduce the cost of transferring the knowledge. Language and culture can be standardized and investments in education made in order to increase the 'absorptive capacity' of the local population.

Overall, therefore, knowledge transfer barriers are likely to be high when:

- knowledge is highly subjective and tacit;
- language and cultural differences are great;
- literacy and numeracy in the foreign state are low; and
- the knowledge-intensive state has military rivals who could acquire its superior knowledge from independent states to which it has been supplied.

When transfer barriers are high, knowledge will be 'internalized' to keep it under the control of the home nation; it will be exploited within the empire rather than sold to independent states under treaty arrangements.

12.9   THE EMPIRE AS A FREE TRADE AREA FOR PRIVATE GOODS

Civilian knowledge does not, of course, relate exclusively to the provision of local public goods. As the theory of the multinational firm clearly indicates, civilian knowledge relates to the supply of ordinary private goods as well – consumer products, production equipment and so on (Dunning, 1981). Private goods are purchased by individual buyers who have exclusive use of the items they purchase, and this makes it easy for private firms to appropriate rewards from the superior knowledge that they embody in these goods. Thus knowledge relating to private goods is normally generated and exploited by private firms, as explained above.

Firms have a choice of where to produce their goods and which contractual arrangements to employ for this purpose. They may produce goods in their home country for export. Alternatively, they may produce abroad in the country in which the good is consumed, or in some third country where resources are cheap. In principle, they can license or franchise foreign firms to produce them. But given the practical difficulties of licensing and franchising, as described above, firms may instead 'internalize' the exploitation of their knowledge by setting up wholly-owned foreign subsidiaries. This strategy transforms the knowledge-intensive firm into a multinational firm.

Firms producing or selling abroad may face discrimination: exporters may face tariffs, or demands to comply with local requirements imposed to protect local producers, whilst multinational investors face risks of punitive taxation or expropriation. It is therefore more secure to trade and invest within the boundaries of an empire. Firms headquartered in the home country are most secure of all, while those based in the metropolis are in a good position to lobby for their specific requirements. Entrepreneurial individuals who recognize this may migrate to the metropolis in order to obtain imperial patronage for their business operations. Thus where an empire encourages private enterprise, immigration will be stimulated, and trade and investment are likely to flourish (Jones, 1998; Moore and Lewis, 1999).

To maximize the benefits a successful imperialist will promote free trade. Tariffs will be used sparingly as a revenue-raising device. A common external tariff may be adopted so that the costs imposed by the tariff are borne, at least in part, by territories outside the empire. This may also be seen as a method of weakening the power of rival empires.

Home country lobbyists may, however, argue for tariffs on imports from the rest of the empire, in order to protect themselves from internal competition, especially from new member states. Such protective tariffs will distort trade within the empire and result in overall losses. The taxable wealth of overseas territories will be diminished by more than the taxable wealth of the home territory is increased; successful imperialists will therefore resist lobbying of this kind.

With a common external tariff, there are significant benefits to enlarging the empire simply on account of the new opportunities for trade that are created when a new member joins. Indeed, there are increasing returns to size of empire. Each new territory that joins a small empire has only a few other territories with which to trade, whereas a territory that joins a large empire has many territories with which to trade. Thus the marginal benefit from enlarging an empire tends to increase with the size of the empire. This effect may be counteracted by diminishing returns, however, if the territories that join later are smaller or have less economic potential than those that joined first. Since a knowledge-based state is likely to expand by occupying the most attractive territories first, it is indeed probable that, beyond a certain threshold, diminishing returns to size of empire will set in. This can explain why, even when there is a dominant global empire, it does not necessarily absorb the whole of the world.

The advantages of an empire as a free trade area should not be exaggerated, however. The empire is useful only if independent territories would otherwise be reluctant to trade with each other. If all nations were sufficiently enlightened, they could negotiate a free trade area by treaty (Alesina et al., 1995). The resulting federation would not only match the empire in terms of trade creation, but might actually surpass it, as unlike the empire no one territory would be strong enough unilaterally to impose protective tariffs against the others.

12.10   THE KNOWLEDGE-BASED STATE: A SUMMARY OF ITS ROLES

The preceding discussion has identified six types of goods and services. The state is involved, directly or indirectly, in the provision of all of them (see Figure 12.1).

Although the state is not directly involved in the provision of private goods, it is responsible for the framework of law under which they are produced and sold. It may specify standard weights and measures, allowing customers to compare accurately the prices quoted by competing suppliers. It may establish anti-trust measures to foster competition in supply, provide sound currency through a central bank and so on.

Where public goods are concerned, the state may regulate the provision of utility services. Network externalities create economies of scale in many

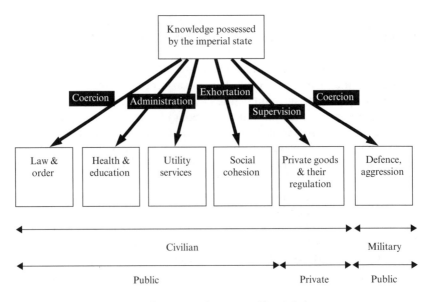

Figure 12.1   Six areas of state application of knowledge

of these industries, and it requires price regulation to prevent the abuse of natural monopoly power. In certain cases the state may build and operate the network infrastructure itself. It may raise finance from both taxation and government loans. It therefore needs an accurate system for assessing taxable capacity and for checking that taxes have been paid. It needs to create efficient financial markets that provide adequate liquidity and thereby facilitate the sale of government bonds.

Where health and education are concerned, the state has an important administrative role, particularly where universal education for children is provided and where there is universal health care as well.

In providing law and order the state must legislate against crime and provide an efficient system of policing, justice and punishment. Coercion needs to be applied against persistent criminals, but those who exercise it need to be held accountable in order to prevent abuse.

The exercise of force is also an important aspect of the provision of defence. A credible threat of retaliation must be presented to potential aggressors. In addition, the imperial state can use its military power to take control of other states, either to pre-empt aggression or simply to expand its territorial boundaries of control.

Where social cohesion is concerned, exhortation and leadership by example is more important than coercion. National pride is generally sustained through the voluntary commitment of the citizens rather than through compulsion or fear. Elite groups, including political leaders, need to provide positive role models that promote responsible behaviour and raise people's aspirations.

Legislation, regulation, administration, coercion and exhortation all depend on knowledge of various kinds. Unlike an individual firm, which can prosper on the basis of highly specialized knowledge, a state requires a broad base of knowledge to fulfil all the roles described above. An imperial power does not require superior knowledge in all these areas, but its superiority in certain areas needs to be supplemented by adequate knowledge in all the other areas if it is to prove successful.

12.11   THE CULTURE OF IMPERIALISM

Transferring knowledge to a foreign location does not necessarily involve transferring the knowledge to indigenous people. Knowledge can be transferred by population movement instead. Short-term visits from the home country may be made, medium-term assignments can be arranged, or permanent expatriation may occur.

Where military knowledge is transferred through occupation, for example, very little of the knowledge may be transferred to indigenous people. Whilst local militia may be formed, their subordinate role may exploit natural abilities and rely on only the most basic knowledge acquired from the imperial power. The superior knowledge may remain in the hands of senior officers posted from the home country. The more tacit the superior knowledge, the greater the cost of transferring it, and the stronger the incentive to retain the knowledge in the expatriate community.

Where civilian knowledge is concerned, there is a stronger case for transferring knowledge to the local population. It is difficult, for example, to provide policing or deliver health-care without relying on people who speak the local language and have local knowledge. A particular issue arises in the case of law and order. Whilst law itself is explicit, it is also complex. Furthermore, much of the law involves the formal codification of informal custom. Customs are also complex, and if they are not codified in law then they must be acquired through a process of social assimilation. With so much tacit information involved, there is a strong incentive for an imperial power to economize on the cost of transferring knowledge by leaving informal local customs intact and confining its own customs to the expatriate population. As a result, only the formal part of the legal system is imposed on the indigenous population.

It is difficult to have different social customs prevailing in the same locality: the scope for misunderstanding, and the consequent risk of incitement to violence, is too great. This favours a policy of residential segregation, based on a division between indigenous and expatriate populations. While each area is subject to the same formal laws, local customs vary. People entering other areas are expected to conform with local customs, although they may be discouraged from crossing boundaries. Where there are different indigenous peoples, each may be encouraged to populate its own area; but if trust between these groups is low, they will tend to segregate spontaneously anyway, as each person will prefer to live near to people from the same group.

This discussion indicates that where the costs of transferring knowledge are high, little education and training will be offered to local peoples. As a consequence, these people will be excluded from positions of responsibility which, in the judgement of the imperial power, require access to the superior knowledge. In addition, they may be segregated into ghettoes. This will occur if the knowledge embodied in informal social customs is considered too complex to be explained and assimilated; it will be reinforced if it is also believed that local people have little respect for the formal law.

The culture of the imperial power will have a significant impact on the extent to which job discrimination and residential segregation occur. An elitist imperial power will equate the sophistication of its civilization with the complexity of its knowledge and its customs, and exaggerate this complexity in order to suggest greater sophistication. It will fail to appreciate the complexity of other civilizations and so further exaggerate its own superiority by regarding indigenous peoples as primitive and backward. This emphasis on their 'otherness' may exaggerate perceived barriers to knowledge transfer. As a result, the elitist state may well decide that knowledge transfer is uneconomic and so resort instead to discrimination and segregation.

Democratic imperial powers, on the other hand, will value the economic advantages of possessing a relatively simple culture that others can absorb, and will be less concerned about how their culture appears to others (Jones, 2006). This makes education and training more viable, promotes the wider dissemination of superior knowledge, and thereby makes job discrimination and residential segregation unnecessary. Whilst some segregation may still occur as a result of individual decisions, it will not be imposed as imperial policy, because it will be recognized as a cause of increased personal transport costs and reduced labour market flexibility.

The terms 'elitist' and 'democratic' must be construed as labels for different cultures rather than literal descriptions of political systems. Elitist imperial powers tend to emphasise the 'high culture' of fine art and pure science, whilst democratic imperial powers tend to emphasize applied art and science, in the form of artisan skills and engineering know-how. Elitists develop elaborate social customs, command of which distinguishes the upper classes from the lower ones. Democrats use simple customs which are common to the mass of the people in a relatively classless society (Casson, 2006). Democratic culture is better adapted to imperialism because it reduces the cost of knowledge transfer and so facilitates territorial expansion.

12.12   THE METROPOLIS

It is a mistake to assume that all parts of a territory are integrated into an empire to the same extent. The discovery and exploitation of superior knowledge benefits from an advanced division of labour in which many different types of specialist are located close to each other so that they can share their knowledge and coordinate their decisions on a face-to-face basis. This encourages the agglomeration of knowledge-intensive activities at a dominant hub in each territory. Transport and communication linkages radiate from this hub (Chinitz, 1960).

The skeleton around which a mature empire is built is a network of trunk-line linkages between the imperial metropolis and a set of local satellite hubs in the foreign territories. The concentration of long-distance transport and communication on these trunk lines reflects economies of scale in infrastructure.

Each hub has a hinterland which provides a supply of supporting services. An empire needs a strong supply of knowledge workers – political and military leaders, bureaucrats, merchants, entrepreneurs, scientists, engineers, artists and artisans. In addition, military superiority requires a supply of young fit and well-disciplined people. Substantial investments in education and training are necessary in order to renew these stocks from one generation to the next.

An elitist empire will tend to rely on its home territory for its key workers, as it does not trust people from foreign territories because it has not invested in their education. By contrast, a democratic imperialist can recruit more widely; in particular it can select the most able people from throughout the empire and educate them to join the governing elite. Given the low cost of assimilating its culture, it may also be able to recruit from other sources, including rival empires.

If the home territory has a large population an elitist empire may be able to recruit sufficient people from within it to administer a large empire; otherwise imperial expansion will be constrained by human resources. A democratic empire is not constrained in this way, and can become large even though its home territory is quite small. As it expands, the pool of human resources from which it can recruit expands along with it, and so expansion becomes self-reinforcing to some degree.

Given the importance of long-distance communication, economic logic suggests that the imperial metropolis and its foreign satellites will each be based around a natural harbour (for a sea-based empire) or a river confluence (for a land-based empire). In some cases, however, administrative centres may be placed near to ports rather than in them, leaving the immediate environs of the port available for transhipment and manufacturing activities, and insulating the knowledge-workers from the physical distractions associated with them.

An entrepreneurial imperial state will recognize that many of the economic opportunities waiting to be exploited will appear on the periphery of the empire rather than at the core. Whilst the key ideas on which knowledge superiority is based may have been developed in the home territory, profitable applications are likely to appear in foreign territories – particularly those rich in natural resources. Mining opportunities in the home territory may be exhausted, for example, so that the superior mining technologies developed for use on the home territory must now be exploited abroad. The development of new resource-based opportunities abroad also encourages new investments in transport and communications networks.

In an entrepreneurial empire, trunk-line communications do not merely relay instructions from the centre to the periphery but, most importantly, convey commercial intelligence from the periphery to the centre. This intelligence relates to new projects formulated often by enterprising expatriates, which are passed up to the centre for a decision on whether finance will be made available. In this context, the centre acts as an investment banker, evaluating competing demands for a limited supply of finance. Given the difficulty of on-the-spot inspection to verify the details of each proposal, the reputation of the applicants is crucial. Reputation will be based not only on track record, but also on the opinion of peers, transmitted to the financiers through social networks. To reinforce their cases, applicants may travel to the metropolis to advocate their case in person, and may seek out patrons who can arrange introductions for them.

The range and quality of the facilities available in the metropolis is likely to be a major factor in the success of an empire. Elitist imperialists are likely to invest heavily in town planning, architecture and landscape in order to give an impression of sophistication and power. However, the resulting proliferation of large public buildings with wide spaces between them may impair efficiency, as functional requirements are sacrificed for aesthetic appeal. In particular, efficient social networking generally requires close physical proximity, and the crowded conditions of a private business district, with small offices in closely-spaced buildings, would often be more appropriate. A democratic state is likely to invest in public buildings on a more 'human' scale. This will promote communication between administrators, improve public access, and provide a work environment similar to that of the private sector.

12.13 THE BOUNDARIES OF EMPIRE

The fact that knowledge is a global public good does not mean that a knowledge-driven empire will control the whole world. Barriers to knowledge transfer vary between territories because of linguistic and cultural differences, as already explained, and in certain cases – such as extreme cultural differences – the benefits of transferring knowledge will be less than the cost. This implies that, other things being equal, imperial government will be applied to territories where knowledge transfer barriers are moderate; if they are low then superior civilian knowledge will be exploited through treaty arrangements, as described above, whilst if they are very high they will not be exploited at all.

Even where knowledge transfer barriers are low, knowledge may not be exploited, simply because it has no relevance to the territory concerned. If an empire is based on superior knowledge of mining techniques, for example, then it has no relevance to territories that have no mineral deposits of any value. Similarly superior knowledge of pastoral agriculture – for example, animal breeding – may have little relevance to a territory whose soils are more appropriate to arable farming.

Geographical distance may also play a part. Although geographical distance increases the costs of transmitting knowledge, the effect is often marginal; the most substantive impact of distance is usually on the cost of transporting heavy and bulky goods – for example, mineral and agricultural products. There is little point in transferring superior knowledge to a foreign country if there is no effective way of marketing the output produced with the aid of this knowledge. Thus when distance is an important factor, empires will tend to be spatially compact. The relevant distance is not necessarily the distance from the imperial metropolis, however. In many cases the resources of a foreign territory can be exploited within the territory itself – for example, for local consumption – or can be exported to neighbouring territories; in this case the cost penalty is related not to the distance from the centre of empire but rather to the distance from the nearest imperial territory, or from the nearest country that trades with the empire on a regular basis. Although the distance from the furthest regions of the empire to the imperial metropolis may be quite large, dependent territories will tend to be clustered into groups which are reasonably self-sufficient so far as trade flows are concerned (a similar point is noted in connection with multinationals by Rugman, 2005).

In this connection, it is not necessarily distance 'as the crow flies' that counts, but rather the distance involved when the traffic is routed along the imperial infrastructure. A territory that is physically close to existing imperial territories may be treated as if it were quite remote if there are no established connections. Natural obstacles such as mountains or dangerous seas can exert considerable influence on the boundaries of empire, and conversely, new knowledge that helps to overcome them – for example, tunnelling and shipbuilding technologies – can modify these boundaries in a significant way.

12.14   COMPETITION BETWEEN EMPIRES

So far the analysis has concentrated on relations between a single empire and a set of foreign territories. This is not unusual in the analysis of empires – indeed many studies focus simply on relations between a single imperialist and a single foreign territory. In reality of course, the boundaries of empire are strongly influenced by competition from other empires. No single empire has a natural monopoly on new knowledge. Knowledge is heterogeneous – there are many different things to know, and different things have different fields of application, as indicated above. Thus a country which is rich in coal is likely to develop superior knowledge of coal mining, whilst a country that has fertile land but no minerals is more likely to develop superior knowledge of agriculture.

When superior knowledge is distributed across a number of different territories – each of which has imperial potential – competition can emerge in several different ways. Two imperialists may wish to develop the same country for different purposes; thus if a territory has both fertile land and mineral deposits then one imperialist may wish to take control to exploit the mines and the other to exploit the agriculture. Alternatively, they may wish to develop it for similar purposes, for example, mining.

In either case, if competition were subject to the rule of law, as discussed above, then the two imperialists would bid against each other by offering better and better deals to the indigenous people (or to whoever owned the territory). Eventually one imperialist would drop out of the bidding because the terms had become too demanding. The successful bidder would obtain control of the territory at this price (provided that the price equalled or exceeded the reservation price set by the representatives of the local people). The imperialist that took control would expect to realize a surplus equal to the difference between the maximum price it could have afforded to pay and the actual price. This surplus would not reflect the superiority of the imperialist's knowledge over the knowledge of the present owner of the territory but its superiority to the knowledge of the best alternative owner – namely the rival imperialist that dropped out of the bidding.

In practice, of course, competition between imperialists is not usually resolved in this way. Instead it is resolved by use of the force. This force is not deployed primarily against the indigenous people, but against rival imperialists. Local people may be so weak in military terms that they will readily surrender when threatened with force. In the case discussed above, for example, the two imperialists would go to war over the disputed territory. This war would not necessarily take place in the territory itself. The theatre of war may be located in the home territories, on the basis that the victor can walk into the disputed territory afterwards because local resistance will be so weak. Once again, it is not the superiority of the successful imperialist over the indigenous people that is crucial in this outcome, but its superiority over the rival power.

The military outcome is less satisfactory than the outcome under the rule of law. Quite apart from the waste incurred in military conflict (the diversion of effort from civilian activity and the damage and destruction that ensues), it is quite possible that the country with the inferior knowledge may prevail. This will occur if the imperialist with the truly superior civilian knowledge has inferior military knowledge and vice versa.

For any given territory anywhere in the world there will be a number of potential imperialists interested in taking control because they believe that their knowledge is superior to that of the indigenous people. The exceptions are territories that are so impoverished or remote that they attract no attention from imperialists at all. Unless imperialists are interested in acquiring options to exploit these territories in future should new knowledge emerge, these territories will be ignored and the local people will retain their sovereignty. This is not necessarily good for local development, however, if potential improvements in local public goods are not made as a result.

Other territories may attract interest from a number of different powers. Under a rule of law, the local people could play these rival empires off against each other, negotiating through their representatives for the best possible deal. It is possible, however, that the imperialists may be interested in a territory that is much larger than the boundaries of the territories controlled by local nations. The local nations may therefore need to federate in order to negotiate with the imperial powers. If they fail to federate then they will find that their negotiating position is weakened as the powers attempt to play off the different nations against each other.

Where there is no rule of law rival empires may go to war. Rival local nations may get drawn into the conflict as different imperialists sponsor different nations by supplying them with arms. Local rivalries and animosities then become mixed up with imperial rivalries. This means that where there is a victorious imperialist there is also a victorious local nation, and this may lead to a localized 'settling of scores' after the war.

Warfare may be not be conclusive, however. If the military knowledge of the imperial powers is equal then they may fight to a stalemate where no one can gain control of the entire territory. The territory may then be partitioned along the 'front line' prevailing at the end of the war. As explained above, such divisions may lack economic logic; the partitioned territories may be small, and the boundaries arbitrary, so that no territory is really viable as an economic entity, and they cannot be united because of animosity between the rival powers.

Imperial rivalries may also make home nations reluctant to rely on treaty obligations. There is a risk that by staying out of a territory a rival power may be induced to enter it. It is possible to reinforce a treaty by agreeing to intervene to defend a territory against invaders – but this is only an effective deterrent to potential aggressors if they regard the pledge as credible. If an imperial power is concerned that rivals may discount its treaty commitments to weaker states then it has a strong incentive to occupy them instead. Even though it trusts the local people to honour the treaty, it cannot trust its imperial rivals to respect it. This creates additional costs for both the home nation – namely the additional expense of occupation – and for the foreign nation – the loss of sovereignty involved.

From the standpoint of rival imperialists, competition creates not only frustration but waste. There is therefore a strong economic incentive to collaborate with fellow imperialists in order to collude against the local people in a disputed territory. Under a rule of law, this reduces the payment to local interests, and without a rule of law it avoids the costs of war. Efficient collaboration would also avoid the wasteful division of territories described above, and focus instead on allocating entire territories to particular powers. For example, an auction market could be established between the powers in which all the vulnerable states that are ripe for takeover would be auctioned internally to the highest bidder. Other things being equal, this would favour the bidder with the superior civilian technology, and would result in imperialists being matched to territories on the basis of the suitability of their knowledge to the particular territory concerned.

However, states with military superiority but without civilian superiority may object to basing rewards on civilian superiority alone. They may demand compensation for agreeing not to exercise their military power. The other states may agree to this, provided that they accept the claims of military superiority. If, these claims are rejected, however, then war is likely to ensue. The military powers will prevail, provided that their claims to superiority are genuine.

Given that there is competition for every territory, there is also competition for the control of the territories in which the imperial powers themselves are based. Some territories are far more suitable than others as an imperial base. As already noted, natural harbours and river junctions are particularly useful as hubs of imperial networks. If in addition they are served by fertile hinterlands rich in mineral resources, they will be extremely attractive. Competition to occupy such territories is likely to be particularly fierce. This suggests that in order to retain control of their home territory, imperialists need significant military power. Thus the military power deployed to defend the borders of empire may first have been refined through battles to defend the home territory.

12.15 DEVELOPING AND MAINTAINING SUPERIORITY

Superiority is a relative concept. So what determines who is superior to whom? The size and quality of the population of knowledge-workers is an important factor in civilian superiority. A large home territory can support a large population, and so too can a compact metropolis that attracts immigrants, as noted above. High density living can impair quality of life, but it can also enrich it through easy social networking and ready access to cultural facilities. An intelligent and entrepreneurial indigenous population in the home country is undoubtedly an advantage, but so too is a welcoming attitude to able immigrants and a convenient location at the hub of a transport and communication network.

A rich and fertile hinterland is not only useful in maintaining a high standard of living, but is also a spur to developing new knowledge in order to exploit local resources. The characteristics of the hinterland, as reflected in the type of resources to be found, will influence the type of civilian knowledge generated. Having been refined through local applications, it can then be transferred to similar territories throughout the world. A fertile hinterland is not essential, however; a large population can be sustained by imports (financed out of the profits of empire), provided that transport facilities are good.

The culture of the home nation is also an important factor. As already indicated, a nation with a democratic culture coupled with an outward-looking attitude is more likely to identify profitable applications for its superior knowledge than an elitist and inward-looking one. It is also more likely to assimilate ideas from abroad and thereby create a synthesis of the best ideas.

In principle individual nations could specialize in gaining superiority in different types of knowledge. Thus small nations with limited numbers of knowledge workers could gain superiority in small niches whilst larger nations could win superiority in whole areas of knowledge. In practice, however, the logic of imperial competition works against small niche players. Any imperialist that occupies or governs a territory must supply it with a wide range of local public goods, as noted above. It cannot simply pick the knowledge that it wishes to supply and leave others to fill in the gaps. There is a minimum critical mass of human resources that is needed to supply a full range of local public goods to a foreign territory. If a nation lacks this critical mass then it cannot fulfil an imperial role.

This does not mean that nations cannot specialize in developing different types of knowledge, but only that they must include certain core types of knowledge within this portfolio. Thus different imperialists could specialize in knowledge relating to agriculture, mining or manufacturing provided that they covered the core subjects too.

The scale of human resources available is also important in military defence. The outcome of war is determined by a combination of superiority in armaments and superiority in the size of the fighting force. Superiority of armaments will reflect the size and quality of the human resources devoted to their development, whilst superiority in the size of the fighting force is directly related to the number of able-bodied people that can be recruited. In each case it is the size of the population relative to that of the strongest rival that is the key factor.

A nation with a small population will find it almost impossible to match a nation with a large population if it relies solely on its own resources. The only way that a small nation can match a large one, given the substantial economies of scale that exist in the relative size of military forces, is to recruit from the foreign territories of its empire and, if necessary, from rival imperial powers as well. Attracting personnel from rival powers has the added advantage of weakening the competition – it is an example of the 'dirty tricks' described earlier.

Type of industry is not the only dimension along which imperialists can specialize their knowledge; they can specialize geographically too. It has already been noted that the rewards obtained from the local application of industrial knowledge depend on the distance between the territory concerned and the nearest territory within the same empire. The greater the distance, the smaller the rewards. If the territories are contiguous then the border can be shortened by eliminating the internal division. By expanding from one territory into adjacent territories, economies of scale in defence can therefore be obtained, as the area encompassed by the communal border increases more slowly than the area enclosed. This reduces the cost of defence per unit area and thereby increases the value of each territory. This is an economy in the absolute size of a defended area, as opposed to an economy in the relative size of military forces, as discussed above.

12.16 SUPERIOR KNOWLEDGE: WHERE DOES IT COME FROM?

The origins of superior knowledge are not very well understood. Chance discovery obviously plays an important part – someone sets out to answer one question and answers another instead, or sets out to prove an 'obvious' point and finishes up proving the opposite. Such discoveries are most likely in societies that encourage natural curiosity, where speculation is welcome and ideas are discussed and disputed. They are unlikely to occur in a society in which an elite group claims to know all the answers already.

Knowledge does not consist of a set of isolated discoveries, however, but rather a collection of related discoveries, set within a broader framework which indicates how these discoveries are to be understood. It is often a synthesis of different discoveries, rather than any single discovery, that leads to superior knowledge of the kind that can be exploited by an imperial power. A new synthesis can be achieved without any new discovery, simply by analysis and reflection on what is already known, although in practice many new syntheses are created as a result of some new discovery being added to the collection and its implications being teased out.

Entrepreneurial imperialists put knowledge into action; they are interested in both the intrinsic and the instrumental value of knowledge, as discussed above. Once curiosity has been satisfied, their agenda moves on to exploring practical applications. Provisional knowledge is refined by experiment and then codified for general implementation. In a democratic culture implementation is simplified so that as many people as possible can be involved.

Historically, two main types of superior knowledge have been employed by imperialists – technological and institutional. Each of these can be subdivided into further categories relating to the specific type of knowledge (for example, the modern disciplines involved) and the field of application (for example, the types of goods to which the knowledge can be applied). Unfortunately, however, there is no space for such refinement here.

Prominent applications of superior technological knowledge that appear in the literature of imperialism include:

- improvements in arable farming, animal husbandry and the training of animals (for example, war-horses);
- discoveries of new natural resources (for example, plants, trees and minerals) and their sources of supply;
- new production technologies (for example, cooking, metal refining, fermentation, preservation, water management);
- new sources of power (for example, windmills, water-wheels, steam, internal combustion, electricity);
- new methods of measurement (for example, land surveying, time-keeping, weighing, development of standard units);
- discovery of scientific laws for the production of wholly synthetic products (for example, pharmaceuticals, computers);
- new transport technologies: larger ships, railways, motorways, air-craft, and so on;
- new technologies of communication and record-keeping: writing, printing, photography and film, radio and television, libraries and archives, and soon.

Prominent applications of superior institutional knowledge include:

- new religions (for example, Christianity, Islam), and new sects or denominations of established religions (for example, Protestantism); these are institutionalized in churches, mosques, and so on;
- new moralities (for example, compassion, chivalry, personal freedom, human rights) institutionalized in voluntary organizations, schools, hospitals, and so on;
- innovations in law (for example, private property, trial by jury, market regulation, incorporation of private firms);
- new political systems for the representation of opinions (for example, council meetings, Parliamentary democracy);
- new systems of planning and strategizing backed by state bureaucracy (for example, state treasuries, tax assessment techniques, statistical offices, standing armies).

Innovations have costs as well as benefits, and these costs can be very high in the short run. Innovation based on superior knowledge involves a process of 'creative destruction', and those who suffer from the destruction are not always fully compensated by those who gain (Schumpeter, 1934). Notwithstanding these qualifications, theory suggests that imperialists can derive significant long-run benefits from exploiting these types of innovation, and that foreign states within their empires can often benefit from them too.

12.17   THE RISE AND FALL OF EMPIRES

If the rise of empires is accounted for by the discovery and exploitation of superior knowledge, then what accounts for their subsequent decline and fall? Environmental change, depletion of natural resources and organizational over-complexity have all been advanced as explanations (Dark, 1998). Whilst such factors can be readily accommodated within the framework of this theory, the theory itself suggests a very simple explanation, namely the eventual obsolescence of the superior knowledge.

Two aspects of obsolescence must be distinguished. In the first, the superiority obsolesces but the knowledge does not. The application of knowledge advertises its existence, and its conspicuous success encourages imitation. The knowledge spreads to rival empires, who then 'free-ride' on what they have acquired, and eventually they catch up with the innovator. In the second case, the knowledge itself obsolesces as new knowledge appears to displace it. In practice, the two processes are often linked. As knowledge spreads, the people who absorb the knowledge for the first time find that their existing beliefs are challenged; this 'creative tension' encourages them to challenge not only their existing beliefs but the new knowledge too. As a result, they are able to recognize limitations or defects in the knowledge that those who have always known it may have failed to detect. If they are entrepreneurial they will perceive an opportunity to use their refinement of the knowledge for their own benefit.

Rival empires can emerge from inside or outside the boundaries of the innovating empire. While outsiders can only observe from a distance, insiders have a closer view; they can develop their own ideas based on the education they have received, and if these ideas are rejected by the empire they can exploit them independently, perhaps under the patronage of other states.

An entrepreneurial empire will recognize the threat of obsolescence and take steps to counteract it. It will commit to continuous improvement of its knowledge base. It will feed back information from the practical application of knowledge at the frontier in order to refine it in the metropolis. This reflects a view that there is always more to be learned and that it is always possible to do better. The opposite view turns established knowledge into dogma and regards further improvement as impossible.

It is difficult for any society to sustain entrepreneurship through successive generations. Entrepreneurial attitudes are often forged in adversity. Adversity provides a sharp choice between giving up, and playing the role of 'victim' of circumstance or of oppression, or gaining control of the situation. Conversely, prosperity blunts the issue by giving people a comfortable life for relatively little effort. These social factors reinforce the 'catching up' process described above. Those who live off the profits of empire are not motivated to advance knowledge in the same way as those who aspire to share in them but are excluded from them.

An entrepreneurial empire will take steps to involve local people in the process of feedback and knowledge improvement and to reward them accordingly. It will promote the recruitment of able people from rival empires as well as taking steps to retain its own most able people. Where entrepreneurship is weak, however, and the surplus from empire is declining as knowledge obsolesces, the profit-earning elite may decide to maintain their living standards by increasing imperial taxation. For example, the home territory may impose tariffs against the other territories in order to extract further rewards. As able people in foreign territories become increasingly excluded from the benefits of membership, a sense of exploitation, and consequent alienation, may promote dissent and rebellion. The resultant costs of policing dissident groups further reduces the profits of empire.

This loss of internal social cohesion is often identified as a proximate cause of imperial decline. Theory suggests, however, that external competitive forces will be important too. As noted above, potential imperialists are always looking for opportunities to take over territories controlled by others, and any emergent weakness that is detected in an empire will incite its rivals to attack it. Having identified the most vulnerable territories, potential imperialists may attempt to destabilize them politically by supporting dissidents and rebel groups. Where 'dirty tricks' are readily available, it may prove unnecessary to commit to all-out war. If sponsored dissidents succeed in gaining independence for their territory then their financial sponsors will expect to acquire a commensurate degree of control.

The development and subsequent obsolescence of knowledge must therefore be analysed against the background of continuous territorial competition between potential imperial powers (that is, the market for territorial control is 'contestable', as defined by Baumol et al., 1982). The development of superior knowledge, either by chance or design, provides a temporary competitive advantage for a nation which, under certain circumstances, it pays to exploit by occupying or governing other territories. This may involve taking over territories from other empires – either by fighting for them, destabilizing the rival's local administration, or simply waiting for the rival empire to disintegrate before picking up the pieces.

At any one time, no single empire may be dominant. Different empires may specialize in exploiting different varieties of knowledge or in controlling particular regions where they operate a free trade area. As new discoveries are made the boundaries of empires will shift as some territories become more valuable to one empire and less valuable to another. Sometimes the shift may occur peacefully through voluntary treaty arrangements, whilst in other cases it may be effected through military force. There is no guarantee that the empire with the best civilian knowledge will prevail in a territorial contest; it is military knowledge that will usually be decisive. But military empires that lack superior civilian knowledge have little incentive to occupy and govern foreign countries as it is more economic for them to raid them or to demand tribute instead.

Thus the empires that dominate at any time will be based on a combination of superior civilian and military knowledge. Their geographical scope and their persistence over time will reflect their ability to counter obsolescence through continuous improvement. Entrepreneurial nations with democratic cultures are most likely to succeed in this.

12.18   A REVIEW OF CASE STUDY EVIDENCE

The theory set out in this chapter has many applications. The simplicity and generality of the definition of empire that is employed means that the theory can be applied to a wide range of different empires, at different times, and in different parts of the world. In some cases the theory merely confirms what other theories already suggest, but in other cases it leads to contrary predictions. In particular, the theory explains a number of apparent anomalies that other theories do not directly address.

It explains, for example, why imperialist so often trade and invest outside their empires as well as within them. Because the knowledge exploited by an imperialist is a global public good, there may be many territories to which the knowledge can usefully be transferred that the imperialist would not wish to occupy or govern. These territories will generally be the subject of treaty arrangements instead.

It also explains why nations with small home territories can often be successful imperialists. It is their knowledge rather than their natural resources that are key. Indeed, lack of natural resources in their home territory is often a spur to expansion abroad. Location of the metropolis is crucial to small imperial nations, however; an island in a major sea-passage, a peninsular controlling a surrounding sea, or a river confluence are ideal hubs for an imperial transport and communications network.

A systematic test of the theory would be based ideally on continuous longtitudinal study of the occupation and control of each individual territory in the world over a very long period of time. This would make it possible to examine the impact of competition between states by assessing how far the occupation and governance of any given territory was related to superiority in locally relevant knowledge. It would also indicate how far the local occupiers were drawing on outside knowledge supplied under treaty arrangements, and how far surpluses were being expropriated by outsiders through raids.

Data limitations make such an exercise impossible, however. Although some relevant secondary information can be obtained from national and regional histories, it is not comprehensive and is not available on a comparative basis. A more modest approach is to focus on the most valuable territories – those that have attracted a succession of imperialists, who have used them either as their headquarters, or as key hubs in the imperial networks of trade and administration. Some of these hubs were seized from indigenous peoples, whilst others were acquired from defeated earlier empires.

Another approach is to focus not on the territory that is occupied but on the imperialists themselves – that is, on the sources on knowledge rather than the local applications of it. In terms of the theory of the multinational enterprise, this corresponds to taking the 'home country' approach rather than the 'host country' approach described above. This approach involves identifying all empires – that is, states that control more than one territory – and examining the connection between the knowledge they possess and the territories they control. The difficulty with implementing this approach is that there is no definitive list of empires that can be used for this purpose. Furthermore, if there were such a list it would be very long.

A first step is to select a small sample of empires for detailed case study analysis. This cannot be a representative sample, however, because the population from which it is selected is not known. Large and long-lived empires are much better known than small and short-lived ones, and also normally leave much better records in terms of documents and artefacts. It is therefore difficult even to stratify the sample so that a lot of small empires are included. It is therefore proposed to test the theory, at least initially, on the set of fourteen empires listed in Table 12.2. This sample provides a reasonable spread in terms of size and longevity and covers most (though not all) parts of the world. Some empires have been especially included

Table 12.2   Factors in the rise and decline of some major empires

Empire	Growth factors	Decline factors	Stereotype
Greek	Navigation and shipbuilding Naval tactics Productive agriculture supporting high degree of urbanization Mathematical skills Local democracy Efficient commercial law Toleration of foreign merchants	Poor work ethic Under-investment in defence	Enterprising intellectuals
Roman	Civil engineering: roads and bridges Mechanical and hydraulic engineering Military weapons and tactics	Poor leadership Under-investment in defence	Classic imperialists, bringing civilized society to vanquished barbarians
Hun	Nomadic mobility Horsemanship and archery Bravery and hardiness Charismatic leadership	Lack of settled agriculture and bureaucratic structures No written language	Warrior tribesmen living off plunder and tribute
Arab	Horsemanship and archery Religious commitment Mathematical, literary and medical skills Charismatic leadership Effective military tactics	Intolerance Internal feuding	God-fearing warriors and erudite scholars
Viking	Seamanship Bravery and hardiness Saga culture	Lack of settled agriculture and bureaucratic structures	Raiders negotiating for tribute

Table 12.2   (continued)

Empire	Growth factors	Decline factors	Stereotype
Norman	Productive agriculture Entrepreneurial town planning Construction engineering (castles and cathedrals) Efficient bureaucracy and financial system	Remained small and stable	Noblemen and chivalrous knights
Mongol	Nomadic mobility Horsemanship Bravery Charismatic leadership	Lack of settled agriculture and bureaucratic structures	Raiders seeking plunder and threatening massacre
Portuguese	Navigation and shipbuilding Effective royal patronage Mining technology	Under-investment in defence Small country with limited capacity	Explorers and adventurers
Spanish	Navigation and shipbuilding Papal sponsorship Mining technology	Under-investment in overseas assets Weak defence of shipping routes Over-reliance on Papal sponsorship	Aristocrats seeking wealth for conspicuous consumption
Dutch	Sophisticated commercial law Personal ambition and Protestant asceticism	Small country with limited capacity	Collegial businessmen
French	Mathematics and engineering Efficient bureaucracy	Late industrialization Inferior military tactics	Elitist bureaucrats
British	Naval supremacy Civil engineering Mining and railway technology Efficient legal and financial system	Failure to develop electrical and chemical industries Under-investment in defence	Ambitious artisans, gentleman traders and Christian missionaries

Table 12.2   (continued)

Empire	Growth factors	Decline factors	Stereotype
Soviet Russia	Military supremacy in rockets Space exploration Surveillance and intelligence-gathering Mathematical skills Heavy engineering	Inability to produce high-quality mass consumer goods Over-reliance on quantity-based planning using production targets	Revolutionary dictatorship focused on rapid industrialization
USA (quasi-imperialist)	Engineering technologies Efficient constitution and legal system Systematic planning and organization Enterprise culture	Parochial outlook Cultural blindness	Industrious profit-seekers, apostles of freedom

Sources: Barck and Lefler (1968), Bell et al. (1995), Boxer (1969), Braudel (1975, 1978), Cain and Hopkins (1993), Davis (2000), Diffie and Winius (1977), Elliott (2006), Engerman (1998), Fieldhouse (1973), Hartz (1964), Hyam (1976), Kennedy, (1987), Kennedy (2002), Quinn (2000), Rosencrance (1985), Seeley (1883), Starr (1977), Steensgaard (1982), Turner (1893), Wallerstein (1980).

because of the importance of their legacy (for example, Greece and Rome) or because of their topicality (for example, the USA and Soviet Russia). In every case, the availability of relevant primary sources and multiple secondary sources authored by reputable academics also is a criterion.

A key requirement for the application of the theory is that it should be possible to identify the types of superior knowledge on which each of these empires is based. In the light of this, the table presents a preliminary assessment, based on secondary sources, of the superior knowledge that was exploited in each case. The table also indicates some of the specific factors that may have triggered decline. Future research will seek to validate these preliminary assessments, and investigate in detail whether the evidence is in agreement with the theory in each case.

The key factors identified in Table 12.2 are classified in terms of the main types of knowledge in Table 12.3. This table identifies knowledge relating to four different types of civilian local public good, as well as military knowledge and knowledge relating to private goods. For each category, the technological and institutional aspects of the knowledge are distinguished, and geographical characteristics conducive to local

Table 12.3   Key factors supporting a successful empire

Type of knowledge as indicated by field of application	Technological aspects	Institutional aspects	Geographical characteristics favouring local application
Civilian local public goods			
Law and order		Efficient criminal law, policing, justice, punishment systems	Moderate density of population
Health and education	Knowledge of medicine, natural remedies and synthetic pharmaceuticals	Culture of compassion, cleanliness, empowerment in families and schools. Professional accreditation systems	Mild climate with few diseases
Utility services (especially transport and communications)	Civil engineering skills (e.g. bridge-building) and supporting trades (e.g. carpentry) Navigation skills Mechanical and electrical engineering	Efficient tax system and capital market for financing large infrastructure projects	Convenient sources of power (wind, water, coal, oil, etc.)
Social cohesion	Local public transport and social facilities to encourage meetings and foster collective action	Religious and moral systems conducive to building trust	Moderate density of population
Military:			
Defence and aggression	Metallurgy (for armaments) Animal breeding and training	Charismatic leaders trained in military schools	Large young male population

Table 12.3 (continued)

Type of knowledge as indicated by field of application	Technological aspects	Institutional aspects	Geographical characteristics favouring local application
	(e.g. for horsemanship) Explosives Missile technology	Culture of bravery, glory, self-sacrifice Logistical systems Strategic thinking	
Private goods	Sophisticated production machinery High-quality mass-production techniques	Efficient commercial law encouraging business partnerships, share-holding Sound currency Sophisticated marketing	Natural resources in accessible locations: fertile land, mineral deposits etc. Access to rivers and seas to facilitate long-distance trade

exploitation of the knowledge are noted. Each of the factors noted in the table is likely to contribute to the geographical expansion and the longevity of an empire.

12.19 CONCLUSION

This chapter has presented a new theory of imperialism, grounded in the economic theory of entrepreneurship. It is based on an analogy between a multinational firm and an empire, considered as a multinational state. It presents new hypotheses which relate the rise and decline of empires to the development, exploitation and subsequent obsolescence of superior knowledge. Knowledge can be classified as public or private, civilian or military and global or local. There are six main types of knowledge that are particularly relevant to imperialism. A successful imperialist must possess knowledge in all these areas and have superiority in some.

Knowledge itself is a global public good. An entrepreneurial nation that believes that it possesses superior knowledge will wish to exploit this knowledge globally. But there are barriers to knowledge transfer which make some methods of exploiting knowledge difficult, for example, licensing knowledge under treaty arrangements. When knowledge transfer barriers are high there are powerful reasons for 'internalizing' the exploitation of knowledge within an empire through occupying, and possibly governing, foreign territories. Because knowledge transfer barriers vary according to location and the type of knowledge involved, imperialists may use a mixture of territorial control and treaty arrangements in their global strategy. The theory suggests that a nation with a combination of superior civilian and military knowledge is most likely to resort to territorial control. The nature of the civilian superiority is a key factor in determining the geographical configuration of the empire.

The theory is based on economic reasoning in which imperialists act in a rational way. Entrepreneurial imperialists maximize the economic rewards from superior knowledge subject to the constraints that they perceive. Some of these constraints arise from competition with rival empires. Because imperial competition is not governed by a rule of law, however, the interplay of rational strategies may well lead to wasteful outcomes. In particular, superior civilian knowledge may not be used if it is not possessed by the superior military power. Thus the rationality of individual states does not lead to a collectively rational outcome. This contrasts with competition under the rule of law, as analysed in conventional economics, where military superiority is irrelevant and superior civilian knowledge prevails.

A combination of civilian and military superiority has the potential to deliver substantial improvements in local services and quality of life. But while local facilities and infrastructure may be improved, local people may be excluded from some of the benefits. An elitist imperialist may fail to transfer the superior knowledge through education, and as a consequence, may resort to job discrimination and residential segregation. Thus economic benefits in terms of certain local public goods – for example, health – may be offset by costs in terms of other local public goods, in particular, social cohesion.

As stated at the outset, it is not the purpose of this chapter to pass judgement on imperialism. The analysis clearly indicates, however, that imperialism has the potential to generate both significant benefits and significant costs (O'Brien, 1988). The balance of costs and benefits will depend upon the different types of knowledge that are transferred to a territory, the culture of the imperialist, the culture of the local nation, and the geographical characteristics of the territory involved. This chapter provides an analytical framework that can be used to address these issues on a systematic comparative basis. It is therefore hoped that this chapter will stimulate not only theoretical research but also empirical research – both to test the theory and to assess the relative benefits of cost of empire on a case-by-case basis.

ACKNOWLEDGEMENTS

We are grateful to Jean Boddewyn, Peter Buckley, Danny Van Den Bulcke, Janet Casson, Niron Hashai, Seev Hirsch, Valerie Johnson, Patrick O'Brien, George Tridimas and Alain Verbeke for advice and comments on this chapter. Previous versions of the chapter were presented to the Association of Business Historians Annual Conference at Queen Mary, University of London, June 2006, the European International Business Association meeting in Fribourg, December 2006, and the Conference of Trademarks and Brands at Queen Mary, University of London in January 2008.

REFERENCES

Alesina, Alberto, Roberto Perotti and Enrico Spolare (1995), 'Together separately? Issues on the costs and benefits of political and fiscal unions', *European Economic Review*, **39**, 751–8.
Arrow, Kenneth J. (1962), 'Economic welfare and the allocation of resources for invention', in R. Nelson (ed.), *The Rate and Direction of Inventive Activity*, National Bureau of Economic Research, Princeton, NJ: Princeton University Press, pp. 609–26.
Barck, Oscar T., Jr and Hugh T. Lefler (1968), *Colonial America*, 2nd edition, New York: Macmillan.
Baumol, William J. (1993), *Entrepreneurship, Management and the Structure of Pay-offs*, Cambridge, MA: MIT Press.
Baumol, William J., John S. Panzar and Robert D. Willig (1982), *Contestable Markets and the Theory of Industry Structure*, New York: Harcourt Brace Jovanovich.
Bell, Morag, Robin Butler and Michael Heffernan (1995), *Geography and Imperialism, 1820–1940*, Manchester: Manchester University Press.
Boddewyn, Jean J. (1988), 'Political aspects of MNE theory', *Journal of International Business Studies*, **19**, 341–63.
Boddewyn, Jean J. (2003), 'Understanding and advancing the concept of "Nonmarket"', *Business & Society*, **42**(3), 297–327.
Boxer, C.R. (1969), *The Portuguese Seaborne Empire*, London: Hutchinson.
Braudel, Fernand (1975), *The Mediterranean and the Mediterranean World in the Age of Philip II*, London: Fontana.
Braudel, Fernand (1978), *Expansion and Reaction: Essays on European Expansion and Reaction in Asia and Africa*, Leiden: Leiden University Press.

Brewer, Tony (1990), *Marxist Theories of Imperialism: A Critical Survey*, 2nd edition, London: Routledge.

Buckley, Peter J. and Mark Casson (1976), *The Future of the Multinational Enterprise*, London: Macmillan.

Cain, Peter J. and Anthony G. Hopkins (1993), *British Imperialism: Innovation and Expansion 1688–1914; Crisis and Deconstruction, 1914–1990*, London: Routledge.

Casson, Mark (1982), *The Entrepreneur: An Economic Theory*, Oxford: Martin Robertson (New edition, Cheltenham, UK and Northampton, MA, USA: Edward Elgar, 2002).

Casson, Mark (1997), *Information and Organisation*, Oxford: Oxford University Press.

Casson, Mark (2006), 'Cultural determinants of economic performance', in David Throsby and Victor Ginsburgh (eds), *Handbook of the Economics of Culture and the Arts*, Amsterdam: North-Holland, pp. 359–97.

Chinitz, Benjamin (1960), *Freight and the Metropolis*, Cambridge, MA: Harvard University Press.

Colley, Linda (2006), 'The difficulties of empire: present, past and future', *Historical Research*, **79**, 367–82.

Dark, Kenneth R. (1998), *The Waves of Time: Long-term Change and International Relations*, London: Continuum.

Davis, R.R. (2000), *The First English Empire: Power and Identities in the British Isles, 1093–1343*, Oxford: Oxford University Press.

Diffie, Bailey W. and George D. Winius (1977), *Foundations of the Portuguese Empire, 1415–1580*, Minneapolis: University of Minnesota Press.

Dunning, John H. (1981), *International Production and the Multinational Enterprise*, London: Allen & Unwin.

Elliott, John H. (2006), *Empires of the Atlantic World: Britain and Spain in America, 1492–1830*, New Haven, CT: Yale University Press.

Engerman, Stanley L. (1998), 'British imperialism in a mercantilist age, 1492–1849: conceptual issues and empirical problems', *Revista de Historia Economica*, **16**, 195–231.

Fieldhouse, David K. (1967), *The Theory of Capitalist Imperialism*, London: Longman.

Fieldhouse, David K. (1973), *Economics and Empire, 1830–1914*, London: Weidenfeld & Nicolson.

Furubotn, Eirik and R. Richter (eds) (1998), *Institutions and Economic Theory*, Ann Arbor: University of Michigan Press.

Gellner, Ernest (1987), *Culture, Identity and Politics*, Cambridge: Cambridge University Press.

Greif, Avner (2006), *Institutions and the Path to the Modern Economy: Lessons from Medieval Trade*, Cambridge: Cambridge University Press.

Hardt, Michael and Antonio Negri (2000), *Empire*, Cambridge, MA: Harvard University Press.

Hartz, Louis (1964), *The Founding of New Societies*, New York: Columbia University Press.

Hyam, Ronald (1976), *Britain's Imperial Century, 1815–1914: A Study of Empire and Expansion*, London: B.T. Batsford.

Jones, Eric L. (2006), *Cultures Merging*, Princeton, NJ: Princeton University Press.

Jones, Geoffrey G. (ed.) (1998), *The Multinational Traders*, London: Routledge.

Kennedy, Hugh (2002), *Mongols, Huns and Vikings*, London: Cassell.

Kennedy, Paul (1987), *The Rise and Fall of the Great Powers*, New York: Random House.

Moore, Karl and David Lewis (1999), *Birth of the Multinational: 2000 Years of Ancient Business History from Ashur to Augustus*, Copenhagen: Copenhagen University Press.

North, Douglass C. (1990), *Institutions, Institutional Change and Economic Performance*, Cambridge: Cambridge University Press.

O'Brien, Patrick K. (1988), 'The costs and benefits of British imperialism, 1846–1914', *Past and Present*, **120**, 163–200.

Olson, Mancur (1965), *The Logic of Collective Action*, Cambridge, MA: Harvard University Press.

Passavant, Paul A. and Jodi Dean (eds) (2004), *Empire's New Clothes: Reading Hardt and Negri*, London: Routledge.

Penrose, Edith T. (1959), *The Theory of the Growth of the Firm*, Oxford: Blackwell.

Quinn, Frederick (2000), *The French Overseas Empire*, Westport, CT: Praeger.

Rosencrance, Richard (1985), *The Rise of the Trading State: Commerce and Consequence in the Modern World*, New York: Basic Books.

Rugman, Alan (2005), *The Regional Multinationals: MNEs and 'Global' Strategic Management*, Cambridge: Cambridge University Press.

Samuelson, Paul A. (1954), 'The pure theory of public expenditure', *Review of Economics and Statistics*, **36** (4), 387–9.

Schumpeter, Joseph A. (1934), *The Theory of Economic Development*, trans. R. Opie, Cambridge, MA: Harvard Univeristy Press.

Seeley, John (1883), *The Expansion of England: Two Courses of Lectures*, London: Macmillan.

Starr, Chester G. (1977), *The Economic and Social Growth of Early Greece, 800–500BC*, New York: Oxford University Press.

Steensgaard, Niels (1982), 'The Dutch East India Company as an institutional innovation', in M. Aymard (ed.), *Dutch Capitalism and World Capitalism*, Cambridge: Cambridge University Press, pp. 235–58.

Turner, Frederick J. (1893), *The Significance of the Frontier in American History*, reprinted in *Frontier and Section: Selected Essays of Frederick Jackson Turner*, Englewood Cliffs, NJ: Prentice-Hall, 1961, pp. 37–62.

Wallerstein, Immanuel (1980), *The Modern World System II: Mercantilism and the Consolidation of the European World Economy*, New York: Academic Press.

Williamson, Oliver E. (1985), *The Economic Institutions of Capitalism*, New York: Free Press.

13.   Conclusion

13.1   INTRODUCTION: THE PROBLEM OF EXPLAINING SUCCESS

The theory of entrepreneurship set out in this book was originally developed to 'plug a gap' in economic theory. There are various symptoms of this gap, including the lack of a convincing account of market processes, and the omission of strategic leadership from the theory of the firm. In conventional economics the existence of firms and markets is regarded as given rather than as something that needs to be explained.

Conventional economics, it is often pointed out, is inherently static; even growth is often analysed as a steady-state process. By recognizing the importance of a specific class of people dedicated to the pursuit of change, the study of entrepreneurship transforms static analysis into dynamic analysis. According to this dynamic analysis, the pace of change adjusts to the threats and opportunities faced by the economy. Increasing demand for change translates into increasing demand for entrepreneurs, which increases prospective profits, and triggers a corresponding increase in their supply.

Perhaps the most fundamental problem with conventional economics is that it does not have a satisfactory theory of success. It does not explain fully why certain people are able to derive so much profit from the market process, nor why some small firms grow into successful large firms whilst many others fail. A successful economy depends on the cumulative effects of numerous initiatives undertaken by successful people. The limited supply of potentially successful people is a major constraint on national economic performance. Increasing this supply is an important policy issue, and so too is unlocking the full potential of the supply that is already available.

In a free enterprise system, new markets typically evolve from the market-making activities of entrepreneurial firms. The projects undertaken by successful entrepreneurs transform the structure of the economy. New industries are created, cheaper production methods are adopted, and more efficient methods of management and administration are introduced. These changes stimulate value productivity and raise the standard of living. They also help the economy to adapt to changing conditions. In the face of overpopulation, raw material depletion or adverse climate change, innovations are required, not so much to make things better, as to prevent them becoming worse. Volatility in the environment not only creates new opportunities for improvement, but also new threats that need to be countered using innovative ideas.

But what is the meaning of success in this context? At a personal level, success can be measured subjectively in terms of happiness or quality of life, but the most common indicators are materialistic – either wealth or income. Some people derive huge incomes from successful speculation – in property or bonds, for example – whilst others achieve success through highly-paid jobs or celebrity status.

Conventional economists typically ascribe personal success to luck. Some people, by chance, just happen to be in the right place at the right time, and get to win prizes that less fortunate people miss. This account raises more questions than it answers, however. Can people make their own luck? Do lucky people tend to share certain characteristics, and if so are these characteristics a cause of their luck? How is it that so many lucky people seem to be associated with the same clubs, societies or families? Do people join these clubs only once they get lucky, or do they get lucky by joining these clubs? If there are certain characteristics that make people lucky, can anyone acquire these characteristics by studying the right subjects or adopting the right role models, or do they have to be born with them?

The dilemma that economics faces in explaining success is that it really has no theory of failure. The problem is not that no one is successful but rather that everyone is successful – in their own way. If everyone is perfectly rational and well informed, and therefore makes no mistakes, then no one ever fails in the decisions they make. If someone is better off than others then it is simply that they have been endowed with more resources than others, and not that they make better use of the resources that they have. There is no waste in the system because mistakes are never made.

A similar problem in explaining success arises at the national level (see Chapter 3). The success of a national economy can be measured in terms of standard of living or quality of life, although in practice it is often measured more materialistically in terms of productivity levels or productivity growth. Productivity estimates are often derived from production functions, which list the key factors that economists believe influence output – namely endowments of land, labour and capital. A production function indicates the maximum output that can be obtained from a given set of endowments. Rational agents, it is postulated, will always operate on the production frontier. This means that there is no waste: a given amount of output is always produced with the minimum quantity of inputs needed to produce it. This view contrasts sharply with the views of political observers and business commentators, who regularly point to widespread waste in the economy. So how can these two views be reconciled?

Economists have sought to address this problem in various ways. One is by asserting that some people use better technology than others. This allows them to generate more output from a given amount of resource than other people. But since technology is a public good – it can, in principle, be shared – the question inevitably arises as to why some people have access to the best technology when others do not. Once again, the problem is to explain failure rather than success. The paradox is not that some people use the best technology, but that many people do not.

A deceptively simple answer is that there is some widespread obstacle to adopting new technology. As noted in Chapter 1, it is often claimed that people face a psychological obstacle to innovation. They prefer a traditional technology even when a modern technology is superior. This naive psychologism leads to the conclusion that traditionalists need to be forced to modernize their technologies for their own good. Persuasion, manipulation and coercion are all justified by the need to overcome this obstacle. But this is not very good economics. For if people genuinely prefer traditional methods then they will be better off with them, in terms of quality of life, and forcible modernization will only make them worse off.

Another reason why people might reject modern technology is that they are unaware of its existence, or are unwarrantably sceptical about its value. In this case, it is not their preferences that are wrong, but their judgement. Conventional economists normally address this issue through uncertainty. The introduction of uncertainty involves a rejection of the notion of perfect information. Once people lack perfect information, they are liable to make mistakes.

Rational agents will, nevertheless, handle uncertainty is a specific way. If rational agents all have similar preferences and access to the same information, then they will all take similar decisions. As a result, they will all achieve the same degree of success in the same situation – either they will all succeed or they will all fail. The theory cannot therefore explain the success of one person, or one country, relative to another.

The normal response to this is to postulate that people differ in their degree of risk-aversion. Risk-aversion measures a particular aspect of a person's preferences – roughly speaking, the weight they attach to a loss as compared to a gain of equal size. Highly risk-averse individuals, for example, will tend to avoid financing long-term projects that less risk-averse people are quite happy to finance.

This suggests that the greatest success will tend to come the way of the least risk-averse. But it also suggests that the least risk-averse people will tend to incur the greatest losses. It does not therefore provide a theory of systematic success. From this point of view, success results from a combination of low risk-aversion and good luck, and so luck remains a key determinant of success.

The obvious route to take at this point is to argue that people differ in their judgement rather than just in their preferences for risk. This is the approach taken by the theory of the entrepreneur set out in this book. Differences in judgement can be based on differences in the endowment of information. If someone knows more about a given situation than someone else then they are less likely to make a mistake and so are more likely to succeed. Furthermore, perceptions of risk are subjective – other things being equal, the more information a person possesses, the less risk they perceive. If someone regularly has more information than other people then, on average, they will achieve greater success. They may appear to take more risks than other people, but if other people had the same information they would realize that in fact the risks were not that great.

As in conventional economics, the theory of entrepreneurship postulates that everyone acts rationally; but because some people have better information than others they appear to be more rational, and less risk-averse. In fact it is just that their information is better.

13.2   INFORMATION AND ITS INTERPRETATION

There is an obvious limitation to a theory of entrepreneurship based on differential endowments of information – namely that it does not explain where these endowments come from. Endowments of information are not fixed. Information can generally be obtained at a cost – although the cost is sometimes prohibitive. The key to modelling entrepreneurship, therefore, is to understand the structure of information costs (see Chapter 2).

Information costs are incurred in collecting information, storing it, retrieving it, and applying it to make decisions. Information can be collected first-hand, through direct observations, or second-hand through social contacts or the media. It can be stored in the head, or in paper-based or electronic record-keeping systems. The processing of information raises complex strategic issues, and the quality of decisions finally made will reflect the success with which these issues are addressed by an information processing system. Successful entrepreneurs, therefore, are people who invest in systems of information support that feed them with the sort of information they need in order to make good decisions.

Information is a product that raises serious issues of quality control. Acting on mistaken information can lead to worse results than acting on no information at all. Someone who knows that they are ignorant will normally be prudent, but someone who wrongly believes that they are right is likely to make an expensive mistake. Multiple sources of information are often useful as a means of cross-checking the key information used in a decision.

Even more important, perhaps, is the fact that information does not speak for itself. Most decisions do not hinge on self-evident facts, but on the interpretation of questionable reports or observations. The interpretation of information requires a theory. Furthermore, relevant information is often only partial – some of the most important information required for a decision is often missing altogether. Information can also be confusing – a mass of information may be available on unimportant aspects of a decision at the same time that information is in short supply on other aspects. Irrelevant information needs to be discarded so that the relevant information can be properly understood, and theory is needed to inform this selection process.

But while theory is needed to make sense of information, theory itself can be a source of error. There are often competing theories, so that judgement is required to determine which theory is used. A realistic theory of entrepreneurship must therefore take account of the theory-dependence of decision-making (see Chapter 8). Theory-dependence does not undermine rationality, as is sometime suggested, because decisions remain rational within the context of the theory used. Indeed, it is difficult, if not impossible, for a decision to be rational if not based upon some kind of theory. It is simply that in conventional economic models the people who take decisions are assumed to use the same theory that the modeller uses. This does not apply, however, in the theory of the entrepreneur.

When formulating a theory of entrepreneurship, therefore, it is more appropriate to take theory as an endowment rather than information itself. Theory guides the sort of information that people seek out, the way they interpret it and the decisions that they make. Differences in theory are therefore crucial; access to superior theory is the key to success where judgemental decisions are concerned. A superior theory provides a superior model of a situation in which a decision needs to be made. It identifies key factors better than other theories, and guides the entrepreneur towards the most relevant sources of information. All theories have their limitations, however, and so theories often work better in some types of situation than in others. An entrepreneur committed to a particular theory may well succeed in certain areas, therefore, whilst failing in others.

13.3   THE CONTRIBUTION OF THE THEORY OF ENTREPRENEURSHIP: A SUMMARY

A theory of entrepreneurship based on rational action principles can explain a great deal about how good judgement is supplied and the contribution that it makes to the performance of the economy. Because the theory retains rational action principles, it is possible to predict how entrepreneurs will behave on the basis that they will make the best possible use of the judgement that they possess.

An entrepreneur who believes that they have discovered an opportunity will normally set up a firm to exploit it. The firm is a convenient institutional device for appropriating profit from an opportunity because it allows the revenue derived from the opportunity to be separated from the entrepreneur's other income, and the expenses of the project to be separated from the ordinary expenses of consumption. Within the firm, the entrepreneur will normally occupy the key decision-making role – for example, managing director or CEO. An entrepreneur with a high reputation will not normally own a firm outright; he/she will either be a minority shareholder or perhaps even just a salaried employee.

An entrepreneur needs certain qualities – not only the good judgement required to identify the original opportunity, but also sufficient basic business knowledge to take charge of the firm and to recruit suitable employees. He/she also needs social networking skills to attract customers, business partners and so on. In other words, the personal qualities of the entrepreneur depend not only on the function of the entrepreneur – namely judgemental decision-making – but also on the entrepreneur's role as the manager of a firm.

The situation is illustrated in Figure 13.1. The function of the entrepreneur, which appears on the extreme left of the figure, determines the role that the entrepreneur plays, which in turn depends upon the institutional framework in which he/she operates. Typically, this framework will include a system of company law that allows the entrepreneur to set up and manage a limited liability joint-stock company.

The requirements of this role dictate the personal qualities that the entrepreneur needs. Some of these qualities are innate, whilst others are acquired. Many of these qualities are personality traits, and the emergence of certain traits within the population as a whole may be encouraged by national or local culture, as illustrated in the figure.

These qualities dictate the way that the entrepreneur perceives the environment in which he/she is operating, and thereby determine the entrepreneur's behaviour. While the entrepreneur's actions reflect the *perceived* state of the environment, the outcome of the entrepreneur's behaviour

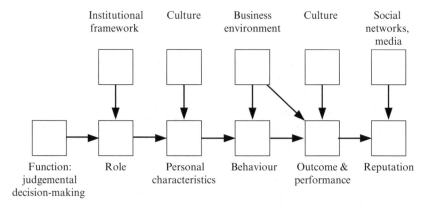

*Figure 13.1   Alternative aspects of entrepreneurship and the relations
between them*

reflects the *true* state of the environment. If the entrepreneur's judgement is good then their perception will be accurate; as a result, the entrepreneur's expectations will be fulfilled, and personal performance will be deemed satisfactory. If the entrepreneur's judgement is poor then the outcomes will, on average, be worse than predicted; possibly so bad that the firm fails.

Whether other people are satisfied with the entrepreneur's performance also depends upon whether the entrepreneur's objectives harmonize or conflict with their own objectives. One of the objectives of a competitive market economy is to align the interests of the entrepreneur with those of the customers served, but this does not always occur because of institutional deficiencies, as discussed below.

The performance of the entrepreneur – by whatever criterion it is judged – will affect the entrepreneur's reputation. The impact on reputation will depend upon the strength of social networks through which gossip flows, and also upon the vitality of the media and the interest that they take in the performance of entrepreneurs. If the entrepreneur's reputation is enhanced by the running of an exceptionally profitable business, then it will become easier for the entrepreneur to borrow funds, and this will facilitate the future growth of the firm.

Although the connections between these various aspects of entrepreneurship are fairly obvious, there has been considerable confusion in the literature over the definition of the entrepreneur. It is a major strength of the theory in this book that it clears up these confusions once and for all. Whilst the canonical writers such as Schumpeter, Hayek and Kirzner have correctly concentrated on the function of the entrepreneur as the foundation of theory, other writers have followed the 'general dictionary' approach of defining the entrepreneur in terms of the role, for example, the role of founder or manager of a small business. Other writers – notably the authors of self-help management books – tend to define the entrepreneur in terms of the possession of desirable qualities, or the admirable manner in which he/she behaves. Finally, popular culture over the last twenty years has increasingly identified the entrepreneur with successful performance, as measured by wealth and celebrity status. All of these aspects are connected, as the figure makes clear, but they cannot all be taken as the defining characteristic of the entrepreneur. Taking the function as the defining characteristic and applying rational action principles shows that all the other characteristics commonly associated with the entrepreneur can be viewed as consequences of this function, as predicted by the theory.

13.4 ENTREPRENEURS AND MARKETS

One reason why conventional economics does not have a satisfactory theory of success is that it does not offer a convincing account of how markets really work. As a result, it understates the potential for generating personal profit from the market system. Historical evidence suggests that most markets evolve on the initiative of entrepreneurs. Someone spots an opportunity – often it is an opportunity to solve a problem that several other people have experienced but which they do not know how to solve for themselves. The solution is embodied in a product that is sold to the people with a problem. The product is sourced from people who have another sort of problem – namely they are looking for a more productive use of the resources that they control. Matching the surplus resources of the producers to the frustrated demand of the consumers generates gains to coordination. The entrepreneur appropriates some of these gains in the form of profit.

Whenever the business environment changes, the entrepreneur who is the first to recognize the change and to appreciate its implications acquires a temporary monopoly. The entrepreneur can devise and implement a project to exploit the opportunity for change – for example, introducing a new product. This monopoly has psychological roots – other people do not recognize the opportunity and therefore believe that the entrepreneur is making a mistake. Once they realize that the entrepreneur is right, however, they will begin to imitate the innovation, ensuring that in the long run the monopoly will be undermined and competition will prevail. But although the market may have begun and ended in a state of competitive equilibrium, the crucial process of adjustment was stimulated by the potential for, and realization of, a temporary monopoly profit.

With a steady stream of changes in the business environment, such profit opportunities occur on a regular basis. A continuous flow of transitory incomes aggregates into a steady long-term flow, and entrepreneurs who can sustain such a flow can become very rich. Just because entrepreneurial profits are temporary, therefore, does not mean that they can be ignored so far as the distribution of income is concerned.

In conventional economics, monopoly profit is generally regarded as a bad thing, whereas in the theory of entrepreneurship it is regarded, up to a point, as a necessary reward for the entrepreneur. This is because the theory of entrepreneurship recognizes the fixed costs of discovering opportunities, which conventional theory does not. Likewise, conventional economics highlights the value of short-run static competition between a fixed number of firms in a given market, whereas the theory of entrepreneurship emphasizes long-run dynamic competition based upon freedom of entry – the ability of entrepreneurs to set up new firms to compete with established ones.

The emergence of an enterprise culture over the last twenty-five years has, however, promoted an uncritical and misleading view of the relation between entrepreneurship and the market system. Entrepreneurs are said to require not only freedom of entry, but a variety of other freedoms as well. Some writers liken market competition to a Darwinian process in which the most successful entrepreneurs drive out the less successful entrepreneurs, who are unfit to survive in the struggle for market share. It is suggested that Darwinian competition works best when there is no limit to the competitive strategies that entrepreneurs can employ. In fact, however, market competition works best when the strategies available to entrepreneurs are restricted to those that operate in the public interest.

Competition in product markets is favoured by economists because it benefits the consumer. Firms compete to offer the best deal to the buyer, and the only firms that survive are those that can match the best deal on offer. But firms can, in principle, compete in other ways. Just as nation-states compete through warfare (see Chapter 12), so entrepreneurs can, in principle, compete through force. An entrepreneur could burn down a rival's plant in order to corner the market. They could even devise an innovative way of breaching their rival's security system in order to achieve this aim. Such resort to violence is common, for example, when a successful drug dealer seeks to expand into a rival dealer's territory.

Competition of this kind leaves the consumer confronting a monopolist – the role of competition is simply to select the most vicious supplier. Instead of competition selecting on grounds of economic efficiency, it selects on aptitude for violence. To ensure that competition selects the right sort of firm, the law commonly rules out resort to violence as a competitive strategy.

An entrepreneur who is denied access to violence can still resort to 'dirty tricks' however, for example, head-hunting a key employee from a rival firm, merely to disrupt their rival's production team. This strategy exploits a common weakness in employment contracts which forces firms to invest in employees even though they are free to quit at short notice.

The most common forms of 'dirty tricks' are based on information warfare. These involve misleading consumers about the product, or about a rival product – either by making false statements or simply by concealing the truth. An innovative entrepreneur could make false claims for their product, suggesting, for example, that it can cure certain problems that in fact it cannot. False statements could also be made about rival products – for example, suggesting that they are more expensive than they really are. Defects in the product could be deliberately concealed, or the virtues of competing products concealed when describing competitive options to potential customers.

The law in most countries addresses some of these issues, but certainly not all of them. Misleading 'trade descriptions' may be outlawed, as may over-zealous advertising. But concealing defects is not necessarily an offence unless health and safety issues are involved, and even then the issue may be disputed in the courts. Negative advertising can sometimes be controlled by libel law, but smears directed at competitors by sales staff are usually difficult to prosecute for lack of evidence. Concealing the advantages of rival products is normally regarded as legitimate, even where it is the poor and vulnerable who are most likely to suffer. The principle of *caveat emptor* is traditionally invoked to justify these weaknesses, but despite the longevity of this tradition it represents an institutional defect in the market system.

Confusing the customer is also possible. For competition to work efficiently, consumers must be able to compare the products offered by alternative suppliers in order to determine which provides the best value for money. Entrepreneurs supplying inferior products may be able to confuse consumers by offering discounts on inflated prices, or concealing 'small print' in the sales contract.

More subtle 'dirty tricks' may involve persuading customers that they have a problem that they do not really have. Health and beauty products are often sold by persuading consumers that they have an image problem or an odour problem; the customer is then sold a solution that merely gives them peace of mind – it does not need to solve a physical problem since such a problem did not exist in the first place. While it may solve a psychological problem by supplying self-confidence, this psychological problem might well be tackled better by more honest means. The only people usually protected against such manipulation are children, and then only when adults are directly affected – for example, where advertisers are exploiting children's 'pester power'.

In general, therefore, competition does not always reward the entrepreneurs who offer consumers the best value for money. Due to defects in the law, competition may select for dishonesty instead. Although dishonest people may eventually acquire a bad reputation and be forced to quit the market, reputation mechanisms are often imperfect and the process of elimination is slow.

Better legislation cannot cure the problem entirely. Legislation is often difficult to enforce, particularly where consumer problems are of a highly subjective nature – as in the case of beauty products. The people best able to control abuses are entrepreneurs themselves. In many industries, trade associations – non-profit organizations owned and controlled by member firms – regulate competition to protect the reputation of the industry as a whole. There is always a risk, however, that such associations can develop into cartels, and thereby restrict the entry of new firms and discourage entrepreneurs from outside the industry. Furthermore, even if the association acts responsibly, offenders may escape detection and, if caught, may quit the association (although in some cases leaving the association may be punishment in itself).

The simplest and most direct way to ensure that competition acts in the consumer interest is to ensure that entrepreneurs themselves want to behave honestly. Given that there are often opportunities to profit from deception, this means that rational entrepreneurs must face some compensating cost of deception. The most obvious cost is guilt incurred through dishonesty – or, equivalently, loss of the happiness that comes from behaving honestly. These emotional incentives are likely to be the consequence of the entrepreneur's allegiance to certain social groups and the values they espouse. Religious conviction, family tradition, or community solidarity may all underpin the honesty of an entrepreneur (see Chapter 11).

Unfortunately, some exponents of entrepreneurship argue that honesty and integrity are not fundamental to successful entrepreneurship. From the standpoint of an individual entrepreneur, this is certainly correct – substantial profits can be made by misleading other people. It is also true that entrepreneurs need to maintain a degree of secrecy in order to appropriate profit from their discoveries, and in this sense they cannot afford to share everything they know openly with other people. Withholding information from rivals is one of the rules of the 'entrepreneurial game', and it is justified by the need for profit to cover the fixed cost of discovery. Secrecy is therefore warranted provided that a project is in the public interest. Withholding information from consumers, however, is against the rules of the entrepreneurial game – or should be. It not only makes unprofitable projects profitable but, through unfair competition with rival projects, it can make profitable projects unprofitable too. To get the best out of entrepreneurs, therefore, it is necessary to formulate a sophisticated set of rules, and the most cost-effective way to enforce these rules is through an ethic of 'fair play' – in particular, fair play for consumers based on traditional values of honesty in business.

So far as national economic success is concerned, policy must not only encourage the supply of entrepreneurship, but also embed entrepreneurship in a web of personal and social obligations that curb profitable abuses by voluntary means. This is not just a matter of discouraging firms from lobbying for protection or subsidy, as is sometimes suggested, or of regulating trading practices by law. It involves promoting non-profit voluntary associations that align entrepreneurship with the social interest. Profit should not be the sole objective of entrepreneurs. Entrepreneurship should be regarded as a game with rules designed to benefit the customer and society as a whole. Whilst the rules of the game should protect the entrepreneur's profit, and the secrecy needed to achieve this, they should also protect the customer against abuses by the entrepreneur. Although the state has a role as umpire and final arbiter, the most effective results will be achieved by encouraging entrepreneurs to affiliate to voluntary associations that promote wider social goals.

13.5 ENTREPRENEURS AS PROFESSIONAL COMPETITORS

Entrepreneurs can be criticized not only for damaging the interests of consumers through unfair trading practices but also for undermining cooperation within society as a whole. Competition between entrepreneurs may not only encourage the deception of customers, but also promote aggression and hostility towards other entrepreneurs. Some entrepreneurs show little or no compassion towards the rivals with whom they compete.

It is generally entrepreneurs rather than consumers that initiate competition in product markets, and it is entrepreneurs rather than workers that initiate competition in the labour market. Entrepreneurs quote prices to consumers – it is only in auction markets that consumers quote prices to entrepreneurs. Entrepreneurs normally refuse to haggle with consumers, and where they agree to haggle they usually have a strategy for outwitting the consumer in the process. Similarly, it is entrepreneurs that usually advertise job vacancies and determine the wages or salaries offered.

Entrepreneurs interview job applicants, rather than the other way round, and they exercise more skill in negotiation processes than the applicants with whom they deal. Because entrepreneurs specialize in making markets, they quickly acquire more experience of negotiation than ordinary customers and workers, and they maximize the benefits of this experience by controlling the market-making process.

When an entrepreneur enters a market they know that if they succeed they will take profit away from other entrepreneurs. In conventional economics, each entrepreneur in a competitive market makes only a normal profit. A new entrant operates on too small a scale to have a significant impact on other entrepreneurs. In practice, however, every entrepreneur supplies a slightly different product from every other entrepreneur, and when a new entrepreneur enters a market the entrepreneurs who produce the most similar products will be obliged to reduce their prices, and hence accept lower profits, in order to survive. In some cases they will not survive at all. The more successful the entrant, the greater the probability that established firms will be wiped out altogether.

Furthermore, it is not only established entrepreneurs that suffer from new entry. Their employees may suffer too. They will lose their jobs and may have to accept employment elsewhere at lower wages – particularly if they are not eligible for the new jobs created by the entrant because they require different skills. There may be knock-on effects on the supply chain too, if the new entrant obtains supplies from different sources to established firms.

The social justification for competition is that the benefits conferred by the new entrant exceed the losses sustained by established firms (after taking account of knock-on effects on customers, employees and suppliers). The harshness of competition stems from the fact that losers often receive no compensation. If the beneficiaries are wealthy, or the losers poor, then competition can widen social inequality. But irrespective of this, competition can undermine social solidarity by making the losers resentful of the winners. This is not just a question of jealousy – the losers may resent the fact that they were not consulted about the entry process.

It is often said to be a strength of competition that it is impersonal. Access to the market, for example, cannot be restricted by ethnicity or social class, so long as no licence is required to enter. However, the fact that entrants require no licence means that they do not have to compensate potential losers out of the profits they make. Whilst entrants are obliged to negotiate with the customers they intend to serve and the workers they employ, they are not obliged to negotiate with the rivals that they intend to displace. This means that even when losers can, in principle, be compensated by an entrepreneur and other beneficiaries, the compensation is never actually paid.

It is not surprising, therefore, that potential losers often object to innovations. Political interventions may occur as a result. In some cases, government may legislate to prohibit certain types of innovation, or attempt to vet each innovation before it is licensed to proceed. In most free-enterprise economies, however intervention involves compensating losers out of general taxation. This response may be triggered automatically – for example, through progressive income taxation – or by special measures triggered by pressure-group lobbying.

Pressure-group lobbying is not necessarily bad in this context, provided it is focused on compensation rather than prohibition. The efficiency implications of compensating losers are very different from the efficiency implications of prohibiting innovation. While prohibition may result in net social loss, compensating losers may result in net social gain. While commitment to compensation may raise the overall tax bill, and thereby discourage innovation by raising the marginal rate of taxation of profit, it can also generate social gain by increasing social harmony, thereby reducing the costs of conflict within society as a whole.

A simple way of reconciling entrepreneurial competition with social harmony is for entrepreneurs themselves to show compassion for those who lose from their innovations. If an innovator dominates a newly-established market then they will be able to appropriate all the benefits of their innovation for themselves. They may earn sufficient profit to compensate the losers and still retain net profit for themselves. Whether they actually choose to compensate the losers depends on whether they feel a social obligation to the losers or not. As before, the strength of such feelings will depend on the social institutions to which the entrepreneurs belong.

Where an entrepreneur has entered an established market, complete monopoly power is unlikely, and so many of the benefits of the innovation may accrue to consumers through competition with imitators or established producers of similar products. An entrepreneur may not be able, therefore to appropriate sufficient profit to compensate losers in full. Since it is unlikely that the customers of the new firm will wish to offer compensation to the firms they no longer patronize, the losers cannot be compensated in full except by the intervention of the state. It is still open to entrepreneurs, however, to restore a degree of social harmony by offering token compensation – which could be targeted on the biggest losers or on the poorest ones.

Entrepreneurship, therefore, is not incompatible with either an honest society or a compassionate one. Indeed, national economic performance is likely to be highest in societies that promote not only entrepreneurial innovation but also honesty and compassion, and do so by offering entrepreneurs a wide range of voluntary associations to which they can affiliate. Entrepreneurs who cultivate good reputation within such institutions will align their values with those promoted by the leadership of the society, and as a result of this they will align their values more closely with the interests of society as a whole.

When national success is measured narrowly by rates of small-firm formation, or by indices of manufacturing productivity growth, societies based on a ruthless Darwinian view of competition may well appear to perform well. But when success is measured by sustainable quality of life, or other broadly-based indicators, then socially-embedded entrepreneurship is likely to achieve better results. Honesty and compassion reduce social conflict and thereby lower the cost of coordination. Whilst anti-social innovation becomes more costly with social embeddedness, socially beneficial innovation becomes easier and, as a result, the private decisions of entrepreneurs become more closely aligned with the interests of society as a whole.

13.6   ENTREPRENEURSHIP AND THE FIRM

In conventional economics, the entrepreneur is missing not only from the market, but also from the firm. Most theories of the firm talk about the resources of the firm, the organizational structure of the firm, and the boundaries of the firm, without mentioning the entrepreneur. Whilst the existence of the entrepreneur – as the founder or owner-manager of the firm – is sometimes implicit in the discussion, the role of entrepreneurial judgement in the performance of the firm – its growth and profitability in particular – is rarely given the prominence that it deserves (see Chapter 4). Yet the theory of the firm is an adjunct of the theory of the market, and the entrepreneur is a leading player in both. Indeed, the entrepreneur is the interface between the firm and the market because the entrepreneur decides the firm's market strategy.

Introducing the entrepreneur into the firm has widespread ramifications. In conventional economics the firm is usually regarded as the owner of a production plant, whereas in the theory of entrepreneurship it is marketing rather than production that is regarded as the core activity of the firm. Conventional economics draws a sharp distinction between the firm that decides how to produce in the most cost-effective way and the market that decides what should be produced in the first place. However, the menu of products from which the market chooses is set by entrepreneurs. They formulate the products that are on the menu and decide the prices asked for them. Market-making entrepreneurs are therefore responsible for many of the decisions that conventional economics ascribes to impersonal market forces.

The entrepreneur's product concept, as reflected in design and quality, is crucial to the firm's success. The firm is, in this sense, the institutional embodiment of the vision of the entrepreneur, as encapsulated in the product. The breadth of this vision is a key determinant of the size to which the firm can grow (see Chapter 1). A product that solves a universal problem of common occurrence will be supplied through mass production to a global market, and where this market requires local sourcing the firm will become multinational. By contrast, if the product responds to purely local needs, and is required only occasionally, the potential exists for only a small local firm.

The product concept developed by the entrepreneur determines not only the scale and geographical spread of the firm, but also its degree of vertical integration (see Chapter 9). Economists usually analyse vertical integration in the context of successive stages of production but in the theory of entrepreneurship integration between production and marketing is more important than integration between one stage of production and another. Entrepreneurs usually establish firms as market-making institutions and only become involved in production through backward integration. It is a mistake to think of entrepreneurs merely as producers, as noted in Chapter 1; while entrepreneurs often engage in production, they usually do so as an adjunct to marketing. Firms that engage only in production are usually dependent on the marketing-making firms they serve, and most of the strategic decisions are taken by the latter.

Furthermore, economists often analyse vertical integration in purely static terms. The theory of entrepreneurship, by contrast, provides a dynamic perspective. Firms may integrate backwards into production in order to maintain secrecy about their innovative product concept; they cannot trust an independent licensee or subcontractor to respect their intellectual property. Furthermore, innovative products often raise significant problems of quality control, caused by lack of experience in production. In order to check quality, and learn about improvements that need to be made, an innovative firm may need to own and control production for itself. Although conventional static theory recognizes that quality control raises problems of asymmetric information that encourage vertical integration, the link between asymmetric information and the novelty of the product can only be clarified by a theory of the entrepreneur. The same is true of interrelated investments – another classic issue in the theory of vertical integration. Minor incremental innovations are unlikely to require interrelated investments, since many of the production resources required for the innovation can be obtained by adapting existing equipment and facilities, but major radical innovations are likely to require a range of new equipment and facilities. To coordinate the resultant set of investments, so that their scales are compatible and their timings are synchronized, vertical integration is likely to be required. The degree of vertical integration effected by a firm is therefore a consequence of the breadth of vision of the entrepreneur. The larger and more radical is the vision, the more likely it is that vertical integration is required to implement it.

Breadth of vision can also explain product diversification. A radical innovation may need to be exploited through several distinct but related products. An innovation in consumer marketing based on psychological insight, for example, may have implications for a number of different products consumed by the same social group (see Chapter 10). Maximizing profit from the innovation may require the firm to take control of the production of each of the products.

It is not only the entrepreneur's vision that affects the behaviour of the firm, however; personality can also be a significant influence (see Chapter 6). New products often diffuse slowly. To build up a customer base quickly, an entrepreneur needs to establish personal relationships with key buyers, such as opinion-leaders, whose patronage will persuade others to follow suit. Using established networks as intermediaries, the entrepreneur will gain access to target customers and create a network based around her/himself as the hub. Social skills help the entrepreneur to recruit and motivate a workforce and management team. As the firm grows, a more sophisticated division of labour will evolve amongst the employees; the entrepreneur must acquire the skills needed to select and retain highly-qualified specialists who may be more expert than the entrepreneur concerning certain aspects of the firm.

While the theory of entrepreneurship does not require a radical revision of the theory of the firm, it provides a welcome opportunity to integrate the many seemingly disparate branches of the theory into an integrated whole. Adding the entrepreneur to the existing theory of the firm is not a complication; it actually simplifies the theory by explaining better how the different branches of theory are related to each other.

13.7   ENTREPRENEURSHIP AND LEADERSHIP: TOWARDS A THEORY OF SOCIAL INSTITUTIONS

The firm is just one of many institutions found in a market economy. Other institutions include social networks, non-profit associations and the state. Furthermore, firms themselves come in different types; while most are organized on a profit-making basis, some are non-profit organizations that simply carry forward surpluses to the future (see Chapter 8). Even amongst profit-making firms, not all firms distribute profit to a specialized group of shareholders; in co-operatives, for example, profits may accrue to employees instead (see Chapter 7).

It is not just firms that compete for resources in the economy. All types of institution compete for resources. Some compete for labour in the same way as an ordinary for-profit firm, but others use unpaid volunteers and compete for the volunteer's time – often against other non-profit institutions. Institutions also compete in supplying goods and services. Charity shops compete on the high street, whilst the charities themselves may compete for the patronage of client groups – for example, providing rival soup kitchens. Competition, therefore, is not confined to for-profit firms. Whatever the objectives of an institution, it will normally face competition from other institutions that employ similar resources or undertake similar activities.

Given that institutions compete, they all have a potential need for the services of an entrepreneur. Indeed, it is unlikely that they would have been set up in the first place if it had not been for the initiative shown by some entrepreneur. Most institutions are set up to implement some project, or portfolio of projects. Costs are sunk both in getting the projects up and running, and in forming the institutions and recruiting members. Someone needs to make the judgement that the prospective benefits outweigh the costs. Since the benefits lie in the future they are uncertain, and opinions may well differ. When most people are sceptical and apathetic, an entrepreneur must come forward to back their own judgement with their own time and money in order to found an institution and get the project 'off the ground'.

It goes without saying that if entrepreneurship is required for almost any sort of institution, then the objectives of an entrepreneur cannot be assumed to be wholly selfish and materialistic. It is often convenient, when modelling ordinary product markets, to assume that venal motives prevail, because very simple predictions about entrepreneurial behaviour can then be made. But it is extremely difficult to construct a theory of charitable institutions on the basis that everyone is selfish.

Furthermore, as emphasized above, venality does not necessarily make someone a better entrepreneur, even when running a private for-profit firm. If success is defined by contribution to social welfare rather than profit per se, then honest and compassionate profit-seeking is most likely to promote success. Venality only promotes success when the rules of the game, as set by politics and the law, allow it to do so.

Unselfish entrepreneurs may prefer to set up non-profit institutions rather than for-profit institutions run in an honest and compassionate way. To avoid confusion, it is sometimes useful to refer to such entrepreneurs as 'leaders' instead. An important role played by many leaders is in the promotion of the values and beliefs on which a successful society depends. They may promote these values through propaganda, persuasion and ritual or through the implementation of projects – such as hospital care or poverty relief – that reflect the values they espouse.

Leaders may also establish research and educational institutions that generate the theories that entrepreneurs use to interpret information, as described above. They may also generate some of the factual knowledge that entrepreneurs use in their decision-making. By promoting values, theories and beliefs, therefore, leaders can influence the behaviour of entrepreneurs. The more 'entrepreneurial' these leaders are – in the sense of using good judgement – the more effective they are likely to be in supporting ordinary entrepreneurs in making decisions when viewed from a social perspective.

The study of leadership endogenizes one of the factors discussed earlier – namely the allegiance of entrepreneurs to particular theories that are shared by members of particular social groups. The more entrepreneurial a leader, the more likely they are to recruit new members and achieve influence for the theories, values and beliefs they espouse. The distribution of entrepreneurial ability across different leaders with different theoretical, moral and social commitments is therefore a significant influence on the attitudes of entrepreneurs and therefore on business behaviour in the for-profit sector as a whole.

This analysis of leadership behaviour suggests an explanation for some of the distorted policies promoted by modern enterprise culture (see Chapters 1 and 8). Modern enterprise culture reflects an essentially Darwinian view of competition, according to which no firm can afford to be honest and compassionate, given that its rivals cannot be expected to behave that way. This Darwinian view became popular in response to the spread of global competition. In the 1950s and 1960s, Western 'national champion' firms, confident of their own superiority compared to foreign competition, adopted increasingly paternalistic policies towards their employees. But as import competition intensified, they abandoned these values as a cost-cutting exercise.

Once Western politicians became convinced that ruthlessness was key to business success, the value that they placed on social institutions wedded to traditional values decreased. In the UK, for example, trades unions that valued cooperation over competition were disempowered, professional associations and trade associations were regarded as mere cartels, building societies were demutualized, whilst religious groups were dismissed as irrelevant. The charity sector was relegated to the role of providing social services 'on the cheap'.

Instead of the non-profit sector setting the values and beliefs on which the for-profit sector acted, the for-profit sector became a model to which the non-profit sector was supposed to aspire. Successful businessmen were hired by government as consultants and promoted as role models for young people. Venal business attitudes were embraced by the media; ruthlessness became a sign of strength and compassion a sign of weakness. Unfortunately, however, ruthlessness encourages crime and undermines loyalty, whilst loss of compassion undermines parenting and the provision of social care. The ensuing breakdown of interpersonal trust is, ironically, bad not only for society but for the economy too. The proliferation of social disruption and anxiety reduces productivity at work. Consumption of luxuries is crowded out by legal expenses, higher insurance premia and by the purchase of new essentials such as home security and nursery care.

A further irony is that those who espouse the values of enterprise culture and seek to promote better decision-making should make such misguided policy decisions themselves. Many politicians seem to believe that introducing venal business values into political policy-making is the key to national economic success. Indeed, political leaders increasingly see themselves as businessmen – competing with each other through the marketing of political party 'brands' in order to maximize their Parliamentary 'market share'. Whilst they may espouse concerns about fragmented or broken societies, they analyse political strategies in terms of venal business values – for example, hiring 'big hitters' and organizing 'negative briefings' in order to destabilize their opponents.

The traditional role of the political leader was focused on providing a moral compass through disseminating understanding of the 'bigger picture' – a view closely aligned with the concept of leadership as set out above. This traditional role requires that leaders understand two things: that the true value of entrepreneurship resides in providing good judgement when it is needed, and that traditional values are needed in order to align competition with social welfare. The business model used by modern politicians, based on Darwinian competition, has lost sight of both these points. In rejecting the ideas on which business was based before the era of globalization, modern politicians have also discarded important truths. Economists have failed to address this problem because of shortcomings in their own analysis. Future research will hopefully address this problem; however, in so doing it will need to give more attention than before to a realistic analysis of the role of the entrepreneur in society. A realistic analysis of this kind must be based on a rigorous theory of entrepreneurship of the kind provided in this book.

Index